ONE MORE RIVER

ONE MORE RIVER

The Rhine Crossings of 1945

Peter Allen

BARNES
&NOBLE
BOOKS
NEW YORK

For my wife, Efrosyni,
who showed great patience during the months
in which I was writing this book

This edition published by Barnes & Noble, Inc.,
by arrangement with Scribner, an imprint of
Simon and Schuster.

1994 Barnes & Noble Books

ISBN 1-56619-747-3

Printed and bound in the United States of America

M 9 8 7 6 5 4 3 2 1

Contents

Illustrations

List of maps

Acknowledgements

I wish to extend my grateful thanks to all who have helped me to
reconstruct these eventful and complicated months of the campaigns.
It is inevitably difficult to pay tributes to everyone; some people have
spent considerable time in locating information, writing me letters, or
affording me the time to visit and discuss the events with them.
Others have been casual, sometimes even unexpected meetings that
have resulted in my learning of their role, however small, and to
them, trivial it may have seemed. I have tried to recreate faithfully
the atmosphere of these battles and am indebted to all who helped
me by giving their recollections, accounts and opinions of events not
always adequately covered in the literature.

Without wishing in any way to depreciate the invaluable help of
others, I would like to pay special tribute to the following, whom I
have listed alphabetically: G. Clout, Department of Printed Books,
Imperial War Museum; General J. Lawton Collins;
Lieutenant-General Sir Napier Crookenden; Colonel B. A. Fargus,
The Royal Scots; Captain R. D. Kennedy, The Argyll and Sutherland
Highlanders of Canada (Princess Louise's); Brigadier M. R.
Lonsdale, DSO, OBE; Major Alastair MacIntyre; Colonel B. E. W.
McCall; Major G. Morrison, DSO, The Gordon Highlanders; Miss
M. J. Pereira, Librarian, Canadian High Commission; John J.
Slonaker, Chief Historical Reference Section, US Army Military
History Institute; Herr Albert Speer; Wynford Vaughan-Thomas,
OBE; Sir Huw Wheldon.

I wish to acknowledge the assistance of the following who have been
kind enough to permit me to make use of their personal
reminiscences: C. Acton; J. Campbell; O. Diels; E. Dixon; W.
Evans; F. J. Fergusson; Edward P. Ford; F. Hagen; L. Jones; W.
Lasser; J. W. MacDonald; W. Mitchell; L. P. Morris; R. Nunn; J.
Piper; H. Pritz; W. Robertson; W. Schaub; J. Shaw; C. Smith; A. P.
Sullivan; J. Walters; D. Warrender; R. Willis.

To the following I am indebted for their time in replying to my
letters, or otherwise giving me their time and aid: Major-General Sir
Alan Adair; H. Gordon Aikman, *The Winnipeg Tribune;* R. T.
Albert; R. Alexander; P. B. J. Baily; Major H. Barker, Seaforth
Highlanders Regimental Association; Colonel J. G. Boulet, Director
of Information Services, Department of National Defence, Canada;
Lieutenant-Colonel D. E. Brand, The Royal Hamilton Light
Infantry; The British Council, Cologne; F. Burger;
Lieutenant-Colonel M. I. Burkham, MBE, The Royal Welch
Fusiliers; Glen Davis; Major J. A. H. Douglass, MBE;
Lieutenant-Colonel M. B. Dunn, The King's Own Scottish Borderers;
G. F. Edwards; T. H. Fitch, The Airborne Forces Museum; T. P.
Frazer; Colonel J. E. E. Fry, Regimental Museum, The Duke of
Cornwall's Light Infantry; H. Gilman; B. Hicks; M. B. Hodges; W.
Holtz; Frau C. Huisemann; E. Jones; Miss P. M. Kelly, Press and
Information Services, The British Embassy, The Hague; Rex C.
Kramer, *The American Legion Magazine;* B. Lewis; Professor Alun
Llywelyn-Williams; L. MacAlastair; Major W. D. McKay, The
Canadian Airborne Regiment; R. A. McLoud;
Militargeschichtliches Forschungsamt; D. Morris; D. B. Nash,
Department of Printed Books, Imperial War Museum; Major R. A.
Nichol; J. P. Parsons; Wilhelm Pohl; Public Records Office; P. Reed,
Department of Documents, Imperial War Museum; The Royal
Canadian Legion; P. Saone; F. Schiller; K. Sommars; Richard J.
Sommers, PhD; Donald Stewart; H. F. Svoboda; M. Tennant; H. W.
Vaughan-Thomas; S. Wallis; R. C. Welch; K. Williams; R. P.
Williams; S. Wilson; Lieutenant-Colonel G. P. Wood, MC, Argyll
and Sutherland Highlanders.
I wish to thank the Regimental Headquarters, The 22nd (Cheshire)
Regiment, for permission to quote from accounts of the airborne
operations in their journal, 'The Oak Tree', 1949.
Finally, a special thank you to my son, Andrew, who spent a great
deal of time helping me with research and produced drafts of the
maps for me.

Peter Allen
October 1978

Foreword

Most accounts of the Second World War in north-west Europe deal at length with the last major German offensive, the Battle of the Ardennes. The remaining months of the war are then rushed through as though they were an anti-climax. In reality the final battle for the Rhineland, and then to cross Germany's greatest river, the Rhine itself, were some of the most desperately fought campaigns of all. Defending their fatherland, the Germans fought with all the courage and determination that such a task engenders. With Hitler threatening death for those who failed him the last measure of fierce resistance was wrung from the Wehrmacht and the Waffen SS troops holding the defences.

Field Marshal Montgomery launched his big push into the Rhineland in early February 1945 with one of the great set-piece battles of the war, supported by an immense artillery barrage that could be heard in England. Lancasters, Mosquitoes and Typhoons roared overhead as massed British and Canadian troops advanced into Germany. But the worst winter for years in Europe was followed by an early thaw that created such floods and mud that tanks sank up to their turrets. The battle was to produce conditions comparable only with the most hideous weeks on the Somme and Passchendaele. Troops floundered in thick mud under heavy German shelling.

To cross the Rhine, the greatest water barrier in Europe, Montgomery mounted a water-borne invasion which in size and complexity rivalled D-Day. He backed it with the biggest airborne assault in history involving thousands of British and American aircraft and gliders, dropping the British 6th and American 17th Airborne Divisions in an unprecedented daylight landing right on top of the German positions. His intention was to create a strong bridgehead from which to mount his final powerful armoured drive to Berlin.

But the battles with the Germans were not the only fights in those

closing months of the war. Among the top Allied commanders there
arose bitter controversies, jealousy and national prejudice that, be-
neath the public accord, nearly wrecked the Allied effort in the final
months.

1 The Bloody Bucket

Great jagged chunks of concrete hung grotesquely from the contorted reinforcing rods that were all that remained of the enemy pillbox. The flotsam of battle lay everywhere—helmets, gas masks, empty ration cans, field jackets covered with blood. Trees exploded with horrifying cracks sending long splinters whirling amongst the advancing American infantry. Mortar bombs and grenades blew gaping craters in the forest floor, Spandaus screeched and hammered forcing the GIs to crouch behind fallen trees or grovel in hollows filled with sodden autumn leaves. An American barrage crashed out in reply and seconds later the woods around the German positions erupted in smoke and flame. For ten minutes round after round slammed into the forest then, suddenly, the shelling ceased. Whistles shrilled, commands were shouted, the GIs scrambled to their feet and staggered forward. Private Hooper from Pennsylvania remembers running along with the rest of his battalion from the US 28th Infantry Division, desperately tired and frightened, eager to throw himself into the next trench. He came across a discarded boot and angrily kicked it aside, then froze in horror and retched as he saw the bloody foot sticking out.

Rivulets streamed from the slopes, washing slurries of mud that oozed into the thick debris on the forest floor. Platoons slithered forward behind men who probed with bayonets, trying to locate the mines. Master-Sergeant Jacobs spent hours of frustration on his stomach in gooey, stinking mud and clinging leaves while he searched to discover the pattern of the minefield. Then, when he was sure they were through, some unfortunate sod trod on another, a mere twenty yards ahead. Most of all the GIs feared the diabolical 'Bouncing Betty', a three-pronged monstrosity that on contact leaped from the ground to explode between a soldier's legs, if not killing him outright, inflicting the most terrible mutilations.

While British Field Marshal Sir Bernard L. Montgomery's 21st

Army Group was preoccupied with clearing the seaward approaches to the vital port of Antwerp, the Supreme Allied Commander, General Dwight D. Eisenhower, designated the American 12th Army Group to make the main offensive into Germany. Early in November 1944 General Omar N. Bradley, the Army Group Commander, ordered General Courtney Hodges's US First Army to advance to the Rhine and cross the river south of Cologne. The US Third Army, under the redoubtable General George S. Patton, would provide support on their south by driving north-east through the Saar. Bradley's newest army, the recently arrived US Ninth Army, was interposed between First Army's northern flank and the British. Under General William H. Simpson, this army was to accompany Hodges's army across the Rhine and encircle the Ruhr.

The attack had begun on November 2nd with a narrow thrust by the lone US 28th Division into the densely forested country south-east of Aachen with the intention of seizing high ground around the town of Schmidt. Hodges intended to anchor the right wing of First Army at Schmidt while the rest of it would pivot towards the Rhine once this objective had been taken. Opposing the American advance was German Army Group B, under Field Marshal Walter Model, a tough and uncompromising soldier who had earned Hitler's acclaim while commanding the German 9th Army in Russia. After the Americans had taken Aachen the German High Command (Ob West) had predicted that their drive would close to the Rhine across the hilly country leading towards Cologne. Model believed that Bradley was specifically aiming for the Bonn area, in which case the American advance would have to cross the river Roer, which meandered right across the American front to join the river Maas at the town of Roermond.

On the plateau at Schmidt were seven dams which controlled the head waters of the Roer. Foremost among these was the mighty Schwammenauel, an immense structure of concrete and earth 188 feet high, 1000 feet thick at the base with a 40-foot roadway on the top. If the Americans succeeded in capturing it they could release 20,000 million gallons of water onto the hapless Germans, thereby cutting their lines of communication. These dams, commanded by the high ground at Schmidt, thus had considerable strategic importance for both sides. It should have been obvious, therefore, that the Germans would never surrender such a key position without a considerable fight. Indeed, Model had reinforced the approaches with a Panzer division and two infantry divisions, and ordered his forces to stop the Americans at the Roer. Yet it was against this formidable force, well entrenched in the strong points within the forest, that General Hodges sent in the newly-arrived and inexperienced 28th Infantry Division.

In their enthusiasm to be first over the Rhine, motivated by the failure of Montgomery's attempt to cross the Rhine at Arnhem, the American commanders—Eisenhower, Bradley and Hodges—simply failed to appreciate how strongly the Germans would resist. They could not avoid crossing the Roer, because by-passing it from the dams to Roermond would have left a sixty-mile gap which the Germans might turn into a salient and thus threaten Liège and even Brussels. Determined to beat Montgomery across the Rhine they failed to recognize the threat posed by the dams.

Just as Montgomery's drive to Arnhem foundered at the failure of his planned rapid advance along the single road from Nijmegen, so now, Hodges's drive for the Rhine was frustrated when the 28th Division failed to secure the important anchor position at Schmidt. It is difficult to understand why Hodges gave the decisive objective of capturing the dams to the untried 28th Division. Nor is it clear why he chose to make his thrust to the Rhine through the difficult wooded country of the Hurtgen forest, for even had his initial attack succeeded the subsequent offensive would have been through heavily populated country; both terrains were unsuitable for the armour upon which American infantry were trained to rely. The country before Ninth Army was, in comparison, relatively open farmland and ideal tank country. It is probable that Bradley simply wanted Hodges's First Army to have the honour of being the first Allied army to cross the Rhine, however he did it. Anxious to win publicity for himself and his army, Hodges obstinately maintained his strategy.

General Stroh's 28th Division's assault had begun quietly enough as his battalions set off through the dense and dark forest of towering fir trees, to seize the high ground around Schmidt. They tramped confidently forward, expecting to reach the Rhine. Ten days later, however, they reeled back, battered and bleeding, with more than 6,000 casualties. Their red keystone shoulder badge was bitterly renamed 'the bloody bucket'. It was one of the war's most costly attacks.

American and German troops fought amongst the trees and bushes in the Hurtgen forest, reliving the horrors of Passchendaele. Terrible losses were sustained from frostbite; soldiers were found dead from exhaustion in water-logged fox-holes. The great forest took on a nightmare quality as men lay alone, cold and tired, staring into the dark recesses, their imaginations playing them all kinds of tricks. Dawn came reluctantly as if afraid to reveal the carnage within the woods.

In at least one battalion morale snapped as a company moved forward under heavy fire for yet another assault. Courageous infantrymen, demoralized by hunger and exhaustion, could do no more, and streamed back in disorder. Both the battalion and company commanders whose troops had broken were immediately relieved of their commands; and in the next few days three more company commanders were also relieved of their commands because of their troops' poor performances. The battle got so bad at one point that one platoon commander refused to order his exhausted men to fight again and was immediately arrested. Hodges made it clear to General Stroh that if he did not get better results it was on the cards that heads might roll higher in the command. Yet as the attack towards the Roer dams ran into deeper trouble, Hodges simply compounded his error by throwing in even more units, in savage but unsuccessful frontal attacks.

So when US First Army's desperate, hard-fought campaign finally fizzled out in the December snows, the Americans had expended some seventeen divisions in return for a few miles of tree stumps, swampy ground torn apart by shells, and shattered, empty villages. The ordinary GI might have established a reputation for dogged courage in the month-long fight but 57,000 men had been lost to enemy shells, bullets and mines, and another 70,000 to fatigue, exposure and disease. First Army alone lost 550 tanks, the equivalent in tank strength to nearly four armoured divisions. The weary troops of First and Ninth Armies gazed disconsolately not on the legendary Rhine but on the obscure, muddy and flood-threatened Roer.

Worst of all, the 20,000 million gallons of water remained in the Schwammenauel. General Bradley now decided that it was impracticable to cross the Roer until his forces had captured the dams. However, his belated decision was to have serious repercussions as Montgomery's British forces were even then preparing to launch an attack from Nijmegen, south between the rivers Maas and Rhine towards Krefeld. It had been arranged by Eisenhower that the US Ninth Army was to be detached from Bradley's 12th Army Group and would advance northwards across the Roer to meet the British. But it was now apparent the Americans could not cross the Roer so long as the Germans controlled the dams at Schmidt, and Bradley was in no hurry to transfer strength from Patton's Third Army to Hodges's First Army, because he was well aware that once the dams were in American hands, he would lose his Ninth Army to Montgomery's 21st Army Group.

As autumn turned into winter the American troops dug in along their front many miles from the Rhine. In due course their failure to seize the Roer dams would wreck the Allied plan to capture the Rhineland and force Bradley's Canadian and British allies alone to take on the weight and fury of Field Marshal von Rundstedt's armies, while the US Ninth Army stood on the banks of the Roer and watched helplessly as the pent-up waters of the Schwammenauel dam roared down and flooded the Roer valley across their path.

The optimistic hopes for an early end to the war in Europe that had been engendered during the Allied race across France and into Belgium during August and early September 1944, had by now dissipated in the slow and bitter fighting of the autumn. Nevertheless, the American, British, Canadian and French armies were within striking distance of Germany, although ahead of them stretched the heavily defended Siegfried Line guarding the approaches to the Rhineland. Once through that, they would be faced with just one more river to cross into the German heartland—the fabled Rhine, a wide and formidable barrier to the Third Reich.

2 The winter of discontent

As Supreme Allied Commander, General Eisenhower—wrote his biographer, Stephen E. Ambrose—'was cast in the role of chairman of an international board of military and civilian directors'. Certainly, after D-Day, he had an extraordinarily difficult task of welding together in north-west Europe the eight armies, from Canada, Britain, America and France, whose commanders displayed varying temperaments and experiences.

Even before the Normandy invasion, for instance, Eisenhower had had differences of opinion with General Marshall, the US Army Chief of Staff, over senior American appointments for 'Overlord'. They had agreed that for the landings Bradley would command the US First Army, under Montgomery's overall command, after which Bradley would assume command of the entire US group of armies and Hodges would replace him as commander of First Army, but Marshall did not like Eisenhower's decision to give Patton the US Third Army. He had been appalled by the press reports of Patton's now-famous behaviour in Sicily which included striking a wounded soldier. Eisenhower had to promise Marshall that, 'in no event will I ever advance Patton beyond army commander'.

Nor did Patton and Bradley get on too well with each other. When Patton landed in France on July 6th 1944 to find Bradley's forces hopelessly entangled in the small fields and thick hedgerows of Normandy's bocage country, he had suggested breaking out on a narrow front with armoured forces supported by artillery. Bradley did so, successfully. But when Bradley ordered Patton southwards first to secure St Hilaire, Fougers and Rennes, then to take the ports of St Lo and Brest, Patton had other ideas: 'General Bradley simply wants a bridgehead over the Selune river. What I want and intend is Brest and Angers.' Angers was a logical point from which Patton could

start his coveted drive to Paris, but it was 100 miles south of Bradley's positions at Avranches and 200 miles east of Brest. This was
not part of the overall plan. Eisenhower, however, said little about
Patton's rapid drive into Brittany, but his aide, Commander Harry
Butcher, commented on 4th August in his diary: 'Ike has been impatient, repeat impatient, and I mean impatient. He isn't excited about
Patton's armoured thrust into the Brittany peninsula, because he
figures all that will fall like a ripe apple.'

In America Patton's spectacular drives made headlines. The press
correspondents liked his excitable, flamboyant personality, in contrast to what they saw as the vapid personalities of Bradley and
Hodges. Montgomery's slow advance towards Caen was also compared unfavourably with Patton's achievements: 'Why don't the British do some fighting?' was the typical attitude. Yet it was hardly a
fair comparison because throughout the fighting in the Normandy
bridgehead, the British and Canadians had dealt with much heavier
armoured attacks than the Americans; indeed by early July the British were engaging seven panzer divisions while less than half a
panzer division appeared on the remainder of the Allied front.

In August Montgomery had turned his attention to what he saw as
the 'big battle'; the need to close up to the Rhine and drive into the
German heartland. His persistent arguments for a thrust into Germany eventually led Eisenhower to allow him to make the ill-fated
'Market-Garden' drive towards Arnhem in September 1944 to
outflank the main German Siegfried Line defences. Although Arnhem was not taken and the British 1st Airborne Division was decimated after Lieutenant-General Brian Horrocks' XXX Corps failed
to break through in time, it had not been entirely fruitless. The capture of Nijmegen had provided an important salient in the northern
end of the German defences and the first foothold across the Rhine.

After 'Market-Garden' the relationships between the Allied commanders grew more strained. Many of Eisenhower's staff thought
him too lenient with Montgomery, who still held very clear ideas on
how the war in Europe should be won. Montgomery favoured a powerful thrust directed towards the Rhine to capture the Ruhr and then
Berlin. Eisenhower believed in an advance on a broad front with all
his armies closing to the Rhine together. (After the war Montgomery
commented bitterly: 'What cannot be disputed is that when a certain
strategy, right or wrong, was decided upon, it wasn't directed. We did
not advance on a broad front; we advanced to the Rhine on several
fronts, which were unco-ordinated.') Although Eisenhower favoured

a broad front, the problems of supplying all eight armies at once would prove too great. He was limited to making advances in turn, according to his appreciation of the strategic circumstances at the time, but it was in this appreciation that he and Montgomery differed. Montgomery argued that Eisenhower's broad front approach would give the enemy time to dig in behind their Siegfried Line defences. Eisenhower, on the other hand, did not think Montgomery could make a single thrust relying only on the inadequate Channel ports to sustain his forces beyond the Rhine. He made it clear that he intended to stick to the pre-'Overlord' plan to advance to Germany on both sides of the Ardennes, which were considered too mountainous for armoured forces. On September 5th 1944 Eisenhower wrote that the broad front approach 'takes advantage of all the existing lines of communication on the advance towards Germany and brings the southern force (Bradley's), on to the Rhine at Koblenz practically on the flank of Montgomery's forces.' He forecast the imminent defeat of the Germans. He wanted to save casualties and ensure that all the armies, and their commanders, got an equal share in the eventual victory. He was, it seems, hoping for a repetition of November 1918 when the Germans signed the armistice while their armies were still west of the border. Such optimism, however, was ill-founded.

The planning for the attack into the Rhineland began just after the failure at Arnhem. The original date to clear the Reichswald, the big German state forest just across the border from Nijmegen that blocked the approaches to the Rhine, was October 10th 1944, but the need to clear the approaches to Antwerp first and so provide a major port nearer to the front than the Normandy beach-head through which supplies still flowed, forced a postponement until November 10th when it was intended that Bradley would transfer the US Ninth Army to Montgomery. But the plan was frustrated again when on October 28th the Germans launched a sudden attack westwards from positions in the Venlo salient on the Maas, which absorbed all the available Allied strength. This attack convinced Montgomery that he could not launch his attack from Nijmegen until the Allies had cleared up to the Maas along its entire length, which would further delay the attack into the Rhineland until January 1st 1945.

Once the Scheldt estuary had been cleared and Antwerp's port opened, Montgomery delegated to the commander of First Canadian Army, Lieutenant-General H. D. G. Crerar, the task of planning the attack between the rivers Maas (the Dutch name for Meuse) and Rhine. No sooner, however, had Lieutenant-General Sir Miles Dempsey, commander of British Second Army, in turn been given the task of studying the problems of a subsequent crossing of the Rhine, than all the planning stopped when, on December 16th 1944, the Germans erupted into the Ardennes.

At General Hodges's HQ at Spa in Belgium, the news of the German attack created great confusion. Because most telephone lines had been cut by the opening barrage and few forward units had time to use their radios, Hodges thought the offensive was intended only as a counter to his own attack on the Roer dams. General Bradley, who was with Eisenhower at Versailles, also thought it no more than a spoiling attack. In fact the Germans were aiming for Antwerp, intent on cutting off and then annihilating the British forces.

In the German centre, General von Manteuffel's Fifth Panzer Army drove headlong into the inexperienced 106th Division and the depleted 28th Division around the Schnee Eifel hills. With six infantry and three panzer divisions, von Manteuffel was aiming for the vital communications centre of St Vith, just over the Schnee Eifel, and for Bastogne in the centre of the Ardennes, another important road junction.

The commander of the 106th Division, Major-General Alan W. Jones, had been told by the commander of VIII Corps, Major-General Troy Middleton, that the withdrawal of his regiments was at his discretion, but in the belief that most of his line was holding, Jones left them where they were. Middleton also told him that a combat command from Ninth Army's 7th Division would arrive early next morning to strengthen his positions. But the snow and the poor roads delayed 7th Division's arrival until the following night and by then von Manteuffel's forces had broken through. Two days later the 106th Division's two regiments surrendered 8,000 men. It was America's greatest loss in the land war against Germany.

On December 19th, Eisenhower called a conference at Verdun of all his top commanders. Although the obvious move was a simultaneous counter-attack from north and south, Hodges's First Army was too busy trying to hold the Germans off and could not counter-attack at all. Patton, therefore, was told to drive for Bastogne in the hope that it might still be in American hands. The conference had not been over long when General Strong, the British G2 (General Staff Officer 2) reported that US 12th Army Group was about to be cut in two. 'At 11 that night, Beetle (Eisenhower's Chief of Staff, General

Walter Bedell Smith), phoned Ike to say that the G2 now figured
that the whole German effort was towards Namur and that at the
current rate of progress the Boche might well be there in 48 hours.
As a result of the enemy's offensive and his paratroop operations in
the areas of Malmedy and Spa, Hodges's signal facilities had been
disrupted, which left the SHAEF G2 a bit confused as to what was
happening.' Strong's recommendation that all troops of First and
Ninth Armies north of the bulge (the huge German salient extending westwards) should be placed under Montgomery's command met
with a stony silence. None of the American commanders relished
being subordinate to the austere English Field Marshal. But later,
when he had had time to reflect, even Bradley had to admit it made
sense and he was finally won over when Eisenhower pointed out it
would assure the use of British reserves, an entire corps of four divisions plus several armoured brigades.

Hitler's operational orders for the battle make it clear that the
Sixth SS Panzer Army facing Hodges was to carry the main burden
of the battle and take the Maas bridges. Bastogne was to be taken by
a *coup de main,* i.e. a sudden, vigorous attack, or simply by-passed by
the drive to the Maas. SS General Sepp Dietrich's Sixth SS Panzer
Army, and von Manteuffel's armies, were to take St Vith, but Montgomery's forces held it for six days before withdrawing. Von Manteuffel pointed out after the war that St Vith held out longer than
expected and prevented II SS Panzer Corps being deployed. This delay not only enabled Montgomery to get Hodges's army ready but
frustrated German intentions and contributed in no small way to their
crippling fuel problems.

Montgomery's policy of rolling with the punches was amply shown
by his withdrawal from St Vith. The American commanders who had
been complacent since the unprecedented advance from Normandy
were stunned at what the 'defeated' Germans had done to them but
were reluctant to surrender any further ground. Montgomery's main
contribution to the 'Battle of the Bulge' was that whereas the Americans viewed it as a series of isolated battles, he saw it from the beginning as a whole and realized the need to protect the all-important
rear areas, especially the approaches to Namur and the Maas. So,
following the precepts of the great Prussian General von Clausewitz,
he exploited the enemy's weakness—an inability to sustain his offensive with poor communications and acute fuel shortages. Before
Montgomery counter-attacked he also wanted to amass adequate re-

serves that would ensure success. He wanted to encourage the enemy to over-extend himself.

Unlike the Americans, Montgomery was not especially concerned that the Germans might reach or even cross the Maas, for he had already positioned British XXX Corps between Louvain and St Trond on the west bank of the river. On December 18th he had sent the 29th Armoured Brigade with their forty-ton Churchill tanks to concentrate at Namur. The next day three battle-experienced infantry divisions, 43rd Wessex, 51st Highland and 53rd Welsh, three more armoured brigades and the Guards Armoured Division—a force of some 90,000 men, 1,200 tanks and 500 guns—moved to annihilate any Germans who crossed the Maas. The 34th Armoured and 6th Guards Tank Brigades moved up to block any German advance towards the big bend in the Maas around Namur.

Montgomery was inevitably criticized by the Americans for his caution and delay in counter-attacking. American commanders still believed that the correct way to contain an enemy salient was to counter-attack immediately from the flanks, a doctrine from World War One. General Joe Collins's US VII Corps had already been pulled back from the Aachen area and Montgomery told Hodges that he wanted Collins, considered to be the Americans' most aggressive corps commander, to spearhead his counter-attack. But first Montgomery wanted adequate time to re-organize and prepare for attack. He wrote: 'The next process was to create a reserve corps in US First Army.' But he believed that as it was being withdrawn from battle it needed a few days' respite. General Collins states: 'I agreed with Monty's plan to build a reserve around the VII Corps but I disagreed with its location. We should have been positioned further east, so as to be prepared to cut into the German salient nearer its base, rather than at its tip. I was confident, and so told Monty, that the Germans would not be able to break through the American front on the north flank of the bulge.'

On the 22nd Hodges sent a combat command of his 3rd Armoured Division from its position astride the Houffalize-Liège road, westwards to the Ourthe river, to form a southwards-facing line adjoining the 82nd Airborne Division. He then assembled the 84th Infantry Division behind the Ourthe near the town of Marche to block the path of the 2nd Panzer Division. While Hodges's manoeuvres were apparently contrary to Montgomery's instructions, Collins states that the piecemeal commitment of divisions of VII Corps was made by Hodges with the approval of Montgomery. This contradicts

Montgomery, who explains that the piecemeal commitment of VII Corps was the result of II SS Panzer Corps coming into contact. 'The divisions of this corps (VII),' Montgomery wrote later, 'intended as reserves, thus became engaged in the battle'. In any case Hodges was determined not to allow the Germans an unimpeded dash for the Maas and he moved forward. When darkness fell on the 22nd a strong easterly wind brought heavy snow and the ground froze hard, enabling both the American and German armour to move freely.

Meanwhile, in a swirling snow storm, Patton simultaneously rushed an infantry division into the line north-east of the city of Luxembourg to strengthen the American position in the southern part of the bulge, and sent the veteran 4th Armoured in a drive to relieve Bastogne. Since withdrawing before the enemy's first onslaught Third Army had made an unprecedented change in direction and it now lost no time striking northwards, spurred on by the ebullient Patton's order to 'Drive like hell!'

When December 23rd dawned clear and cold the weather gave a long-awaited advantage to the Allies. From dawn American fighter-bombers and medium bombers pounded the German columns while C-47s were out in force dropping supplies by multi-coloured parachutes to the surrounded troops at Bastogne. General Joe Collins and the commander of the 2nd Armoured Division, Major-General Ernie Harmon, planned to attack with armour soon after dawn on Christmas Day. Ernie Harmon roared loudly: 'The bastards are in the bag! In the bag!'

This was indeed the high water mark of the German Ardennes offensive. On Christmas morning the 2nd Armoured Division, with attached British armour and supported by US fighter-bombers of IX Tactical Air Command, began to destroy the 2nd Panzer Division, which at the height of its success had run out of petrol at Celles, as Montgomery said it would, four miles or so from the Maas. Von Manteuffel—and Hitler—had failed in their gamble that the tanks would reach and capture the big Allied supply dumps. Harmon's attack succeeded more because of this lack of fuel than anything else. Perhaps if Hodges had not committed VII Corps piecemeal the subsequent destruction of the panzers would have been absolute. In any event the price the Germans paid for their sixty-mile advance from their frontier was the destruction of more than eighty much-needed tanks in the snow before the Maas. Their Ardennes offensive was broken and, with the relief of Bastogne, Eisenhower ordered the main counter-offensive to begin. As Montgomery put it, promptly:

'This battle is finished—the Germans have shot their bolt.' He knew they could not stand losses of the scale the Allies had inflicted upon them.

The Battle of the Bulge reflected on the reputation of several Allied commanders. Hodges's reputation in particular was very much sullied by his handling of the initial German attack and by his subsequent performance. In contrast, Patton emerged as a national hero in America on the strength of his drive northwards with thousands of vehicles during that terrible winter. But his achievement was mainly a logistical one. Whereas the main German offensive was against Hodges's First Army which fought off four panzer corps of Sixth SS and Fifth Panzer Armies, Germany's élite, Patton's drive was chiefly against four weak infantry divisions that the German Seventh Army had placed in his path to delay the advance.

General Bradley's reputation was also damaged by his handling of the campaign, but in this case, unjustifiably. His own HQ at Luxembourg City was badly placed south of the 'bulge' to direct his armies to the north of it. Montgomery's appointment to command Bradley's armies to the north was thus a logical and effective measure, but was interpreted by many commanders and correspondents as a reflection on Bradley's ability. This was later exacerbated by Montgomery's retention of the First and Ninth Armies, which, although it was in line with Eisenhower's plan for Montgomery to make the main thrust to the Rhine with Ninth Army, could not be seen as anything but a censure by Eisenhower himself on Bradley's performance. As Bradley retained only Patton's Third Army it was inevitable he would denigrate the role of First Army and exaggerate Patton's part in an attempt to convince American opinion he had personally played a major role.

Although Montgomery had commanded more American troops during the battle than any of the American commanders, his austere personality—and his nationality—made it difficult for the American press to fête him. So although he really played the major role, this was not fully appreciated in America. In any case he gave a press conference on January 7th which struck a particularly sour note with the Americans. 'As soon as I saw what was happening,' he said, 'I took certain steps myself to ensure that if the Germans got to the Maas, they would certainly not get over that river. When the situation began to deteriorate . . . national considerations were thrown overboard. General Eisenhower placed me in command of the whole front.' He explained how he had employed the 'whole available power of the British group of armies'. He concluded on what seemed to the Americans a condescending note. The operation, he said, 'was one of the most interesting and tricky I have ever handled.'

General Sir Francis de Guingand, Montgomery's Chief of Staff, sensed the threatened rift in Anglo-American relations and flew to Rheims to discuss the situation with Bedell Smith, his opposite number. Then, after a meeting with a very worried Eisenhower, he flew back to Montgomery's HQ at Hasselt and explained the dangerous implications. 'His reaction was characteristic of the man. "Give me a writing pad," he said. And he proceeded to draft a really generous signal to Eisenhower saying he would do anything to help.' Back to Brussels went de Guingand and at a war correspondents' committee meeting he then gave 'what I hoped was a fair appreciation of Montgomery's and Bradley's part in the Ardennes battle—and also the reasons for Eisenhower's recent re-grouping of First and Ninth US Armies.'

But Montgomery's version of the battle almost destroyed the amicable relations of the joint Allied command. The efforts of Eisenhower and his team were gravely threatened, and the dissent was fanned by the press in both Britain and America. Renewed suggestions were now made by the British Chiefs of Staff that Montgomery should be made sole ground commander. When Bradley heard of this he went straight to Eisenhower and insisted that his boss explain how he intended to respond. Eisenhower impatiently retorted that he did not intend responding. 'You must know,' Bradley declared, 'that after what has happened I cannot serve under Montgomery. If he is to be put in charge of ground forces, you must send me home, for if Montgomery goes in over me, I will have lost the confidence of my command.'

Eisenhower was taken aback by this outburst from the usually equable Bradley: 'Well, I thought you were the one person I could count on for doing anything I asked you to,' he retorted. But Bradley couldn't be calmed. 'You can, Ike,' he replied, 'I've enjoyed every bit of my service with you. But this is one thing I cannot take.'

Eisenhower promptly sought a way of appeasing Bradley, and in a telephone conversation with Churchill on January 9th, after talking about press coverage generally, he saw a chance to praise Bradley and his fine work; it had been submerged, he said, by Montgomery's command of two American armies. Accordingly he awarded a Bronze Star to Bradley and used the citation to praise him for his 'important part in the battle'. Churchill followed this with his own public congratulation to Bradley, thus restoring his stature in American eyes.

But Bradley had other worries and while American troops were clearing the last Germans from the Ardennes in late January, he was concerned about the planned shift in emphasis in the forthcoming attack from his US 12th Army Group to the British 21st Army Group. In spite of his attitude, however, Eisenhower had not wavered in his determination to return to his strategy that the main effort should be in the north and aimed at the Ruhr. The realignment of American troops that had resulted from the Ardennes counter-offensive inevitably dictated that the main attack should be Montgomery's.

Bradley objected to leaving Simpson's Ninth Army under Montgomery. He also wanted to hold on to his First and Third Armies and to use the impetus of the 'Bulge' counter-offensive to drive on towards the Rhine, thus by-passing the troublesome Roer dams at Schmidt. Eisenhower's plans were not wholly incompatible with this for while he advocated the main thrust in the north, he still favoured a broad front advance to close up to the Rhine before launching the main attack across it.

But the British Chiefs of Staff thought that Eisenhower would not have enough strength to close up to the Rhine along the entire front, and considered it unlikely, therefore, that an attempt to cross the Rhine could be made before May. This was quite apart from proposed converging attacks by Montgomery's Army Group with Ninth Army in the north and Bradley's Army Group driving towards Frankfurt in the south. The British wanted a single, powerful thrust, preferably in the north, where it would pinch the Ruhr, thus crippling Germany's war output. They insisted that 'one man should be directly responsible.'

On the question of the concentration north of the Ruhr, Eisenhower was mindful of the activities of the Germans in the Colmar Pocket, a big German bridgehead on the Rhine between Strasbourg and Mulhouse. He was now aware that to concentrate north of the Ruhr for a successful invasion of Germany he had to have the remainder of the front secure along a firm defensive line. It was a logical precaution to avoid having German troops west of the river while his army was trying to get across.

As for a ground commander, Eisenhower's view was that it would be a needless duplication in the chain of command. Bradley, Devers and Montgomery were, anyway, virtually commanders-in-chief of their own sectors. Montgomery in particular, who had emerged into the New Year with control of the biggest army group and was confident of retaining this force intact, saw no reason for an intermediary between himself and Eisenhower. He now had first call on resources and he had an assurance that his group was earmarked for the big push over the Rhine, and he thought, to Berlin.

Eisenhower saw that the key to the drive for the Rhine was the strength of the new Russian offensive towards Silesia, the third major industrial area of Germany. If this was weak the Germans would be able to keep 100 full-strength divisions on the western front, but if the Russian offensive was strong, then he believed the Germans could not retain more than 85 divisions in the west. He wanted to mobilize more French manpower as well as additional American divisions. Many of his American infantry divisions, however, were seriously under-strength as a result of the American belief that it would be armour that would win the war. This had not proved to be the case at all; and as the Allies battled into the Siegfried Line and the German cities it was to become increasingly an infantry war. If Eisenhower managed to meet his schedule they would have 85 divisions by May, including eight French, although he added, 'they are a questionable asset', a comment on De Gaulle's intransigence and not on the French fighting quality. If any German pockets remained west of the Rhine, Eisenhower calculated he would need 45 divisions for defence and reserve, but only 25 if the enemy defences west of the Rhine were cleared. Only the Rhine offered a safe defence line against an enemy attack from the Siegfried Line.

The final SHAEF plan implementing Eisenhower's concept of how the last campaign should operate was produced at a series of meetings between 14th and 20th January by Bedell Smith, Lieutenant-General Carl Spaatz, the commander of the US Strategic Air Force, and the British officers on his staff, Generals Strong and Whitely. Eisenhower outlined this plan in a seven-page cable to Combined Chiefs of Staff in America. His operations would fall into three phases: the destruction of enemy forces west of the Rhine, the crossing of the river and the destruction of the enemy forces east of the river, and the advance into Germany. The main crossing would be north of the Ruhr but only 35 divisions could be got over the Rhine on Montgomery's front. So while the Allies would not be as strong as Eisenhower wished at that point, he would at least have the reserves to make a supporting attack in the south, and the flexibility to switch the attack elsewhere should Montgomery run into strong resistance.

In considering operations from Frankfurt, which would be the main objective after the Rhine crossing on Bradley's front, he admitted that the advance north to Kassel would be over difficult country for mobile warfare compared to the north German plain, but added that after reaching Kassel it would be possible to advance in several directions, including north to link up with Montgomery. He was aware that the crossing in the north would be opposed by the heaviest concentration of German forces. 'It may, therefore, be necessary to divert enemy forces by closing and perhaps crossing the Rhine in the Frankfurt sector . . .' He was thus preparing a situation that would allow Bradley to run the last campaign, the drive on Berlin. But he could only do this when Bradley was over the Rhine. So he could justify to himself the initial assault by 21st Army Group while deliberately planning to switch the major thrust later to US 12th Army Group. It was a way of using the British and Canadians as an anvil.

Ever since Normandy the Rhine had dominated Allied strategy. It was the greatest barrier to breaking into the German interior and the enemy's major communication network for coal and armaments. It was also the key to their vital industrial heart of Germany, the Ruhr. Once the Allies were across the Rhine, the Wehrmacht would no longer have the weapons, transport or fuel with which to oppose the Allies in battle. The east bank would also provide a springboard from which to launch their main operations into Germany. Each of the Allied commanders had his ideas on how the Rhine should be reached and each could produce arguments for their priority. But the river had so occupied the Allied planners that they had been blind to the recurring threats from the German forces who had savaged them too many times: at Arnhem, the Venlo salient, Hurtgen forest, Ardennes and the Colmar Pocket. Considering the destruction wreaked on the enemy at Falaise in 1944 and their headlong retreat into Belgium and eastern France in August and September, their ability to turn and fight was all the more remarkable. What the Allied commanders seemed to overlook was that while their own communications from Normandy were getting ever longer and harder to maintain, the German communications from the Ruhr were getting shorter. Although many of the newly-created German divisions, especially the Volkssturm, were woefully short of heavy weapons, they were more than capable of defending prepared positions. And as the front line was driven in, so the enemy concentration became greater.

Having failed in their gamble in the Ardennes, the Germans now prepared to defend their fatherland from behind the formidable concrete and steel Siegfried Line, and to use every natural obstacle to hinder the Allied advance.

3 A typical Monty set-up

By the end of January 1945 the German Commander-in-Chief, West, Field Marshal Gerd von Rundstedt, had been forced to squander most of his slender reserves in the Ardennes, losing a phenomenal 120,000 men—killed, wounded or missing—600 tanks and assault guns and 1,600 aircraft. He had argued against the whole idea of the offensive, but as a loyal General Staff officer had obeyed Hitler's commands. After the war he said: 'I wanted to stop the offensive at an early stage, when it was plain that it could not attain its aim, but Hitler furiously insisted that it must go on. It was Stalingrad No 2.' The effect of this appalling wastage meant that the German Army would now have to defend the Rhineland with much depleted forces based on fixed defences and backed by such mobile forces as could rapidly deploy wherever an Allied thrust developed. Von Manteuffel summed up the situation after the Ardennes failure: 'Hitler started a "corporal's war". There were no big plans—only a multitude of piecemeal fights.'

Hitler would not listen to the advice of his top commanders and insisted that it was possible to defend the Rhineland and stop the Allies getting to the Rhine, and thence to the Ruhr. He still had 85 divisions west of the Rhine to hold back Eisenhower's armies, but whereas the Allied divisions were in the main at full combat strength, the German divisions were generally undermanned. Model's Army Group 'B' in real terms had the equivalent of only six and a half divisions; many formations were composed of second-rate troops that were either under- or over-age, or suffering from physical disabilities.

The northernmost German armies were commanded by General Johannes Blaskowitz's Army Group 'H', comprising 85,000 men. Under its command were the Twenty-Fifth Army in Holland, under General von Blumentritt, and the First Parachute Army under General Alfred Schlemm. Schlemm's front extended from the Rhine, six miles west of Emmerich, south-west to Gennap on the Maas and thence along that river to St Odilinberg. The army comprised four corps which varied considerably in strength.

The right wing of the army was held by XLVII Corps, the Wehrmacht's No 1 mobile reserve, commanded by General der Panzertruppen, Heinrich Freiherr von Luttwitz, one of the most experienced commanders of mechanized forces in the German Army. Although his corps was no longer the powerful panzer force that had broken through US First Army's front in the Ardennes, it was still a formidable mixture of paratroopers from General Plocher's 6th Parachute Division, moved from Holland, and two of the Wehrmacht's best panzer divisions, the 116th Panzer and the 15th Panzer Grenadiers. Both panzer divisions had suffered heavy losses in the Ardennes and were refitting at Marienbaum, a small town astride the main road from Nijmegen to the important Rhine bridges at Wesel. The corps' front ran from the Rhine to Udem, a fortified town lying to the south-east of the Reichswald.

From Udem to Weeze the front was held by II Parachute Corps under another very experienced commander, General Meindl. This corps included the 7th and 8th Parachute Divisions, known to be tough and fanatical Luftwaffe troops, but it also included General Fiebig's 84th Infantry Division, known to be weak. This division had been destroyed in the Falaise Gap in August 1944 but had then reformed in Holland in September. But as recruits to the German Army were increasingly drafted into Himmler's Waffen SS divisions, only the residues went into the regular army. The detachments that now formed part of 84th Division included the 719th Regiment made up of old men, and the 176th Regiment who were nearly all semi-invalids. The division was deployed along the defences astride the approaches to the Reichswald but Schlemm had no illusions about their ability to stop a strong Allied attack. He was relying upon them only to hold up the Allies for a few hours while he rushed in reinforcements from General Erdmann's 7th Parachute Division based at Venlo. As a gesture to strengthen the 84th Division, after appeals from Fiebig, Schlemm reluctantly sent three battalions of first-class paratroopers from 2nd Parachute Regiment.

South of Weeze to south of Venlo General Straube held the front with his LXXXVI Infantry Corps comprising 180th and 190th Infantry Divisions commanded by Generals Klosterkaempen and Hammer respectively; they were both good divisions, the 180th being mainly parachute troops. The last sector of the front was held by LXV Infantry Corps with just one weak Landwehr division under General Kuehlwein, charged with protecting the area from south of Venlo to Roermond.

Thus Schlemm had his strong parachute and panzer divisions deployed on his northern front covering the Rhine approaches while in the south only the weakest forces were stationed. Schlemm was also keeping his powerful panzers in a fairly central position behind a weaker screen of infantrymen; he could then respond to any attack by moving his armour quickly to contain the threat.

Although the German forces had suffered major defeats in the Ardennes, they were by no means beaten and, as Hitler's directives made plain, they were expected to fight courageously and ferociously in the defence of their country. In the northern sector there were three lines of defences barring the way eastwards from Holland to the Rhine and the Ruhr. The Germans had employed the experience gained from constructing defences in the First World War in creating the complex defence system they called the *Westwall,* better known to the British as the Siegfried Line, which extended from the Dutch border to Switzerland.

First in order of approach from Nijmegen was the outpost position of the main defences, a double line of trenches in front of the Reichswald and protected by an anti-tank ditch. In this area every farmhouse and village had been transformed into a strong-point, with machine-gun emplacements and reinforced cellars in the houses that doubled as effective shelters against bombing and shelling. This complex, manned by Fiebig's 84th Division, was connected by trenches extending 2,000 yards from the forward minefields in the forest. Both main roads which intersected the defences, the Nijmegen–Cleve road in the north and the Nijmegen–Mook–Gennap road running south, were well defended with road blocks, anti-tank guns in concrete emplacements and a variety of obstacles including ditches, barbed wire and concrete and steel obstructions.

Three miles back from the outpost positions were the main Siegfried Line defences. They ran through the Reichswald from north to south, then along its southern boundary as far as Goch, a formidable fortress-town encircled with anti-tank ditches and fortified houses. In the north the other ring-fortified town of Cleve was similarly defended. The approach from the west to Cleve ran through a narrow defile known as the Materborn Gap, near Nutterden, defended by trench systems extending to the hills just west of the town. To the south of Cleve another trench system completed the encircling defences of the Reichswald.

Eleven miles further south, guarding the approaches to the Rhine at Xanten, was the third defence system, the Hochwald Layback. This was a series of deep trenches and anti-tank ditches about a mile wide protected by a continuous barrier of barbed wire. In this area too, all the buildings, towns and villages had been converted into small fortresses.

Schlemm's plan for defence was thus based on the Siegfried Line, about which the German commanders had varying opinions. In Schlemm's view: 'The Führer envisaged huge concrete fortifications, several kilometres in depth, behind which the Reich was secure.' General Straube declared afterwards that in his section of the *West-wall* the defences were farcical: 'It wasn't a wall, it was an idea,' he said contemptuously. Albert Speer, Hitler's Armaments Minister, claimed: 'Hitler believed in the strength of the *Westwall* as a defence'.

In the past few months considerable work had been done to strengthen the *Westwall*. The Germans had built additional trenches, weapons pits and anti-tank ditches covered by concrete pillboxes, each of which was supported by adjacent boxes along the entire length of the line. In the Goch–Asperden area, and at Materborn, large numbers of concrete fortifications had been constructed to protect the vulnerable flanks; this was especially necessary in the south where the relatively open country extended to the Maas. These structures contained no heavy armament but were skilfully sited so that an infantry attack against one would immediately come under withering Spandau machine-gun fire from the others.

The task of organizing the assault into the Rhineland had been given to the Canadian First Army, commanded by Lieutenant-General Crerar, but as some of its units were still clearing German pockets along the Channel coast, Montgomery reinforced Crerar's forces with Lieutenant-General Brian Horrocks's XXX Corps from the British Second Army. XXX Corps was withdrawn from its positions in the Ardennes as soon as possible and sent north to concentrations near Nijmegen. There it was further strengthened by the addition of the 15th Scottish Division from XII Corps. The composition of armies and corps was a flexible matter depending upon the tasks required of them at any one time. Now that British Second Army was given a static role of holding the line along the Maas and planning for the actual crossing of the Rhine, most of its strength was allocated to the Canadians.

Crerar delegated to Horrocks's staff the initial moves in the battle, now officially designated Operation 'Veritable', but issued a directive for guidance: 'To clear the Reichswald and secure the line Gennap–Asperden–Cleve.' Crerar assumed that the enemy would strongly man and defend his several lines of organized defences and on January 25th directed that the 'operation, as a whole, will comprise several phases and, after each phase is completed, it will be necessary to move up the artillery and supporting weapons and commence the next phase with co-ordinated and heavy fire support and with controlled movements.'

XXX Corps' front was pinched by a bottleneck some two miles in extent between the northern edge of the forest and the low-lying polder land that stretched north to the Rhine. The country was heavily fortified with an anti-tank ditch, concrete emplacements, barbed wire and dense minefields. Canadian Army Intelligence reported it to be held by only about 8,000 men of the 84th Division but Horrocks had no doubt they could be quickly reinforced if necessary. It was now estimated by Intelligence that although on D-Day + 1, the enemy forces could concentrate only one extra infantry division, by the third day they could have an additional complete panzer and a panzer grenadier division at their disposal, while within a week two more infantry divisions would be able to join the forces blocking the approaches to the Rhine. Speed on the Allied part was therefore of the essence.

Horrocks's first objective was to smash the 84th Infantry Division in a spectacular lightning thrust and then seize the high ground at Nutterden which was the 'door' controlling the approaches to Cleve. Then he could move his supporting weapons swiftly to back up the attack on Cleve and the subsequent breakout onto the plain beyond. Initially then, the attack would be a race for Nutterden, for once the enemy realized the direction of the British attack they would rush their reserves to hold the bottleneck at the adjacent Materborn Gap, just west of Cleve. Any mistake at that point could have a decisive effect on the battle for the Rhineland because the Germans would have time to move their mobile reserves, identified as 116th and 15th Panzers, into the Siegfried Line. This would force a costly, protracted battle on XXX Corps trapped in the gap, while the enemy counterattacked against their flanks.

Horrocks was therefore resolved to ensure success by using the maximum force right from the outset, supported by an overwhelming concentration of artillery. His attack was going to be a great set-piece battle using the three British divisions, 15th Scottish, 51st Highland and 53rd Welsh, supported by two armoured brigades, 6th Guards Tank Brigade with 15th Scottish and the 34th Armoured Brigade with the other two divisions. Additional support in the initial attack was to be provided by the 2nd and 3rd Canadian Infantry Divisions.

The main thrust to seize the vital ground at Nutterden and the town of Cleve was entrusted to the 15th Scottish Division, which under their redoubtable commander, the seven-foot-tall General Barber, had a deserved reputation for making determined assaults. The division would have to break through the formidable Siegfried Line defences before Nutterden and would be supported by an immensely strong armoured breaching force of Crocodile flame-throwing tanks, mine-exploding tanks, bridging tanks, and all the Churchill gun-tanks of 6th Guards Tank Brigade. After breaking through they would then drive at full speed for Cleve to grab it before the enemy could fall back from the forward defences or reinforce the town with his reserves.

The 15th Scottish Division would advance in two columns but they would be exposed to a flank attack from the south by German armoured forces believed to be positioned in the forest. Air reconnaissance had mistaken 36 enemy self-propelled guns seen in the Reichswald for tanks (of which there actually were none in the forest, although they were positioned further back and could move in quickly). Therefore to protect the Scots, Horrocks directed the 53rd Welsh Division to advance along 15th Division's southern flank and seize the low hills, known as features, on which the Germans had located artillery to command the roads to the north. Any German counter-attack, it was predicted, would be launched from the forest since there were good roads transversing it from Goch northwards to Kranenburg and Cleve. The Welsh had been assigned a very tough task: to fight through the dense woods fast enough to capture the roads and deny them to the enemy before he moved reserves along them.

Further south of the Welsh, the 51st Highland Division were in turn to cover their right flank, taking the extreme south-western tip of the forest and also clearing the roads southwards from Nijmegen towards the Maas, and south-eastwards towards the strategic strongpoints of Hekkens and Goch. Montgomery stressed the urgency of securing the east bank of the Maas as soon as possible to establish

bridgeheads that would relieve the anticipated congestion at Nijmegen and Grave.

It can be seen then that only when the key objectives of Nutterden, the Materborn Gap, and Cleve were in Allied hands could Horrocks send his reserve divisions to exploit the breakthrough. Guards
Armoured Division was to race eastwards through Cleve and sweep
onto the rolling countryside on the principle of Captain Liddell
Hart's 'expanding torrent'; that is, to punch a hole in the enemy's
front and pour armour through, then to fan out and overrun the
enemy ground before he can regroup.

The other reserve division, the 43rd Wessex Infantry, would pass
through the southern outskirts of Cleve but then veer south, around
the far end of the Reichswald and head for Goch, there to meet the
51st Division coming around the south of the forest. This encirclement would trap any German forces remaining in the Reichswald, or, by its threat, oblige them to make a hasty withdrawal, leaving the way open for Canadian First Army to drive on Calcar, the
Rhine bridges at Wesel and south to Geldern to link up with the
Americans who were to advance north from the Roer.

Although the two Canadian infantry divisions were to protect
XXX Corps' left flank, this role did not satisfy the commander of 11
Canadian Corps, Lieutenant-General G. G. Simonds. Simonds wrote
to Crerar drawing his attention to what he described as the 'unfortunate situation which would develop if no Canadian regiments took
part in the initial attack'. He was anxious that after all the hard
fighting the Canadians had done since Normandy they, too, should
not be deprived of their share of the honour of reaching the Rhine.
Simonds's protests were heeded, for first the 3rd and then the 2nd
Canadian Infantry Divisions were added to Horrocks's already considerable forces.

To move as fast as possible, the 15th Scottish Division were going
to by-pass the main Nijmegen–Cleve road at Wyler, where there
were very strong enemy positions anchoring the northern end of the
Siegfried Line, and seize the strategically important road further east
at Kranenburg and Nutterden. Now the 2nd Canadian Infantry Division was directed to take Wyler and protect 15th Scottish's communications. Because the 2nd Canadians were providing the front-
line screen, they would have to assemble quickly after XXX Corps'
attack had started and so their objectives were deliberately limited.
To their north the 3rd Canadian Infantry Division now had a role in
the battle, too. They were to clear the flood plain that extended north

to the great westward bend in the Rhine near Emmerich. The plain was dotted with heavily defended strong-points manned by about 3,000 Germans, which the Canadians would clear as they made a great left hook to join up with the Scots at Cleve.

Montgomery, Crerar and Simonds also agreed that after the Reichswald was cleared, the two Canadian infantry divisions plus the Canadian 4th Armoured Division would exploit the left wing during the advance to the Rhine. Eventually the advance would become a two corps attack with 11 Canadian Corps operating between the Rhine and the Cleve–Xanten–Wesel road, when Simonds would also command the British 11th Armoured and the 43rd Wessex Divisions. Horrocks's XXX Corps would maintain its advance on the right flank, making a great wheeling movement, and both corps would close to the Rhine at Wesel.

The underlying principle of Operation 'Veritable' would be much the same as that undertaken by the British–Canadian forces in July and August 1944; Canadian First Army would attract the enemy reserves on the one flank enabling the Americans on the other flank to break out. The Canadian First Army, including XXX Corps, was to attack in great strength on February 8th, penetrate the Siegfried Line and take the ring-fortified towns on their way southwards. Then, on February 10th, when the Germans were moving to counter this threat, General W. H. Simpson's US Ninth Army was to attack across the Roer and advance northwards, squeezing the enemy in a vice. Montgomery believed that once their main defences had been breached the Germans would have to fall back to the Rhine, but he was not particularly worried if, instead, they elected to fight west of the river, for he knew the Allies possessed overwhelming superiority in weapons and men and complete domination of the air. The enemy would be destroyed and when the remnants withdrew British Second Army would be poised to launch its attack at any point along 21st Army Group's front.

For Operation 'Veritable' some major problems still remained. First, success depended on achieving complete surprise for if the Germans got wind of the offensive they would doubtless move their reserves before it started and block XXX Corps' path. Second, the supporting attack by US Ninth Army, Operation 'Grenade' as it was called, was essential to protect the right flank and keep the enemy's last mobile reserves busy, otherwise XXX Corps would face very strong forces in prepared defences. The key to Operation 'Grenade' was still the

Roer dams. In the previous November, as we have seen, the Americans had suffered heavy casualties in Hodges's actions against these dams, diplomatically termed by Montgomery as a 'strategic reverse'. Now Hodges, with Bradley's connivance, was again showing reluctance to seize the dams. The third problem was the weather. Only if it remained cold and the ground hard could the mass of armour and transport move at will.

It would not be easy to maintain the surprise. Operation 'Veritable' was the biggest Allied offensive since Normandy. An enormous concentration of men, tanks and guns were moving into the outskirts of Nijmegen and the adjacent woods, involving the most intricate staff work. Ultimately there would be 200,000 men in all, including infantry, supporting artillery, engineers, armour, signals and pioneers. A force of about 500 tanks would be backed by a further 500 specialist armoured vehicles, known as the 'funnies'—the brainchild of Major-General Percy Hobart, Montgomery's brother-in-law.

Several important 'funnies' would play a big role in the forthcoming operations, not only on the British and Canadian fronts but on the American front, too, where there were no bridgelayers nor, initially at least, mine-clearing tanks. Flails were adapted Sherman tanks, equipped with a system of chains on a revolving drum to beat the ground ahead of the tank and explode the mines, so clearing a path for the following tanks and infantry. 'Crocodiles' were Churchill tanks equipped with flame-throwers. Of the many types of flame-throwing tanks produced by several nations in the war, none was so formidable or feared as the British Crocodile, which could shoot its fiery jet up to 120 yards. The AVREs (Armoured Vehicles Royal Engineers) were Churchill tanks equipped to do a variety of specialist tasks. All carried the 'Petard', a short-barrelled mortar that could hurl a heavy, high explosive charge, known as a 'flying dustbin', against concrete bunkers, gun emplacements, sandbagged houses and so on. Another AVRE carried a box-girder bridge for crossing anti-tank ditches or steams. Some AVREs carried large bundles of wood, called 'fascines', up to eight feet in diameter for dropping into ditches either to support a bridge or for the tanks to drive over. Two other vehicles were much used in the battles to cross the Rhine—Kangaroos, converted Canadian Ram tanks used as armoured personnel carriers, and Buffaloes, heavy American amphibious armoured vehicles that could carry up to thirty troops, a 25-pounder gun or a Bren carrier.

As the preparations neared completion, the weather began to turn for the worse. Following the exceptionally cold winter an early spring thaw set in. The mild weather melted the frost and iron-hard fields and unsurfaced roads began to soften; soon the landscape had turned into grey-brown expanses of liquid mud. Fifty companies of Royal Engineers, 29 companies of Pioneers and three specialist road construction companies of the Engineers worked around the clock to shore up roads that were breaking down under the combination of thaw and heavy traffic. They rebuilt 400 miles of road and constructed 100 miles of new roads. Canadian Lumberjack companies cut and prepared 36,000 logs for 'corduroy' road construction in the forest. But the thaw and rain also affected the level of the Rhine, and on February 5th, when it was higher than at any time for forty years, General Blaskowitz ordered his engineers to blow up the main dyke at Erkolom, four miles east of Nijmegen. The Rhine poured through the breach and slowly but surely began to inundate the polder land across which the Allies were to advance.

A re-appraisal of Allied plans was immediately necessary. With both flanks flooded (the Maas had overflowed too) Horrocks decided there was 'no room to be clever'. There would have to be a frontal assault across flooded and swampy ground against well-fortified positions held by a determined enemy. Montgomery, who had bitter memories of similar, disastrous assaults in the First World War, was far from happy, and some Allied commanders thought the operation should be called off, or at least postponed. But it was too late for that, and Montgomery no doubt realized that, with the American commanders pressing Eisenhower for a renewal of their advances, he might lose the initiative altogether. It was not a situation a commander would choose, yet with almost unlimited air support and a massive weight of artillery Horrocks thought it possible to pound the defenders into the ground and destroy their communications. Once that had been achieved the three infantry divisions, 15th Scottish, 51st Highland and 53rd Welsh, would roll forward in a solid mass and burst through the surviving Germans before they had time to re-organize. It was, however, necessary to alter the arrangements for the 3rd Canadians. Because of the floods they would exchange their tank support for that of Buffaloes of the Engineer regiments, which would enable them to make an amphibious assault over the now-flooded country north of the Nijmegen–Cleve road. For the added protection of darkness and to avoid congestion with the 2nd Canadians, the 3rd Division's assault was put back until 6 pm on the 8th.

The historic town of Cleve had to be taken quickly. When General Crerar asked Horrocks: 'Do you want the town of Cleve taken out?', he meant totally destroyed. It was an unpleasant decision to take but as all the German reserves had to pass through Cleve to reach the bottleneck at Nutterden it would be a race between them and 15th Scottish. As Horrocks reasoned, 'the lives of my own troops must come first, so I said, "Yes" '.

But heavy bombs in front of a force making a swift advance have the effect of destroying or blocking roads, thereby necessitating detours or lengthy road clearance. This was a particular problem around Cleve where the roads were few, with soft ground on either side. The British had already experienced this problem in Normandy in 1944, when the town of Caen had been destroyed by RAF Lancasters: the advancing armour had been held up by the roads and the consequent delays had enabled the Germans to regroup. Accordingly Horrocks now asked for incendiaries and anti-personnel bombs to be dropped on Cleve and also Goch. The RAF replied that such concrete installations as those of the Siegfried Line could only be destroyed by heavy 'blockbuster' bombs capable of penetrating the concrete. Reluctantly Horrocks agreed but specifically asked that only airburst bombs should be used in the area through which the Nijmegen–Cleve road ran for the last four miles.

Once the bombers had left the area the artillery could concentrate on pre-selected targets in the path of the advance. It was an inventive fire plan. The opening barrage would cover the front of four divisions and be delivered by well over 1,000 guns. It would last for two and a half hours, smashing enemy batteries and mortar positions. Then the guns would fall silent and a smoke screen, 13,500 yards long, would be laid across the front of the German lines. Horrocks predicted this would lead the enemy into believing the attack was beginning, whereupon they would surface and fire into the smoke. British and Canadian locating units would then pin-point the positions of the German guns before the full weight of the Allied artillery opened fire again to pulverize the enemy gun sites. In addition the gunners would let loose a 'pepper-pot' barrage. This invention of the artillery was designed to neutralize enemy targets by the co-ordinated fire-power of every tank, machine-gun, heavy mortar, anti-tank gun and light anti-aircraft gun of the participating divisions, in all some 5,000 weapons. Then a full five and a half hours after the opening barrage, all guns would fire a round of yellow smoke signalling the advance. The troops would advance under their powerful barrage to the accompaniment of Mosquitoes, Spitfires and Typhoons roaring overhead.

RAF support extended to pre-battle attacks on bridges and railways behind the breakthrough sector to hinder German attempts to bring up reserves from the south and across the Rhine. On February 6th 2nd Tactical Air Force flew 800 sorties, one group going for railways and road transport to the east of Nijmegen and deep into Germany while another group attacked railway bridges and junctions; especially important was a damaging attack on a fuel storage dump at Emmerich. To conceal the intended assault area, air attacks were made over the whole front of British Second Army. The 84th Tactical Group would provide close support for the ground forces by attacking enemy communications and headquarters and maintaining a 'cab-rank' of fighter-bombers overhead to strike at any target called for by the army. 83rd Tactical Group was to deal with any counter-effort by the Luftwaffe and also to destroy communications in the German rear. Finally at the last moment Bomber Command would attempt to destroy the Rhine bridges at Emmerich and to trap the German remnants and hinder reinforcements.

Although the Luftwaffe was no longer a serious menace it was still capable of sudden strikes with its Messerschmitt 262s. These were excellent twin-jet aircraft, their high speed enabling them to sneak in at low level and evade the anti-aircraft guns. Pierre Clostermann, a Free French fighter pilot, remembered how 'the Messerschmitt 262s were becoming a distinct nuisance. Those blasted jets were appearing on our front in ever-increasing numbers. Every day at dawn and at twilight they came over, singly, ground level, to take their photographs. Every now and again, just for a change, patrols of six, or even twelve, came and machine-gunned or bombed our lines'.

Meanwhile, troops continued to arrive at Nijmegen amidst the closest possible security. The 6th Guards Tank Brigade and 34th Armoured Brigade, however, posed a special problem as so many Churchill tanks in the area were difficult to conceal and enemy reconnaissance aircraft could not fail to observe them. The tank brigades therefore painted out all tactical signs so that their formations could not be identified. Specialist camouflage units moved in to conceal as much as possible of the armour and once in position no tank movement was allowed by day or night.

Inevitably the build-up was too big for complete concealment but the direction of the attack still remained unexpected. General von Blumentritt subsequently remarked that 'At one particular time it seemed as though the Canadians in the area of Nijmegen, Grave and S'Hertogenbosch, were really preparing for an attack to the north.' But on February 6th, General Schlemm, who was becoming increasingly worried about the build-up and anticipated an Allied attack, asked the Luftwaffe to carry out a reconnaissance over the Canadian lines.

Messerschmitt 262s swept low over the front and brought back photographs that showed unmistakable signs of troops assembling for an attack. Schlemm now became convinced that the Allied big blow was about to fall on his front, despite assurances from O.K.W. to the contrary. Only the previous day the Chief Intelligence Officer at von Rundstedt's HQ had sent a memo to all key staff officers of Army Group 'H': 'Allied activities west of the Reichswald are intended to deceive us regarding the real centre of the coming attack. It is possible that a subsidiary offensive by the Canadians in the Reichswald area might be launched to draw our reserves but the appreciation that the main British attack will come from the big bend in the Maas (at Venlo) is being maintained.'

Nevertheless the German High Command was not happy and on the maps at von Rundstedt's HQ at Zeigenberg, British XXX Corps was labelled 'whereabouts unknown'. Schlemm, however, had a strong hunch it was about to be launched against his northern front and consulted with his corps commanders. Both Generals Straube and von Luttwitz agreed with him that an attack was imminent and Schlemm went again to his commander, General Johannes Blaskowitz, to get approval to reinforce his positions in the Reichswald. Blaskowitz remained unconvinced and retorted that everything indicated it was all part of a big Allied deception plan. He even produced photographs of British guns deployed on the Canadian front; under a magnifying glass they were revealed as dummies; that, Blaskowitz insisted, made it clear that Montgomery was bluffing. Montgomery *was* bluffing—the guns were meant to be seen as dummies. The real ones were further back and ready to take their place the night before the attack started.

Schlemm was not convinced. What, he argued, was the point of the British making a costly assault across the Maas when they already had a bridgehead over the Waal (a branch of the Rhine) at Nijmegen? Blaskowitz could not agree, in spite of the opinions of von Luttwitz and now Meindl, too. General Fiebig, whose 84th Division would take the full force of any attack, also thought it unlikely, pointing out that the thaw had made impossible any large-scale ar-

moured attack into the Reichswald. When questioned by Blaskowitz
about this, Schlemm had to admit that the deep patrols he had sent
into the Canadian lines had reported that there were only Canadian
troops there. Unknown to the Germans, Montgomery, with his usual
caution and far-sightedness, had issued an order forbidding any British officers from the assaulting divisions to go to the front unless
wearing the slightly different Canadian battle dress. So although
Schlemm's patrols made several sorties they found only 2nd Canadian Division troops holding the line; Horrocks's XXX Corps were
well back for the time being.

In spite of all the evidence Schlemm doggedly maintained his
viewpoint: 'The British-Canadian attack had been expected since the
end of January and the Forst Reichswald was the most likely place
for the attack.' In some exasperation, Blaskowitz turned for advice to
Schlemm's predecessor, the man who had organized the First Parachute Army and was the founder of Germany's airborne forces, Colo-
nel-General Kurt Student; he had been severely wounded in an air
raid the previous autumn. Student supported Blaskowitz and claimed
that the evidence from Holland reinforced his opinion that the next
big attack would be an American crossing from Roermond with a
supporting British attack from Venlo. At worst, Student affirmed, the
attack from Nijmegen would only be a holding attack by the Canadians. This attack, Blaskowitz could point out, he had already countered by ordering the dyke to be blown, flooding the country north of
the line Wyler–Donsbruggen–Cleve, which would prevent the Canadians out-flanking the Siegfried Line. But he had reckoned without
the resources of British 79th Armoured Division which even then
was moving forward its Buffaloes and swimming tanks to carry the
Canadians into battle across the floods.

Montgomery's extensive and devious plans to deceive the enemy,
which included 'leaking' information about an attack by the two
Scottish divisions northwards to liberate the rest of Holland, had thus
succeeded in persuading the Germans that they should expect the
British Second Army and the Americans to storm the rivers Maas
and Roer further south. Only Schlemm and his corps commanders
close to the scene remained unconvinced. Now, on his own initiative,
Schlemm gently edged the 7th Parachute Division from the area they
held opposite British Second Army and moved them north to Geldern at the south end of the second defence line of the Reichswald.
This was done in spite of Blaskowitz's assurances that 'there is no evidence of large enemy concentrations in the Nijmegen area'.

On the day that Schlemm's reconnaissance aircraft had alerted him
of the danger of an Allied attack, the RAF also carried out sweeps
over the Rhineland. They brought back disturbing reports of strong
enemy formations moving northwards to the Goch area from Cologne, which suggested that von Rundstedt was moving reinforcements from the front opposite the Americans in the belief that it
had been held. They were more probably the Panzer Lehr, another
redoubtable panzer force which had now been withdrawn from the
Ardennes and was being sent north to refit. Allied intelligence remained unaware, however, of other moves that Schlemm was making
to stiffen his front around the Reichswald. He had even persuaded
Blaskowitz to let him have an additional regiment from Blumentritt's
Twenty-Fifth Army to strengthen Fiebig's 84th Division. Still
Schlemm was not happy about the position in the forest.

Within the Reichswald were four artillery battalions of 184th Artillery Regiment equipped with 105mm and 150mm guns and some
anti-tank guns. There were also a number of static 88mm anti-
aircraft units deployed along the Siegfried Line with another fifty or
sixty further back between Emmerich and Goch. These formidable
guns had been converted to a dual purpose, as anti-tank and anti-
aircraft weapons, but they were placed by Army Group under a separate anti-tank commander, causing a furore with Schlemm who
wanted them under Fiebig's control. He made repeated requests to
Blaskowitz for this change in command, but eventually got a sharp
rebuke denying his request. Hitler would not, under any circumstances, allow the change of command because it meant moving them
out of the hallowed Siegfried Line. Blaskowitz, who had twice before
in the war lost his command after contradicting the Führer, was not
going to risk it again. The guns remained where they were: as a result they were handled by untrained men, which coupled with an
acute ammunition ration of only 20 rounds per gun, made them
largely ineffective. Had Schlemm been permitted to move them forward to support Fiebig, they could decisively have affected the outcome of the battle in favour of the Germans. As it was, the only
heavy weapons available to Fiebig were the 36 self-propelled guns of
655th Heavy Anti-Tank Battalion that Canadian Intelligence had
mistaken for tanks. These would have to oppose the 4–500 tanks in
the initial Allied attack. Nevertheless the situation was not as one-
sided as this seems, for the German weapons were very heavily armoured, could out-range the Allied tanks and would be firing
from prepared positions, often in ambush. Commendably though,

Schlemm went on with his covert preparations: 7th Parachute Division, now at Geldern, were put on the alert to move at short notice and the 15th Panzer Grenadiers got ready about fifty tanks to move at equally short notice.

Other factors helped redress the balance towards the Germans. The soldiers in this area were comparatively fresh, and fighting on their own soil would improve their morale. They had their backs to the Rhine beyond which was the Ruhr and adequate supplies of ammunition and light weapons. The Germans had developed a version of the American bazooka, the *Panzerfaust,* which compensated for the lack of large calibre anti-tank guns. It was a very simple weapon to make, which could be discarded after use in the field; according to Albert Speer, over 1,200,000 were made in January 1945 alone and they proved very effective in the coming battle. Despite the heavy losses of tanks and self-propelled guns, what the Germans still had were in the main superior in quality to the Allied tanks. Although the Allies were numerically superior the Germans in their prepared positions and defences were still formidable foes.

Since halting the German offensive in the Ardennes, in December, the American First Army had been engaged throughout January in clearing the last of the Germans from the 'bulge'. Using the momentum generated by their counter-offensive the Americans developed their operation into an attack into the Eifel mountains along the borders of the Rhineland, beyond which lay the river Moselle and the confluence with the Rhine. However, the deep snow and the fatigue of the divisions after their six weeks of battle were too much and by early February they had been halted by the first, outlying pillboxes of the Siegfried Line. So, while the final preparations were being made for 'Veritable' Allied commanders focused their attention once again on another attack by Hodges's US First Army in a last-minute attempt to capture the Roer dams. The Americans launched an attack on January 30th towards the Urft dam, at the weakest part of LXXIV Corps, held by 272nd and 62nd Volks Grenadier Divisions. Simultaneous attacks were launched against the adjoining LXVII Corps. For several days the rolling country saw fierce fighting and then, unaccountably, 272th Volks Grenadiers on the right of the front withdrew to the second *Westwall* defences. The American 7th Armoured and 78th and 9th Infantry Divisions broke through the weakened front, outflanking the 62nd Volks Grenadiers who streamed back, abandoning their positions. This action enabled

Hodges's divisions to secure jumping-off positions for the main attack on the dams on the high ground near Ruhnberg and Rollesbroich.

In the meantime, the Fifteenth Army forces of General der Infanterie Gustav von Zangen were being reinforced as much as possible. 'The bringing up of the Army Combat School at Wahlerschneid could only temporarily alleviate the situation. Parts of 12th Volks Grenadier Division which at this time were brought up by Army Group by battalions reached the area around Schoeneseiffen first, after 62nd Volks Grenadier Division had lost almost the entire Monschau woods. It could be considered decimated'. During these first days, in a series of desperate house-to-house battles, the Americans fought their way up through the woods and scrubby country around Dreiborn to dig in across the road from Einruhr to Herhahn, within reach of the southern edge of the Urft dam.

At the Urft dam the GIs of 78th Division's 47th Regiment worked their way down the steep wooded slopes to run into a Hitler Youth Camp at Ordensburg-Vogelsang. Although the defenders put up a fanatical resistance the Americans simply steamrollered the way through to the lake. From there they overran the dam quickly only to find the Germans had already destroyed the discharge valves controlling the water to the Schwammenauel dam downstream, thus increasing its level still further.

On February 5th US 78th Division launched a strong attack southeastwards towards the Schwammenauel dam. Sherman tanks of 7th Armoured shot them forward, running over machine-gun positions and crunching across wire entanglements. Behind them the guns thundered over the infantry, shelling the enemy positions. For almost three days the 78th Division fought continuously against the 62nd and 272nd Volks Grenadiers dug in behind concrete strong-points and backed by heavy tanks, in the rolling, thickly forested hills. It was the Hurtgen forest again. But this time, as von Zangen recounted: 'the bulk of these two German divisions were destroyed.' They had been faced with an insurmountable task and had been refused all reserves which the High Command had already committed elsewhere.

On February 6th *The Times* correspondent reported: 'In the vital area of Kesternich and the river Roer dams, the attack by the 78th Division has not slackened and today it was reported within 1,500 yards of the key town of Schmidt . . .' Troops of the division attempted to put a bridge across the stream flowing from the Paulushof

dam near its junction with the Roer, but the Germans laid down a
heavy artillery concentration which stopped the Americans capturing
the reservoir's approaches. The dams still seemed just as unattainable
as in the previous November.

So it was that on the day before 'Veritable' was launched, and
three days before their subsequent attack across the Roer, the Americans were again suffering in their attempt to take the dams. Considering the performance of the British and Canadians in breaking the
Siegfried Line in their attack, the value of Montgomery's specialized
armour was undeniable. But the Americans had insufficient armour,
and Bradley kept Hodges's US First Army short of artillery and new
divisions in order to support Patton's US Third Army. Hodges therefore lacked strength in his struggle to capture the key area from
which the Cologne plain and the Rhineland could be dominated.

The stage was set by nightfall on February 7th for one of the last
great battles of the Second World War. Behind the Canadian screen
lay a vast army. On the start-lines alone there were 50,000 troops
with their 500 gun tanks and 500 specialist armoured vehicles. Behind them more troops and armour were ready to come forward. On
the evening of February 7th it was raining heavily when General
Crerar met with war correspondents and told them of the adminis-
trative foundations of this vast operation, the largest Allied offensive
since D-Day. In his closing remarks he reminded them that as with
the Canadian 1 Corps in Italy, the Canadian First Army in North-
West Europe was only half Canadian, the other half being predomi-
nantly British. For Operation 'Veritable' it would be only a quarter
Canadian; Crerar generously and characteristically asked the newspaper men to give 'proper recognition to the English, Scottish and
Welsh formations' in their dispatches. As Alexander McKee wrote
on January 30th: 'It's a typical Monty set-up. Bags of guns crammed
on a narrow front, all your force at one point and bash in. Unsubtle
but usually successful. Jerry knows you're coming, but he can't do
very much because the gigantic bomber formations we wield will
sweep it like a broom'.

4 The big push

If the British and Canadian soldiers awaited the dawn in a state of great tension, the Germans, too, were apprehensive, concealed in their positions along the far end of the valley against the dark shadow of the Reichswald. Since very late on February 7th, Allied guns in northern Holland had been firing a barrage to distract German attention away from the real assault front. Nerves already stretched taut came near to breaking point when the deceptive shoot began. From the Reichswald the Germans fired flares in the hope of seeing the assault forces moving forward. Flare after flare burst in the cold pre-dawn air, but lit only a silent and watery landscape.

The sound was imperceptible at first, a buzzing in the ears, but as it grew louder, Canadians, British and Germans alike stared up into the heavy overcast sky. The still, dark night began to pulsate as the 'Heavies' of Bomber Command thundered on their way to 'take out' Cleve and Goch, while a smaller group of Stirlings and Halifaxes headed for the fortress towns of Calcar, Udem and Weeze. Allied troops said to one another in relief, 'Bomber Harris is out tonight', confident now in the knowledge that the RAF was with them.

Within minutes the eastern sky was lit by a throbbing glow, slashed through by tracer from German flak guns, and soon the crash of exploding bombs could be heard as Cleve was pulverized. The rain and low cloud prevented almost half the main force attacking Cleve, but nevertheless 1,400 tons of high explosive reduced the centre and southern area of the town to heaps of rubble. The other bombers dropped 500 tons on Goch, creating havoc in the small town, while the Stirlings hammered their own targets. The bombing seemed to go on for a long time, its echoes coming back across the forest, but when eventually the planes turned for home, the Germans fired more flares, certain now that the attack was imminent. The troops of the German 84th Division tightened their grips on

their weapons and stared into the empty expanse towards Nijmegen
where the Allied assault troops were ready.

The 15th Scottish Division's two assault brigades, 46th and 227th
Highland Brigades, supported by the Coldstream and Scots Guards
of 6th Guard Tank Brigade, would take the left flank. Next in line,
53rd Welsh Division's 71st Brigade, with part of 34th Armoured Brigade's tanks, would attack across the open valley towards the
Reichswald. On their right 154th Brigade of 51st Highland Division
with other tanks of 34th Armoured, waited to launch their attack on
the village of Breederweg, with the 1st Black Watch in the lead.

As the Historian of the 4th/7th Royal Dragoons recorded: 'It was
a fantastic scene, never to be forgotten by those who were there; one
moment silence and the next a terrific ear-splitting din, with every
pitch imaginable, little bangs, big bangs, sharp cracks . . . the night
was lit by flashes of every colour and the tracers of the Bofors guns
weaving fairy patterns in the sky as they streamed off towards the
target.' The noise of the barrage was all but unbearable and men
near the guns were deafened for hours. Far forward of the guns the
ground shook continuously and anything loose rattled endlessly. To
talk was impossible; men reported that they felt they were being
hammered into the ground. The thousand-plus guns plastered every
known German battery, mortar position, command post, communication and fortification in the infantry's path.

Hans Gilman was stationed with a Luftwaffe Parachute Regiment
just north of Nijmegen. On the night of February 7th he couldn't
sleep; it was cold and he had a painful back. In the early morning he
got up and went outside. To the west of him, the guns were firing
into north Holland. As he turned to go back to his bunk in a barn,
the sky to the south suddenly seemed to split open—great flashes
seared across the horizon, rippled in waves from end to end, and
then the thunder of the gunfire reached him. His first thoughts were
relief that it wasn't them getting the terrible beating, but one of his
companions, also roused by the noise, put into words what they all
thought: 'My God, the boys in the Reichswald are getting smashed!'

News of the preliminary bombardment reached the HQ of the
German 84th Division at Cleve, at 6 am, but by all accounts there
was very little reaction. The unit commanders urgently predicted a
Canadian attack, but General Fiebig rejected the idea, continuing to
believe that the attack could not be launched over the water-logged
and swampy ground. For the moment he did nothing.

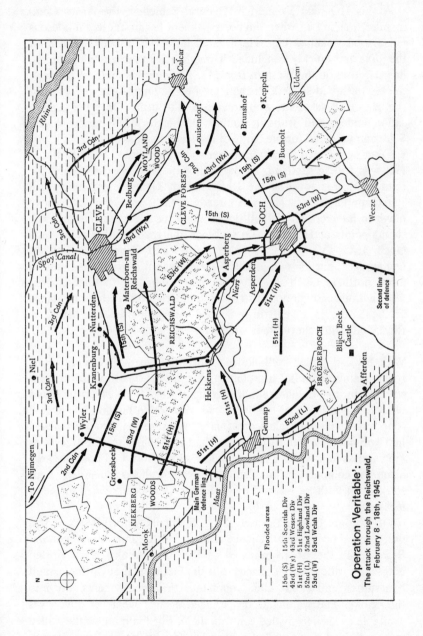

Operation 'Veritable':
The attack through the Reichswald,
February 8 - 18th, 1945

Legend:

- - - Flooded areas

15th (S)   15th Scottish Div
43rd (Wx)   43rd Wessex Div
51st (H)   51st Highland Div
52nd (L)   52nd Lowland Div
53rd (W)   53rd Welsh Div

Labels on map: Rhine, 3rd Cdn, 3rd Cdn, 3rd Cdn, 3rd Cdn, Spoy Canal, Niel, Wyler, Kranenburg, Nutterden, CLEVE, Bedburg, MOYLAND WOOD, Calcar, Louisendorf, Brunshof, Keppeln, Udem, Bucholt, 2nd Cdn, 43rd (Wx), CLEVE FOREST, 2nd Cdn, 43rd (Wx), 15th (S), 15th (S), 15th (S), Materborn-am Reichswald, 53rd (W), REICHSWALD, Asperberg, Asperden, GOCH, 53rd (W), Weeze, Niers, 51st (H), To Nijmegen, 2nd Cdn, 15th (S), 53rd (W), 51st (H), 51st (H), Groesbeek, KIEKBERG WOODS, Mook, Hekkens, 51st (H), 51st (H), Gennep, 52nd (L), BROEDERBOSCH, Blijen Beek Castle, Afferden, Maas, Main German defence line, Second line of defence, N

At his HQ near Emmerich, General Schlemm, the Army Commander, was in bed when the bombardment began but its thunderous noise soon wakened him. He listened for a while to the roaring of the guns and quickly concluded it was heavier than anything he had heard before on the Western front. He made up his mind; this was it, the big push had started. Rising from bed he immediately telephoned the news to Blaskowitz, who prevaricated as usual. Once the conversation ended, and without waiting for his torpid superior to act, Schlemm prepared for the battle of the Reichswald.

First, he ordered General Plocher's 6th Parachute Division, whose HQ was still in Holland, to begin moving to Cleve and block the road eastwards towards the Rhine. Next, General Erdmann's 7th Parachute Division, which was already at Geldern, was told to move north to intercept any Allied thrust along the Maas, to reinforce the strong-points at Hekkens and to block the road south-east towards Goch. LXXXVI Corps was also alerted and General Straube, its commander, put his two infantry divisions in a state of readiness to move north to Goch should the situation demand it. But Schlemm was cautious enough not to strip his southern front at this early stage in the battle, in case British Second Army crossed the Maas, as Blaskowitz still believed they would.

With his cap pulled well down against the weather, General Horrocks clambered into his command post, a small platform constructed by the Engineers half-way up a tree, from which he could observe a good deal of the battlefield over which his divisions would soon attack. He had taken great care to ensure that reports reached him without delay and the Signals had run cables up the tree from the wireless link vehicles parked below so that he could not only hear a running commentary but also talk directly to his commanders. Liaison officers with jeeps stood by to deliver more complicated or secret messages.

At 7.30 am the guns ceased firing. Suddenly, miraculously, it was quiet, an almost painful silence after hours of thunderous gunfire. Breathlessly the troops watched as the thick smoke-screen drifted across the valley. In the Reichswald the Germans thought the assault had started and amid yelled commands their guns opened fire into the smoke. The waiting troops cringed against whatever cover was available as shells whistled towards them. For ten minutes the Allied guns remained silent while the range-finders pin-pointed the German guns that had been lured into revealing their positions. Then, while the Germans were wondering if after all it was only going to be another artillery duel, the British and Canadian gunners sighted their weapons and reloaded.

At 7.40 am the guns of XXX Corps replied. Another stupendous barrage exploded among the German guns and mortars. The bombardment was further increased by the 'pepper-pot' as four divisions' firepower joined in. Through the din the armour could be heard grinding forward to their start lines. RAF Mosquito bombers swept over just above the low cloud; because their targets were thus obscured and because the massive bombardment prevented them from flying lower the pilots had to bomb by instruments alone. There were anxious moments for the forward assault troops as the bombs whistled down barely a thousand yards ahead, yet confidence ran high and many optimistically thought it would 'be a walkover'. Twenty minutes before 'H' hour, 15th Scottish Division's 46th Brigade moved up the Glasgow Highlanders and a squadron of the Coldstreams' Churchills, eastwards from Groesbeek. Other troops came to readiness, tank engines roared and commanders checked final details.

Five and a half hours after the barrage had started the clouds of smoke were pierced by a line of yellow smoke shells indicating 'H' hour. The shouted orders to 'Advance!' were drowned in a bellow of tank engines as the armour moved forward. Churchill tanks, led by the mine-exploding Flails, began to advance. From woods and buildings east of Nijmegen khaki-clad figures—Scots, Welsh, English and Canadians—accompanied the tanks, following the barrage as it moved forward to the enemy lines. It was as if the barrage was a curtain of steel protecting the troops, pre-arranged to advance 100 yards every four minutes; at the end of each twelve minutes all guns fired a round of yellow smoke and increased their range by another 300 yards.

From his observation post, Horrocks watched his men advancing down a gentle valley with small farms on the far side merging against the sinister blackness of the Reichswald, towards the waiting Germans concealed in the forest fringes. In the centre the leading brigades of 15th Scottish and 53rd Welsh advanced across open ground to the east of Groesbeek that was still littered with the skeletons of innumerable gliders of the US 82nd Airborne which had landed the previous September, during the attack on Arnhem.

Two Canadian infantry battalions advanced from their start line along the Wyler–Groesbeek road and tramped eastwards with fixed bayonets. On the right, the French-Canadians of Le Regiment de

Maisonneuve, advancing rapidly behind the barrage, easily drove in
the battered German defenders at Den Heuval. Those that had survived the bombardment put up a token resistance for an hour or so
and then surrendered. The French-Canadians then moved rapidly to
hold Hochstrasse on the main road. On the left the Calgary Highlanders split their force, sending one company to cut the road and
the other eastwards towards the 15th Scottish Division. The Germans
in Wyler were facing north-west and to surprise them the Calgarys
by-passed the village, attacked through Vossendaal, and cut the main
road half a mile behind the enemy positions.

Ed Ford, commanding No 14 platoon of the Calgary Highlanders,
recalls how:

everything was going pretty much according to plan in our sector, with
my platoon on the extreme right of the fan-wise movement, until we
reached a farm outbuilding. Then we ran into a belt of mines, ground
and machine-gun fire. As instructed, I called for smoke and artillery fire
because the attack was grinding to a halt due to casualties from the mines
and gunfire. I barked an order to one of my men, John Shaw, to take a
Bren and give me covering fire. Shaw reacted swiftly and both of us
quickly gathered up all available Bren ammunition, then raced across the
field towards the buildings in Wyler from which most of the fire was
coming. We had all rehearsed house-clearing and No 14 Platoon tackled
the job whole-heartedly once on the objective. In the first building that I
hit, I threw a grenade down the basement stairwell but some fragments
rebounded because the wily foe had rigged up a protective set of mattress
springs. We routed the defenders before the buildings started to crumble
and conscripted some to act as stretcher bearers. One cocky POW
jauntily said over his shoulder to me as he passed, 'I'll be in Canada
before you'. I resisted the urge to boot him on his way.

But the Calgarys had in fact taken a beating from the German machine guns and mortars and when Ford eventually contacted HQ, it
was to find the company commander dead and the HQ personnel in a
state of shock. Ford was now made acting company commander.
'Fortunately I was given the deceased's map and was able to direct
artillery fire from our position late in the afternoon.' As evening
drew rapidly on the Calgarys rushed the village while the defenders
were still reeling and this time succeeded in taking it.

To the right of the Canadians, 15th Scottish Division had been
allocated the entire force of over 170 Churchills of 6th Guards Tank
Brigade for their tough task of breaking through the Siegfried Line

and capturing Nutterden and Cleve. They also had two extra squadrons of the much-feared Crocodiles, two specialist armoured regiments of 79th Armoured and the 2nd Household Cavalry's armoured cars, as well as first priority on the heavy guns and their own divisional artillery. Still more support came from three regiments of mobile artillery and two batteries of self-propelled 17-pounder anti-tank guns. 'Kangaroos' carried the infantry in the initial assault. This massive force was opposed by just two German regiments of infantry, but at least the Germans had made good their defences which in this section were two lines of trenches covered by wire and mutually supporting machine-gun positions. There was a wide anti-tank ditch across the front, beyond which were dug-outs, pillboxes and fortified houses in turn covered by mortar batteries, self-propelled guns and anti-aircraft batteries.

Major-General Barber, the commander of 15th Scottish Division, attacked with his two Highland Brigade Groups, 46th with Coldstream Guards' tanks on the right and 227th with Scots Guards' tanks on the left. First they were to capture the Frasselt road by 4 pm when 44th Lowland Brigade, from reserve, supported by Grenadier Guards' tanks, would advance with the breaching force, pass through the Highland Brigades and launch a night attack to capture Nutterden by 1 am next morning. Then 46th and 227th Brigades would take over again, keep up the pressure, pass through the anti-tank ditch and seize the high ground controlling the Materborn Gap to the west of Cleve before the Germans reinforced it.

The narrowness of the front, together with the few roads, restricted the massive strength of 15th Scottish Division's initial attack. Yet Groesbeek was taken without too much difficulty and the Sherman Flails led the way eastward out of the village, rattling forward into appalling rain and cold, their tracks churning up the mud. One by one they became embedded in the deepening mire. Just one vehicle kept going and with its chains threshing the mud into a whirling curtain, it ground out a path. All the Coldstreams' bigger Churchills followed in line, their wider tracks holding in the mud better than those of the Shermans. The infantry had by now dismounted and as the barrage smothered the ground ahead they kept up with the tanks and pushed forward some 2,000 yards. Outside Groesbeek, No 1 Squadron was further delayed when the last Flail finally became bogged down and the Engineers had to clear yet another minefield by hand.

About the time the Scots were fighting their way clear of Groes-

beek, around 10.45 am, news reached General Fiebig at Cleve that
the German forward defence line had been penetrated, and now he
realized that a major attack was indeed being made against his positions. While he deliberated his next moves, further news arrived at
noon that several divisions were breaking through. Fiebig ordered his
84th Division to withdraw and fall back to the main Siegfried Line
defences, but either his signal did not get through or his units were
unable to move under the terrible shelling, for it was not long before
his staff were reporting that his forward troops were not responding.
Just after noon, Fiebig contacted his commander, General Straube,
and appealed for immediate aid. He later claimed that he had not
been informed by his corps commander of the imminence of an attack.

The Scots pushed on during a pause in the barrage and when it
began again at 2.15 pm 9th Cameronians of 46th Brigade came up
from behind right on schedule and advanced with two companies. In
three-quarters of an hour of driving rain they reached the Gelgensteeg Spur, a high point facing northwards, half a mile beyond the
first German village of Hettsteeg, and commanding the vital road.
They advanced with fixed bayonets expecting the inevitable screeching chatter of a Spandau. Instead they stumbled into crater-torn,
abandoned defences; 84th Division grenadiers had taken such a beating from the artillery that they had withdrawn in spite of the raining
shells. Optimistically the Cameronians pressed on through the defences but tragedy struck when the left company walked into a
minefield. For several minutes, above the roar of the guns and armour, men could be heard screaming in agony as the mines blew up
under them. Several fell against their comrades, knocking them
down, too, and in the brief but bloody holocaust legs and feet were
blown off. The wounded lay in the freezing rain until stretcher
bearers managed to struggle forward and get them out on small
American Weasel carriers.

The surviving Cameronians gingerly left the minefield and pressed
forward. The reserve company, supported by the remaining Churchills of the Coldstream Guards and 141st Regiment's Crocodiles, set
off from the Gelgensteeg Spur, slipping and sliding along its wooded
and ploughed slopes towards Frasselt, a pretty village straggling
along the important Kranenburg–Hekkens road through the forest.
Possession of Frasselt would give the breaching force access to the
anti-tank ditch, several hundred yards further on, and also deny the

Germans the use of the important route through the edge of the forest.

The Crocodiles were ordered to advance in line ahead into Frasselt to flame the houses. To Corporal Ian MacDonald of the Cameronians 'it was an awe-inspiring sight in the wintry gloom, the column of tanks grinding and rattling along and the great gush of flame belching and rumbling to incinerate its target.' The Crocodiles fired at the embrasures of the cellars, their flames immediately absorbing all the oxygen inside, asphyxiating as well as burning the occupants. Before long the Germans were flushed from the hideouts to which they had fled from the Gelgensteeg defences in the face of the barrage, and were rounded up by the Cameronians, moving in behind the Crocodiles. In half an hour the smoking ruins of Frasselt were in 15th Scottish Division's hands together with an entire battery of 105mm guns and a tank destroyer.

On the left flank the 227th Brigade's attack went in with the Churchills of Scots Guards carrying 2nd Argyll and Sutherland Highlanders. The Argylls ventured into the forest, their first day's objective being a line from Klinkerberg, north of Frasselt, north to the triangle formed by the convergence of the road and railway from Kranenburg to Cleve. The Germans manning the defences before the frontier in this sector had withstood the opening barrage well, and when it passed beyond them, they took up positions and immediately opened fire on the assault company with machine-guns, automatics and mortars. The leading formation of Argylls was raked with fire and within a few minutes every officer of the company had been hit and several killed. The Company Sergeant Major took control and rallied the remainder of the unit towards their objective, in spite of well-directed shelling from a battery of 88mm guns in the defence line. The Churchills did their best both to cover the infantry and to knock out the opposition. A slogging match developed in which German mortars and 88mm guns exchanged 'punches' with the infantry's mortars and the Churchills' 75mm guns. Very slowly the Argylls shoved the Germans back and at 11.40 am they moved across the frontier into Germany.

In the meantime the 227th Brigade's reserve company of the Highland Light Infantry had passed through the depleted Argylls' battalion and, now strengthened to three companies, advanced on the left flank into the flooded ground on the way to Kranenburg, the next town along the road to Nutterden and Cleve. In the thick mud the last Flail became embedded after floundering along for several hun-

dred yards. Without the Flails the infantry now had to feel their own
way forward and in so doing blundered into yet another minefield; by
late afternoon, however, they had forced their way across the anti-
tank ditch.

In the gathering gloom of early evening they reached the strongly
fortified town of Kranenburg. The unearthly glow of the artillery's
searchlights bouncing off the low cloud lit the driving spears of rain
as the troops sloshed through a foot of water along the tracks and
road. They could see Kranenburg's conspicuous onion-shaped church
spire, silhouetted by a large fire burning behind it. From fortified positions in the town the Germans counter-attacked. There was a particularly stubborn resistance from a tall narrow house a hundred
yards from the church. Several times infantry attempted to advance
along the sides of the street only to dive into cover when a Spandau
fired upon them. Private Alexander remembers racing with a companion for a doorway across the road while another member of his
platoon engaged the window with a Bren. Alexander had a 2″ mortar
which he held and aimed while his mate dropped in the bombs. The
first crashed onto the roof next door to the Spandau gunner, but the
second went squarely through the window and seconds later the entire front of the house blew out complete with the gunner and gun.
The Highland Light Infantry then fanned out to seize the factory
area around south-east Kranenburg. The fighting in the town was intense but by 5 pm the garrison and 300 prisoners had been taken.

The left flank squadron of the Coldstreams headed out of Kranenburg along the narrow, cobbled road towards Nutterden, the essential
objective some four miles further on behind the anti-tank ditch. The
Churchills smashed their way through meagre defences and shot up
the guards with their machine-guns as they drove through to reach
the outskirts of Nutterden. Thus a little after nightfall on the first day
it looked as though Horrocks's initial objectives were about to be at-
tained. The vital Nijmegen–Cleve road, essential to support the attack on Cleve, had been cut by the Canadians at Wyler and again by
the Scots at Kranenburg. Now the Coldstreams' tanks had reached
Nutterden, the 'door' to the Rhine. But, ominously, the assault was
two hours behind schedule and the armour was in a mess in the appalling mud.

South of the 15th Scottish Division the 53rd Welsh Division were
making their attack into the forest. For them, it would be one of the
most unpleasant weeks of the war as they fought their way deeper
into the Reichswald against mounting German opposition. General

Ross planned to employ 71st Brigade—comprising 4th Royal Welch
Fusiliers, 1st Oxfordshire and Buckinghamshire Light Infantry and
1st Highland Light Infantry—initially attacking due east to break
their sector of the Groesbeek defences. They would then drive on to
capture the Branden Berg feature, the high ground dominating the
forest to the south-east. This would let 160th Brigade—comprising
6th Royal Welch Fusiliers, 4th Welch Regiment and 2nd Monmouthshire Regiment, plus the 1st East Lancashire Regiment from
158th Brigade—pass through and break the Siegfried Line entrench-
ments where they ran through the forest. 1st East Lancs and 6th
RWF were to attack at night supported by tanks and Wasp flame-
throwers. Then while the 1st East Lancashires held the defences, the
rest of the brigade would push on along the northern edge of the forest on a narrow front and seize the Stoppel Berg feature, occupying
the north-east corner of the Reichswald, to secure the track along
which the reserve division, 43rd Wessex Infantry, were to advance
from Cleve to exploit the breakthrough. This track had been located
by Dutch resistance workers and recommended to the Wessex's commander, Major-General Thomas; he in turn asked the Welsh Division to capture it as soon as they could. A major problem facing the
Welsh was that all roads through the Reichswald lay parallel to the
front which meant that while they would have to use forest tracks,
the Germans had good roads on which to move swiftly to counter
any thrust.

The 83rd Regiment, Royal Artillery, its batteries all territorial
units from South Wales, opened fire in support of 71st Brigade and
for four hours bombarded enemy positions around the Branden Berg
feature. By noon on February 8th the 4th Royal Welch Fusiliers
were about a thousand yards from the forest edge where they paused
to allow the 1st Oxford and Bucks Light Infantry and the 1st Highland Light Infantry to pass them. These regiments pressed on to the
anti-tank ditch. While the Churchills engaged the enemy, the AVREs
moved up and dropped bridges in two places. Straightaway platoons
of infantry ran across followed by the tanks which then took aboard
the troops and headed for the forest.

The rain and mud affected the Flails on this front and before they
had advanced much beyond the start-line they, too, became bogged
down along with the AVREs and their unwieldy loads. Fortunately
147th Regiment's Churchills kept going, even though the tracks were
ridged with mountainous mud. The leading battalion burst into the
forest to find a desolate scene. Trees lay smashed among craters,

their broken branches twisted and gaunt like scarecrows, and the
smell of cordite and spent explosive hung in the damp air, almost
overpowering in its intensity. Further in the forest was a tangle of
scrubby undergrowth in which the soaking trees dripped water continuously. John Piper recalls that they

were dripping wet and our boots were caked with thick mud when we ran
the final dozen yards from behind the tank and threw ourselves into the
forest. Shells were still flying over and exploding in the woods with
tremendous cracks. The Churchill smashed its way into the trees,
knocking down a couple of broken trunks before stopping. There was an
explosion just in front of it and the tank backed out, and then roared in
again. As it did it fired its gun at nearly point-blank range. Almost
immediately we heard shouting and about a dozen Jerries came stumbling
out, torn and wounded and a couple in tears.

The troops from the 176th Grenadiers of 84th Division were dazed
and told their captors that the advance had seemed unstoppable.
Their communications had been destroyed by the shelling which had
also blown in the saps under cover of which they were supposed to
withdraw. They were in a state of panic and believed themselves
abandoned by their commanders.

As 4th RWF advanced into the forest they encountered great
wooden blocks set up as tank obstacles. None of the Churchills could
penetrate the forest to begin with and they had to wait until 71st Brigade had taken the forest edge. This was a formidable obstacle of
young trees interspersed with older areas of thickets and scrub, separated into blocks by straight rides running deep into the forest. Private Dick Hughes recalls that 'the long straight paths through the
forest were death traps. The Germans had placed anti-tank guns at
the end of them and shot up any tank as it moved into view. They
also had machine guns sited among the fallen trees which made it
near impossible to move forward.' In fact, General Schlemm used the
terrain to full advantage: the glades were mined and the battalions of
2nd Parachute Regiment were dug in at every approach. These narrow rides caused increasing communication problems for the Welsh
as the in-going ammunition carriers and out-going ambulances could
not pass each other; a one-way traffic system had to be established.
The few roads in the area, built to take logging trucks and only covered with sand, immediately collapsed in the milder, wet weather.

The defenders at the forest edge were soon pushed back, as the assault troops made for the Branden Berg feature. 'We had already left

the tanks behind and the barrage had ceased in our area,' recalls John Piper. 'As we advanced we ran up against enemy well-entrenched in dug-outs. As soon as you moved into the darkening woods they opened fire. When that happened we sent a section around the position while another drew its fire. Every time the enemy saw they were being "left-hooked" they pulled back to avoid being cut off.'

The brigade unrelentingly shoved the Germans back. Private Phil Morris remembers fighting for the Branden Berg feature:

It was a sort of low hill in the forest on which German paratroopers were manning trenches covered with barbed wire; many were roofed with logs in turn covered over with turf and bushes making them very hard to clear. They had plenty of machine guns and a couple of self-propelled guns. My section were sent to clear out a trench running across the front between dense thickets of pine scrub. Our sergeant took us forward, crouching as we ran to a pile of fallen timber on our side of which was a pool of black, oily water. The Germans opened fire with a machine gun from a covered position that was so well concealed we hadn't even seen it. We had no alternative but to leap into that stinking pool and it was bloody freezing. Three men tried to move to our right to outflank the machine gun, but the gunner saw them and they were raked with fire, killing one and wounding the others. While the gun was occupied with them, we threw several grenades which just exploded on the top in a cloud of earth and did no harm at all. But we immediately came under fire from another position a hundred yards to the left of the first one. I was sent back to our platoon commander to get a tank and scuttled back while the battle raged all around. The Captain was wounded but carrying on; he got a radio message back and a tank came up about quarter of an hour later. It was guided to the problem machine-gun position by our sergeant and put a shell straight through the embrasure from about 70 yards away.

By 3.30 pm, however, they had taken the feature. When the Oxford and Bucks Light Infantry finally occupied the high ground they found the artillery had demolished most of the enemy positions there.

The 6th Royal Welch Fusiliers continued their advance along a treacherous track under heavy and accurate mortar fire. In a sudden burst of enemy fire, HQ Company was hit and its commander, Captain L. Evans, killed. William Evans remembers:

tramping along in a column with the rest of my platoon between the trees along the sides of a slope. Mortar bombs were dropping and every now

and then another tree was blown down. Just above us on another track a
couple of tanks were roaring away as they moved further into the forest.
Suddenly someone shouts for us to run "like 'ell" and when I looked up
this tank was sliding tail-first over the edge. It crashed through the trees
like they was matches and we ran like hares.

This particular track later became known as 'Chewing Gum Alley'
and claimed a heavy toll of vehicles. The confusion delayed the assembly and it was 10.30 pm before the two leading battalions, 6th
RWF on the left and 1st East Lancs on the right, were ready to attack towards the anti-tank ditch.

The tanks shot the 6th RWF forward into the forest at 11 pm. The
only illumination was from the blinding shell bursts and the weird,
artificial moonlight of the artillery's searchlights. But it seemed that
the enemy were pulling out of their forward positions and indeed by
midnight the battalion was through the defences and consolidated in
positions to mop up enemy stragglers. Then the 6th RWF had a well-
earned breather.

On the right of the 6th RWF, the 1st East Lancs did not reach the
Kranenburg–Hekkens road until the early hours of the morning,
and after a brief battle secured a crossing which they then firmly held
with two companies. Thus one of the first routes by which Schlemm
hoped to reinforce Materborn from Hekkens and Goch south of the
Reichswald was now blocked by the Welsh Division who dug in in
case the enemy should try to regain the road. The rest of the battalion then pushed on beyond the road for another 150 yards until they
ran into a system of trenches which they took with a spirited attack
aided by mortars.

The most difficult advance on the first day, however, was on the
extreme right, where the 51st Highland Division's task was to clear
the main road running parallel to the Maas from Mook to Gennap.
The Divisional Commander, Major-General Thomas Rennie, decided
to launch his attack with 154th Brigade reinforced with the 5th/7th
Gordons, from 153rd Brigade.

The 1st Black Watch assaulted the village of Breederweg and
carried it without too much difficulty by following the rolling barrage
in best World War One style. They quickly passed through the village but ran into an anti-tank obstacle. Well concealed in nearby
houses, Germans opened up with Spandaus, killing three officers; the
rest of the company immediately sought cover. Pinned down by continuous fire the acting company commander called for support from

the tanks of 107th Regiment. A troop under Lieutenant Walker approached and opened fire with 75mm guns and Besa machine-guns. Shell after shell crashed among the enemy positions but still they replied with heavy firing. When he discovered that the company commander and platoon commanders of the Black Watch company were dead, Walker dismounted from his tank and, assuming command of the infantry, rushed the houses from front and sides as the tanks kept up their supporting fire. Amid a bedlam of noise and clouds of smoke laced with flame the Scots broke in and drove the enemy back with ruthless bayonet charges.

Tank officers in the battle of the Reichswald often spent as much time on their feet as they did in their vehicles. Walker and his troops of Churchills now went forward to aid a Gordon company trying to force its way through fortifications at the forest edge. Walker's tanks attacked these anti-tank gun emplacements and several times he had to dismount in the face of heavy fire to lead his tanks to their targets by running in front and ensuring they gave maximum support to the battling infantry. Walker only withdrew when it became too dark for the tanks to fire effectively; he was later awarded the Military Cross.

With no sign of the fierce fight diminishing Brigadier Oliver, Commander of 154th Brigade, ordered his reserves, the 7th Argyll and Sutherland Highlanders, to attack. Their added weight then forced the enemy to withdraw. The brigade was then relieved by 152nd Brigade who sent the 5th Cameronians into the forest.

Then 153rd Brigade attacked on the left to hold the high ground in the south-west corner of the Reichswald, force the Germans from the thick Kiekberg woods and cut the Mook–Gennap road. The narrowness of the front forced them to use the same axis as 154th Brigade and so the leading battalions of 5th Black Watch delayed their own attack until 4 pm. The 1st Gordons followed an hour and a half later. It was still raining and, as elsewhere, the tanks became bogged down, although a couple of Flails thrashed a lane through the first minefield. Behind the Flails an AVRE bridge-carrier dropped its bridge over the anti-tank ditch, which was particularly helpful when late that night a solitary Weasel carrier used the bridge to get up to the forward troops with 500 tins of self-heating soup, the only hot food XXX Corps' assault troops got that night; for the rest it was cold stew carried up in the morning.

So, as night fell on the first day, Horrocks was both pleased and worried. The advance had gone well and most of the objectives seemed secure, although they were hours behind schedule and the plight of the tanks in the dreadful weather was a serious setback. The 3rd Canadians were about to launch their assault northwards into country now under three feet of water and 15th Scottish Division's 44th Brigade was on its way to breach the main Siegfried Line defences with a mass of armour; by the following morning the situation would be clearer. Two things, however, worried Horrocks. The delays were giving the Germans extra time in which to bring up their first reserves and the flooding caused by the atrocious weather was raising the level of the river Roer and increasing the doubts about US Ninth Army's ability to launch Operation 'Grenade'.

Montgomery was keeping a close watch on the battle, using a number of personal liaison officers who kept him informed of the progress of each division. He was satisfied that all the formations had achieved their objectives and that their casualties had not been severe, yet he stressed to General Crerar that there must be no weakening of pressure: air reconnaissance had indicated that there was a general northwards movement of enemy troops across the Geldern–Wesel road. Moreover, he was seriously concerned about the bad state of the ground: 'in spite of the special provisions for the creation of new tracks and the improvement of those existing, it was clear that we should continue to have grave difficulties in the maintenance of our communications.'

At his headquarters, General Schlemm, too, had followed the development of the battle and was concerned at the rapid penetration made by the Allies of his forward defences; he might not have time to get his reinforcements forward. He contacted von Luttwitz, Commander of XLVII Panzer Corps, still at Marienbaum, and warned him to be ready to make a counter-attack with his panzers as soon as the direction of the main Allied thrust became clear. Thus, on February 8th, when night fell over the embattled Reichswald, both sides were preparing for the battle to increase in intensity in the coming hours.

5 'We're going to hang out the washing...'

By February 8th the flat land north of the Nijmegen to Cleve road was a huge lake extending for ten miles up to the Rhine at Millingen and nearly forty miles eastwards to Rees. These floods hampered 3rd Canadian's operations and so 79th Armoured Division provided Buffaloes armed with machine-guns, Polsten 20mm cannon and PIATs (anti-tank weapon similar to the bazooka) and also Terrapin amphibious trucks and Weasels. Major-General Spry's 3rd Canadian Division was to float over the submerged anti-tank ditches, wire entanglements and minefields. The division had already had considerable experience of amphibious operations in Normandy, and later along the Scheldt estuary, and had already earned the nickname of 'Water Rats'.

At 6.30 pm that day the command was given to advance. The Buffaloes reverberated as their great engines accelerated, then they jerked forward, slewing on the muddy ground and rolled into the swirling flood water, throwing backwash high in the air. Two companies of the North Shore Regiment pushed quickly forward towards the main dyke which they seized while the Germans kept under cover from the combined attack of artillery and RAF Typhoons. Among the prisoners taken was an infantryman who spoke of his terror in a machine-gun emplacement on the dyke. All day the battle had raged to his south, gunfire echoing continuously, and when darkness fell the sky was lit by the flashes of the guns that threw into relief the trees and isolated houses. Then he heard the unmistakable sound of heavy engines, the roar of armour. He and his comrades had been crouching behind their gun peering into the darkness and rolling smoke when to their horror the Typhoons had suddenly roared out of the night: 'They came right at us, flying low over the water with their huge engines which seemed to fill our gaze, and then the shrieks of the rockets speeding towards us. Next moment the dyke seemed to erupt and the fighters swept over so low we all dived into the water. They kept coming back to machine-gun us.' Then the dyke was over-run by the Canadians.

The North Shore Regiment left sufficient men to hold the dyke and round up survivors while the rest set off to clear the nearby village of Zandpol, sailing forward under cover of the artillery shells pounding into the flooded ground ahead. When necessary any air strike pre-ceded them and then when close enough the Buffaloes' automatic weapons opened up as the barrage lifted. Finally the infantry dis-mounted and splashed forward to seize the position before the de-fenders could recover.

On the brigade's right, the French-Canadians of Le Régiment de la Chaudierre spent most of the night wading through waist-deep water towards Leuth, just inside the Dutch border. As Corporal Paul Saone advanced through freezing cold water that swirled waist high, holding a Bren over his shoulder, his feet slipped on the stones be-neath the water. He stumbled, fell forward and would have gone under if the man behind had not snatched his webbing and hauled him back. Next moment a machine-gun fired at them and he was thrust right under by his companion. The machine-gun fell quiet and Saone splashed onwards, completely soaked. The regiment's progress was slow and it was early morning before they attacked the small garrison at Leuth and captured the village.

The right flank attack by 7th Brigade was spearheaded by the Regina Rifles with DD (Duplex Drive) Sherman tanks of the 13/18th Royal Hussars in support. These tanks had been evolved for the Normandy landings and were standard Shermans modified to 'swim' by means of screens that could be raised to provide buoyancy and a propeller. The Reginas' area had escaped serious flooding and they attacked under cover of a smoke screen towards Zyfflich and the mile-long Quer dam, just inside the German frontier.

During the day RAF Spitfires had attacked enemy positions along the dam, in preparation for the Canadian attack. But towards the end of the afternoon, the Quer dam was blown up by the Germans, on the orders of Blaskowitz, who was again trying to stop the Canadian advance by flooding the plains. The Reginas had to wade through the swirling water while the tanks forged ahead, led by a Flail of the 1st Lothian and Border Horse. When the Flail reached the village it rolled in along the street firing its gun and blasting each house in turn. Soaking-wet Canadians then rounded up the Germans as they were flushed from the cellars, taking two hours to complete the village's capture. Dawn was breaking when at last the enemy gave up.

On the right of the brigade, 1st Canadian Scottish ran into difficulties in their attempts to take Niels, some three and a half miles northeast of Zyfflich. Having set a compass course across the dark water, there was a fault in the navigation and they ran into a group of fortified houses about a mile south of the objective. Here they made a strong attack covered by the machine-guns and PIATs, leaping overboard to take the houses by storm. But their battalion commander thought the advance troops had reached Niels and promptly ordered his Command Group to follow up. When they came out of the darkness correctly at Niels, in their Buffaloes, the Germans, who had clearly heard the fighting a mile south, opened a withering fire, wounding the CO and killing four others. The battle continued until daylight when the other companies, having overcome the enemy in the south, arrived at Niels and helped to take the village.

How important tactically was the attack by the 3rd Canadian Division? After Simonds protested against the use of his Canadian infantry solely as a screen behind which XXX Corps would assemble, Montgomery had agreed they should be given the role of protecting the left flank of 15th Scottish Division while they made their dash for Nutterden and Cleve. At that time the numerous German strongholds dotting the flood plain could have been used as a base for a counterattack, or to reinforce their defences at Wyler, Kranenburg or Cleve. But when on February 6th the Germans blew out the dyke at Erkolom, the resultant floods not only hampered the Allied advance but also cut off the German strongholds. This had virtually eliminated their threat, except for artillery, and the rocket-armed Typhoons were admirably equipped to deal with them. Thus, the amphibious assault by 3rd Canadians cost many lives without having a major effect on the tactical situation, for by the time they reached Cleve, 15th Scottish were already there. The Canadians might have been better employed as additional reserves for XXX Corps, but that would not have pleased Simonds, who, throughout the campaign to cross the Rhine, insisted on an independent role for his tough Canadian infantry. They took persistently heavy casualties as a result.

On the front of 15th Scottish Division the plan stipulated that it was time, albeit two hours late, for the reserve, 44th Lowland Brigade, to pass through Frasselt and seize the heavily defended area around Nutterden in order to open the northern axis to Cleve. By the time Nutterden was captured, 46th and 227th Brigades would have re-fuelled, drawn ammunition, eaten and rested, and would resume the attack, keeping pressure on the Germans to deny them time to regroup.

Already the 2nd Gordons, temporarily attached to 44th Brigade, had been ordered to Nutterden to hold the area recently taken by the Coldstreams' tanks. They made a rapid advance along the main road on the left flank and rushed a bridge across the main anti-tank ditch before the enemy had time to destroy it. Fiebig had earlier been commanded by Schlemm to hang onto the defences in front of Nutterden until the 6th Parachute Division troops arrived; they were travelling by road from Holland but had to take the long way around the east bank of the Rhine to cross at Emmerich. The remnants of the 84th Division tried to defend as best they could, but with close support from their Scots Guards tanks, the 2nd Gordons brushed aside any defenders who had not fallen back and advanced to Nutterden where they linked up with the Coldstreams. Fiebig's troops fell back to positions at the far end of the village which they endeavoured to defend until the paratroopers arrived.

In their assembly area at Nijmegen 44th Brigade had waited all day to begin the task of breaking the formidable defences of the Siegfried Line, of which the most important feature was a huge anti-tank ditch. This was between twelve and fifteen feet wide and averaged eight feet in depth; the sides sloped so that it was only about six feet wide at the bottom where some four feet of water sloshed around. On either side of the ditch, there was a continuous belt of mines and trenches connected by saps every 500 yards or so, to cover the defenders as they moved from one side of the ditch to the other, either to reinforce a position or withdraw. The ditch was strongest in the Kiekberg woods and at Wyler, and in the Frasselt sector it was heavily defended by outposts and numerous fortified houses commanding the open countryside over which any attack would have to advance. The entire area across the 44th Brigade's line of advance was reinforced with concrete emplacements for anti-tank guns and masses of thick, rusting barbed wire wrapped in impenetrable coils around steel stakes.

The strong breaching force comprised Grenadier Guards' Churchills, Crocodiles of 141st Regiment, one and a half squadrons of Flails of the Lothian and Border Horse, a squadron of AVREs with bulldozers to cross ditches or maintain roads, a battery of self-propelled guns and another mass of Kangaroos to carry all the infantry. Two main axes had been assigned to 15th Scottish Division, the hard-sur-

faced main road to Cleve, code-named 'Skye', which was used by
227th Brigade, and to the south a narrow, unsurfaced track bordered
by deep ditches along which 46th Brigade passed, code-named 'Ayr'.
Because of the stubborn and protracted resistance at Wyler the main
'Skye' route could not be used, and both brigades were told to use
the 'Ayr' track. 'Ayr' was becoming badly rutted because in addition
to 46th Brigade's assault forces, supporting armour, trucks, bridge-
carriers and guns were all moving along to cover the advance to
Cleve.

Lieutenant-Colonel P. T. Wood, acting commander of the Divisional Royal Engineers, became anxious when it was obvious that
congestion was diverting the breaching force on to the main road
'Skye' to Frasselt. He decided to reconnoitre a new route and went
forward on a motor-bike to 44th Brigade HQ. In the pouring rain he
found a way across the main road at Kranenburg over a bridge west
of the town. A bulldozer from 20th Company, RE, made a 12-foot-
wide track behind Wood's motor-bike. The wet road was covered by
wet leaves and twigs and now and then Wood had to dismount and
lift mines before the bulldozer could follow. In the eerie quiet his
men reached the north end of the road that ran south through Frasselt towards Hekkens. Wood then roared off to report that the armour could get through to its start line, although on the way he had
to stop several times in pouring rain to remove trailing telephone
wires that wrapped themselves around the wheels. Eventually the
bike got irretrievably stuck in a water-filled shell hole and the inde-
fatigable Wood had to struggle back on foot.

While the 44th Lowland Brigade was advancing the German Intelligence at Oberkommando West was very perplexed. The general
opinion was still that the attack into the Reichswald had been made
by two Canadian infantry divisions with only a Canadian armoured
brigade in support. Intelligence was pensive—was this the true offensive or not? Fiebig still did not think the attack was an attempt to
break the Siegfried Line and held to the opinion that the appalling
conditions of both roads and tracks made it too difficult to maintain
a strong offensive. In the darkness of that first night, so he later
claimed, he was not aware that British units were operating on his
front; he says the first time he knew this was on the morning of February 10th when his headquarters was attacked by units of the 43rd
Wessex Division. This is difficult to understand since his Army Commander, Schlemm, had been able to persuade Army Group that this
was the real thing and included both British and Canadian forma-

tions. On the morning before the attack began Fiebig had held strong positions 7,000 yards in front of the Siegfried Line defences with no less than seven battalions, but by nightfall on February 8th they had been broken and decimated.

Fiebig's 84th Division suffered some 3,000 casualties, including 1,200 prisoners. The whole of 1051 Grenadiers, a battalion of 1052 Grenadiers and a battalion of 84th Fusiliers had been captured or killed; all except three battalions of 84th Division had been engaged. Schlemm was now even able to persuade the lethargic Blaskowitz that the situation was critical and to release the 7th Parachute Division, parts of which Schlemm had already sent into battle, despite OKW's directives that Army Group 'H' was not to release any reserves until the situation clarified. Yet 7th Parachute Division could not immediately help as they were widely scattered and had to be committed to battle in drips and drabs. Schlemm was therefore distinctly pessimistic. The Siegfried Line had been broken at every place the Allies had attacked. It confirmed his long-held doubts of the effectiveness of the *Westwall*. There seemed to be nothing to stop the British driving on to seize Cleve before he could get his reserves forward.

General Schlemm's First Parachute Army had experienced a traumatic twenty-four hours. The five and a half hour barrage had all but broken his forward troops. The air-raids that had opened the offensive had been worse than any previously experienced on their front. Schlemm reflected bitterly that not a single Luftwaffe aircraft had been seen, that the Allies had roamed the sky at will. He saw only one hope of holding Cleve until his reserve troops arrived. He had to defend the Materborn feature, two hills a mile south-west of Cleve running north and south near the village of Materborn-am-Reichswald. The lower south-westerly ridge went north-west of Materborn while the higher easterly ridge went through Bresserberg. It had to be reinforced immediately if it was to be denied to the British and Schlemm began urging the 6th Parachute Division, now on its way from Holland, to get there first.

Day merged into night as the 44th Brigade endured the bumping of the Kangaroos, roaring and belching clouds of choking exhaust. A short distance beyond Groesbeek the gunfire intensified briefly. 'It percolated through to us', one soldier recalls, 'soaked through, cramped and half asleep, that we had crossed the frontier, we were in Germany.' Colonel Lord Tryon led 4th Tank Squadron of the Grena-

dier Guards of 6th Guards Tank Brigade, under the command of the
44th Brigade for this operation.

I went on ahead of the battalion in my scout car to keep in touch with
the commander of 44th Lowland Brigade, Brigadier the Hon. H. C. H. T.
Cummings-Bruce, who was moving along with 46th Brigade's HQ. The
route up was blocked by a mass of vehicles all trying to get forward,
progress was very slow, and the going indescribable. On the way I passed
a considerable number of dejected looking German prisoners, most of
whom had been so dazed by the preliminary bombardment that they
surrendered without a fight. I found 44th Brigade HQ and a site for my
own battalion HQ nearby. It was raining and very unpleasant, but there
was no shelling by the enemy.

The Lowlanders rumbled along through what had once been the
billeting area for German troops manning the forward defences.
Those buildings that still remained bore slogans painted in big white
capital letters: 'WIR GLAUBEN AN ADOLF HITLER!' appeared
on several and on them all was: 'EIN VOLK! EIN REICH! EIN
FÜHRER!'
    The AVRE bridge-carriers ran into trouble as the roadway nar-
rowed amongst the trees, and they kept hitting the branches which
broke the supporting cable holding the front of the bridge in the air
and caused them to drop onto the road in front of the tank. Moving
off the road, however, had disastrous results. They all wallowed
along, stopping constantly to pull each other out of the mire whenever it was possible. After seven hours of chaos the 6th King's Own
Scottish Borderers reached the assembly area. 'From about 18.00 onwards I spent my time like the proverbial Sister Anne, hopefully
looking to see if anyone was coming,' reported Tryon.

But I had to keep reporting no-one in sight, and the Brigade Commander
had continually to put off H-hour. Finally in the small hours the column
started to rumble by; even then our troubles were by no means over, for
one of the AVRE bridge-carriers decided that it had carried its bridge far
enough; the wire holding the bridge snapped and down it fell into the
road. All the vehicles then had to go over this entirely superfluous bridge.
Needless to say after a few had passed over, one RE contrivance pulling
a sledge arrived and got well and truly stuck. No sooner had we sorted
this out than one of the AVRE bridge-carriers, going around a corner on
our one and only road, over-balanced and toppled over side-ways.
However, everything has to come to an end sometime and finally, at
04.00 the attack on the Siegfried Line went in.

Although by now the assembly area was a shambles, nevertheless just
before daybreak, eight hours behind schedule, the attack on the Siegfried Line was launched. The mist had gone and even the rain had
ceased and a great panorama of rolling upland and pastures, much
like Normandy and tactically excellent tank ground, could be seen,
broken only by a few small hills, some lightly wooded, of which the
Hingst Berg dominated Nutterden. Away to the south the downland
was edged with the dark line of the Reichswald; the squat shapes of
Churchills grouped in the muddy fields were visible as they ploughed
on with the Welsh Division (at that time 4th Welch Regiment were
advancing along the forest edge). On their left the ground dropped
away to the floods where the Canadians' Buffaloes surged through
the watery landscape.

The Lothians' Flails led the attack, clearing a path through the
minefields. Behind them the AVREs with fascines were followed by
the bridge-carriers, both ready to provide crossings over the ditch.
Then came the much-feared Crocodiles. The infantry rode into battle
in the Kangaroos, their officers controlling the supporting artillery
fire from the Churchills and using their radios. Almost medieval in
their organization and steady advance the Lowlanders went forward
to break the Siegfried Line.

Major G. E. Pike was with the breaching force: 'The squadron
was equipped with Churchill tanks and organized into four troops,
each of three tanks. I was allotted one tank from Battalion HQ to act
as my HQ tank. It was fitted with two wirelesses whereas Squadron
Commanders' tanks then had only one set.' Pike's instructions were
to cross the minefields ahead as quickly as possible and establish a
close bridgehead. 'For this task I could use the company of 6th
King's Own Scottish Borderers and troops of 141st Regiment's Crocodiles from 6th KOSBs if I required them.' As the battle developed
and the supporting armour and troops began to arrive Pike had to
act fast.

I decided to use my squadron, less two troops with the breaching force.
This allowed one troop to support each lane and a squadron HQ to
support the centre lane, and ensured that 6th KOSBs would get the
support of the remaining two troops for their operations in the
bridgehead, however heavy casualties might be in the breaching force.
The breaching force arrived in Frasselt without further incident but there
were still no signs of the Flail Squadron or troop commanders. I held a
quick Orders Group at which I found that the Troop Sergeants and the
Liaison Officer of the Flails had not been briefed, and had no idea where

their lanes were, or where to expect the minefield to begin. I therefore put
a troop leader of mine in charge of each outer lane, and my
second-in-command in charge of the centre lane. In view of the wireless
plan this was obviously far from ideal as he had no communication with
the Flails, AVREs or Kangaroos except via me. Flailing operations
started some 30 minutes later.

Captain P. E. Du Villiers, with 279th Field Company, Royal Engineers, had travelled forward in a Kangaroo to Frasselt: 'On arriving
opposite to lane 2 there was no halt and the gun tank commander
gave the order to move forward. We turned left along the track to the
south side of the Frasselt church. When the gun tanks got past the
cemetery they opened out to the sides and started shooting. The
Flails went on along the track and we followed in the Kangaroos
with a sergeant and four sappers marking the track on the right hand
side as we went.'

At Pike's instructions the Flails beat their way forward together,
their whirling chains sending up great clods of earth and mud; the
noise was indescribable, for added to the crack of small-arms and the
'whoompf!' of exploding mortar shells the Flails reverberated on the
ground and the occasional mine exploded sending fragments smashing against the reinforced belly plates. They beat two wide lanes up
to the anti-tank ditch, breaking the trenches on their way. At the
ditch the Flails beat their way to the flanks to allow the AVRE
bridge-carriers to pass through. The Flails then took up positions and
reverting to their roles as gun tanks began shelling the German positions to cover the activities of the AVREs. Their instructions were to
continue firing until the bridges were laid and the carriers had backed
away, then they were to form up once more, cross the bridges and
beat a path forward to Schottheide.

The bridging operations were difficult. The sides of the great ditch
had been softened by the downpour and there were doubts whether
they would support the weight of the bridge. But the sappers laid
flexboards on the approaches to lane 2 and immediately they were
ready the signal was given and the remaining Flails formed into line
ahead and beat their way forward across the bridge. Behind them
came the Squadron HQ followed in turn by 'C' Company of the
KOSBs and the remaining two troops of tanks. 'Traffic continued to
flow,' Du Villiers reported, 'until a Bren Carrier towing a 6-pounder
anti-tank gun got onto the bridge and jammed the gun fast between
two girders. Nothing would move that gun quickly, so we directed

the traffic, which had started to queue up, along the south side of the
ditch and over lane 3. This of course was not such a good surface as
lane 2, but it worked all right.'

The KOSBs that couldn't cross on lane 2 fell back before intensive
mortar and machine-gun fire, the bullets 'whanging' off the Kangaroos. They went to lane 3's bridge which was a box girder supported
on the fascine. Another company of KOSBs rushed forward to link
up with those already holding out on the far side of the ditch.
Behind them Churchills bombarded enemy positions with their
75mm guns, pounding the defences and keeping the Germans occupied while the infantry deployed. The rest of the Grenadiers' tanks
crossed the ditch soon after and forged ahead on much better ground.
According to Sergeant Robertson of the KOSBs:

The mortars were worse than the shells, because you couldn't hear them
coming, they just dropped around us and we had no time to dodge into
cover. A tank came up from behind and began churning forward towards
the trenches where Germans were firing at us with a Spandau. We ran to
get behind the tank but it began slewing from side to side as though the
driver didn't know what to attack first. We kept close and the next thing
we knew we were right on top of the Germans; the tank simply crushed
the gun into the earth.

The long-delayed attack on Schottheide began. 'A' and 'B' Companies stormed Schottheide in an attack that drove the Germans back
in a wild mêlée. The Germans were disconcerted by the force of the
attack and seemed utterly shocked by the speed with which the supposedly impenetrable anti-tank ditch had been crossed. 'It was obvious,' said Robertson, 'that in this sector the Jerries hadn't much fight
left in them. They came from their defences and trenches about the
village and surrendered, throwing their weapons down in front of
them.' The KOSBs rounded up large numbers of prisoners as their
companies stormed forward and consolidated their positions. Once
clear of the anti-tank ditch, waves of Kangaroos rumbled across the
rolling ploughland, stopped before the village, where the infantry dismounted, and rushed the objectives on foot. Entire units of Germans
ran forward in columns led by their NCOs to surrender.

Ahead of the King's Own Scottish Borderers lay the Reichswald
through which ran a direct road to the Materborn feature. It was
vital that the Lowland Brigade push forward with all speed and take
advantage of the shelling but the road was dominated from the north
by the 150-foot Wolfsberg from which the Germans fired on traffic

below. The Royal Scots Fusiliers were supposed to pass through the KOSBs and seize the Hingst Berg to the east of Nutterden and the Wolfsberg a mile further south, but they were hopelessly delayed by the terrible road conditions and had no hope of coming up in time to exploit the success of the KOSBs. Brigadier Cummings-Bruce had no option but to order the tired KOSBs to continue supported by tanks.

'A' Company now went for the Wolfsberg, fanning out across the rolling country to make their attack along a broad front. Their Kangaroos revved up and charged the hill, slipping and sliding but gradually clawing their way up the slopes. Several carriers exploded with clouds of smoke and flame; in one, every man was killed. It was a battle of extremes in which entire German companies gave up while individual groups fought to the death. But by early afternoon the enemy had broken and fallen back in panic.

The Lowlanders had at last forced a way through the Siegfried Line. A derogatory cheer was raised at the height of the battle when the KOSBs' Regimental Sergeant Major hoisted a quantity of washing on the Siegfried Line. At last the British could fulfil the promise of the famous 1939 song; 'We're going to hang out the washing on the Siegfried Line . . .' Many men remembered another incongruous sight—a solitary German woman hurrying along a track as fast as she could away from the fiercest fighting. She was middle-aged, dressed in black and beside her strode a British soldier in full battle order carrying her suitcase.

To the right of the 44th Lowland Brigade, 4th Welch now led the way along the northern edge of the forest intent on capturing the hills leading to the Stoppel Berg feature. Gradually they made their way towards the ridges in the darkest parts of the forest. Forward troops several times fired on one another, only stopping when the outraged language from both sides revealed their identity. Horrocks marvelled at the 'stoicism of these youngsters', whom he called the 'cutting edge of the vast military machine'. The forward troops were often no more than a couple of young men crouching in a trench, quite alone in the sinister darkness, ahead of them the never-ending rows of trees, dripping rain and minefields. The boys from the Welsh mining valleys went through the same horrors as the youngsters from the Pennsylvania mining towns had done in the Hurtgen forest months before. Sergeant Willis remembers advancing along a sunken lane in the forest:

On either side of the lane were muddy banks topped with masses of dead and soaking bracken. It was pouring with rain and the soil was washing

down the banks in muddy little landslips of earth and stones. Suddenly a
machine-gun opened up on us from somewhere in the trees and thick
undergrowth. One of my men fell and I scrambled from the bank. We
were like rats in a barrel in that bloody lane. I jumped for the top of the
bank, pulling at the bracken to try and heave myself up into cover at the
top. But the ferns pulled out by the roots and I got showered with mud. I
sprawled down the bank again, which probably saved me because the
German stopped shooting at me, probably thought he'd hit me. For God
knows how long I lay in the mud and shivered with fright and cold while
the machine-gun rattled on. Then some of our boys came up and hit it
with a captured *Panzerfaust*.

Major 'Barney' McCall, commanding 'Able' Company of the 4th
Welch, largely made up of 'boys' from the mining valleys around the
Rhondda, remembers

advancing up a steep ridge in the darkest part of the forest with great
caution. We made our way through the trees and suddenly encountered a
German pillbox from which a couple of Spandaus opened up a scathing
fire. We all went to ground while I tried to work out some way around
the pillbox but every time we attempted to move the Spandaus sent a hail
of fire smashing through the trees, splintering them and tearing off slices
of bark which showered onto the men below. I sent an urgent message
back to the Commanding Officer, Lieutenant-Colonel R. G. F. Frisby,
'Look, for Christ's sake, send us some tanks.' But the answer came back
saying: 'You'll have to manage . . .' I then sent a blistering appeal: 'If
you don't send some . . . tanks, we can't get up. Why don't you come
and see for yourself.'
   This produced a result and Colonel Frisby arrived to have a look at
our problem and agreed to send us some tanks. About an hour later a
Churchill and a Crocodile arrived and set about the pillbox, quickly
shooting it and flaming it. We then went over the ridge very cautiously,
not sure what we would find. To my surprise, I could see a great many
small lights, which seemed to be strung through the trees, just like fairy
lights. We crept closer and found a German Field Dressing Station. There
were a number of Germans about and they started dodging around in the
darkness during which our boys hit several of them. One German popped
his head out of a tent and was nearly shot, but the rifleman recognized he
was a doctor just in time. We easily captured the station and sent the
prisoners back.

Plans to capture the Stoppel Berg had been made two weeks before
and the well-rehearsed programme now went into operation with 4th
Welch giving way to 2nd Monmouthshires attacking with tanks. A

private from Raglan was there: 'We tramped along with the tanks roaring along behind us, crashing straight through the trees, which were mostly little more than saplings just there, snapping them off and rolling over the stumps. When they came to thicker, mature trees we had to guide them forward. It was pretty frightening then, very scary, with these enormous tanks grinding around and suddenly coming out of the thickets like charging elephants.'

In a couple of hours the Monmouthshires and their tanks had advanced over about 2,000 yards of thick forest. Isolated battles continued to flare up and every now and then the rattle of the tanks' machine-guns evinced their contact with German units. A German Oberleutnant dismally told his interrogators: 'It was very bad in there, we could hear the tanks coming nearer and all we could do was dig in and wait. Suddenly to our right a tank crashed out of the trees and fired its machine-guns. We scrambled away straight into your infantry.' Most of the German prisoners taken were relieved it was all over.

At 11 am the 6th RWF left their positions astride the Siegfried Line and went to secure the north-west corner of the woods, overlooking the all important Materborn feature. Major Hughes of 'A' Company and Captain Sharpes of 'B' Company rode forward on the tanks, beating off the localized opposition. One eyewitness told how a Churchill came up to assist in overcoming a machine-gun emplacement.

As the tank came forward and turned into a ride, an anti-tank gun fired from the trees, hitting the tank squarely and killing the driver. The tank commander clambered out while under machine-gun fire and although wounded, immediately scrambled across to another tank and took command. This tank revved up, slewed on its tracks and smashed its way into the trees on the right, while we engaged the anti-tank gun as best we could to hold the gunners' attention. The tank crashed forward and suddenly burst into view behind the gun. Its guns killed the gun crew and then the tank accelerated right over the gun, crushing it into the pine needles and mud.

Eventually the Fusiliers reached the forest edge from where they could see both the Materborn road where it left the Reichswald, and to their delight, Germans moving along it—infantry, motor vehicles, staff cars and even a few tanks, on their way to the defence of the Materborn feature. They were the advance units of 6th Parachute Division, apparently unaware of British troops in the forest. The

Churchills quickly manoeuvred into positions and opened fire. At the
same time a signal was sent to Divisional HQ for artillery support
and the Medium and Field guns promptly opened fire too. Direct hits
began thumping down among the column, blowing trucks to bits,
scattering the infantry and knocking out tanks before the survivors
scattered in panic and movement along the road ceased.

The Materborn feature was also under attack from the left, from
6th Royal Scots Fusiliers. While they and their tanks drove for the
north-west ridges, the KOSBs and a squadron of Grenadiers' tanks
headed east to seize the Materborn feature above Cleve. The KOSBs
moved off in their armoured array once more. A German paratrooper watched from a bunker: 'We could hear the British coming,
the noise of their advance was overwhelming and sounded like hundreds of tanks. Then we got our first glimpse of the huge column advancing, dipping and rising along the hilly road.' The impact of the
Kangaroos was terrifying as they forced their way through a double
line of trenches and weapon pits supported by pillboxes. There was
uproar, too, as the Grenadiers' Churchills shot their way into battle,
their 75mm guns firing at almost point-blank range into the enemy
positions. Fritz Hagen was a member of an anti-tank gun crew and
remembers how they

took aim at a British tank that was roaring away, skidding and sliding but
getting gradually nearer. Our first shot ricocheted off its front armour.
We saw the tank's gun swing towards us but the tank was slipping around
so much, the gun couldn't train properly, and we hurriedly loaded and
fired again. This time we hit it on the turret and knocked the gun out. But
by then more tanks were pressing closer and infantry were beginning to
by-pass us as they struggled up the slope. Our gun was too heavy to move
and all we could do was swing it onto another target, but this time
flame-throwing tanks began attacking the nearby emplacements and as
the position was hopeless, we started back up the hill but a shell burst
very close and the shrapnel caught me and another soldier. Then the
Tommies overran us.

The Crocodiles were ordered forward to clear out the stubborn defenders. One Crocodile member recalls:

We had been ordered to pressure up on the approach and to concentrate
on the pillboxes and emplacements. There was a terrifying fight going on
with the mass of armour advancing on a broad front, explosions
everywhere and the infantry pressing on behind the tanks. We headed for

a concrete emplacement from which a couple of machine-guns were
playing havoc with the infantry. As we turned right to attack, a
self-propelled gun fired at us but missed, its shell exploding some feet
behind us. Before it could fire again it was in turn hit and seemed
disabled. We rattled on and the order was given: 'Flame gun, fire.' There
was a roaring noise as the yellow jet shot straight out, then bubbled along
the ground and flickered over the bunker. The undergrowth burst into
flame and clouds of smoke blotted out our view. The Croc' slewed again
and we could see a German soldier writhing in flames.

Farm buildings and houses that had been wrecked by bombardment
and bombing were set on fire by the Crocodiles. Increasing numbers
of prisoners were taken as the enemy fell back from their forward
positions. Dusk was falling and the Scots found resistance hardening
as more paratroopers arrived and joined in. These troops often employed a trick; they would shout 'wounded' and wave a white flag in
mock surrender, then when any Scots troops went to round them up,
other paratroopers nearby would fire on them. It took only a short
time for the KOSBs to recognize this pattern after which the white
flag no longer afforded sanctuary. As the first night in Germany descended it was chaos, gunfire and flames all around. It seemed that as
the Scots knew they were in Germany at last, it didn't matter any
more what damage they did.

By nightfall, then, on February 8th the Scots were through the Siegfried Line, but at his command post Horrocks was distinctly worried.
Cleve should have been taken eleven hours earlier and reports indicated that German resistance was stiffening and increasing numbers
of parachute troops were moving into the battle area. These parachute troops from the Luftwaffe were an élite fighting force, fanatical
soldiers who were ready to die for their Führer rather than surrender.
Continuing RAF reconnaissance reported more enemy reinforcements moving westwards towards the Rhine from inside Germany,
while US flights further south had seen troops and armour still heading northwards through Cologne. Montgomery's strategy for the battle
was to draw the enemy troops towards the Canadian Army's offensive to enable the US Ninth Army to cross the Roer and take the
Germans in the rear. But by the early hours of February 9th, Horrocks was only too aware that the overall situation at the south end
of 21st Army Group's front was deteriorating. The endless downpour
and melting ice had swollen the usually turgid Roer to a racing torrent and there was increasing doubt as to whether the Americans

could risk a crossing under those conditions. Even worse than the state of the river was the knowledge that Hodges's US First Army was still unable to capture the Roer dams.

Dawn was breaking on February 9th, some fifty miles south of the Reichswald, when US First Army launched yet another attack to take the Schwammenauel dam. The previous day the 311th Regiment of 78th Division had recaptured Schmidt and a senior officer had told press correspondents: 'This time we are here to stay.' The 78th Division had then been withdrawn after their three-day ordeal and the fresh 9th Infantry Division ordered to capture the remaining dams by morning.

At the approaches to the dam the enemy withdrew in an ordered way to fresh positions, holding back the Americans with machine-guns and mortars and with supporting fire from artillery on high ground east of Schmidt. But it was obvious to the Americans that this resistance was intended to give the German engineers time to blow up the dam. Its massive structure had already withstood several direct hits from RAF Lancasters the previous October, but this would not prevent German engineers, with full knowledge of its construction, from destroying it. By hanging onto the dam since November they had won two months' time, delayed the Allied advance and had been able so far to dictate events in the battle for the Rhineland.

The Germans had already placed explosive charges in the inlet gate to the tunnel and other carefully measured charges at the outlet gate. They were much too clever to destroy the dam and release its 20,000 million gallons in one devastating deluge that would wash away all in its path but subside a few hours later; the Allies would soon replace their losses. Instead, by jamming both inlet and outlet gates they could keep the Roer flooded for several weeks. In a private letter to me Albert Speer writes that 'The decision to blow up the Schwammenauel dam was made by Hitler on advice from the *Generalstabs*. The economic consequences were regretted, as valuable land was to be unusable for many years due to the destruction caused by the water.'

Private Tony Sullivan, with the 9th Division, recollects that

It was almost dark by the time we got within reach of the dam. The woods were very dark and there was a wisp of snow in the air, it was very cold. My section had just managed to dislodge a group of Germans from dug-outs controlling the way to the dam itself; on our right the huge twin outlet pipes ran down the steep hill into near darkness. Our sergeant shouted for us to get on up the hill and we had just grabbed our weapons, which included a light machine-gun, when there were several sharp bangs—they echoed and reverberated down the valley and the next moment this enormous jet of water literally soared out in a huge arc and plunged down the hill. The noise was terrific and further down we could see our troops scrambling out of its path. We all stood around for a moment, not sure what to do, and I suppose, thinking it was all over, but the next moment the German artillery began shelling us in earnest and we had to take cover.

The German guns at the northern end of the dam combined with small arms and mortars to drive the Americans back from the dam. Despite the ferocious fire, American engineers got to the dam's control buildings. After some discussion the commander decided to find out whether there was any chance of the dam itself being blown, because his men were still scattered all over the slopes and would have been swept away in the event. Lieutenant Maurice Phelan, of the divisional engineers, took four men and crept into the conduits and tunnels, searching for more explosives. It was pitch dark in there and the lights from their torches threatened to bring down enemy fire from any Germans still working or hiding in the maze of tunnels. But the Germans had gone and they found no more explosives. Outside, the bitterly cold night was torn by gunfire that would go on for several more days until the Americans finally cleared the enemy from the area around the dams.

It is, admittedly, difficult to see how the Americans could ever have taken the dams while the Germans were controlling them, and able to blow them up at will. An airborne force could have seized them in a *coup de main* but would not have guaranteed an easy approach for the ground forces and could have produced another Arnhem. Perhaps the remedy lay in bombing the Roer dams, but in the event it was not done. The attack, by whatever means, should have been pressed on much more strongly in the autumn of 1944 when the waters' release would have had fewer consequences for the Allies.

The situation was now clearly serious. Canadian First Army had succeeded in drawing out the enemy reserves, but far from the Americans taking these in the rear, the Germans were protected by the floods from American interference. The dreadful weather had by now stopped the Allied Tactical Air Forces' operations and supplies to the ground forces were becoming all but impossible. By comparison, the Germans were, for the time being at least, free of the Allies' devastating air power, and could move easily along the surfaced, unflooded roads they still controlled. Both Generals Straube and von Luttwitz were moving their corps forward and it looked as though they would win the race for Cleve and Goch.

6 The race for Cleve

By the evening of February 8th, Lieutenant-General Horrocks was eager to press on to complete the capture of the initial objectives. Although at 3 pm that day 15th Scottish had reached the Materborn feature in time to forestall the German 7th Parachute Division, they did not completely dominate it; the enemy were still holding the eastern slopes. The latest report was that the Germans were also moving into Cleve and this was enough for Horrocks to judge the moment right to unleash the reserves. The signal was sent to the 43rd Wessex Division to 'press forward' at midday on February 9th, to take first Cleve and then Goch, Weeze and Kevelaer. Guards Armoured Division at Tilburg were also warned to be ready to move from midnight.

However, the appalling state of the roads had not been made entirely clear to Horrocks and he admitted that he committed the first of his reserves at the first opportunity because he was afraid of losing momentum. At that time he was suffering one of his periodic bouts of fever, the result of severe wounds sustained in North Africa in 1943, and his high temperature affected his judgement. In his memoirs, Horrocks frankly confessed that the decision was the worst mistake he made in the war. But to be fair to him, he was engaged in a battle of rapidly increasing ferocity and complexity.

The whole operation hinged on catching the Germans off balance and thrusting the British infantry and armour through their positions before they could organize their defences. Although the element of surprise had been lost, the break in the weather had seriously slowed the attack and the Germans had had time to react; Horrocks had only hours to get onto the plains beyond Cleve. If this plan failed there was the daunting prospect of his divisions, their armour inextricably bogged down in the mud, being attacked on the congested narrow front between the Maas and the Rhine north-west of Cleve and Gennap. It was against this background that Horrocks ordered the 43rd Wessex Division forward. It was absolutely essential to maintain the momentum of 'Veritable' and keep up the pressure on the Germans.

At his headquarters, near Koblenz, von Rundstedt contemplated a map of the Reichswald. The Wehrmacht's oldest and most senior officer rested his bony knuckles on his desk and fixed the map with stern and tired eyes. In February 1945 von Rundstedt was greatly distressed by his inability to command the German armies in the west as he saw fit, despite Hitler's earlier promises that he would have 'far-reaching powers'. The frustration and worry robbed him of rest and sleep to the extent that he drank heavily before retiring each night. Since the Ardennes campaign he had been persistently arguing with Hitler that the *Westwall* could not stop the Allied armies. Hitler personally reassured him that the *Westwall* would stop the Allies, but von Rundstedt insisted that he did not have enough men to hold all the defences and the entire front as well. Hitler was infuriated and flew into a tantrum, forbidding any evacuation of the defences.

Although the combined air and ground attack at Arnhem, in September 1944, had alerted him to the danger of an Allied thrust to the Rhine around the northern tip of the *Westwall,* either through apathy, tiredness or disillusion, von Rundstedt totally miscalculated the present Allied plans. He later admitted he had not foreseen a large-scale attack through the Reichswald; Montgomery's deception plans had misled him. The German High Command now realized the strategic importance of the Reichswald attack; if the Allies broke through the main defences there was little to stop them advancing to the Rhine. Von Rundstedt now sent a signal to General Blaskowitz, the Army Group Commander, that Cleve had to be held at all costs; it was essential to contain the Canadian advance and prevent a breakthrough to the Rhine.

Von Rundstedt was only too conscious of the immense importance of the Ruhr, a fact that Speer had been at pains to impress upon Hitler. So, with the Americans held on the Roer, he hesitated no longer about committing reserves and, without consulting Hitler, ordered General Heinrich von Luttwitz to send his XLVII Corps into the battle to secure Cleve. If it had already fallen, then he was to try to recapture the town. Von Rundstedt had confidence in von Luttwitz; he was one of Germany's most experienced and auspicious commanders. His XLVII Corps, comprising the 116th Panzer Division and the 15th Panzer Grenadiers, was reinforced by the 346th Infantry Division brought from east of the Rhine. In addition he would assume control of all the parachute divisions moving into the area. His meagre fifty tanks at least included Germany's best, the Panther and the super-heavy Tiger. Von Rundstedt signalled Blasko-witz that there would be 'incalculable' results of any breakthrough.

Major-General Ivor Thomas, the Commander of 43rd Wessex Divi-sion, had trained his men hard, bringing to the task all the qualities of his quick and creative mind, paying particular attention to street fighting. He had kept his men in readiness at St Oedenrode while waiting to join 'Veritable'. The division was now to go along the main Cleve road, by-pass the town and press on towards Bedburg and take the fork right, around the smaller Forest of Cleve, and south to Goch where they were to meet up with the 51st Highland Division fighting along the southern edge of the forest.

Night had fallen on February 9th by the time 43rd Wessex's 129th Brigade left Nijmegen on the road to Kranenburg. Sleet swirled around the leading troops of 4th Wiltshires, huddled on the cold steel of Sherman tanks of the Nottinghamshire Yeomanry (Sherwood Rangers). Behind them stretched a sinuous column of bridge-carriers and Crocodiles, trucks and self-propelled guns, all trailing along in icy rain. Since the 44th Lowland Brigade had passed along the road the night before the track had worsened and was littered with aban-doned vehicles.

The flooding also worsened as the column neared Kranenburg and by the time the 129th Brigade waded into the village after midnight, averaging only two miles an hour, the half-frozen troops were ex-ecrating those at HQ who had sent them on this mission; they pre-dicted with perverse glee that they were going to meet with disaster.

Lieutenant-Colonel J. E. L. Corbyn, the CO of 4th Wiltshires, was perplexed to find the HQ of the 44th Lowland Brigade still in Kranenburg. The 44th Brigade itself had not yet reached Cleve but had been halted two miles west of the town by a German road block. However, a secondary road was discovered, leading through a gap in the woods towards the southern area of Cleve, and Corbyn ordered his column along it. A mile or so along this road, 4th Wiltshires en-countered a fallen tree adjacent to German outposts. The enemy opened fire from their positions, the bullets scything like hail amongst the vehicles. In an instant 'C' Company leapt off the vehi-cles and scattered into the trees, while tanks of the Nottinghamshire Yeomanry rumbled forward and dealt with the machine-guns. Scouts

searched for the road to the south-east, but before long they emerged
from the woods into the houses in the southern outskirts of Cleve.

Cleve had suffered terrible destruction from the Lancasters. The
'blockbusters' had blown enormous craters so close to each other
that the rubble and debris of one spilled over into the next. Engineers had to bring up their bridge-carriers to cross the worst holes
and allow the tanks access to the town. The stench was awful; leaking gas, burnt rubber, gutted buildings, cracked sewers that spewed
effluent into the craters. Later the division's armoured bulldozers
would come and shove the rubble back into the craters to restore the
roads to use. Collapsed walls revealed the upper floors of houses
from which people's belongings tumbled out. Private Warrender remembers that: 'It made me think of my home and my things and my
children's treasures just poured into the street and trampled into the
dirt. And we added to the chaos. Our tanks fired into every house,
which exploded in flames, flying bricks and glass.'

The 129th Brigade broke through the outer defences of Cleve and
were on top of Fiebig's Divisional HQ just as he was struggling to
control the situation and deploy his reinforcements. Wilhelm Pohl
was a signaller at Fiebig's HQ and remembers the consternation
when the first British troops overran their outposts: 'A runner came
back to the large house we were occupying, to say that troops,
identified as British, were entering Cleve from the direction of
Esperance, a small village just south of the Materborn feature. General Fiebig became very excited and asked for confirmation that they
were British, not Canadian, then sent signals to our main HQ. I
heard that parachute infantry were arriving from Holland but apparently nobody at our HQ was sure where they were. Then our
building came under fire from small arms and mortars. We spent
about ten hours under increasingly heavy fire and saw several British
tanks moving along the roads.'

Schlemm had been relying on his troops manning the defences on
the eastern slopes of the Materborn and Bresserberg features to bar
the way to a British advance to Cleve, while von Luttwitz's panzers
were moving to establish defensive positions at Udem and Cleve. Already the first arrivals of General Erdmann's 7th Parachute Division
were stiffening the remnants of Fiebig's 84th Division and digging in
to block 15th Scottish's advance from the crest of the feature. The
defence line across the forest from south of Materborn to Hekkens
and Gennap was being held in the north by battalions of 16th Parachute Regiment, in the centre by 7th Division's 20th Parachute Regi-

ment while three battalions of 2nd Parachute Regiment from the 2nd Parachute Division were deployed from Gennap to the southern end of the line. Schlemm was in for an unpleasant surprise, however, on the morning of February 10th when he found that more British infantry and tanks were in their rear in southern Cleve. Horrocks's decision to send in the 43rd Wessex Division was now having its effect, confusing and demoralizing the enemy and hindering his reinforcements in their attempt to consolidate behind the front-line formations.

The battle in Cleve developed into a bewildering mêlée that the official Historian of the 43rd Wessex Division described as 'like a riot in a wild western town'. Groups of 129th Brigade and of German parachute troops hunted for one another among the ruins. Private Warrender found himself 'in a couple of ruined houses with Jerries popping up all around. They seemed as confused and frightened as us. Sometime just before dawn shells began to explode around us and after a couple of men were injured by shrapnel, we were ordered back to another row of houses. But the shells followed and in the dim light, and clouds of smoke, a huge Jerry tank very slowly moved after us. We fired a couple of mortar bombs at it and watched one bounce off the beast. We could hear the rubble being crushed under its tracks. Then we lay doggo and to our relief it moved off.'

The battle raged throughout the day as the enemy mounted fierce attacks supported by tanks which almost overran the Wiltshires' positions. But each time they were driven off. In the neighbourhood of the cemetery the fighting for control of the Materborn road reached new heights as the shelling and mortaring grew worse. As evening drew on the Germans still held out but could not continue without support from the rest of the division.

As February 10th dawned wet the 43rd Wessex's column stretched back in a long immobile procession; the leading elements were in woods south of Cleve, the remainder of the column wound back to Nutterden where the Tactical HQ was held up in the traffic jam. Behind this, 214th Brigade stretched back to Kranenburg, while 130th Brigade was still in Nijmegen. Major-General Ivor Thomas was still trying to get his second brigade group forward to support the 129th with which communications had been lost, for he had had alarming reports, so far unconfirmed, of the fighting in Cleve. During the planning, Dutch Resistance had revealed that a concrete road had been built south to Materborn, to enable German tanks to move rapidly to Cleve. Thomas now heard that the Welsh had taken the

Stoppel Berg and the northern tip of the forest and had opened the
road. At a meeting with Thomas, Montgomery stressed the absolute
importance of getting into the open country beyond Cleve as soon as
possible. Therefore, although it was late afternoon and the early winter evening fast approaching, Thomas sent Brigadier Hubert Essame's 214th Brigade along this road to relieve the 129th Brigade so
that they could move out of Cleve and along the road towards Bedburg, the route to Goch.

The 43rd Reconnaissance Regiment's 'B' Squadron set off down
the road but in their struggle to reach the open ground east of the
forest at Saalhof, they went straight into prepared enemy defences
guarding Materborn-am-Reichswald village. Their armoured cars
were badly shot up by anti-tank guns. When the 5th Duke of Cornwall's Light Infantry's 'D' Company carriers tried to get forward to
tackle the defences they found their way blocked by the litter of armoured cars. It was already late afternoon by the time the infantry
formed up in the shelter of the woods and then, led by Major Mike
Lonsdale, stormed the village defences and dislodged the Germans.
Carriers could at least move up now to continue the advance. The
Commanding Officer of the 5th Duke of Cornwall's Light Infantry,
Lieutenant-Colonel Taylor, would have liked to by-pass Materborn
but the ground was too soft for the armour, so there was no alternative but to capture the village and open the road through it. In the
early evening, they attempted to advance and relieve 129th Brigade
but the enemy was still firmly established behind strong defences. In
the rapidly failing light 'B' Company went on foot between the Materborn feature and the forest to try and distract the enemy and permit the armour to crash through the village. 'C' Company went north
while 'D' Company under Lonsdale attempted to move right and attack from the south-west. All these attacks ran into opposition and
there was much confusion in the dark. Finally Taylor called a halt
until daylight.

As the Germans struggled to organize their defences, the rising
floods washing across the Nijmegen–Cleve road brought confusion to
the British ranks. General Barber was exasperated to find that, after
15th Scottish Division's magnificent break through the Siegfried Line,
they were being deprived of their chance to take Cleve by the immobile mass of troops and armour on the flooded road. He had intended
leaving his 44th Lowland Brigade on the Materborn feature to stop
any German attempt to prevent his 227th Brigade advancing along
the road from Nutterden to capture Cleve. His third brigade, the

46th, was already assembling a column of armour, guns and infantry
to pass through Cleve, once it had been captured, and advance towards Calcar on the road to Wesel. All these plans were being held
up by the 43rd Wessex's mass of guns and equipment stuck in the
congestion on the flooded road. Indeed, throughout the night and
early morning there were endless confrontations between commanders of units that found themselves in each others' way. 'In the circumstances,' said Essame, 'it is not surprising that the contacts of many
of the commanders involved had been of a character which cannot be
justly described as being noteworthy for their cordiality.' A Wessex
driver who overheard one such confrontation between an irate Scot
and an equally angry Devonshire man reckoned that had the Germans heard the language they would have gone home in shame. Nevertheless, in the face of the delays to the Wessex, Barber was forced
to abandon his plans to capture Cleve that day.

Meanwhile on XXX Corps' right, 51st Highland Division had
been clearing important German positions in the Kiekberg woods on
their way south to cut the Mook to Gennap road. The German
anchor position was strongly defended by some 2,000 men of the
2nd Parachute Regiment sent to reinforce the 84th Division Grenadiers. Enemy resistance had held up 153rd Brigade's advance until 4
am on February 9th when their artillery blasted the Germans and enabled the brigade to rush the defenders and drive them off the ridges.
According to Corporal Lamont: 'There was a concrete pillbox half
hidden in undergrowth. Every time we tried to get forward the Jerries
opened fire on us. Then our guns plastered the area sending great
masses of earth and bits of trees flying in all directions. One of the
shells blew up right in front of the pillbox's slit and the gunner fell silent.' In the wake of the artillery, 107th Regiment's tanks attacked
and broke a way through the wire enabling the troops to follow further down the valley towards Gennap.

By evening, 1st Gordons had advanced to within a few miles of
Gennap. For a while the rain had ceased and the moon came out
shedding a cold light over the battlefield. Major Martin Lindsey led
his men forward to break through strong German defences, a mile
and a half from Gennap, that included wire entanglements anchored
to concrete and steel obstructions and ditches to hold back tanks.
Every house and farm was fortified and every approach covered by
machine-guns. Undaunted and yelling wildly, the Gordons stormed
each of the defences in turn, breaking through the wire with their
tanks and charging over the ditch into the fortified houses. Private

Ian Miller was with a platoon ordered to wipe out the defenders of a farm from which machine-guns and a *Panzerfaust* were supporting another group of houses on the Mook–Gennap road, itself under attack by another company of Gordons. 'We went forward in darkness, trying not to be seen in the light of exploding shells and mortars. We got within fifty yards when the patchy clouds cleared and the moon came out. Our platoon's 2″ mortar lobbed three bombs, one at least hit the farm which was already ruined. Then their bazooka landed a shell a few feet from the mortar, injuring two men; I think one died afterwards. We rushed the farm but they belted us with the machine-gun and we fell back after taking more casualties. I remember seeing two men hanging onto one another as they staggered back and then I tumbled into a ditch and lost sight of them. We lay there for some while before one of our tanks came up. It passed us and headed for the farm. Suddenly there was a jet of flame from its gun and a bang as it fired an HE shell and blew the farm to bits.'

Several hours later the Gordons broke through and formed up in preparation for the attack on Gennap, a vital link in the German fortifications and a key crossing over the river Niers which would enable the 51st Highland Division to debouch on Goch. It had been a confused battle and the men were scattered in the darkness. There were also other divisional formations in the area and their gunfire echoed across the country. Lindsey became worried lest they encounter these other troops in the dark and inflict casualties on one another. He displayed considerable panache in dealing with the problem—he sent word back to the regimental pipers at Company HQ to play their regimental march, 'Cock o' the North'. Unfortunately it is not recorded what the Germans thought when they heard the pipes in the dark, but as they had a healthy respect for the Scots their feelings would hardly have been improved when they heard the distant answering pipes of the Queen's Own Cameron Highlanders of Canada, who were on the left of the Gordons.

It was vital that the key crossroads at Hekkens were taken with all speed as they controlled all communications south of the Reichswald. The roads from Gennap to Cleve and Goch to Kranenburg passed through this junction, which was also an anchor position of the main Siegfried Line defences. The 152nd Brigade had by now started their attack at dawn through the forest towards the Kranenburg–Frasselt–Hekkens road. Across their route stubborn units of German 180th Division, mostly parachute troops, still fought on. The 5th Seaforths made the initial attack in the cold of dawn through a ghostly world of grey trees, mist and the lingering smoke of battle. Alex McKenzie recalls how 'I had just taken a swig of water from my bottle, thinking how bloody cold it was, and was moving on again when all hell broke loose! The enemy let fly from hidden positions— they must have been lying in the freezing forest for hours—and we all ducked and darted behind trees. As we did the Jerries broke from cover and came at us like madmen, leaping over the broken branches and drainage ditches, firing as they ran with Schmeissers and rifles, while their machine-guns supported them from the flanks. Someone bawled "fix bayonets!" and we up and charged them yelling and screaming louder than the Germans. It was a bloody battle, slipping, sliding and slashing with bayonets but we drove them back.' The Seaforths routed the enemy counter-attack and, taking advantage of their momentum, pursued them all day. Late that night they reached the Kranenburg–Hekkens road where they halted in the face of the defences just beyond, a southern extension of those breached by the 1st East Lancs the night before.

On the right, the 2nd Seaforths were also moving through the dark forest and, like all formations in the Reichswald, running into extremely strong and stubborn defences. Bill Corker was a Troop Sergeant in 'Able' Squadron of 107th Regiment which was on the point of being recalled to the rear assembly area when 2nd Seaforths requested urgent help. Although Corker's tank was critically low on fuel and needed more ammunition, he insisted on going into battle again. The troop advanced through the forest but, in the dark, lost contact with the infantry. They were rumbling in the direction of the defences when without warning the Germans poured an intensive fire from well-entrenched positions. In quick succession the lead tank was hit followed by the troop leader's tank. Disregarding the concentrated fire, Corker sat on top of his tank in order to control his guns with greater accuracy, and knocked out the first *Panzerfaust,* then charged and ran over a second. Corker went on attacking to counter the enemy fire, seemingly oblivious to his danger, while the other two tanks got going again, manoeuvred into place and then poured their combined fire power onto the enemy positions.

In the tanks' wake the infantry stormed the trenches which they occupied after bitter hand-to-hand fighting, when the remaining paratroopers streamed through the woods. After consolidating their position the Seaforths prepared for a dawn attack on the next very strong sector of the Siegfried Line, guarded by three big pillboxes. These were constructed of concrete two feet thick with four-inch steel em-

brasures and were surrounded by barbed wire entanglements and
thickly sown mines connected to trip wires. The defences had been
planned early in the war and designed to resist attacks by infantry
and conventional armour. To overcome them the specialist armour
attached to 152nd Brigade moved forward to put into operation what
was called 'The Drill'. Here, as in similar situations elsewhere,
Churchill gun tanks moved in, first firing smoke shells, to isolate the
target pillbox from its supporting strong-points, then firing HE into
the embrasures to soften them up and force the defenders to keep
their heads down. An AVRE from 1st Assault Brigade, Royal Engineers, then closed in to fire its 290mm Petard mortar, loaded into the
front of the short barrel from a hatch in place of the co-driver's position. The Petard hurled its 40-lb 'Flying Dustbin' blowing in the already weakened embrasure. The *coup de grâce* was then adminis-
tered by the dreaded Crocodile of 1st Fife and Forfar Yeomanry
which sent a flaming jet of fuel through the shattered embrasure.
After this devastating and concerted attack which often lasted fifteen
minutes, it was rarely necessary to repeat the performance at the
other pillboxes. No matter how heroic the defenders, few dared to
face the Crocodile.

With the pillboxes eradicated the brigade continued its advance
and wheeled right towards the strong defences guarding the Hekkens
road junction. Here they came under devastating mortar and shell
fire and although the tanks managed to cross the road, north of the
junction, they were stopped by a wide ditch. Unable to cross without
the specialist equipment which was far behind, they withdrew a little
and shelled the enemy. When the 5th Seaforths caught up they tried
to rush the defences by crossing the ditch but were hopelessly pinned
down. 5th Camerons came up in support but although a series of
dauntless bayonet charges wiped out five machine-gun posts, they,
too, were finally pinned down in the ditch while the enemy pounded
them with mortars. In response to frantic signals Divisional HQ ordered 154th Brigade to relieve the Seaforths and Camerons, pass
through their positions and take Hekkens.

In the meantime, XXX Corps was closing in on Cleve. The 44th
Brigade's 6th Royal Scots Fusiliers finally got clear of the congestion
and made a determined assault with Wasp flame-throwers against a
German strong-point on the Cleverberg, the high ground dominating
the northern approaches to Cleve. But when the German troops retreated into the town they were mistaken by the 5th Wiltshires for
German reinforcements and the 43rd Wessex's divisional artillery

1 General Johannes
Blaskowitz,
Commander of
Army Group H
(First Para Army
and 25th Army)
during the entire
Rhine campaign
2 Major-General
Martin Fiebig,
Commander of 84th
Infantry Division in
the Reichswald

3 Argyll and Sutherland Highlanders and Scots Guards' tanks advance towards
Reichswald on February 8th
4 Fascine and bridge-carriers moving into Reichswald

5 The devastation of Cleve

6 The 2nd Gordons and Scots Guards' tanks in Kranenburg

7 Highland Brigade moving into Cleve

opened fire onto the Cleverberg killing and wounding many Scots before urgent messages halted the guns. Despite their many casualties the 6th RSFs soon began entering Cleve.

Further north the 3rd Canadians were also closing in. After taking Kekerdom and Millingen, the most westerly German town on the Rhine, their Buffaloes plunged on through swirling flood waters that threatened to swamp their low freeboard. Shells screamed out of the night and tore the freezing water into huge gouts. Mortar bombs pitching into the water reminded one Canadian from the coast of Nova Scotia of 'plunging gannets'.

After surviving the carnage at Niels, Brigadier Spragge's 7th Canadian Brigade seized Keeken and then drove on for the fortified Custom House on the Alter Rhein in a move to outflank the northern German defences. The Custom House fell after a desperate battle involving the Buffaloes' cannon, mortars and artillery 'stonks'. Only one objective remained to General Spry's 3rd Canadian Division, to advance eastwards over the water-covered plain to the Spoy Canal which connected the Alter Rhein to Cleve, thus completing the encirclement of the town. The capture of the Spoy Canal was allotted to 9th Canadian Brigade, under Brigadier J. M. Rockingham, but although they fought a bitter, night-long battle they could not yet dislodge the Germans and had to fall back with heavy casualties. The Spoy Canal remained in German hands.

The blowing of the Roer dams had raised the river to incredible dimensions. Behind the raging Roer flood, General Simpson seethed in frustration. He had a huge army poised to make one of the most powerful assaults by American forces in World War Two. He had eleven divisions totalling 300,000 men with a further 75,000 from General Collins's VII Corps on loan from First Army, ready to make a simultaneous attack along his southern flank. The US XXIX Tactical Air Command had 375 fighter-bombers waiting to pound the enemy defences and armour. Over 2,000 guns, one for every ten yards of front, and around 1,400 tanks and armoured vehicles stood waiting, impotent behind the Roer. Yet all along the front from Linnich to Duren the usually turgid Roer roared and tumbled, flecked with dirty foam, bloated from its normal 25 yards to an average of 300 yards, and in places up to a mile wide.

Montgomery arrived to confer at Simpson's HQ at Maastricht. His engineers had said that there was no hope of American support until the river subsided, which would take at least eleven days, but Simpson's engineers feared it would be nearer fourteen. The consequences of this situation were undeniable and in stopping the American offensive the Germans had achieved a triumph which they might still turn into a decisive victory. XXX Corps would have to bear the full weight of the German counter-attack. The Germans would attempt to destroy British and Canadian formations before the American attack, then, using their excellent system of roads running north and south, turn what was left of their forces on the Americans and possibly beat them too. On 28 March, Eisenhower was to tell reporters: '. . . as you know, the conditions on the Roer river, with the ability of the Germans to flood the Roer river, held the rest of that attack (Grenade) up until February 23rd. I'll confess to you now that those were the two most anxious weeks I have spent in the campaign.'

Generals Crerar and Horrocks had both hoped, when the ground had been frozen, that they would be able to move quickly enough to capture a bridge over the Rhine, but the rain, floods and stubborn German resistance had denied them that. Welsh troops in the Reichswald had had to suspend operations for several hours while their engineers tried to create a road surface out of the wretched ribbons of mud that wound through the shattered forest. The other divisions were little better off. If only the weather would clear there were swarms of fighter-bombers on airfields in Belgium and Holland ready to destroy the enemy armour. But in the meantime the British and Canadian divisions that had fought continuously for three days and nights had, somehow, to get second wind and fight on.

On February 10th Canadian First Army's Intelligence reported: 'If the enemy has forces available either from the Hochwald or from across the Rhine he will be tempted to try and regain Cleve or at least to seal it off. If he cannot do so then he must hold Goch and also cover the nearest Rhine crossings.' Montgomery faced a dilemma. His northern attack was in imminent danger of becoming completely immobile in the floods along the Dutch border, while German reinforcements were moving across the relatively high ground from the east. He had either to break out rapidly from the narrow floodlands, and take on the best divisions of the German army in the west with his already weary forces, or call off the offensive. This would inevitably lead Eisenhower to cancel his thrust and switch it to Bradley, who was even then urging to be given the opportunity. Montgomery's single-minded determination to beat the Russians to Berlin and the Baltic coast would never allow him to let Bradley lead the drive into Germany.

In the absence of American support Montgomery's decision was to reinforce XXX Corps with all speed. Accordingly he approached Eisenhower with the request to move some American divisions from the US Ninth Army northwards along the Maas to British Second Army to replace British divisions he wanted released for battle. Eisenhower immediately agreed and assured Montgomery of his full backing, letting him know he had no intention of changing his overall strategy. It was clear, Eisenhower admitted, that a bad blunder had been made over the Roer dams, an error that went back to Hodges's abortive attack the previous autumn. But eventual success for 'Veritable' seemed inevitable and so British 11th Armoured and the 52nd Lowland Division went north to reinforce Crerar's forces.

But if Montgomery had Eisenhower's backing, not everyone was so sympathetic. At the end of January Patton had been very angry when orders from SHAEF had limited his activities to 'active defence'. An explosive situation had been created by the orders passed on by Bradley, that the main drive would be made by Montgomery's 21st Army Group. Patton stormed at Bradley that he was the 'oldest leader in age and combat experience in the United States Army in Europe and that if he had to go on the defensive he wanted to be relieved.' Irritable and still rankled by his failure in the Ardennes, Bradley was himself bitterly envious of Montgomery's freedom of action, and he advised Patton that, while his orders were in no way countermanded, he would permit him to conduct his defensive activities as he thought best. It was a tacit understanding that Patton could go his own way once more; that he could again absorb badly needed supplies which should have gone to Hodges's First Army. Bradley secretly wished Patton to continue his offensive in the Eifel sector for which he had argued so long but in vain with Eisenhower.

To Bradley, then, the news of Montgomery's problems was not unwelcome. Although on February 10th, Bradley was in the throes of yet another squabble with Patton, he still found time to telephone his crony and give the news of Montgomery's débâcle in the north: 'Monty's alleged attack is the biggest mistake Ike has made in this war!' he crowed. Derisively, he claimed that 'Veritable' was hopelessly bogged down, 'Grenade' had been stopped and would now be scrapped. He confidently predicted that the Allies' main drive would now be switched to Patton's front in the south.

7 The Germans hit back

At 2 pm on February 11th the Wessex's 214th Brigade sent the 5th Duke of Cornwall's Light Infantry to attack Materborn village. The supporting Shermans of 4th/7th Dragoon Guards raced across the open ground skirting the forest while 6-pounder anti-tank guns of 59th Anti-Tank Regiment knocked out two German tanks that moved to intercept. Simultaneously there was a devastating concentration of fire from Divisional artillery's three Field Regiments which all but demolished the village. Major, now Brigadier, Mike Lonsdale recalls that 'when we charged into the village, with the tanks racing along in front, the Germans were dazed by the artillery concentration, and those that hadn't bolted didn't put up much resistance.' Four officers and 174 other ranks surrendered at Materborn; they 'could no longer endure the British and Canadian bombing, shelling and mortaring.'

The second wave of the attack, led by Lieutenant-Colonel Ivor Reeves' 7th Somerset Light Infantry, ran into pockets of enemy troops holding out in the ruined houses scattered along the Bedburg road and were forced to spend time clearing them out. Jack Walters, with the 7th Somersets was with the leading company: 'the village was pretty well demolished and we didn't expect any opposition, but no sooner did we enter the street than we came under sniper fire from the ruins. We ran for cover behind a tottering wall and one of our blokes lobbed a grenade. There was a bang and we rushed the house but came under fire from a machine-gun. He suddenly stopped and we reckoned another platoon had got him.' When the defenders were finally wiped out the Somersets broke clear of the village and pressed on after the retreating Germans. For over half a mile a running battle developed along the narrow road skirting southern Cleve as British and German troops darted from one ruin to another.

The Somersets' 'C' Company under Major Durie ran into a hail of Spandau fire from strong positions at the key crossroads 400 yards

ahead, which became known as 'Tiger corner' and controlled the
roads between Cleve and Goch. It was held by 6th Parachute Division troops. Jack Walters has a vivid memory of 'German paratroopers running between the strong points, with their long camouflaged smocks flapping around their legs. They were heavily
armed with plenty of automatic weapons.' As the Shermans closed up,
one was hit and exploded in a sheet of flame killing all the occupants, but the others saturated the enemy with a mixture of HE and
machine-gun fire. No 13 Platoon under Lieutenant Lawson inched
forward clearing each house in turn, fighting in the blazing ruins of
red-tiled houses and their adjoining sheds and barns. As the winter's
day drew to a close, and the freezing sleet hissed in the fires, the
crossroads was gradually overwhelmed. The tanks surged forward
and drove off the last defenders who limped back into the gathering
night.

The troops were exhausted, hungry and half-frozen, yet ahead
stretched 1,000 yards of heavily defended road to Hau that still had
to be taken to prevent German reinforcements reaching Cleve. A platoon was sent to probe the way. 'It was murder,' Jack Walters said,
'every move was met by machine-gun fire as the Jerries seemed to
have a Spandau behind every tree and bush and in every ditch. We
went back and took cover at the crossroads. Behind us was some
woodland and there was a terrific racket coming from a couple of
guns firing from inside the woods, but we couldn't see where they
were aiming because so many shells were being fired from Hau.' The
Somersets took five hours to fight their way along the nightmare
road, measuring success in yards at a time. By midnight, Hau was
still ahead of them and troops were all in. Lieutenant-Colonel
Reeves ordered his men to advance straight down the road to seize
the critical bend in the road near Hau, ignoring the enemy to either
side who would be dealt with by the following companies. The men
were weary and more intent on getting their objective so as to rest
than on killing the Germans. Behind 'C' Company the rest of the
Somersets dealt with the enemy in isolated houses along the road
while 'A' Company, under Major Roberts, broke away and attacked
Hau village; hand-to-hand combat continued all night in houses and
orchards. By early morning, however, thirteen hours after the first attack, the Somersets had consolidated their positions.

As 44th Lowland Brigade moved forward to Cleve the 43rd Wessex's 129th Brigade resumed their advance to the east. In the lead 4th
Somerset LI moved from the factory area across the suburbs and out

along the Bedburg road next to the Spoy Canal. To their right was a narrow belt of deciduous woods, mostly bare birches and beeches, which had been heavily mined. Major Cooke-Hurle's 'D' Company led the way. Some German infantry dug in at the side of a railway embankment resisted strongly, but it was only a matter of time before they caved in to the stronger forces. The 43rd Wessex still had to take vital high ground at Bedburg which involved them in bitter fighting around the sanatorium there. But by late afternoon on February 11th they had broken free of the congestion around Cleve and could begin their advance along the roads leading to Pfalzdorf and Goch.

The latest reports at Fiebig's HQ in Cleve were showing increasing confusion. From prisoners and dead enemy Fiebig knew he was fighting the 43rd Division, but it became increasingly evident during the morning that this division was being displaced by fresh formations coming in from the Materborn feature. Fiebig's 16th Parachute Regiment on the eastern slopes of the Bresserberg had already reported troops and armour moving down from the hills into Cleve. At the same time other reports from his Grenadiers in south-east Cleve reported the British moving eastwards out of Cleve. That morning Fiebig sent an urgent message to General von Luttwitz, in whose corps his division was now operating, that he could not hold Cleve much longer. Then in the early afternoon a new bombardment descended on Materborn village from the feature to the west. Before long frantic messages were flooding into Fiebig's HQ about the destruction of the village which protected the south-western approaches to Cleve.

The decisive assault on Cleve itself began on February 11th when the 15th Scottish Division finally attacked. The 227th Brigade and their Scots Guards' tanks bore down from Donsbruggen north of the forested high ground, and 44th Brigade with the Grenadiers' tanks from the hills to their right. The German 6th Parachute Division attempted to drive back the 5th Wiltshires long enough for the panzers to arrive. Lieutenant A. Fussey's 7th Platoon counter-attacked and after a bitter struggle managed to trap a group of paratroopers in the ruins; surrounded and unable to break out, 180 paratroopers surrendered. Desperately, the Wiltshires regrouped and prepared for another enemy attack, conscious of their dwindling ammunition. But the attack did not come; instead, to their great relief, at about 10.30 am the KOSBs and the Royal Scots arrived. A veteran of 5th Wiltshires recalled how he was shot through the hand in the last German attack and had been sent to a dressing station. He had not been there long when someone yelled that tanks and infantry were coming in. 'A few minutes later we saw them tramping along the road and someone shouted, "It's the 'Jocks'." '

Slowly the pincers closed as the Argylls of 227th Brigade from Donsbruggen skirted the wooded Tiergarten and moved in from the northern extremity of the Materborn hills. Scots Guards' tanks with 2nd Gordons drove along the northern edge of the forest belt that extended a wooded finger into the heart of Cleve. At dusk the 2nd Gordons had reached the crossroads at the edge of the woods, still 500 yards from the railway station. A Scots Guards' tank trying to move along the débris-covered road near the water works found its way blocked by a huge crater whereupon it turned left across some rubble. There was a bang as a projectile from a rocket launcher glanced off its side. At first the commander couldn't locate the weapon but when a second projectile exploded just in front he caught a glimpse of two Germans scurrying behind a half-ruined building, one carrying the rocket launcher and the other a couple of missiles. The tank gun traversed, the gunner aimed, fired, and the wall exploded in clouds of flying bricks. But the Germans had moved back just in time. 'Our commander got angry,' Andy Brown recalls, 'and ordered me to drive after them. I went straight over the rubble and there were the Germans struggling to reload. Our machine-gun blasted away and they dropped the "bazooka" and ran like hell into another ruin while I drove over it and charged the ruin which collapsed on top of us. The commander just managed to get his hatch slammed shut before a shower of bricks hit us. But by then he had calmed down and we backed out leaving two very lucky Jerries to leg it away.'

The KOSBs meanwhile skirted the worst craters, scrambling over mounds of débris, ever ready to dive for cover if the Germans suddenly opened up with machine-guns. The Gordons and Argylls on the left and right respectively forced their way in from the north-east and in the failing light the inevitable happened, the Lowlanders and Highlanders opened fire on one another. For several stormy minutes a private war developed until they recognized each other and stopped before too many casualties were incurred.

But the main objective of the attack had succeeded. The Germans were withdrawing eastwards, and 3rd Canadians had now arrived on the west bank of the Spoy Canal and had advanced into northern Cleve to threaten communications in the German rear. The enemy hurriedly abandoned his defences and retreated towards Calcar. By midnight the Canadians had taken control of the Spoy Canal from the Alter Rhein to Cleve and Fiebig had withdrawn completely in the face of overwhelming force. The Germans had lost Cleve.

Taking Cleve had been made infinitely more hazardous because of the appalling conditions to which it had been reduced by the bombing. As General Essame said: 'What will always rankle in the minds of those who fought at Cleve is the oafish stupidity of the attack by Bomber Command, which, with its deep cratering, had completely blocked the roads within the town.' Seven months after Caen, the error had been repeated at Cleve and those who had again advised the use of heavy bombs carried a major responsibility. If Cleve had not been attacked at all the 43rd Wessex Division would have been able to pass quickly through in the critical hours before dawn and get two brigades in Materborn, which would have forestalled the German paratroopers and enabled the Wessex to begin their encircling movement of the Reichswald two days earlier than they did.

Horrocks had captured Cleve and turned the northern end of the Siegfried Line, but only just. Given the atrocious weather it was no mean achievement. Yet they had been lucky for there had been several failures of communication, the most dangerous of which had been the erroneous information about 15th Scottish Division's progress which had resulted in chaos when 43rd Wessex had been committed along the only available axis. Clearly the Germans, for their part, had put too much reliance on their Siegfried Line defences, despite their almost unanimous criticism of its effectiveness. Schlemm had entrusted the first line of defence to the very weak 84th Division and while he had not expected them to hold up an Allied attack, he had thought it would give him time to move in his tough parachute reserves. This was fine in principle but did not take into account the reliance Montgomery placed on his powerful artillery, or the ingenious specialist tanks which had already proven their worth in breaking the Atlantic defences in Normandy. In such a situation Schlemm needed prompt reinforcement but it is apparent that both von Rundstedt and Blaskowitz badly miscalculated the strength and direction of the attack and hesitated too long. It had to be seen if von Luttwitz's redoubtable panzer corps could now retake Cleve and delay the offensive.

Von Luttwitz's corps, the Wehrmacht's No 1 reserve, had fought against and earned the respect of all five Allied armies. While it was

no longer the powerful force that had driven through the US First
Army in the Ardennes, it still possessed about 90 tanks, including
large numbers of the well-tried Mk IV equipped with a new long-
barrelled 75mm gun, the Panther and the Tiger, with an 88mm gun.
More dangerous still was the Jagdpanther, an 88mm high-velocity
gun mounted on a turret-less Panther tank chassis, a really devastating anti-tank weapon with which both of XLVII Corps' divisions
were equipped. Von Luttwitz hoped to drive through the remnants of
84th Division and recapture Cleve before the British could consolidate there. He compared the Allied push between the Maas and
Rhine, which was clearly aimed at crossing the Rhine, with the German Ardennes offensive for the Maas. In both offensives a combined
armoured and infantry force had attacked a weakly held front intent
on achieving a rapid breakthrough. In both cases the offensive had
been held up in the critical first three days and the defenders had
been able to bring up reserves. Von Luttwitz was critical of Montgomery's decision in the Ardennes to concentrate first on the defence
line and believed he should have attacked immediately with his superior armoured strength. He himself wasn't going to make the same
mistake; he intended to smash the Allied offensive with his superior
tanks. It would be a vain hope.

Von Luttwitz's first objective was to seize the Materborn feature,
but when he reached Udem he was shocked to learn that, despite reports, not only had Cleve completely fallen but that the British had
pushed forward and occupied Hau, from where they could cut the
Cleve to Goch road at the eastern end of the Reichswald. German
Intelligence reports told of the arrival of large numbers of British
tanks, many with the new 17-pounder guns. Von Luttwitz knew he
would also have to contend with the overwhelmingly strong British
artillery which could destroy his forces before they could get to grips
in the open country east of the forests. For the moment the weather
was keeping the Allied air forces grounded but von Luttwitz had no
illusions of what could happen if the weather cleared. He decided,
therefore, to send his divisions westward into the Reichswald where
they would suffer less from the artillery and armoured forces. He ordered the existing forces to block the way to Calcar and the Rhine
while 116th Panzer Division deployed west through Bedburg and
15th Panzer Grenadiers, under General Rott, cleared the area from
the smaller Forest of Cleve to the *Westwall* defences in the Reichswald. The remnants of Fiebig's 84th Division he reduced to a Battle
Group under von Waldenburg's 116th Panzers. Both divisions were

now directed to reach the Cleve–Hekkens road, then swing right to drive for the Materborn feature from the south, the very move antici- pated by Horrocks when he had sent the Welsh to take the forest.

Since February 10th, the 53rd Welsh Division's 160th Brigade had been driving down the eastern edge of the Reichswald forest to break out opposite the Forest of Cleve. The Welsh were to clear up enemy resistance and open routes that would improve their supply position. It seemed a fairly straightforward task but they did not know that von Luttwitz's XLVII Corps was about to strike his powerful counter-blow.

The advance continued on February 11th when 6th Royal Welch Fusiliers, with 'D' Company leading, set off with a squadron of Churchills. They descended the eastern slopes of the Stoppel Berg, followed by the 2nd Monmouthshires and in a steady, day-long downpour sloshed their way to the Materhorn–Hekkens road in the heart of the forest. Meanwhile 158th Brigade, on their right, crossed the road and made for the village of Am Klosterhuf from which they would seize a crossing over the river Niers leading to Goch. It was 10.30 pm before both Welsh brigades were ordered to halt and pre- pare for the following day. But while the Welsh rested, huddled in their greatcoats, von Luttwitz's 15th Panzer Grenadiers were still moving closer to the Forest of Cleve.

At the southern edge of the forest the Highland Division's 154th Brigade spent all day moving forward over the ploughland which was now a sea of glutinous mud. At 3.30 pm Brigadier Oliver sent 1st and 7th Black Watch for Hekkens, a mile away. It was defended by the 20th Parachute Regiment who had a forward defence line of Spandaus dug in behind earthworks covered by barbed wire. Maxi- mum artillery support was ordered and all guns turned on Hekkens.

The barrage crashed out on time and the troops flinched as shells began to crash into enemy positions sending up clouds of earth, stones and flying metal, opening a path for the infantry. They set off at the run, while on the flanks, the Crocodiles shot their flaming jets amongst screaming defenders. One Black Watch soldier recalls see- ing 'this Hun coming out of the smoke, his uniform torn, staggering with his face in his hands. One of the lads grabbed him and shoved him towards our lines. The bloke kept muttering "Danke, danke".' By 7 pm the strong-point had fallen, 200 prisoners had been taken and Hekkens was in Scottish hands. The remaining troops withdrew from their right-hand positions and fell back towards Gennap.

Major-General Thomas Rennie, commander of 51st Highland Division, now directed his 153rd Brigade to take the Dutch town of Gennap on the Nijmegen–Goch road. Their path was crossed by the river Niers, which was in spate like all the rivers that winter. Two troops of Buffaloes from 77th Assault Squadron RE and 11th Royal Tanks moved up to the river to ferry supplies and troops once the banks had been secured. That night the leading platoons of 5th Black Watch stealthily crossed in assault boats, gently dipping paddles to propel themselves across the dark, deep river. On the far bank, the men grasped clumps of waterside grass to steady the boats and crept ashore to surprise the unsuspecting guards. Within minutes the banks were taken and the rest of the battalion and their heavy equipment, carriers, anti-tank guns and vehicles streamed across in the Buffaloes. Maintaining their surprise they advanced along the river bank and attacked Gennap from the north-west.

The next morning the battalion HQ of 1st Gordons moved into the town and occupied the cellar of a house in the main street next to the Black Watch HQ. All the while the Germans shelled the area, especially around the site of the demolished bridge where the sappers were struggling to build a new one, and the German paratroopers, barricaded in virtually every house, shot at anyone moving along the rubble-strewn streets. The Gordons set out to clear the houses, using a method they had developed in street fighting in Holland. Their mortar and machine-gun platoons held the enemy's attention by bombarding the front of the house while infantry attacked each one in turn through the back garden. Donald Stewart remembers that 'We crept through the garden of a house, some lads slipped over the wall to the next one and positioned themselves to either side of the door. At a nod the door was kicked in, a grenade lobbed through. There was a bang and a cloud of smoke and flame. Then a Sten magazine was emptied inside. After that we rushed upstairs and dealt with any survivors.'

During the night fresh orders arrived from Brigade HQ that 1st Gordons were to take high ground north-east and east of Heyen from where German shelling was hitting the river Niers crossing. The village a mile south of Gennap would be simultaneously attacked by 5th/7th Gordons on the left who would take the remaining high ground. Major Lindsey spent five hours in his ill-lit cellar, working out the complex operation, co-ordinating the fire plan and ensuring that his communications worked. 'A' and 'D' Companies set out to capture two rows of houses just beyond the railway line and 'B' and

'C' Companies were ordered to take a sandy ridge criss-crossed with trenches and foxholes. 'C' Company quickly reached the outskirts of Heyen but was stopped by a Spandau which Alec Lumsden, the commander, thought was in a ruined church. Lindsey told them to await first light before attacking the gun and to dig in around a few houses at the roadside. Morrison's 'B' Company was sent up just behind them and some reinforcements of mortars and anti-tank guns were sent to Lumsden. All the battalion's objectives had been taken except a hillock east of Heyen which overlooked Gennap and that, too, would have to await the morning. Just as Lindsey had wearily settled on the one bunk in the cellar command post, and rolled himself in a blanket, the telephone jangled—it was Alec Lumsden reporting that his company was under attack from Heyen. Lindsey acknowledged and told him he would order up artillery at once.

Frank Philip, the Battery Commander, was already at his radio. Three miles back his eight guns stood loaded in a field. By each gun a sleepy sentry stood in the gun-pit, wrapped in his greatcoat, but ready to pull the firing lanyard immediately the tannoy crackled. At the Battery Command post and the Troop HQ duty officers sat drinking tea or reading. When the telephone rang the routine slipped automatically into gear. The Signals Officer took his place and was commanded to tell all stations to open immediately in case of telephone failure. The other companies were alerted and jeep drivers went to man their radios—all possible communication lines were opened. As soon as the battery confirmed its readiness Lindsey went upstairs and stood outside to watch. The rain had cleared and stars twinkled in the cold air. It was less than a minute since Lumsden's call until there were sounds of distant gunfire, then a delay of five or six seconds until the faint hum of a shell which grew rapidly in noise, zoomed overhead and crashed down behind 'C' Company.

In the cellar Frank Philip urgently conversed with his forward observation officer by telephone, asking if it was safe to bring the fire any closer to the threatened company. They were interrupted by the thud of boots on the stairs and a breathless corporal burst in: 'No-fourteen-platoon-is-surrounded-sir . . .' he gasped. Even as he was gabbling, Lumsden rang again to report the incident was in hand. It turned out that a fighting patrol had thrown a phosphorus grenade onto the thatched roof of a house setting it alight. As the men ran out, silhouetted against the flames, the Germans had opened fire. One German officer was foolhardy enough to stand in the road bawl-

ing: 'Come out you English swine!' The platoon commander's batman shot him dead.

The capture of Gennap by 51st Highland Division was another
important step forward, especially now that the American operation
'Grenade' had been delayed. From Gennap, 51st Division would
swing eastward, skirting the Reichswald to attack Goch, but, with no
American offensive to draw off the Germans along the Maas, the
Scots would have their right flank wide open to an enemy counter-attack from the area of Venlo or Roermond. Possession of Gennap
would go some way towards alleviating this problem as Montgomery
could now get into the battle his reserve divisions from British Second Army, the 52nd Lowland and 11th Armoured. They would debouch into the open country along the Maas where the Americans
should have been and would prevent German movement north towards the Reichswald. Thus, the 51st Division could now drive for
the important, key defences of Goch, the last major bastion before
the open country leading to the Hochwald Layback positions and the
Rhine.

At daybreak on February 12th, 53rd Division's 160th Brigade continued its advance through the same dreary woods that had been
their lot for the past five days. The 2nd Monmouthshires struck out
to clear the north-east corner of the Reichswald which brought them
to the road along which 7th Somersets had battled some hours before. 'After another morning scouting through the dark woods,' said
Corporal Edwards, 'we saw daylight through the trees ahead and realized we had reached the end. It seemed marvellous after a week of
mud and dripping trees and we cast caution to the wind and ran
ahead. Thank God there were no Germans waiting for us, but as we
broke out of the forest we saw troops bearing down on us. A few
shots were fired before someone started shouting, "Welsh! Welsh!"
and from the other side a voice yelled, "Somersets!"' The Monmouthshires were through the Reichswald.

At the same time, 6th Royal Welch Fusiliers reached the Cleve–
Asperden road about a mile and a half from, and parallel to,
the vital Cleve–Goch road. There the battalion dug in to plan the
next move, leaving 4th Welch to take over the advance. They ran
into the 115th and 104th Panzer Grenadiers, under direct orders
from von Luttwitz to stop the British advance. The Welsh battalions
fought stubbornly with small arms and mortars against the very
spirited German attacks but as soon as the divisional artillery was

turned against them the Panzers broke under the deluge of explosives
that rocked the forest and felled huge trees, and finally they fled with
heavy losses. At the end of five exhausting days in the forest, therefore, the Welsh had not only found the strength to meet the Panzer
onslaught, but had also destroyed eight 88mm guns, a number of
Mk IV tanks, some Jagdpanthers and countless mortars and machine-
guns.

On the high ground east of the Reichswald, other German formations driving for the forest ran into the 43rd Wessex moving south
from Hau and Bedburg. The enemy launched three successive attacks
against 7th Somersets, who, like the Welsh, stood firm. The attacks
were driven off by combined infantry, tank and artillery fire.

By late afternoon on February 12th, therefore, von Luttwitz's attempt to relieve Cleve had foundered upon the Welsh and the Wessex Divisions. Next morning von Luttwitz was forced to admit defeat
and decided to go over to the defensive. In spite of his criticism of
Montgomery's caution in the Ardennes, his own much vaunted
counter-attack had failed, largely because instead of establishing a
defensive line for which he had had several days to prepare, he had
committed his forces piecemeal and had seen them driven off. He
was forced to fall back on Goch, where he should have been in the
first place.

Now that Cleve was irretrievably lost, Schlemm ordered von Luttwitz to fight on a line extending from Hasselt on the Calcar road,
along the Eselberg ridge, that ran just south of Bedburg, to the
north-west corner of the Forest of Cleve. Von Luttwitz deployed his
divisions plus 346th Infantry Division from across the Rhine. Fiebig's 84th Division was strengthened by more paratroopers and positioned on the right. The 15th Panzer Grenadiers were deployed left
of them, north-west from Udem on a four-mile front along the Eselberg as far as Moyland, a village between Cleve and Calcar. Both
had units of 116th Panzers for heavy support and 116th's commander, General von Waldenburg, was given the task of co-ordinating the entire defence, including more paratroopers from 180th Division if needed. By late on February 13th there lay across the path of
the 43rd Wessex Division's main axis a strong force of tanks, self-
propelled guns, machine-guns and mortar batteries. On the right
flank they spread into Moyland Wood on the main road to Calcar
along which 15th Scottish Division's 46th Brigade were advancing
from Cleve.

Notwithstanding his concern for the men, whom he visited as often as he could, Lieutenant-General Horrocks told Major-General Ross that, regrettably, his exhausted Welsh Division had to continue their attacks; the initiative couldn't be lost. The RAF had reported heavy rail traffic heading westwards from Germany to the Rhine all day on the 12th, but bad weather was preventing air strikes. The enemy had recovered from his initial shock and was pouring in all his reserves, many from across the Rhine, now that the Roer floods protected his southern flank.

Orders were issued for the final clearance of the forest to begin on February 13th. The 71st Brigade, of 53rd Welsh Division, would take command of 1st/5th Welch, and what was left of 147th Regiment's tanks, to drive through the centre of the forest and break out onto the Cleve–Asperden road opposite Wilhelminenhof; the rest of 158th Brigade, 1st East Lancs and 7th RWF were ordered to swing right and clear the south-eastern defences, from where they would head into open country and capture the Asperberg bridge.

At 10 am 1st/5th Welch began their attack. It was a hard fight against enemy self-propelled guns fired down the rides, often for several hundred yards. All the enemy had to do was camouflage a gun and wait; a British tank or carrier would nose into the ride and after a moment to aim, the German fired. Emlyn Jones's platoon had been pinned down for the umpteenth time that morning: 'We were waiting for a tank to come and drive the Jerries out; after what seemed ages it eventually arrived. Our sergeant jumped onto the back of the tank to direct the commander, a young ginger-haired chap, then dropped off. As the tank revved up there was a hell of a bang and smoke poured out as the tank ran off the track and crashed into the trees. We stared horrified while our sergeant leapt up and ran to the tank, but there was another explosion, a sheet of flame and that was that.' It took 1st/5th Welch until midday to get to Wilhelminenhof and by then eight of the sixteen tanks they had started out with had been knocked out. They dug in at their objective to allow 1st Oxford and Bucks Light Infantry to take over.

In the meantime, the 7th RWF in the south-east of the forest passed through a quarter-mile strip without encountering much opposition and emerged near the Asperberg bridge where the Niers is about twenty feet wide and runs deep between steep banks. It lies on the edge of the village with a large farm to its right. The road runs along the edge of a narrow belt of woodland for about 300 yards, beyond which is a clearing with a small wood crowning a feature on the far side.

Hugo Pritz, a young German paratrooper and part of a machine-gun team dug in on the slopes of the wood above the river Niers, could see the British coming from the woods: 'I remember my gunner muttering that we had been told it was impossible to get through the forest.' As the 'Tommies' fanned out across the farm-land, Pritz fed in the ammunition belt while his mate fired and for several minutes the gun vibrated and its ammunition belt jerked forward in short bursts; then the belt jammed. Shells—he presumed from tanks, but more likely from anti-tank guns—began to explode on the slopes around him. Not far to his right a tall birch received a direct hit. 'I was kneeling down by the gun and glanced up at the terrific crack! The whole tree shook violently and then toppled over, hitting the ground so hard that I swear it bounced two metres high, just missing a couple of men.'

For hours the 7th RWF committed companies in an effort to reach the bridge but suffered heavily as machine-guns raked them with cross-fire. They had a number of hand-operated flame throwers with which they intended to flush the enemy from their defences, but they could not get close enough. When they mounted a last attack in the late afternoon, there was a loud explosion, and smoke poured from the bridge. Gerald Thomas remembers 'having a bit of a breather and watching another company having a go. We couldn't see the bridge because of the smoke but we knew it was at the end of a finger of woodland. As our boys tried again there were a couple of bangs which at first I thought was a Tiger tank firing. I remember thinking, Christ, that's all we need, then some of the boys started pointing at a cloud of smoke. They seemed pleased it was blown because there wasn't any point in trying to get it any longer.' Hugo Pritz also remembers the bridge being blown. 'It did not please us much be-cause we couldn't get back over it and would have to withdraw under fire or in the night, back towards Pfalsdorf where our HQ was sup-posed to be.'

After the Asperberg bridge was blown the fighting died down rap-idly. Aerial reconnaissance next day confirmed that the bridge was in the river. Although for another three days the Germans held out around the bridge site, 51st Division finally came up from the south of the river to attack—and capture—Asperden.

The level of the river Roer, meanwhile, was at last falling—it was still 400 yards wide north of Julich, but had shrunk to 300 yards south of the town—and behind it the powerful US Ninth Army was waiting to drive forward for the Rhine. Everything seemed set for XXX Corps to implement phase two of the operation, which was to capture Goch and break through the second line of the Siegfried Line defences.

8 Battle for the Goch escarpment

The shells exploded in rapid succession, flinging clouds of mud, earth and stones in every direction. The 5th Wiltshires, caught on the exposed slopes of the ridge south-east of Bedburg, dodged, threw themselves flat, shuddered at near misses, then scrambled up and raced on through a curtain of shrapnel and flames. Rain poured down as they stumbled along, desperate to gain the start-line on the ridge for 4th Wiltshires' attack on Trippenburg and the vital crossroads at which met the roads from Cleve, Goch and Calcar.

In Trippenburg and its approaches, German 6th Parachute Division troops lay in trenches awaiting the assault with 116th Panzers' armour. 'It was very tense waiting for the British attack', recalls one paratrooper. 'We knew they were on the ridge and wondered how they had survived our shelling. Just after noon the rain eased a little and we were told the attack was imminent. Then we heard the distant rumble of heavy guns and waited, slowly counting the seconds, before the shells screamed into our lines.'

The Divisional artillery had turned its guns on Trippenburg while the 4th Wiltshires advanced with Shermans of 8th Armoured Brigade's Nottinghamshire Yeomanry. But one by one the Shermans bogged down in the deep, red mud of the ploughlands. Infantry struggled on while the paratroopers tore into them with machine-guns and hundreds of mortar shells. They reached Trippenburg in the late afternoon and began clearing the scattered farms and adjoining barns and sheds. Everywhere the Germans retaliated with machine-guns and mortars. Even though they lacked armour the Wiltshires set about driving the enemy out. Small groups of men raced for each building, seeking cover behind walls from where they lobbed grenades; before the smoke cleared they emptied automatics into the buildings. Private Warrender remembers seeing 'three or four of our

lads running for a barn. They got within a dozen yards when a stick
grenade was flung from an upstairs window and blew our lads over.
No-one got up but immediately several Mills bombs were "bowled"
through the window of the barn and the explosions blew the tin
sheets off the roof.'

At nightfall the 4th Wiltshires took refuge and a breather. But
their rest was brief for less than a mile away two enemy divisions
were mustering for a counter-attack. The Wiltshires kept their heads
down while paratroopers and panzer grenadiers backed by Tiger
tanks and Mk IVs launched the assault. 4th Wiltshires put up a phenomenal resistance, driving off the enemy infantry, but the German
tanks lumbered back and forth through the ruined village pursuing
the 'Tommies', overrunning one entire company. At last the German
armour stopped, hesitating to go too far without infantry support.

On the ridge the order to advance was given at 11 am. The 5th
Wiltshires tramped forward to relieve their comrades and secure the
positions for the 43rd Wessex's 130th Brigade to launch its assault
towards Goch the next day. They hadn't got far when their 'A' and
'D' Companies were forced to the ground by converging fire from
machine-guns backed by self-propelled guns. On the right, 'C' Company had also run into the 1st Panzer Genadiers' infantry and were
fighting them hand to hand. Bayonets flashed and glinted in the rare
bright sunshine, grenades flew, and all through the sunny afternoon
the battle raged. It took another couple of hours of night fighting before the 5th Wiltshires could regain Trippenburg, pass through and
at long last capture the crossroads a quarter mile east of the Forest
of Cleve. Over 200 men had been killed but the two battalions had
won the high ground in time for 130th Brigade to pass through.

General Straube was responsible for the defence of Goch, while
von Luttwitz concentrated on the front from the east of Goch to the
Rhine. German reconnaissance aircraft were now reporting another
big Allied formation assembling south of Cleve and apparently heading for Goch—this was the 15th Scottish Division's 44th Brigade with
the armoured breaching force. Schlemm was of the opinion that the
thrust by 51st Division might therefore be only a feint towards Goch
by the devious British. But Straube was unsure and remained cautious. He wanted to retake Gennap and seal off the western approaches to Goch by throwing the British back across the Niers. On
February 12th he sent two companies of 2nd Parachute Regiment
and a battery of self-propelled guns from the Siegfried Line to
Thomashof, a strongly defended hamlet south of Goch, to contain

any attempt by 51st Division to swing southwards around the town and drive for the Rhine.

In the meantime, General Klosterkaempen sent paratroopers from his 180th Division to counter-attack at Heyen where the 1st Gordons were dug in, just south of Gennap. The unexpected appearance of the paratroopers took the 1st Gordons by surprise as no one believed the Germans would attempt to retake the village which they had abandoned twenty-four hours before. There was a sharp engagement but eventually the Germans were driven off by a sustained mortar attack. Straube had to report to Schlemm that Gennap was being defended by a British force of 'Grade One' infantry, backed by armour and self-propelled guns. He made his report and then asked permission to pull back two miles to the Broederbosch Woods.

But he wasn't quick enough and before he could establish his force the British attacked again. This time it was the 'crack' 32nd Guards Infantry Brigade; although the Guards Armoured Division was still immobile behind the floods, Horrocks used its infantry to reinforce his southern flank. Straube had to report that the Guards had driven through the woods before Hommersum, although taking heavy casualties from mines, and by nightfall had fought their way into Germany and taken the village of Hommersum itself. General Klosterkaempen had been instructed to hold the village only long enough for Straube's LXXXVI Corps to establish another defence line before Goch. An anti-tank ditch was hastily improvised by enlarging and flooding a *beek* (drainage ditch) which extended from the Maas to the moat of Blijen Beek castle. The new defences were south of Broederbosch and included the small village of Afferden. Straube dug in and prepared to defend the line to prevent more British divisions crossing the Maas and joining the battle; in addition to the 52nd Lowland Division, German Intelligence reported that the 3rd Infantry Division was also coming forward. The new German positions were intended to stop another British drive outflanking German defences before Goch and sweeping in a great arc south-east towards Wesel and south to meet the Americans when eventually they crossed the Roer.

At his new HQ west of the Rhine at Xanten, to which he had moved on February 8th, General Schlemm made it absolutely clear to von Luttwitz that Goch was critical to the defences of the Rhineland and like Cleve was an 'at all costs' position. So, too, was Calcar. It was von Luttwitz's responsibility to prevent the British reaching Calcar and Goch by their drives east of the Forest of Cleve.

Canadian First Army's assault had driven them back almost thirty miles and only Goch and the Hochwald Layback remained before the Rhine. Nor could Schlemm ignore the threat from US Ninth Army beyond the Roer. He realized that any more divisions thrown against the British offensive would leave fewer to oppose the Americans; he already had elements of nine divisions trying to stop the Allied drive south.

The Germans were not the only ones making changes in their troop dispositions. A fundamental change in Allied organization occurred on February 14th when General Crerar decided it was time to operate a two-corps front. The original front had expanded to fourteen miles and two more divisions had come in to protect the flanks. In spite of the continuing bad weather and ground conditions Crerar thought the tasks ahead could best be tackled by dividing responsibility between two commanders.

Horrocks's XXX Corps on the right would take Goch after which they would drive south-west down the Maas to Venlo, and south-east towards the Rhine to link up with the Americans when they came over the Roer. The left attack would be handled by Lieutenant-General G. G. Simonds's 11 Canadian Corps. Simonds wanted a change of plan, however, and was urging Crerar to allow him to attack north of Nijmegen, to the west of Arnhem which he would by-pass, and then drive along the east bank of the Rhine which had been Montgomery's intention in the airborne attack on Arnhem in the previous September. Crerar, however, would not be diverted from 'Veritable' and refused Simonds's request. His immediate objective was to take over the battle for Moyland Wood, and then capture Calcar. Following this his axis would split, one heading for Marienbaum, Xanten and the Rhine, the other going through Udem to the Xanten to Geldern road.

The first axis would break through the defences in the direct route along the road to Xanten, one end of the phase three line; the other axis would out-flank the defences, take von Luttwitz's concentration area at Udem followed by the defences near their south end and secure the Geldern end of the line. For this task Simonds was given 46th Brigade, from the 15th Scottish, 43rd Wessex and 11th Armoured. These moves would fulfil Crerar's third objective for 'Veritable', to break through the Hochwald Layback and secure the line Xanten to Geldern inclusive.

South of the Reichswald, the 51st Division were beginning their moves to close on Goch. The 154th Brigade was now ordered to cross the river Niers from its position in Hekkens to capture Kessel. The Niers bridge south of Hekkens had been blown and the Buffaloes came up to ferry troops across. On the night of February 13th/14th two assault companies of 1st Black Watch were taken across followed next day by their equipment. Then 7th Argylls followed, passed through the Black Watch and attacked Kessel, which they took after bitter fighting. With their right flank secured by 52nd Division, plus 32nd Guards Brigade which was to attack Straube's new defence line, the 51st Highland Division now prepared to advance on Goch.

On the far side of the Reichswald, 43rd Wessex's 130th Brigade moved through rolling farmland dotted with substantial farm complexes which the Germans had fortified heavily. 'A' Company of the 4th Dorset Regiment attacked a farm and was met by machine-gun and mortar fire. Their own mortars bombarded the farm but the German Spandaus drove them back. The platoon commander called for a PIAT to launch projectiles at the farm. 'The first rocket smashed a great hole in the wall near a window frame,' said 'Bill' Williams. 'The next hit the tall roof, blew the tiles to bits and started a fire. Brens and mortars kept firing and after a final rocket blew in a wooden wall of the barn, we went in again. This time the Jerries had been plastered and we got little opposition. Inside was a hell of a mess; several Jerries had been badly wounded and lay around screaming.'

In his caravan at Cloister, Major-General Ivor Thomas, 43rd Wessex's commander, deliberated on the battle. His division had run into fierce opposition as, like the Scots a few miles east of them in Moyland Wood, they had encountered von Luttwitz's formidable defences. With no obvious signs of a break in German morale the outlook was far from rosy. But Thomas believed that if he struck with his reserves at the right moment he would break the German resistance, as they must be as tired as his own troops. He ordered Brigadier Essame's 214th Brigade, which had been resting since their attack on Bedburg three days before, to capture the eastern end of Pfalzdorf. A third battalion was to go forward in Kangaroos and cut the Goch to Calcar road at the villages of Schroenshof, Bergmanshoff and Imigshof. Their attack would be strengthened by 4th Somerset Light Infantry and would be launched at midday on February 16th from a start-line running between Blacknik and Berhovel, 800 yards east of the Forest of Cleve. This point was still in enemy hands and 130th Brigade was instructed to secure the start-line. This drive would isolate the fortress of Goch from reinforcement, cut off the

retreat of those German forces holding the Asperberg bridge site and
help the Welsh. Upon the success of this operation the entire action
would depend.

At 9.30 am the following day Shermans from 4th/7th Dragoons
lumbered forward in the renewed drive to secure the Eselberg ridge
for 214th Brigade to begin. Major Allen's 'C' Company of 5th Dorsets made a fighting advance along the main road to Blacknik and
then Major Hartwell's 'D' Company took over and fought its way
through bitter opposition to deploy to the left of the road on a ridge
extending to Louisendorf, south-west of Moyland Wood. 'We were
told to dig in, but the earth was so sloppy that all we could manage
was a mud hole,' remembers Brian Hicks. 'We lay there while a German gun in the woods to our right shelled us, blowing fountains of
mud everywhere and from each crater, clouds of choking smoke
began drifting around making it difficult to see. A tank passed us to
take on the German gun. This cheered us up until the German shot
back at the tank and more shells came even closer. After a near miss
the tank moved off the ridge and drove closer to the gun.'

The infantry kept close behind the divisional artillery barrage,
each section with its own tanks sweeping forward and providing
cover from the Spandaus. As they passed through Blacknik the Shermans set every house on fire with their main guns and then poured
machine-gun fire into the German troops streaming from the blazing
ruins. As the afternoon wore on the ploughlands were dotted with
blazing buildings and thick smoke writhed upwards in every direction. By 5 pm the Somersets had advanced 2,500 yards and overrun
three lateral roads. 'D' Company thrust forward through small farms
and orchards until German paratroops holding strong positions in a
group of farms on their left opened heavy, accurate fire.

Men raced across the fields and flung themselves into shallow
ditches and depressions when Spandaus raked the ground. They lay
there, clutching weapons, waiting for the order to break for the farms
again. The distant barrage cracked and rumbled, the noise overlaid
by the thump of mortars crashing into the ground. Sergeant Colin
Smith raised his head and peered across through weeds and broken
winter sedges. He recalls that

a ball of fire whizzed from a ruined building, snaked along the ground
and exploded with flames and smoke where three men huddled. Smoke
rose in choking clouds, from which a soldier staggered, coughing and
rubbing his eyes. A Spandau hammered and he was flung grotesquely to

8 Montgomery and Horrocks stop for lunch in the Reichswald

9 The 160th Brigade, 53rd Welsh Division, nearing Goch

10 Refugees mix with soldiers on the road to Goch

11 Horrocks and Montgomery with Barber, Commander of the 15th Scottish Division

12 Simpson (US Ninth Army), Montgomery, Hodges
(US First Army), Collins (US VII Corps)
13 American pontoon bridge collapses during Roer crossings

14 The US 102nd Division moves along the Roer

15 Welsh troops advancing towards Weeze

the earth. The platoon on the right opened up with a 2″ mortar, its bombs bursting either side of the ruin, until one smacked right into it, killing the *Panzerfaust* team and sending bricks and splinters in every direction. Then the platoon was racing for the left hand farm, Stens blasting from the hip, grenades flying and Brens tearing wicked slivers of wood and glass which whirled around inside the farmhouse.

The Somersets tore into each farm and by sheer force overcame the German paratroopers, whose tired and shocked survivors were sent to the rear. In this way they advanced nearly five miles.

Essame now prepared to deliver his decisive thrust. On the outskirts of Bedburg the 5th Duke of Cornwall's Light Infantry had waited all afternoon in Kangaroos. With them along the road were Shermans of 'B' Squadron, 4th/7th Dragoon Guards. By launching an attack with the speedy Kangaroos and Shermans, Essame aimed to rush the enemy positions, and allow the infantry to pour from the carriers and swamp the opposition.

In the gloomy twilight Essame gave the order to advance. As Private Wallis remembers it, 'We had been sitting in, or on, the Kangaroos for hours. Then one of the lads pointed in the direction of the CO, Taylor, who was hurrying from the signals truck. Someone shouted and our drivers yelled for us to get in. The rest was drowned in the roar of engines and we were off, trundling south along the narrow road in a long column.' The mass of armour surged past the woods to Blacknik, still smoking from the Dorsets' battle the night before. They swept onto open country and rapidly formed up into five powerful columns. A mighty roar of tank engines blasted through the night and the five columns charged for the villages of Schroenshof, Bermanshoff and Imigshof, 6,000 yards ahead. 'We heard the tanks coming, the noise was terrific, it filled the night,' a trooper of 2nd Parachute Regiment wrote later. 'In the dark all we knew was the Tommies were sweeping forward and we had practically nothing left with which to stop them.'

The charging infantrymen were the last straw; as Thomas had hoped, it proved too much for the enemy, who began pulling back in great haste. By 8 pm the armoured force had cut the Goch–Calcar road. Essame now prepared a daring manoeuvre, described as 'high military art . . . to be attempted only by those prepared to take risks and then only by troops of the highest quality led by experienced commanders.' The 4th Somerset Light Infantry would make a night attack over country which had not been reconnoitred as it lay ahead

of the start-line recently won by the 7th Somersets and the Duke of
Cornwall's Light Infantry.

Before the armoured attack by the DCLI, it had seemed to the
Germans defending the escarpment in front of Goch that they could
rest awhile in the safety of darkness. Then the armour had roared
out of the night and the ensuing battle lasted until the early hours of.
the morning, before petering out in desultory shelling. In trenches
and defences the Germans now stood down to eat and draw ammunition; only sentries patrolled. It seemed they had the night to prepare
for the next attack. But, unknown to them, half an hour after midnight, 4th Somersets were silently creeping forward towards the all-
important escarpment. Occasional flashes from guns shed some light
on the soft, muddy, treacherous ground, criss-crossed with trenches
and ditches. Suddenly a German shouted a challenge. Barely had it
died away when a Spandau opened fire, its screeching chatter deafen-
ing in the silence. Grenades were thrown and in a welter of bangs the
gun stopped. But the advantage of surprise was lost and other Spandaus opened fire. Startled German paratroopers flung away mess tins,
grabbed weapons and rushed to positions to find the Tommies already breaking through. More machine-guns swung around to join
in. Major Beckhurst pulled back his 'A' Company a short way in the
face of cross-fire from the trenches and called for artillery support.
The artillery's Forward Observation Officer sent back the co-or-
dinates: moments later the Field Regiments opened fire. Shells
zoomed over into the target area, pounding the enemy's concentration, blowing the wire defences apart and killing the machine-
gunners. The moment the barrage ceased 'A' Company raced in
with bayonets fixed, yelling like madmen, through a wire fence
straight into the enemy positions. The enemy fought briefly but soon
gave up. The German commander surrendered with his remaining
men and in good English said he had never expected the British to
attack by night. By dawn 4th Somersets had a front 1,000 yards long
on the wooded escarpment overlooking Goch. With the 43rd Wessex
Division astride the Goch–Calcar road and holding the escarpment,
Straube's LXXXVI Corps in Goch could no longer maintain contact
with von Luttwitz's XLVII Corps holding Moyland Wood and Calcar. Altogether it was a major reversal for the Germans.

On February 16th the 53rd Welsh Division's commander, Major-
General Ross, departed on sick leave and Brigadier Elrington, of
71st Brigade, took over. Soon afterwards at 11.30 am Elrington issued orders for the final phase of the battle of the Reichswald. He

told 71st Brigade's new commander, Lieutenant-Colonel T. McLeod, to attack north of the river Niers to support the 51st Highland Division's attack on Asperden and Hervost which would begin at 10 pm that night. The 71st Brigade's task was to secure a line north-east of the Asperberg bridge and cut the Hau to Asperden road. On their right 158th Brigade would advance with one battalion and both brigades would receive artillery support.

At 8 pm the divisional artillery fired its preliminary bombardment. Five Medium Regiments plastered the German positions around the Asperberg bridge where the 7th Royal Welch Fusiliers had been repulsed three days before. Hugo Pritz was still dug in with the paratroopers just north of the Asperberg bridge. 'We waited for days, getting anxious as the British began to close in behind us, we knew they had got over the river further west. It was dark and cold and we were settling for another long night. The roar of the heavy guns roused us and briefly we wondered what was going on. But not for long. Seconds later the shells began to scream towards us and explode everywhere.'

At the cessation of this 'softening up' the attack began. A heavy rolling barrage covered the infantry's attack and while the shells tore up the farmland, smashed trees and blew up farms and houses in front of them, the 1st Oxford and Bucks Light Infantry, with 7th RWF to their south, began their advance. The 7th RWF, who had already suffered heavy casualties attacking the bridge, were again unlucky when the barrage fell short injuring and killing a number of men. And the advancing troops were still fired on by 88mms. 'It was bloody awful racing down that road,' said John Piper, 'but we made it.'

By 10 pm 1st Oxford and Bucks Light Infantry had crossed the road to either side of Asperberg and seized the village in a headlong charge, firing after the retreating defenders who made off eastwards towards a small belt of woodland. The 7th RWF ran into heavy machine-gun fire from the woods and ruined buildings but by 11 pm they, too, had taken their objective and the last remaining corner of the Reichswald had been captured.

Jubilantly the brigade HQ decided to consolidate and sent forward carriers towing 6-pounder anti-tank guns, signallers, ammunition carriers and medical units to catch up with the infantry. But as the column moved across the dark country enemy fire hit them without warning. In moments carriers were on fire, trucks exploded and men lay dead. This signalled a renewal of the battle and parties of zealous paratroopers holding out in cellars and trenches around the Asper-berg feature launched an onslaught. Inculcated in the belief that they were the élite of the German Army, they were prepared to die fighting. A platoon of Oxford and Bucks Light Infantry near the vil-lage were astonished when eight fanatical paratroopers attacked in a style that was pure Hollywood; they walked eight abreast, each man carrying a Spandau firing from the hip. The startled troops recov-ered, opened fire and killed all eight.

Next day 53rd Welsh Division's 160th Brigade cleared the narrow belt of farmland between the Reichswald and the Forest of Cleve, encountering no opposition. It now remained for 71st Brigade to draw up between the 51st and 43rd Divisions attacking Goch; the Welsh Division had completed the capture of the Reichswald, an op-eration that cost them over 3,000 casualties, more than a third of all their casualties in World War Two. The division's achievement was a major factor in breaking the formidable enemy defences, and their defeat of von Luttwitz's offensive cleared the way for the 43rd Wes-sex to gain the Goch escarpment.

February 17th saw Major-General Thomas exploiting his success still further with 130th Brigade clearing the Forest of Cleve. At 11 am that day, 214th Brigade was ordered south to consolidate the di-vision's strength on the Goch escarpment to prevent the Germans recapturing it, and 7th Somersets and 1st Worcestershires set off. They fought a desperate battle all afternoon, inching their way for-ward bit by bit. The Panzer Grenadiers hit back with all the weapons they could muster, including six-barrelled *Nebelwerfers,* or 'moaning minnies', which blasted from each barrel in turn and were so danger-ous their own crews stood well clear. 'After being hit by *Nebel-werfers* a brush and shovel was used to clear up.' Around Berg-manshoff the Duke of Cornwall's Light Infantry endured German artillery fire that many thought the heaviest and most accurate of the campaign. With the Ruhr just across the river Rhine, the Germans had no shortage of ammunition and even artillery batteries from across the Rhine joined in with long-range shelling. But by nightfall a signal reached Thomas that 'they now looked down on the chimneys of Goch on a front of 4,000 yards'. Behind the troops the ground was cluttered with abandoned enemy equipment and just below them stretched the first of Goch's formidable anti-tank ditches.

The German garrison in Goch, including 180th, 190th Divisions and the 2nd Parachute Regiment of Straube's LXXXVI Corps, fe-verishly prepared to defend their anchor position in the second line of the Siegfried defences. They hurriedly sandbagged positions, dragged artillery pieces into new pits and checked machine-guns. Self-propelled guns and tanks rumbled up to block any routes into Goch. Pillboxes, minefields and wire entanglements surrounded the town. Every approach was covered by mines and tripwires. But there were no anti-tank guns—a fatal error, as would become clear within a short time.

9 Breakthrough at Goch

While the British and Canadians were fighting the Germans to the point of exhaustion, Eisenhower was growing more confident of his armies closing to the Rhine. On February 20th, while the battle was raging in Goch, he told General Marshall, 'All our preparations are made, the troops are in fine fettle and there is no question in my mind that if we get off to a good start . . . the operation will be a complete success.' He was referring especially to Simpson's US Ninth Army that was completing its preparation to cross the Roer and launch 'Grenade', an operation that would catch the Germans in the rear, relieve the pressure on Canadian First Army and eventually destroy all German forces west of the Rhine on Montgomery's front. He went on: 'If the weather improves with the advancing spring, I feel that matters will work out almost exactly as projected.'

But if Eisenhower felt satisfied with the way things were going, Patton was increasingly impatient. He had liberally interpreted Bradley's instructions to undertake 'active defence', had fought his way through the *Westwall* and had driven along the north bank of the Moselle on the way to the Rhine. Now he went to Bradley to ask for extra divisions to broaden his attack, emphasizing that most American troops in Europe weren't fighting, which was an exaggeration. Ninth Army's inactivity behind the Roer was only caused by First Army's failure to capture the dams. Patton's Third Army had already begun the offensive that would accelerate into his momentous drive to the Rhine. The US Seventh Army had just cleared the Colmar Pocket and was closing along the upper reaches of the Rhine. Patton was riled because he had not been officially given the honour of reaching, and crossing, the Rhine first. He warned Bradley that 'all of us in high positions will surely be held accountable for the failure to take offensive action when offensive action is possible.' Bradley,

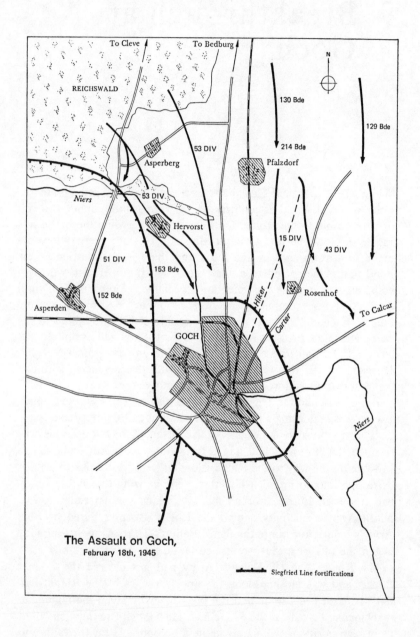

The Assault on Goch,
February 18th, 1945

Siegfried Line fortifications

whom Eisenhower was relying on to keep the troublesome Patton in check, calmed him down, repeating that Eisenhower's decision was to attack north of the Ruhr. He added: 'Regardless of what you and I think of this decision, we are good enough soldiers to carry out these orders.' US First and Third Armies had the task of crossing the Rhine in the Frankfurt region and he suggested that Patton should take the opportunity to refit his troops for the decisive blow they were to strike.

But Patton wouldn't listen. He ordered a reconnaissance in force which he then increasingly strengthened until all his troops were committed. He started two strong thrusts, one towards Bitburg and the other towards Trier, which had frustrated him the previous October, when he had claimed he had insufficient troops. For this new drive he wanted to use the 94th Infantry Division supported by the armoured division he had previously lacked. Patton went to Paris, ostensibly on leave, and 'borrowed' the 10th Armoured Division. This was supposed to help him clear the Saar-Moselle triangle and not to capture Trier, but Patton cajoled Bradley into including that city in the Eifel operations.

Third Army cleared the Saar-Moselle triangle but instead of returning the 10th Armoured Division in the last week of February the wily Patton sent it into battle at Trier. Determined German resistance frustrated Patton's hopes of taking the town, and the 10th Armoured Division came to a halt at the flooded Moselle river when bridging equipment failed to arrive. For nine hours Patton fumed while the Germans shelled. At last the bridging operations were completed and in the face of strenuous enemy opposition 10th Armoured fought its way—at a terrible cost in casualties—into a bridgehead on the far side.

The Supreme Headquarters Allied Expeditionary Forces (SHAEF) ordered Bradley to get the division back again without delay. Once more in trouble through Patton's audacity, Bradley arrived at Third Army's HQ demanding the division. His subordinate was far from abashed and vigorously defended his action, telling Bradley: 'General, Third Army wants to fight. It can do so victoriously if it is allowed. That's all we're asking. The chance to fight for our country and lick the goddamned Hun whom we've got on the run. I asked the corps commanders to come here to outline their situation to you. They will tell you the whole story.'

The argument went on, General Middleton, commander of VIII Corps, explaining the need for 10th Armoured, but still Bradley refused, saying that Eisenhower had been commanded by Washington to keep one armoured division in reserve. Eventually Patton exchanged an infantry division for the 10th Armoured and with that Bradley had to be satisfied. But SHAEF then told Patton directly that he had 10th Armoured for precisely forty-eight hours and then it had to be returned.

At the end of that time, Third Army still had not captured Trier and Patton pestered Bradley to be allowed to keep it a little longer. Bradley replied that SHAEF hadn't contacted him yet, and he would keep well away from the telephone. With that Patton was satisfied and regardless of the plans of Eisenhower and SHAEF went on with his personal battle for Trier, while Bradley went *incommunicado*.

On February 18th the assault on Goch began to take shape. The 43rd Wessex divisional artillery opened fire. Explosions rocked the town, sending great columns of smoke and clouds of dust high in the air. The 44th Lowland Brigade in all its armoured strength moved south from Cleve. The force that had breached the Siegfried Line at Frasselt and opened the way to Cleve brought to bear its great cavalcade of bridge-carriers, Crocodiles, guns, bulldozers and Kangaroo-borne infantry. Two battalions were to attack, 8th Royal Scots on a route code-named 'Hiker' along the railway, and 6th King's Own Scottish Borderers whose axis, named 'Carter', lay through the village of Rosenhof.

The Wessex troops brought up their engineers by night and, taking advantage of the shelling, put several bridges across the anti-tank ditch. As soon as a bridge was finished 7th Somersets' infantry platoons crossed and penetrated the town's outskirts. Two platoons even crossed the second anti-tank ditch and deployed within the town itself, extremely risky while their artillery were shelling. But these attacks by the Wessex on the north-eastern areas of the town were only diversions intended to confuse the Germans about the direction of the main attack.

The task of taking Goch was assigned to the two Scottish divisions, 15th and 51st. The 51st's 153rd Brigade was to attack west of the river Niers, which flowed in a curve through Goch, while 152nd Brigade attacked further south to capture the smaller part of the town. The 15th Division's 44th Brigade was to attack east of the Niers on 'Hiker' and 'Carter' at 3 pm.

Brigadier Cummings-Bruce and Lieutenant-Colonel Lord Tryon went forward together in the morning to have a look at conditions.

To their surprise they almost reached the ditch without encountering any opposition. The enemy was obviously confused about the direction of the attack. After a brief discussion, Cummings-Bruce and Tryon decided that because the movement from the escarpment had attracted little attention and the town seemed so quiet, they would launch their attack at once, using two troops of tanks and an infantry company of 8th Royal Scots.

At 1.15 pm, therefore, the order to advance rang out and a troop of Grenadiers' tanks led off, followed by Major McQueen's 'A' Company in Kangaroos of 49th Armoured Personnel Carrier Regiment, and then another troop of tanks. Churchills of Grenadiers' No 3 Squadron opened fire on the enemy positions while, under cover of smoke, two AVRE bridge-carriers approached. When McQueen's company tried to cross the fire was too heavy. 'Our platoon sergeant yelled to us to get over the ditch,' said Andy Ross. 'We ran for the ditch firing bursts from Stens and scrambled over the edge. It was slippery and I slid to the bottom, but the sergeant bawled at me to get off my backside and we scrambled up the far side. The enemy had Spandaus placed in buildings just beyond and were tearing up the ground in front of us. Several lads were hit and fell back but the rest of us scrambled out and took cover in the ruins.'

On 'Hiker' axis the troops found an intact bridge but as the first tank moved across it, the bridge collapsed. Engineers moved up bridge-carriers and alongside the broken bridge a Grenadiers' bridge-carrier dropped 'London Bridge', as it was called, over the gap. Major Drummond's 'D' Company crossed in Kangaroos but the drivers said they couldn't travel on the railway lines which would rip off their tracks. The company debussed and advanced between an orchard on the right and a two-storeyed house on the left. A heavy burst of shelling knocked out the only wireless set, breaking communications with HQ except for the Gunners Observation-Post tank. This now vital link-vehicle crossed the railway very carefully and stayed with the company throughout the night.

Men grabbed for support as the other Kangaroos lurched forward, raced along the road, across the bridges and into Goch, to deploy between the factories and the railway. 'C' Company, 8th Royal Scots, under Major MacIntyre, followed 'B' Company through and was ordered to a large block of buildings near the railway. Lieutenant-Colonel Pearson, their CO, decided the attacks must go in on foot since the going was so bad beyond the ditch. As the troops advanced across open ground, a large body of Germans, who apparently believed themselves cut off, made a desperate charge through the middle of MacIntyre's company, firing and chucking grenades. The chief effect of this surprise move was simply that 'C' Company's wireless was knocked out. Communications were now an acute problem since neither of the companies in the town had any serviceable wireless and could not contact the battalion HQ.

Meanwhile Major Jackson, in temporary command of 6th King's Own Scottish Borderers, waited for fascine-carrying tanks to arrive. They shed their loads into the ditch, effectively filling it for the KOSBs' Kangaroos to rush over. 'D' Company raced across, bucking and bumping over the ditch, and crashed into the town just as German grenadiers let them have it with a fusillade from *Panzerfausts*. Three carriers were hit and crashed in smoke and flames, but the infantry managed to scramble from the others and stormed the buildings. By the early hours of the morning the Germans had either been killed or driven out enabling the KOSBs to consolidate about the bridgehead and link up with the Royal Scots 'A' Company.

On the left of the last KOSBs' attack, their 'B' Company was violently opposed at the crossing of the Goch to Calcar road. As the leading platoon rushed for the bridge Germans holding the other end hurled stick grenades which exploded amongst them. The Scots pitched grenades back again and for several minutes a grim contest ensued around the bridge. When more KOSBs joined in, the surviving Germans fired several long bursts, flung their remaining grenades and retired into the wrecked streets beyond. Grimly the KOSBs tended their wounded and counted the costs. The leading platoon had lost half its men. The rest of the company dug in to hold the bridge for the armour coming up behind.

The 51st Highland Division mounted its attack from the west. The 5th Seaforths' 'A' Company crept forward in the dark, hardly daring to breathe for fear of alerting German outposts, although the heavy shelling was drowning any sounds the infantry made. Incredibly they crept right to the edge of the ditch. 'Suddenly we were there,' Jimmy Macdonald said; 'it was just a great hole stretching away in the gloom. Then the Jerries woke up and it all started, grenades and machine-guns. But we rushed the ditch and when we got to the other side, they'd gone.' The Seaforths crossed virtually unopposed and then 5th Assault Regiment, RE, brought up an AVRE bridge-carrier which successfully dropped its bridge in place.

The 5th Black Watch marched on into Goch and were on the second bridge almost before they realized it. All the noise seemed to be coming from the other side of the Niers and so the battalion pushed forward to find its objective unoccupied. According to a correspondent at Goch: 'The Black Watch made a night attack into the town and found it lightly held with a few old Spandaus.' In fact the town was being defended very strongly but at that time Colonel Matussek, the German Commandant of Goch, had shifted every available man and weapon to the other side of the Niers. He soon realized his mistake and began to shift them back again later that night. Once again the several British thrusts had served their purpose, confusing the enemy and keeping his forces off balance.

While the Seaforths were mopping up the heavily-defended pill-boxes, which had proved much more vulnerable against the British special armour than Hitler would have imagined, the 5th Black Watch filed into the town along cratered streets, about to consolidate for the night. A message arrived from Brigade requesting the battalion to capture the Monastery Hospital, the German HQ in the area, a large building on the west side of the main square. Without delay Major Brodie went to reconnoitre and after discussion with Major Pilcher, commanding the leading company, they decided to send Bill Chisholm's platoon through the back streets to attack it. The hospital's gateway was guarded by a barricade manned by several men. Brodie himself worked his way forward along the street towards the barricade, keeping well to the sides in the face of spasmodic firing. He took the platoon's mortar out into the street intent on firing a couple of bombs at the barricade. With the mortar man, he crouched in the middle of the road, fairly safe in the darkness as the Germans were firing too high. A couple of bombs burst around the barricade and drove the Germans back into the hospital. Brodie pursued them as far as the medieval-looking gateway, flanked by a long buttressed wall, from behind which a German was shooting. Other enemy soldiers sniped from an elevated tennis court on the far side of the yard. There was a short exchange of shots until a German flung a grenade that exploded with a brilliant flash; a splinter in Brodie's shoulder was the only damage.

A section of Chisholm's platoon now joined Brodie just inside the gate. Other sections arrived and spread out in the courtyard. Dawn was breaking as the group rushed up the steps of the hospital under heavy fire both from snipers located upstairs and from those in the grounds. One Scot fell dead; the others dashed into the shelter of a porchway at the head of the steps and Brodie threw a smoke grenade at the glass door. Fortunately it wasn't a Mills grenade for it bounced back and exploded only feet from him, badly burning his hands and face. As Brodie recoiled in pain the door was pulled open and a German officer emerged with his hands up. Brodie sent him back under escort, and seeing that their officer was being treated reasonably, many other German soldiers also surrendered.

Kenneth Buchanan had meanwhile brought Company HQ forward to a suitable house and soon had a wireless set operating. Brodie reported the situation to the battalion commander, Bill Bradford, stressing how few were their numbers and that they might not be able to hold on if counter-attacked. Bradford told him to get established in the hospital and he would send up a company to support them. Brodie returned to the hospital where he found Chisholm's platoon huddled against houses on the far side, unable to cross the road because of an enemy machine-gunner firing in regular bursts along the main road. Noting the regularity of the bursts, Brodie slipped across the road between them, but the soldier following him caught the full blast and was killed.

Within the hospital they finally set about clearing the cellars. Scots dashed down the stairways after throwing grenades into the semi-darkness. When the company commander arrived he was met by a very correct and elderly German captain, most concerned for his colonel, whom he said was badly wounded. Colonel Matussek was found lying on a stretcher surrounded by his attentive staff, most chagrined at being captured, explaining that because the attack had been expected from the north he had carefully chosen this cellar in the south-west. 'D' Company's HQ moved into the hospital and soon afterwards 107th Regiment's Churchills rumbled along the street towards them. Even more welcome was the arrival of a jeep and trailer carrying hot breakfast packed in hayboxes.

While the Black Watch were consolidating in the hospital, 5th/7th Gordons passed through to their objectives east of the main square, and 1st Gordons began their advance into Goch from Gennap. It was about 10 am when the leading companies, 'A' and 'D', set off, under command of Majors Arthur Thomson and Casey Petrie respectively, accompanied by Lindsey and Kenneth McDonald, their new Intelligence Officer.

They took over a house near the Black Watch HQ and while the windows were sandbagged, Lindsey consulted Bradford about the Black Watch's position. The Black Watch had broken in with relative ease but opposition had since stiffened considerably. Although they had captured the blocks to either side of the main road it was

now becoming obvious that it wasn't going to be as easy as expected
and that 5th/7th Gordons were still fighting in Black Watch territory
unable to get to their objectives.

'A' Company set about opening the route south from the main
square. Arthur Thomson and his second-in-command, Bill Kyle,
sought shelter in a doorway to talk briefly, while the din of battle
raged around them. Suddenly as Kyle talked, Thomson reeled back,
shot through the head by a sniper in a nearby school. The young
Kyle took command of the company and progressed in the face of a
crescendo of machine-gunning and mortaring. Casualties mounted
amid the dust and rubble and the infantry had to be supported by
Crocodiles and tanks. But the cratering made the going very difficult.
Desperately a bulldozer was sent for to push the rubble back into the
holes but it was met by heavy fire, which pinged and banged
against its blade until it withdrew. Frustrated and furious, Lindsey
had to halt the attack.

Lindsey decided to have another go at getting south through a
housing estate using 'B' and 'C' Companies. A reconnaissance platoon went to report on the enemy's positions. While they were gone a
troop of Crocodiles and one of tanks came forward in support. An
hour and a half later all was ready and a smoke screen laid to protect
the right flank from the enemy fire.

Under cover of billowing smoke 'C' Company entered the housing
estate with the Churchills shooting into the houses. George Morrison
took 'B' Company through to attack the school and other large buildings along the main road. 'We were sniped at continually from the
houses, but the lads dashed in with grenades and fired their automatics, and we routed them out of the school, taking about ten prisoners.' Hardly had 'C' Company left the estate when mortar bombs
plunged through the smoke, exploding in the area still held by Morrison's 'B' Company. Troops dived for cover into strong cellars be-
neath the shattered buildings where they sat out the earth-shaking
concussions.

Lindsey now sent two companies forward; one to take important
cross-roads south-west of the housing estate and the other to capture
the large farm at Thomashof, to which General Straube had recently
sent his reinforcements. Like most farms in this part of Germany the
buildings were grouped around the farm house, an arrangement that
proved eminently practical. Aerial photographs showed a large farm
house with five big buildings around it and two smaller houses
nearby, while a number of enemy trenches ringed the complex. It

was all set in open farmland with clear visibility so Lindsey planned to attack under cover of darkness.

The platoons of Sergeant Cleveland and Lieutenant Charlie Howitt were ordered forward. A cold, clear dawn was beginning to light the sky. Heading 'A' Company Lindsey followed Cleveland's platoon through an orchard and over a stream to the two nearest buildings. The Germans were by now well aware of the attack and were firing in all directions. In the darkness there was a danger of shooting each other and when Kyle returned from a look outside, his batman fired but fortunately missed. Before anyone could move a Sten blazed. 'You bloody fool', Lindsey shouted, but a man fell into the hay, gasping away his last moments . . . a half-dressed German.

Cleveland's platoon was stopped by two Spandaus in the garden of the building next door, which opened up whenever a movement was made. Lindsey considered that the buildings they now occupied were strong enough to resist the enemy fire, which did not look like it was getting any worse, and decided to bring up another company with tanks. As they had no radio contact there was no alternative but for him to go back.

George Morrison's 'B' Company, meanwhile, had stayed at the school that night. 'At eight in the morning I was told to take out tanks and Crocodiles to this company, and then come back. We had had no food since the previous day, and breakfast was just cooking. So we left four chaps behind to get the breakfast meal cooked, and set off. We hadn't got far when we met a corporal and half a dozen privates from the company at Thomashof. They told us they were the only survivors of the company.' The few survivors, including a stretcher bearer who had been captured but escaped, told what had happened.

Howitt's platoon had gone for a house and found several men standing there. In the deceptive half-light, they mistook the Germans for Gordons and shouted a challenge. Immediately the Germans fired, killing Howitt. The platoon scattered before a strong enemy force which made several attacks supported by mortars and Spandaus. 'A' Company had lost its leader and the youngsters were no match for the fanatical paratroopers. Later Howitt's body and those of ten others were found, another 43 were missing and presumed wounded or prisoners.

Morrison listened to the accounts: 'That didn't sound so good. So we set out to clear the company's area. We were heavily mortared and under fire from 88s so we decided to clear one group of houses on the right flank to get a firm base for the attack.' The company moved forward with its flame-throwers but some of these were defective and didn't function properly, which left the platoons in a very vulnerable position in open fields criss-crossed by Spandau fire.

I got the company in position and had a look across the field. In the main group of buildings I could see hundreds of Boche walking around. Their snipers were very active, and I had no sooner posted one chap at a window than he was killed by a Spandau.

To reach the main group of houses we had to cross 300 yards of open ground. Six Spandaus were firing across this field, and it looked a pretty grim job. I told the tanks and flame-throwers to go in with the infantry, and they set off under cover of smoke.

One of the flame-throwers got right across the field with the leading platoon, into a group of buildings and took 20 Boche prisoner. The young officer in charge, Lieutenant Ventris, had just joined us two days before. He walked right through these Spandau bullets, with a grenade in each hand, and as one of his chaps told me: 'You couldn't help following that man.' He walked back across the bullet-swept field, escorting ten German prisoners—three of the Germans were killed by their own bullets coming back. I found the officer was wounded in the hand and had three Spandau bullets through his ankle. He nearly wept when I wouldn't let him go back.

Meanwhile the next platoon had reached about the middle of the field when every Spandau in creation opened up. They were pinned down. I went out to the tanks and asked them to go forward, but they had run out of flame-throwing material. 'Moaning Minnie' and ordinary mortar bombs were being pumped into the field, but I had to get the lads through, so I sent in the next platoon. Half of them managed to get across, and the rest were pinned down by Spandaus. But they crawled on their stomachs to the buildings.

A gruesome sight greeted 'B' Company for many of 'A' Company's dead lay sprawled on the wire of the outer perimeter.

However, the Germans holding Thomashof now began to 'crumble' and 'B' Company cleared and held the farm. George Morrison was awarded the DSO for his actions. They had taken 140 prisoners, and the rest had gone, leaving their weapons behind. 'Then for the next three days we had to occupy the position, mortared and shelled continually, with 88mm shells smashing through the houses. A medium machine-gun detachment from 1st/7th Middlesex Regiment was sent up to support me and whilst they were resting in a barn a delayed action shell went through the roof and exploded killing twelve of the fifteen men. On the first night the only place available for Company HQ was in a cellar which was full of dead Germans and I rested for a few hours on the floor lying between some—not pleasant.'

But the sojourn at Thomashof had its lighter side too.

It was difficult to get up rations because of the shelling but I had seen there was a sty full of pigs and told my Sergeant Major, Jock Muir, to go and knock one off in spite of the German farmer who remained in the cellar to safeguard his property. The CSM returned to say that one of the company had selected a big one and had tried to kill it by firing a Luger at its head but the bullets just bounced off. I went with him and found the 'so-called butcher' was firing on its forehead, and took the pistol and shot it behind the ear. By this time I realized the shots from the pig sty would attract the farmer and called for Stretcher Bearers and a guard was put on the door to keep the farmer out. He arrived just as the pig was being carried out on the stretcher covered in blankets. We had very good rations from then on!

The battalion now went into reserve to reform and rest.

At my new company HQ in a house in the town I told the company piper to dig latrines at the bottom of the garden. Two hours later when I saw him he was drunk, and as there were no spirits to be got anywhere at this time I eventually succeeded in extracting from him that he had dug up two large boxes of various bottles of whisky, cognac and schnapps which I immediately confiscated for consumption on ration to Company HQ and friends. It so happened that at that time Battalion HQ had lost a few bottles of whisky and I had great difficulty in persuading them that my supply came honestly!

In the action at Thomashof 'B' Company had lost ten men as they crossed the open ground; Lindsey later paid tribute to their commander: '. . . as usual, he was exceedingly brave in what was a very nasty attack . . .' As Lieutenant Ventris, who had been hit five times, was carried away by stretcher bearers after only four days with the company, he commented cheerily, 'it was fun while it lasted.'

By nightfall Lindsey was depressed by the day's losses. With his resources stretched to their limit, Thomashof had been too much. Brigade ordered 5th Black Watch to go up to Thomashof to take over from 1st Gordons' 'B' Company. The Black Watch's 'D' Company would then go on to take an isolated cottage with a commanding view of the road to Goch from where they could shoot any approaching enemy troops.

General Schlemm now sent General Meindl's II Parachute Corps to strengthen his forces between von Luttwitz's XLVII Corps in the north and Straube's LXXXVI Corps in the south. Meindl called in his 7th Parachute Division from positions they were holding in Moyland Woods, but found the 43rd and 15th Divisions were already as far east as Halvenboom and Bucholt and his communications with both Calcar and Udem had been cut. Baulked of his objectives he regrouped and fell back to the next Siegfried Line defences. By the morning of February 22nd, Goch, the anchor in the Siegfried Line, had been taken. Canadian First Army had a line twenty miles long between the rivers Maas and Rhine and with its southern supply route clear from the Maas was ready to surge forward across open country to the important Geldern to Xanten line. This was roughly the limit of the planned advance by the Canadian Army and the line along which the Americans would soon join them as both swung east towards the Rhine.

10 'Moyland, bloody Moyland'

At 11 am on February 12th 46th Brigade's column moved out of Cleve through the north-east suburbs, crossed the canal and drove along the road curving south-east towards Calcar, a key town blocking the approaches along the eastern side of Canadian First Army's front towards the Hochwald defences which controlled the routes to the Rhine at Xanten and Wesel. At this time the rest of the 15th Scottish Division, together with the 43rd Wessex Division were beginning to move out of Cleve, while on the right wing of XXX Corps the 51st and 53rd Divisions were capturing the rest of the Reichswald. As these divisions moved towards Goch it was important that the left flank of the corps should drive as far as it could along the road towards Calcar both to seal off the Rhine crossings and so prevent German reinforcements arriving on the battlefield, and to act as a secure pivot upon which the rest of the corps would swing south-east once the key fortress of Goch had fallen. In Horrocks's original plan Guards Armoured Division should have erupted from Cleve on the first day of the offensive, striking through the shattered Germans to Wesel, but they were still cut off by the floods.

The 46th Highland Brigade's column comprised the 7th Seaforth Highlanders carried by Kangaroos, a squadron of Coldstreams' tanks, Crocodiles of 141st Regiment, a battery of Canadian self-propelled guns and a platoon of Engineers with the Reconnaissance Regiment leading. Once again speed was the essence; in Montgomery's terminology the enemy had to be kept 'off balance' by forcing mobile warfare on them.

A short way along the narrow, poplar-flanked road a Churchill ran over a mine, leaving it stranded in the middle of the road. The floods prevented any way around the tank and so for two hours the troops seethed in frustration and anxiety, sitting ducks for artillery. The

Germans had moved powerful railway guns into position across the
Rhine, firing huge shells onto the road ahead. The armoured cars
pulled up a short way ahead while a detour was cleared around the
stranded tank and eventually at 1.30 pm the first of the Kangaroos
got through and the Reconnaissance Regiment's 'A' Squadron armoured cars set off once more.

The country was very flat with no cover to hide their advance.
Ahead lay the small village of Qualberg, distinguished by its tall
church steeple showing through the mist. In the village houses and
outlying small holdings, 16th Parachute Regiment, backed by advance units of von Waldenburg's 116th Panzers, awaited the British.
As the 'Jock' column reached the outskirts of Qualberg all hell broke
loose. The 'Jocks' were off the carriers in an instant and into cover
alongside the road, then to everyone's surprise the Kangaroos were
told to take the lead. A German self-propelled 75mm gun that had
been patiently waiting backed into a partly-demolished house, saw its
chance and opened fire. In as many minutes four Kangaroos were
knocked out, blocking the road. Two Coldstreams' Churchills went
forward; one manoeuvred close to the Kangaroos and in considerable
personal danger a crew member managed to get a towing chain
coupled to the Kangaroos in turn and pulled them aside. The Seaforths then broke cover and stormed the village with fixed bayonets.
By 3 pm Qualberg was taken although the enemy had retreated only
a short way down the road from where they continued to shell and
mortar the village.

Hasselt was three miles further on and like Qualberg strongly
defended. The Highlanders advanced alongside deep drainage ditches
which made it very difficult for vehicles to get off the road in an
emergency. A church steeple rose ahead of them marking the village.
Two of 116th Panzers' heavy Jagdpanther tank-destroyers had been
positioned and as the column drew near, they opened fire narrowly
missing several tanks, their shells plunging into the soft fields beyond. Whilst the Churchills engaged the Jagdpanthers the infantry
cleared the houses along the single narrow street.

A report now reached the Seaforths that less than a mile away to
the right, the 43rd Wessex were fighting desperately at Bedburg
against strong German formations of infantry and armour. The information suggested that very strong enemy formations from 116th
Panzer Division, with numbers of Jagdpanthers and Tiger tanks,
were also in the immediate vicinity. This report, subsequently found
to be false, put the Seaforths' commander in a quandary: should he

keep up his attack on Hasselt and risk the German armour breaking out of the Bedburg area a mile away to cut off what he thought was a comparatively small force, or withdraw to positions at Qualberg? The rapidly failing light of the wet winter's evening logically pre-scribed temporary withdrawal, but it meant losing momentum at a crucial time. After consultation with Brigadier Villiers, he pulled back his forces and formed a laager for the night.

Later that night the Seaforths sent out fighting patrols to probe Hasselt, creeping forward in darkness to the houses, many now in ruins. There was a lot of muffled noise and the sound of heavy en-gines. Were the Germans going to launch a sudden night attack or wait until early morning? The patrol peered into a darkness faintly il-luminated by hooded headlamps and some storm lanterns. From the activity it certainly appeared that the enemy were pulling back, aban-doning Hasselt. Quietly the patrol slipped away unseen.

Early on February 13th, the Seaforths advanced without tanks. Hasselt had indeed been evacuated and beyond it the floods were washing across the road. Patrols hastened along the Calcar road, wading in places where the river water washed across the Moyland Wood which lined the right of the road for some five miles, rising steeply towards the Eselberg ridge where 15th Panzer Grenadiers were digging in along their defence line.

The Seaforths' worst fears were soon realized; the enemy had blocked the road to Calcar. The 'Jocks' now had to prepare for yet another bloody assault, this time on Moyland Wood. The Germans were again using the natural features to skilful advantage. The Moy-land Wood were heavily defended and would slow the Scottish ad-vance, and would protect von Luttwitz's right flank, enabling him to throw his main forces against the 43rd Wessex whose advance was by now threatening to break through to Goch. Nightfall found 46th Brigade preparing to attack these strong enemy positions.

For the next thirty-six hours a desperate battle was fought for the control of Moyland Woods, which were strategically important be-cause they controlled not only the road to Calcar but also the uplands on their western fringe across which the Canadians would have to advance towards the Hochwald. Cameronians, Glasgow Highlanders and Seaforths struggled to dislodge the German para-troopers and panzers. At the village of Tillesmanskath, for instance, a company of Glasgows, caught in the woods skirting the village by heavy shelling and mortaring, lost all but forty men. Then the Ger-mans moved in the 60th Panzer Infantry Regiment backed by mor-

tars and self-propelled guns which devastated first the 7th Seaforths,
and then the Cameronians in turn, when they came up to relieve the
Seaforths. The situation grew so desperate that Major-General Barber, commanding 15th Scottish Division, detached the 10th Highland
Light Infantry from 227th Brigade just as it was preparing to attack
Goch and sent it to protect 46th Brigade's right flank. Unknown to
Barber, however, Schlemm had also been combing his front for battle groups and had sent in four fresh battalions from General Vadehn's 8th Parachute Division. The paratroopers dug in at a group of
houses in time to decimate the 10th HLI's attack. The next day the
HLI tried again but even before they reached their start-line they
were once more savagely cut down by a parachute battle group.

The 9th Cameronians returned to the battle, this time accompanied by Wasp flame-throwers and attacked the southern corner of the
woods. They set the undergrowth on fire while the infantry charged
in, and in the face of this new and awesome onslaught the Germans
retreated across the Moyland road that bisected the woods, and dug
in in the eastern extension. In their pursuit, the Cameronians encountered a storm of machine-gun fire. George Frazer recalls that as 'we
got near the road mortar bombs began dropping around us. I passed
a chap sitting on the ground, hugging his bleeding legs and repeating,
"Moyland, bloody Moyland".'

On February 14th the already-mentioned changes in the Allied
command structure took place and General Simonds's 11 Canadian
Corps assumed control of the eastern front including Moyland
Wood. The 46th Highland Brigade now passed under his command,
as arranged, together with the 43rd Wessex Division, once they had
completed their drive on Goch, and the 11th Armoured then joining
the battle. The two Canadian infantry divisions now took over most
of the fighting for Moyland Wood from the weary 46th Brigade.

Early on the 14th General Spry, commanding the 3rd Canadian
Division, sent his 7th Brigade south-eastwards from Bedburg. The
left flank attack by the Regina Rifle Regiment with Scots Guards'
tanks aimed to clear the eastern Moyland Wood to which the paratroopers had been driven by the Cameronians. As they progressed
past the north-east end of the woods, supposedly clear of the enemy,
a heavy fire swept them, catching them by surprise and forcing them
to take cover; 60th Panzer infantry had infiltrated back into the
woods during the night. The drive for the eastern woods then had to
be diverted to clearing the northern woods again.

The Royal Winnipeg Rifles entered what was left of Louisendorf

after a fighting advance in Kangaroos supported by tanks, and set
about clearing out pockets of resistance by nightfall. They then exploited northwards to the high ground held by other Scots Guards'
tanks, where they dug slit trenches in which to shelter for the night
while the Scots parked their big Churchills over the top of the
trenches to protect them from mortars and shells. It was 'just as bad
as anything encountered in Normandy', according to the Reginas'
War Diary.

The next morning, the Regina Rifles and their supporting tanks
again tried to clear Moyland Wood of the tenacious paratroopers and
infantry but were cut to pieces by heavy artillery concentrations and
mortar attacks. After hours of punishment the Canadians and tanks
withdrew under smoke cover in the late afternoon.

This northern flank of Canadian First Army's battleground was
held by strong German formations constantly reinforced from across
the Rhine. Two more battalions of 6th Parachute Division had come
in from Holland and moved into the woods. In spite of Lancaster
raids which destroyed most of the bridges, the Germans sent boats
and rafts across in the night; they had to hold the line before Calcar
if they were to stop the Allies getting to the Rhine.

A last attempt to take Moyland Wood was made by the Reginas
on February 18th, the day the assault began on Goch. Supported by
Wasps they attacked the eastern woods and very slowly pushed the
Germans northwards out of their positions until they grimly held
onto an area a mere 1,000 yards by 500 yards. But yet again the Germans found hidden strength and retaliated just when the Reginas
thought they had won. They laid down a furious non-stop fire and
systematically drove them back.

General Simonds now ordered forward Brigadier Cabeldhu's 4th
Brigade, with Shermans of the Fort Garry Horse, to break the hinge
of the German blocking line at Calcar and advance beyond the
Goch–Calcar road. At the same time General Spry's 3rd Canadian
Division tried again to clear Moyland Wood, and pass through to
seize high ground overlooking Calcar.

At first light on the 19th, in pouring rain, 4th Brigade attacked
small villages across their path, fighting doggedly until early afternoon
when the objectives were taken. By nightfall, believing themselves secure, their supporting tanks were withdrawn for fuel and ammunition.
But unknown to the Canadians a battle group from the crack Panzer
Lehr Division was even then advancing from Marienbaum. It struck

the Canadian positions late that night, all but wiping out two regiments.

As dawn broke the panzers attacked again in force, bent on driving the Canadians from the high ground south of Calcar. The battle swayed back and forth across the rolling farmland and orchards, men of both sides staggering through the mud, dodging mortar bombs and shells. The German commander rushed more infantry forward in half-tracks and the strengthened enemy formations surged onwards, driving back the Canadians. For an hour or so they fell back foot by foot, desperately holding on until Shermans of the Fort Garry Horse arrived with the Queen's Own Cameron Highlanders of Canada and tilted the balance. All morning and into the afternoon the fight went on while the rain fell. When the rest of the Camerons came up with their anti-tank platoons the Germans began to reel. Their Jagdpanthers were exposed on the open ground to the full fury of anti-tank guns and started to falter and then stream back to Marienbaum. The Panzer Lehr, doyen of the panzer divisions and terror of the Ardennes, was broken. Schlemm sent them south towards Roermond to refit as best they could.

On February 21st the Canadians systematically began to destroy the woods. The woods were divided into 300-yard belts which the divisional artillery saturated in turn while hundreds of mortar bombs thudded amongst the blazing and shattered trees. The Cameron Highlanders of Ottawa took up positions along the southern edge, preventing the enemy withdrawing and loosed their machine-guns and anti-tank guns in a non-stop torrent of fire. When the Germans were reeling, two companies of Royal Winnipeg Rifles and the tanks of 27th Armoured Regiment, the Sherbrooke Fusiliers, advanced line abreast, each company with three Wasp flame-throwers that squirted a continual stream of fire to set ablaze the cover. Even the weather cleared and the Typhoons struck. With great courage the paratroopers withstood even this inferno and fired their Spandaus until driven back. Their 88mm guns still roared, taking a heavy toll of the Canadians. That night they made two desperate attempts to retaliate but the odds were now decidedly against them and they fell back. Early on February 22nd the Canadians entered Moyland village.

In a message to his troops on February 23rd, Horrocks could truthfully say:

You have now successfully completed the first part of your task. You have taken approximately 12,000 prisoners and killed large numbers of

Germans. You have broken through the Siegfried Line and drawn to
yourselves the bulk of the German reserves in the West. A strong US
offensive was launched over the Roer at 0330 hours this morning against
positions, which, thanks to your efforts, are lightly held by the Germans.
Our offensive has made the situation more favourable for our Allies and
greatly increased their prospects of success. Thank you for what you have
done so well. If we continue our efforts for a few more days, the German
front is bound to crack. [Essame. *The Battle for Germany*]

In two weeks of continuous fighting since the offensive began Canadian First Army had sustained some 6,000 casualties, of which about
4,800 were British. General Marshall's January prophecy that 'the
British divisions of necessity will play such a minor part and, . . .
we (US) are bound to suffer heavy casualties . . .' was, as the last
two weeks had proved and as the two weeks to come would also
prove, fallacious. But help was coming at last. Beyond the Roer, the
mighty US Ninth Army had at last begun their attack.

11 The Yanks are coming!

At 2.45 am on February 23rd, another great bombardment thundered out. More than 1,000 guns of US Ninth Army were joined by those of British Second Army stretched along the Maas from north of Venlo and those of US First Army to the south. For forty-five minutes the sky lit up from south of Duren to north of Venlo. As the bombardment died down the GIs were off. So began the offensive that would roll across the Rhineland and beyond into the German heartland in what has been described as the Ninth Army's most brilliant contribution to the Allied victory in Europe.

Ninth Army Intelligence knew that opposing them would be elements of General Vadehn's 8th Parachute Division (the rest had gone to Moyland Wood), 176th and 59th Infantry Divisions, the 183rd and 363rd Volks Grenadier Divisions plus an unidentified static defence division on the Erft river. There was some confusion about the strength of the enemy armour, but it was believed that either, or possibly both, the 9th and 11th Panzer Divisions were in the Cologne area.

On the afternoon of the 21st General Simpson had considered in detail when to make the crossing of the Roer, and had weighed the calculations of his Engineers that by midnight on the 22nd/23rd the river would be just low enough. Aware of the bitter fighting to his north and the plight of his British and Canadian allies against which the Germans had moved their reserves, Simpson believed that Operation 'Grenade' should be launched before the water level fell to its lowest as the slightly increased risk thus involved would be offset by the Germans' lack of preparation.

From north of Duren to the confluence of the Maas and Roer Simpson had three corps disposed in depth behind a front thirty miles wide. On the south Major-General Raymond S. McLain's XIX

Corps had two divisions. His southern flank was held by 30th Division and to their north, opposite Julich, 29th Division, sharing an eight-mile front. Their southern flank was in turn protected by General Collins's VII Corps, of US First Army, who would attack with them. Eight miles behind his front line troops, McLain had placed his 83rd Division to back up the assault as soon as needed. Eight miles further back again, and able to take advantage of the road network from Aachen, was the 2nd Armoured Division, of Ardennes fame, in a position to rush forward when needed.

Major-General Alvan C. Gillem's XIII Corps in the centre occupied a front only six miles wide, where they had been since the November offensive. Like XIX Corps Gillem had his infantry in front and the 5th Armoured some fifteen miles back at Heerlen. The 102nd Infantry Division held the Linnich area and a three-mile belt to the south, while the four miles north of Linnich were held by the 84th Infantry Division.

Half of the entire front was held by Major-General John B. Anderson's XVI Corps, a new formation still awaiting its first action. From left to right were the 8th Armoured Division, 79th Infantry Division, with only one regiment committed and the rest in reserve, and 35th Infantry Division. This corps was not going to cross the Roer initially because Simpson was concerned at its lack of experience. Instead they would drive north along the west bank, to clear remaining German outposts there, and only cross—unopposed—after XIII Corps had crossed the river and seized the Huckelhoven–Ratheim–Golkrath triangle. Then they would advance northwards, clear the east bank of the Maas and meet Canadian First Army.

The four assaulting divisions fought their first battle against the fearsome river that tossed their boats like corks. Some chugged over in twelve-man assault boats—although there were many engine failures attributed to the cold weather and the occupants had to row—others pulled themselves across in rubber boats, using a cable laid by a patrol that had got over under cover of the bombardment. Motor-driven boats roared across while Tank Landing Craft surged over with a bow wave and wake almost as dangerous to the small craft as the river itself. The swirling Roer tore at the craft, washing them as much as 150 yards downstream to thud into the river bank far from their planned landing zones. Patrols that had slipped across before the general assault grabbed sites to which Engineers in assault boats towed pre-fabricated sections of duck-board bridges fastened to other assault boats. As soon as these were anchored infantrymen stumbled

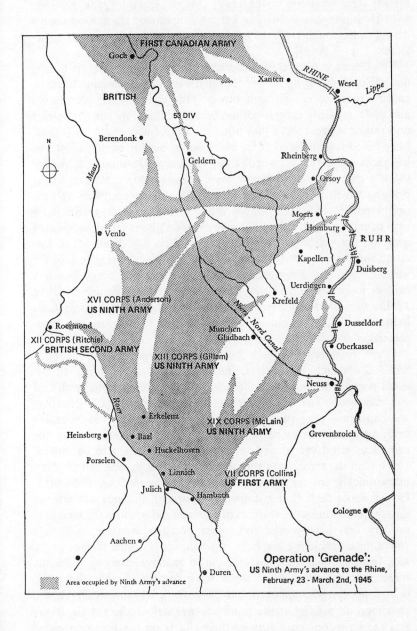

Operation 'Grenade':
US Ninth Army's advance to the Rhine,
February 23 - March 2nd, 1945

across, their weapons at the ready. Major-General Frank Keating, 84th Division, gave priority to getting as many of his anti-tank guns across as he could, ready to hold off the inevitable German counter-attack.

The Germans opened fire soon after the barrage ceased, the bombs and shells throwing up tremendous gouts of water, capsizing boats or causing them to collide with others. One chance shell plummeted alongside a partly-completed footbridge, cutting its anchor cables and raising a great wave that lifted the bridge and dashed it to bits. Men yelled and splashed in the black water, but fortunately most had life jackets and few drowned. Even the Luftwaffe appeared, swooping low over the water, their cannon tearing along the water to the bridges, which were left in splinters with sinking pontoons and assault boats. Field ambulancemen risked their lives to drag back those men caught trying to cross, but many couldn't be reached and floated away on the swirling current. Several Junkers 88s dived out of low cloud and then swerved away as their bombs blew a bridge out of the water. Again the Engineers struggled to complete heavy pontoon bridges to get tanks and tank-destroyers, including British Flails of 1st Lothian and Border Horse and Crocodiles of 141st Regiment, on loan from 79th Armoured Division, across to support the hard-pressed infantry.

Corps Engineers on each front sought to get their bridges assembled and across the river, but with the enemy holding all but small pockets around the bridgeheads, they were continually shelled and mortared. The smoke screens were not particularly effective; smoke screens were started early on 30th Division's front to enable bridging operations to begin, but they had to be stopped when the capricious wind veered and forced all the equipment to be moved. Until 8 am the smoke was very patchy at the south side and the Germans quickly got the range of the bridging operations. William T. Dozier wrote that: 'Later during the morning, bridging activities at the south crossing were temporarily abandoned because the incoming artillery fire there proved too severe and too accurate. Alligators (amphibious vehicles) had been provided for just such an emergency and, being moving targets, were able to continue crossing under the screen. At the same time, shells were coming in near the north bridge, opposite Schophoven, but the fire was inaccurate. During the afternoon all activity at the south site was halted and the Engineers and smoke troops concentrated their efforts on the north crossing,' where a smoke screen three miles long effectively hid operations.

At least the crossings were at places the Germans thought unsuitable, which aided surprise. By nightfall the Engineers had two foot-bridges in use and two treadway bridges nearly finished. Also by midnight on the 23rd Lieutenant-Colonel G. E. Carter's 295th Engineer Combat Battalion had a floating treadway bridge finished at Schophoven. At 1 am 743rd Tank Battalion, 823rd Tank Destroyer Battalion and the Divisional artillery were crossing, fifteen hours ahead of schedule.

At the northern end of XIX Corps' front 29th Infantry Division launched their attack over the Roer opposite Julich. Warren Lasser recalls:

I was in an LVT (Buffalo) that had a hell of a crossing; the water swirled over the sides as shells created waves and fountains. Our vehicle was hit several times by small arms fire and one of the guys was hit in the head when he didn't keep low enough. At the far bank our vehicles rammed the bank which was too steep at that point and our driver turned downstream to a place where the bank sloped. Another LVT crawled out in front of us and hit a mine—there was a sheet of flame and a roar as the tracks were blown off—the enemy then raked it with gunfire and the whole vehicle blew up. That scared us to death as we tried to climb out past the burning vehicle and the Huns raked us too.

A number of the assault force's Buffaloes were wrecked on uncleared mines and others were hit by heavy shelling so that eventually the crossing site had to be abandoned.

There weren't many of us landed before the crossing site was changed said Warren Lasser, and we felt pretty desperate as we dug in under a storm of fire, wondering what was going to happen to us. However, the rest of our regiment began landing a couple of hundred yards away and we just had to sit out the shelling until they broke through to us as the bridgehead expanded. During that time I think about half our number became casualties as the enemy mounted several counter-attacks, each one beginning with a storm of machine-gunning and mortaring before their infantry tried to break through our positions. I guess we must have had a radio link with our combat command because our artillery on the west bank kept a steady fire pouring down in front of us. The noise was terrible as our shells zoomed overhead and exploded in sheets of flame and German mortar bombs thudded down all around.

The Buffaloes began crossing at other points and troops leapt ashore while other vehicles dropped their ramps and disgorged jeeps towing anti-tank guns and carriers. The smoke screen gave some protection, but at dawn the artillery complained so vociferously that they couldn't see the targets that it was stopped. Divisional Engineers quickly moved in with bridging equipment and, working under constant small arms and machine-gun fire, slowly but surely extended their bridges across the racing water. Two bridges were almost completed when the Germans opened fire with heavy guns from their positions near Julich. Several near-misses sent huge splashes high into the air, then the first bridge received a direct hit, tearing a great gap in it. Whipped around by the racing current the furthest end rapidly disintegrated and was swept away. Even as the Engineers cursed, the heavy guns were seeking the other bridge and before long that, too, was gone under a deluge of shells; the swirling water carrying débris, half-sunken boats and pontoons battered the damaged structure until it collapsed.

Troops already across the river pressed on after the enemy towards Julich, the scene of harsh fighting. Still disorganized by the bombardment and under continual air attacks from droves of heavy Thunderbolt fighter-bombers, the Germans could not consolidate. By nightfall the Americans had taken all of Julich except the Citadel, a moated fortress dominating the defence system. By then two foot-bridges and a heavy pontoon bridge were allowing the Divisional troops and armour to stream across and burst over the enemy trenches and defence line.

At his HQ near Xanten, General Schlemm was watching the crucial battle for Calcar when von Rundstedt telephoned to tell him that 'the Americans crossed the Roer this morning.' Schlemm realized that his First Parachute Army would now be crushed by Montgomery's vice. Von Rundstedt explained how following the bombardment the US Ninth Army had crossed along a fourteen-mile section of the river. Schlemm agreed it was bad news and he would have to take it into account as he planned his tactics to prevent the Canadians breaking through the Hochwald, which now became more vital than ever as the only means of stabilizing one front while he switched his forces back against the Americans. He sent word to both von Luttwitz and Straube of the urgency for them to establish their fronts. He also contacted the Army Commander on his southern flank, General Gustav von Zangen, commanding Fifteenth Army, urging upon him, too, the need to secure a firm defensive line to stop the Americans taking his own army in the rear. First Parachute Army's survival, he stressed, now depended upon von Zangen's ability to hold the Americans. But von Zangen was another strong-willed Prussian officer, who, like von Luttwitz, believed in the offensive, and instead of withdrawing to a defensible line he began to commit his forces in a series of counter-attacks. He now used his only available reserves, two battalions of infantry with tanks and some self-propelled guns, choosing to make his attack at Baal.

The American 84th Division troops were taking a brief rest in houses and barns when, without warning, the counter-attack broke. Tiger tanks rattled menacingly from the hilly ground. Walter Mitchell's company had tramped for hours since their landing and were lying about in a ruined shop.

Suddenly, he recalls, a shell slammed into the house across the road, blowing it up. We all scrambled up thinking it was shelling, but men were yelling that German tanks were coming down the street. Our anti-tank section got its 57mm gun into position in quick time and fired at a tank, but the damn shell bounced off it! By now the road seemed to be filling with German tanks and we could see their troops advancing behind them. Our gun got off a couple more rounds before a Tiger tank fired back and that was that. The whole place seemed to be falling to bits as houses collapsed. Further down the road their infantry set up machine-guns behind the piles of rubble and before long our own guys were withdrawing as fast as they could. We were ordered into the cellars, which all had great concrete beams built in and told to sit tight while our artillery took on the Germans.

The American commander radioed his HQ for immediate aid. The American tank-destroyers had not yet crossed the Roer but their Field guns opened fire from the west bank and soon enveloped Baal in clouds of flame, smoke and dust. 'We crouched in those cellars', continues Mitchell, 'while above us the ground shook and we could hear whole buildings crashing down. When a pile of bricks crashed down above us I wondered if we would be able to get out.' But caught in the open the German infantry was badly battered and withdrew in panic, leaving the panzers amongst the rubble-filled streets. They too then came under severe attack as Thunderbolts joined in, destroying several tanks and forcing the rest to withdraw.

On XIX Corps' right VII Corps of US First Army attacked under General Collins, who described the event:

The Roer was still a raging torrent when the VII Corps jumped off at 3.30 am, February 23rd, in conjunction with the XIX Corps of the Ninth

Army on our left. The Germans had earlier destroyed the autobahn bridge at Duren so that the initial crossings had to be made in assault boats. The current was so swift that the boats had to be powered by outboard motors, but in the cold dampness few of them would start, requiring our men to row or paddle across. A few managed to get across, but others capsized or were swamped. Caught by surprise, the enemy offered little resistance at first, but as soon as the crossings were discovered opened up with prearranged artillery fires which, after dawn, were joined by machine-gun cross-fire from the high banks beyond the river.

The enemy guns prevented any bridge construction until after dark when a vehicular bridge was built across the concrete piers of the autobahn bridge at Duren.

The 8th Division immediately moved on Duren and occupied the town. The enemy regrouped astride the plain behind Duren with artillery pieces, self-propelled guns and tanks. The division had only three anti-tank guns east of the Roer due to lack of bridges and suffered heavy casualties when the enemy counter-attacked. Fortunately the enemy failed to press home the attack.

'Further downstream,' writes Collins, 'a pontoon bridge was almost completed when a hidden artillery piece destroyed it with direct hits. At other sites, construction could not start until after dark. No bridge other than the one at Duren was open to traffic until the 25th.' (None of the divisional commanders had exercised their discretion to use smoke and so the bridge sites were naked to German artillery.) 'VII Corps finally succeeded in constructing nine bridges for the 8th and 104th Divisions. By February 26th, VII Corps had a firm bridgehead around Duren which was linked with the US Ninth Army's XIX Corps east of Julich.'

As February 23rd drew to a close Simpson's army had crossed the turbulent Roer along a front of some thirty miles in the face of relatively light German opposition. German defences along the Roer had been swamped and the Americans had twenty-eight battalions of infantry east of the river supported by seven Class-40 bridges, and were already beginning a spectacular sweep towards the Rhine and along the Maas towards the British.

The advance by VII Corps was important to protect Ninth Army's right wing as it began to clear the Hambach forest, from which Simpson feared a counter-attack on Julich. VII Corps' role was similar to that of 51st Highland Division protecting the Welsh in the Reichswald. Of equal tactical importance to the clearance of the Hambach forest was the rapid advance northwards by Gillem's XIII Corps. The 102nd and 84th Infantry Divisions quickly occupied the western extremity of the Linnich–Harff Plateau which indicated to Major-General Gillem that the German forces in the region were weakening. It also promised an opportunity for Anderson's XVI Corps to get a firm bridgehead for their crossing.

On the morning of the 24th von Zangen made renewed efforts to stop the American advance. He ordered the Luftwaffe to destroy the bridges but although they flew many sorties the American anti-aircraft defences prevented them bombing effectively and several aircraft were lost. Next, von Zangen committed the infantry of his reserve 9th Panzer Division which had been moved from Cologne, and which, together with the 11th Panzer Division, had been sent to him by the commander of Army Group 'B', Field Marshal Model. The infantry advanced into the forest supported by a small number of panzers to head off XIX Corps' swing north alongside XIII Corps. There followed a heavy engagement at Steinrass on the northern edge of the Hambach forest when the panzer infantry dug in west of the Erft river tried to halt the American advance. But a combined assault by 30th Division infantry supported by an artillery 'stonk' defeated the Germans and by nightfall the Americans had captured Steinrass and gone on to take Lich.

A general advance of two to three miles was made along the fronts of XIX and XIII Corps. The latter now had a salient six miles wide extending just over three miles towards Erkelenz, a major road junction astride its path. Opposing it were only isolated battle groups as Fifteenth Army began to disintegrate as a result of von Zangen's piecemeal commitment of his forces. XIII Corps' commander, Major-General Gillem, decided it was time to commit his armour in an attempt to break the tottering German defences. Combat Command 'B' went across the Roer by a heavy bridge at Linnich and rolled towards Hottorf ready for the encirclement of Erkelenz. Meanwhile infantry moved against a series of German strong-points in houses and small hamlets dotted along the route across the plain between Roer and Erft. At the end of the day they had a bridgehead twenty miles wide and had taken 6,000 prisoners.

Von Zangen now tried to stem the tidal wave of three whole American corps by moving south elements of 176th Infantry Division with some artillery and self-propelled anti-tank guns, but he made the same error as before and committed them piecemeal. He then threw in the infantry of his 11th Panzer to little effect and in each case withdrawal was forced upon them before they could consolidate; the battle was moving too fast.

In the twenty-four hours since the American attack, General Schlemm, now established at Saalhof, west of Rheinberg, had further considered the strategic implications. He sent some officers to Fifteenth Army who reported back that US armoured forces committed against Fifteenth Army were estimated at three or four armoured corps. Divisions belonging to Fifteenth Army were mostly destroyed already. There was no longer a coherent defensive front. With the British past Goch, the Canadians preparing to hurl themselves at the Hochwald defences and the American army surging north-east to meet them, his forces had to withdraw or be overrun. But Schlemm was no fool, and had paid heed to his Führer's harsh command that no bridges were to be surrendered, on penalty of death. He later remarked to his interrogator, Major Milton Schuman, that 'Since I had nine bridges in my sector, I could see my hopes of a long life rapidly dwindling.' Schlemm decided to call his chief, von Rundstedt. To the embittered and disillusioned C-in-C, he declared that it was imperative to prevent a junction of the two enemy armies. He reported that his paratroopers were holding the 'Canadians', and asked if von Rundstedt had enough men to oppose the Americans, to which his worried chief replied that he had not. Schlemm then offered to release two armoured and one infantry divisions south to the Roer front, which the astounded von Rundstedt accepted with alacrity. Schlemm wrote:

the enemy's attack to the south presented a threat to First Parachute Army. If successful, the attack would reach and roll up from behind not only the *Westwall* but also all fortifications lying behind it and facing west. On the whole, I had the impression that the British-Canadian forces had also suffered heavy losses in the preceding fighting and were advancing only slowly. I therefore believed I could hold the defensive front from between the Rhine and Maas with the forces I had. Little ground would be lost and an enemy breakthrough to the south through this front could be prevented. This plan necessarily depended on the adjacent Fifteenth Army being able to secure the southern flank of First Parachute Army against the US forces.

It is interesting to conjecture that when eventually the survivors of Schlemm's First Parachute Army reached the east bank of the Rhine, he could point out that his forces were considerably reduced to counter the American attack; a useful and perhaps vital excuse

against Hitler's wrath. Von Rundstedt, though, was to take the full
weight of Hitler's fury.

Schlemm maintained that they had expected an American attack
against Model's Army Group 'B' soon after the Ardennes campaign,
but thought the Roer between Duren and Roermond was impossible
to cross due to the flooding. 'I therefore concluded that the main
effort of the US forces would be south of Duren, directed against Cologne, rather than against Fifteenth Army in the direction of
Neuss–Krefeld–Rheydt.' He had had discussions with von Zangen
in January which 'convinced me that Fifteenth Army had enough
forces and prepared positions to repel a US attack and to prevent a
breakthrough towards the southern flank of First Parachute Army.'
This was why Schlemm had weakened his southern flank early in the
month by withdrawing the headquarters of II Parachute Corps, its
troops and 8th Parachute Division and sending them to the northern
wing. Their place was taken by Kuehlwein's inadequate Landwehr
Division. He concluded: 'The transfer to Roermond of units of such
low combat value was an emergency measure, forced by the necessity
of reinforcing the northern flank.' Thus Montgomery's two army pincer movements had succeeded in their aim of forcing Schlemm to
take emergency measures and kept him off balance.

Along the American front 5th Armoured Division was on its way
to Hottorf. On the night of 25th/26th, VII Corps moved the 3rd Armoured Division to Duren from where it was to attack towards Els-
dorf and a junction on the Erft with XIX Corps. Next day the 2nd
Armoured Division's Combat Command 'B' moved south-west to
Julich and then was sent to Steinrass under the 30th Division. XIX
and XIII Corps were preparing to drive forward towards the Rhine.

The original purpose of operation 'Grenade' had been to attack
the Germans in their rear two days after they had turned north
against the assault by Canadian First Army. It was now two weeks
later and the battle of the Rhineland had developed very differently
from Montgomery's expectations. So many German formations had
gone to stop the northern thrust that the Americans had little opposition at all. This enabled Ninth Army to drive very rapidly for the
Rhine as well as fulfilling its intended role of being the right jaw of
Montgomery's vice, meeting the British at Geldern after which both
armies would turn east and run parallel to reach the Rhine in the
Wesel area. Wesel, on the east bank of the Rhine, was an important
centre for road, rail and river traffic and also the site of two bridges
which spanned the river at a point where it is about 400 yards wide;

over these bridges German reinforcements were still crossing despite persistent attacks by Lancasters. Wesel was an ideal area from which the Allied armies could break out into Germany north of the Ruhr. It was intended that once Bradley's armies crossed the Rhine further south, Simpson's Ninth Army, under Montgomery's 21st Army Group, and Hodges's First Army, under Bradley's 12th Army Group, would between them envelop the Ruhr and its vital armaments works. The light opposition to Simpson's Roer crossing and subsequent swift drive to reach the Rhine along some thirty miles of its length, mostly opposite the Ruhr, was to aggravate yet again the delicate, frequently strained relationships between Montgomery, who saw Ninth Army's drive simply as an integral part of his overall strategy to beat Germany, and Bradley, to whom it was another example of American armies making powerful thrusts. He wanted Simpson to charge straight across the Rhine by any available means, bridge, boats or ferries, irrespective of its effects on overall planning; to him Montgomery's control was restricting American initiative and he began agitating again for the return of Ninth Army to his Army Group.

12 The Canadian Blockbuster

By February 23rd the situation in the north Rhineland was looking more optimistic; Goch had fallen and the remnants of the enemy were being cleared from Moyland Wood allowing the 2nd Canadian Infantry Division to push on for Calcar. General Henry Crerar had followed the battle assiduously. He was a fatherly figure, a little older than most of the senior commanders and had not always got on too well with Montgomery, although their relationship had improved since Normandy, probably because Montgomery realized the need to foster good relations with his Canadian allies. Crerar was in any case a good intermediary between Montgomery, who tended to keep himself apart, and his corps commanders, especially the independently-minded Canadian General Simonds who was always eager for an autonomous role for his 11 Canadian Corps. They had a deserved reputation for being determined fighters, especially in attacking, and this quality was about to be given its severest test in the war.

Crerar had anxiously watched his forces struggling towards the Hochwald defences and was distressed at their heavy losses. It was, therefore, a great relief when, on the 23rd, operation 'Grenade' began and his American allies joined the battle to take the Germans in their rear. The Americans, he knew, were meeting with only weak resistance from the mostly second-line German forces in their sector, all that remained after the best divisions had been sent to oppose the British and Canadians, and Crerar rightly judged that the enemy would have to move forces south again to stop the American advance before it gained momentum. It was essential then that XXX and 11 Canadian Corps should increase their pressure still further to hinder and confuse the enemy as much as possible; the more German forces they occupied in the north, the easier it would be for the Americans to race for the Rhine, cutting off the Germans who would have to withdraw. Accordingly Crerar told Horrocks to push XXX Corps' right wing south towards the Americans to make the Germans pull back from the Maas. Jubilant that the Americans were on the move, Horrocks sent the 53rd Welsh Division south from Goch to capture the town of Weeze blocking the way to Geldern where they and the Americans were to meet.

At 1 am on February 24th, operation 'Leek' began. While the usual bombardment softened up the enemy positions, 160th Brigade assembled south of Goch and 'married up' with the Shermans, an important operation ensuring that the armour understood the infantry's intentions. Major Body's 'C' Company, 6th Royal Welch Fusiliers, set off at 5.30 am to mop up a strong-point which would alert the enemy further back. At 6 am 'D' Company, with a squadron of armoured cars protecting their right flank, advanced to secure a bridgehead over the first anti-tank ditch at Weeze, and if possible the second ditch as well. At the same time 'B' Company attacked the village of Hohenhof, 500 yards along the Weeze road, their objective being a group of fortified houses thought to be held by a company of 115th Grenadier Regiment. After a quick advance, they seized outlying houses but came under heavy shelling which cut them off. Lieutenant-Colonel Exham, the battalion commander, ordered 'C' Company to keep up the momentum, by-pass the beleaguered company and seize the adjacent village of Host. Although they tried three times to capture Host they failed when the Germans beat them off with heavy losses in men and tanks.

The acting 53rd Welsh Division commander, Brigadier Elrington, arrived at 160th Brigade HQ that evening and told them he had ordered 71st Brigade to take over, capture Host and then Weeze. At 5 pm the 1st Highland Light Infantry launched their usual furious assault and as their Crocodiles burnt out the houses they ruthlessly cut down the escaping enemy. In 90 minutes the Scots were through the blazing, shattered village and heading for Rottum, the next village which they took by 9 pm. By 9.45 pm the HLI had three companies in or around Rottum and were only 400 yards from the anti-tank ditch at Weeze.

That evening Brigadier Coleman, commanding 71st Brigade, despatched 1st Oxford and Bucks Light Infantry to begin the attack on Weeze itself. They were sent to capture a small wood near the anti-tank ditch. John Piper crept forward with them and remembers that 'it was very dark and the fighting had died down so there were few gun flashes to illuminate the scene. We set off in single file through sodden fields, thinking ourselves lucky, when out of the night mortar bombs began thumping down. We dived for cover. Platoon commanders reorganized us and after about ten minutes we set off a bit faster to get into the woods. It was pretty bad but we finally got amongst the trees and set about clearing the enemy. There was some shouting and an NCO yelled for us to take cover and wait. We were in the wrong wood!'

A hurried orders group was called and some radio signals made to 71st Brigade HQ after which they set off again. The ground was badly flooded and when heavy shelling started troops found the saturated earth gave little protection and casualties were heavy.

I remember digging like a maniac (John Piper recalls) shovelling wet mud that slipped back as fast as I threw it out. Jerry was dead on target with his shelling and a lot of blokes were killed outright. Two of us were desperately burrowing when I heard a shell screaming over. Christ! I had a chill feeling it was mine and hurled myself into a shell hole ten feet away. The shell slammed into the ground about ten feet the other side of our miserable scrape, killing my mate who had jumped the wrong way. I staggered out of the hole and promptly got blasted backwards by what I think was a mortar bomb. My back was hurt and I lay there for about an hour until helped back by a stretcher party.

Eventually the Oxford and Bucks LI took the wood although their casualties were heavy.

Operation 'Daffodil', which involved 160th Brigade, plus 13th/18th Hussars and the 53rd Reconnaissance Regiment, taking over the front then held by the 8th Brigade of 3rd Infantry Division who had been in the battle for some days, was the familiar Montgomery operation, a direct attack to draw attention, then a 'hook' around the flank obliging the enemy to face in two directions and threatening his rear communications. The 158th Brigade was going hell for leather along the railway line to the west of Weeze to go in opposite 160th Brigade. A squadron of the Reconnaissance Regiment and the Nottinghamshire Yeomanry drove south-east to protect the flank.

The remnants of the Oxford and Bucks LI attacked from the north and experienced heavy fire and floods. The net closed with the advance of 4th RWF with Shermans of 4th/7th Dragoons. At 3 am the enemy lost control of the anti-tank ditch in the northern sector and by first light the armour was across and breaking into the town.

Under cover of smoke, the 7th RWF attacked, making good progress until they were near the big bend in the Niers that looped to within a hundred yards of the town. Franz Schiller, a paratrooper defending Weeze remembers that 'the Tommies started their attack before daybreak, coming across the flat country from the river. By the time it was getting light we could see them through breaks in their smokescreen running forward in scattered groups while their mortars and guns fired into our positions. A couple of panzers sent to head them off began shelling and machine-gunning. It looked as though we would hold them off for a while, but then a group of British tanks came racing out of the smoke, throwing up spray like warships. I saw shell-bursts near our tanks and they began pulling back.'

An armoured force, 'Robin Force', under command of the 1st East Lancs, crossed the Niers a mile and three-quarters south of Weeze, threatening to cut off the defenders. By evening Weeze was almost surrounded and although enemy artillery near Geldern was still shelling, the end was not far off. In the dark of night a patrol of the Highland Light Infantry probed deeply into Weeze; the enemy had gone and the town was strangely quiet, even the civilians had been evacuated, and at first light Coleman sent the 4th RWF across the Niers in assault boats to occupy Weeze up to the main road. On that day 3rd Division took Kurvenheim on their way south along the Maas and news came in that the Americans were only twenty miles away.

On February 26th Lieutenant-General Simonds launched operation 'Blockbuster', fulfilling Crerar's plan for the final phase of the drive to the Rhine; a deliberate assault across the plateau between Calcar and Udem against the strong enemy defences in the Hochwald. It was the inner arc of XXX Corps' huge right swing with its pivot near Calcar, aimed at clearing the outer axis of Geldern, Bonninghardt and Wesel. The operation would secure the Geldern to Wesel road where they anticipated joining up with the Americans.

Von Luttwitz's last bastion was the Hochwald Layback, which crossed the two main roads leading to Xanten. The Goch to Xanten railway cut the forest in two. North of the railway the Hochwald commanded the country to the west while south of it, the smaller Balbergerwald was itself dominated by high ground near Udem. The approaches were covered by three trench systems 500 yards apart, defended by wire and heavily sown with mines to strengthen the anti-tank defences. Schlemm had recently removed fifty 88mm guns from the Siegfried Line and placed them among the already formidable defences.

It has never been adequately explained why Crerar chose to attack Xanten across such heavily defended ground when the 53rd Welsh and the 11th Armoured were already well south of Goch and swinging left to outflank Xanten and the Hochwald, which would have almost certainly forced a German withdrawal. If Crerar ever considered letting the Hochwald 'wither on the vine' is not known, since Canadian official history is silent on the subject. It is true that Simonds's 11 Canadian Corps were already across the Goch to Calcar road and since Crerar wanted to use the roads leading from Calcar to Xanten and from Udem through Sonsbeck to Xanten, his Canadian troops were well placed to move quickly towards the Hochwald. Up to this point most of Canadian First Army's offensive had been with British troops and although Simonds had been pressing to use his Canadian infantry divisions since the planning of 'Veritable' they had been squeezed out of the battle early on. In the last week they had again joined the assault in the battle for Moyland Wood and by the 23rd they held a line running more or less north-east and south-west about five miles from Cleve, from which they could move on towards the Hochwald. 'The country before them was rolling, with no special heights between Canadian forward positions and the high ground east of Udem, some four miles to the south,' recorded the Historian of the Argyll and Sutherland Highlanders of Canada. There were few good roads and the many tracks crossing the countryside had been reduced to a poor state by the weather and the shelling. Numerous farm buildings had been converted to German strong-points and between these mutually-supporting emplacements there were rarely more than 500 yards of open country.

Once the Canadians got through this formidable belt of German defences they would run into Udem, surrounded by a deep anti-tank ditch with but one opening and bristling with defences. East of Udem was a low-lying area of marsh and woods that stopped about 1,500 yards from the edge of the dark Hochwald, and between the two there was only a bare, gradually rising plain, with a few scattered houses. The plain was mined, crowded with trip wires and crisscrossed with weapon pits for the defenders. It was also, of course, covered by fire from the forest, and ranged accurately by high trajectory weapons away to the eastward. A high railway embankment ran through the Hochwald, just south of the gap which was about 300 yards at its widest. The ground rose towards the eastern end of the gap, reaching some 230 feet high at its narrowest part, known as Point 75.

Simonds never committed his plan for operation 'Blockbuster' to writing but his aim was to smash a hole through the enemy defences with a great artillery concentration and then pour his infantry and armour south-east at first, then due east through the Hochwald gap. The 2nd Canadians would take the Hochwald and 3rd Canadians the Balbergerwald. Crerar sanctioned this broad outline for a set-piece battle.

Simonds's plan hearkened back to the First World War when the great offensive on the Somme and Passchendaele had opened in just that way. Even the terrain had much in common with the battlefields of thirty years before. Once the breach was made Simonds's forces would drive towards the railway cutting through the forest and then swing east along the railway. He planned for his engineers to tear up the railway track as they advanced to make a roadway enabling 4th Canadian Armoured Division to make a rapid breakthrough towards Xanten. It was a bold plan but over-ambitious when account is taken of the formidable German artillery and the fanaticism of the defending parachute and panzer troops.

The 4th Canadian Armoured Division, to whom Simonds had given the onerous task of capturing the gap, split its forces into two groups, 'Tiger' comprising the Algonquin Regiment and the South Albertas' tanks, and the rest of the division known as 'Lion'. 'Lion' was to seize the high ground east of Udem after which 'Tiger' was to drive through the Hochwald gap.

'Lion' was further divided into five groups. The first two, 'Snuff' and 'Jerry', were mainly armoured with squadrons of Canadian Grenadier Guards and the British Columbia Regiment respectively, two companies of infantry in Kangaroos and a troop of Flails; they were to seize areas half-way to the high ground. 'Jock' and 'Cole' would follow up with more tanks, two companies of infantry each, a few self-propelled guns and two Crocodiles, to mop up enemy positions and join the first groups. The last group, 'Smith', contained the tanks of the Governor-General's Foot Guards (21st Armoured Regiment) and the Lake Superior Regiment and they were to seize the high ground ready for 'Tiger' force to begin its drive for the Hochwald.

At nightfall 'Snuff' and 'Jerry' forces lined up in exact battle order in Cleve and moved off at 6 pm, followed three hours later by 'Jock' and 'Cole'. But the night was full of trouble. Soon after leaving

Cleve, part of one force took a wrong turning and it needed a great effort by the brigade staff, including Brigadier Moncel, to get them sorted out. They drove on in heavy drizzle until they reached the point where they left the roads and set out along cross-country tracks. The two armoured groups churned and slid their way over the fields, the heavy tanks reducing tracks to ridges of deep and glutinous slime in which lighter vehicles became trapped. At 3.30 am the columns halted while labouring vehicles struggled to catch up and those that had become bogged down were winched or pushed out. Despite its tribulations 'Snuff' and 'Jerry' reached their start lines in time for the attack at 4.30 am.

The atmosphere was tense. Canadian troops preparing to move off at 4.30 am were puzzled to hear the sounds of approaching armour. John Armstrong with the Canadian Grenadiers was 'checking something at the back of the tank when somebody nudged me to listen. Sure enough we could hear tanks. We thought it was one of the other groups that had got bogged and was only now arriving. Then without warning all the guns behind us opened fire. My God, but they made a noise.'

If the German panzer attack surprised the Canadians, it was nothing beside the reception the Germans rode into as serried rows of 25-pounders fired continuous salvoes. Clearly they knew the Canadians were massing for an assault and had hoped to disrupt it before it got organized. But they found the artillery too much: they took heavy casualties before falling back, as the order to advance rang out among the Canadians and the 2nd Division roared forward.

The opening barrage had destroyed many of Schlemm's recently emplaced 88mm guns but the remainder, backed by several Panther tanks, took a heavy toll of the Canadian tanks, leaving almost 100 smoking or wrecked. Brigadier Moncel struck with 4th Canadian Armoured Brigade between the two infantry divisions, intent on gaining the ridge north-east of Udem, but found it 'ringed with anti-tank guns'. By the time the objectives were won the battleground resembled the shell-torn slopes of Vimy Ridge in the First World War.

The South Saskatchewan Regiment drove for high ground dominating the ridge south of Calcar and took it after a fierce fight, in accordance with Simonds's plan to deceive the enemy and draw his reserves away from the main attack into the Hochwald gap. Les Fusiliers Mont-Royal, on the left flank, also broke through to their objectives. On the right flank of the brigade's attack, the Queen's

Own Rifles of Canada had the task of capturing positions blocking the Calcar–Udem road just north of Kapellen.

Supported by Shermans of 6th Armoured Regiment (1st Hussars), a platoon attacked enemy strong points in three farm buildings in the village of Moeshof. Spandaus immediately opened a terrible cross-fire killing the platoon commander and most of the men. With the enemy still attacking, Sergeant Aubrey Cosens was posthumously awarded the vc for his heroic attacks on their strong points; he was killed on his way back through the shelling to report that resistance in Moeshof was over.

Meantime, the Governor-General's Foot Guards, of 'Smith' group, carried the Lake Superior Regiment and the Argylls into the assault across open ground strewn with mines. Walter Roberts of Toronto recalls how 'We broke out from the start line and raced across flat country rising to the ridge. Before we had covered a hundred yards the Jerries were shelling us, the ground was bursting in explosions and I could hear the stones and fragments clanging off the tank. The infantry hanging on to us were suffering as we bucked and jolted along. A couple of tanks close by brewed up, one with a hell of a bang that threw the infantry off. Then we were hit in the drive sprocket. There was an explosion, a jolt and the track reeled off. I don't know what happened to the infantry, I think they grabbed rides on other tanks still passing.' Although the objectives were taken, thirty-five tanks were destroyed.

For all the apparent confusion, 'Blockbuster' was gradually evolving, although more slowly than planned because of the mud and difficulties in deploying. Nevertheless, Simonds was ready to thrust forward towards the main Hochwald positions now that his 4th Canadian Armoured Brigade was astride the gap between the Hochwald and the Balbergerwald. The 10th Infantry Brigade, under Brigadier Jefferson, was ordered to penetrate the gap and open it to the armour to rush Xanten. First 'Jock' and 'Cole' would open the gap and then 'Smith' force, followed by 'Tiger', would attack in waves to drive through to Xanten.

An hour before dawn 'Tiger' force formed up for the attack against the Hochwald gap. 'Once more nature took a hand,' wrote the Argylls' Historian, 'as bad as ever, the mud impeded progress of the force to such an extent that it was not ready to move forward until five hours after its scheduled starting time. This delay made the fatal difference that at first light on the 27th the force found itself in the open area before the Hochwald instead of further on in the woods.' In the woods the 146th Panzer Artillery waited until the Canadians were streaming down the slopes before opening fire with anti-tank guns. Otto Diels, a gunner, remembers that

The Canadian tanks were ploughing through deep mud and seemed unable to maintain their usual speed, some could be seen sliding and looked difficult to control. We laid our gun on the leading tank but by the time we were ready to fire, it had already been hit and we swung our gun to another, but that too, stopped with smoke pouring from it. The third tank at which we aimed fired first and a shell burst only yards in front of us, the fragments clanging off our gun's shield. Quickly we re-aligned our gun but once again a shell burst close by, this time fragments injuring one of our loaders. Then the tanks seemed to falter and we fired, our shot glancing off a Sherman tank. All the while the Canadian gunners were firing tracer as markers for their tanks and shells were whizzing around us. The battle went on for a long time and twice more we were lucky when enemy shells narrowly missed, but eventually the Canadians fell back, but a lot of us had been injured.

While the main force strove to penetrate the Hochwald gap, the Canadians sent another force of South Albertas' tanks and the Algonquins' Carrier Platoon south to bisect the railway and dash for the forest while the main force was occupying the enemy. Frank Fergusson was with the Algonquins and remembers advancing in Kangaroos with a troop of Shermans for protection.

We left the assembly area and headed towards the railway leaving the main battle raging on our left—we could see our Shermans floundering in the mud amid blazing wrecks from which smoke was beginning to obscure our view of the forest. Our group ploughed its way through very soft going, then swung eastwards onto the slopes rising towards the forest. We were all pretty tense and no one spoke as we crouched inside the Kangaroo; it was noisy and we couldn't hear much of the battle. Then suddenly we heard a terrific crack! Our sergeant risked a peep over the rim of the carrier—'Jesus!' he yelled, 'they've hit the lead tank.' Next thing we knew was an absolute deluge of shelling. Our driver shouted that the Germans in the forest had seen us and were shelling with dozens of 88s dug in along the forest edge. It was murder, caught in the open and with nowhere to turn, we hadn't a chance. Six or seven carriers went up in flames and men were scrambling from them and diving for cover in shell holes, often to be hit by the scores of shells zooming in continuously. The tanks were shooting back but hadn't the range and they too got pasted. We all hung on, white-faced and swearing as our carrier

driver lurched and swerved to dodge the shells, then we copped one right
on the nose which stopped us dead in our tracks, sending us flying around
inside like so many peas. One man was knocked out and another gashed
his face really badly, but the driver was killed instantly. There were
smoke and flames and men yelling to get out. We scrambled out and
flung ourselves into the first shell holes. The whole group seemed to be on
fire but a couple of tanks came back, picked us up and withdrew.

The German 88mms knocked out thirteen Kangaroos and eleven
Shermans, completely stopping the advance.

Still the battle raged. The main 'Tiger' force still fought to capture
the important gap and eventually managed to get close enough for
the leading companies of Algonquins to rush the anti-tank ditch and,
under fire from paratroopers hidden in the woods to either side of the
gap, search out a path through the minefield. They broke through the
knee-high wire entanglements in broad daylight with supporting fire
from the Shermans and reached the trenches. With bayonets and grenades the indomitable Canadians fought their way through the
trenches right up to Point 75. Every German mortar, gun and tank
within range was ordered to shell the area from north, south and
east; a tremendous volume of fire was hurled onto the Algonquins'
positions in the worst shelling the Canadians had hitherto experienced. They were forced to draw back to slit trenches in the open before the gap. Crerar summed up the situation: 'The American attack
led to the strategic defeat of the enemy but it did not immediately
have any substantial effect upon our own hard battle between the
rivers.'

The situation was serious. At 8 am on February 28th Lieutenant-
Colonel Wigle, commanding the Argyll and Sutherland Highlanders
of Canada, held a briefing with his commanders and explained the
situation. They were to advance eastwards over the heights taken by
'Smith' force, through the scrubby woods and thence up over the
open ground to the gap; in fact they were to take over 'Tiger's' tasks.
Before an hour was up, the Argylls' companies advanced quietly
through Kiesel, and onto the heights where an occasional 88mm shell
slammed down near them. But casualties mounted as they neared the
gap and by 2 pm they were under constant sniper fire. By 5 pm the
enemy had really begun to paste them: as John Campbell from Mon-
treal recollects, 'It became impossible to go on, the ground was almost bubbling with explosions and the noise was terrible, felt as if

someone was hitting me on the head, I found myself walking with my eyes closed.' They were forced back and retreated to low ground as night fell again; they had lost three of their four rifle company commanders. Wigle, nevertheless, reorganized his shattered companies and ordered a new attack at 2.30 am.

They fought their way forward in conditions not seen since Flanders thirty years before. The woods were full of German paratroopers sniping and flinging grenades, while Spandaus tore gaps in the advancing men. Splashing and stumbling the Canadians fought their way between the trees, not letting up until the Germans withered before them and began slipping away; by the time the sky grew light the Argylls were in the gap and holding it firm. But as John Campbell recalls,

at around 7 am the Germans counter-attacked. We were in their recently evacuated trenches when they came at us from the woods. For about an hour it was pretty desperate and one of our companies, I heard later, was overrun. The German paratroops were mostly armed with Schmeissers and Spandaus while we had only rifles. There wasn't time to reload after emptying a magazine and then it was bayonets. My buddy, Eric Kennedy, loosed off all his bullets when a veritable horde of Jerries came out of the woods, and then found he'd lost his bayonet. He snatched up his trenching tool just as a paratrooper swung at him with his machine-gun, and brought it down on the German's helmet with a great clang. They both rolled in the trench and someone else finished the German with a bayonet. But they took a heavy toll of us before they finally broke off and retreated amongst the trees.

'B' Company fought a day-long battle against persistent German attacks that completely isolated them from the rest of the battalion. At noon the Canadians heard the sound of tanks clanking through the woods. Several Tiger tanks backed by infantry appeared, clearly determined to wipe out the Canadians. One Tiger suddenly made a break and crashed forward over the slit trenches, its gun swinging towards the house where the company HQ was located. There was a swoosh as a PIAT bomb was fired, followed by a mighty explosion and the Tiger blew up. The Canadians gleefully watched as the rest of the force fell back after the shock of the Tiger's demise. But they reformed in the woods and came back. The German commander's tank stopped in front of the house, the lid opened and he leaned out, bawling for the Canadians to surrender. Captain Perry, the company commander, took careful aim and shot him through the head; as he tumbled back into the hatch a hail of fire swept the tank, PIAT bombs crashed and the tanks hastily withdrew.

In a fury the enemy attacked again and again, but the Argylls fought as men inspired; they stopped the enemy every time. Eventually when Wigle heard of 'B' Company's situation he sent forward Captain Pogue and Lieutenant Maxwell to bring out 'B' Company. They came back with just fifteen men alive and five badly wounded. The enemy's tanks and guns had created a hell in the woods but the position had been held.

Montgomery had placed Crerar in charge of 'Veritable' and although he constantly visited the battle he did not interfere with Crerar's handling of it. General Sir Miles Dempsey, Commander of British Second Army, was frequently advised or even commanded to make changes to operations while Crerar was largely left alone so long as he conformed to Montgomery's overall plan. Montgomery could be ruthless when circumstances demanded it. He would accept whatever losses were necessary to gain the objective. It was vital to get the Hochwald and he knew the Canadians could do it.

The fighting for the Hochwald erupted again on March 1st when the 2nd Canadian Division tried desperately to get its 4th and 5th Brigades through the gap, but both were badly mauled. The Essex Scottish Regiment was decimated when they were caught in the open although their 'C' Company managed to beat off several enemy attacks, its commander, Major F. A. Tiltson, winning the Canadians' second VC for his heroic action. On the right of the front, Major-General Spry's 3rd Canadian Division drove for the Tuschen Wald, a small extension of the Balbergerwald, but although they got a foothold they were driven out again by a strong enemy armoured counter-attack. Between the infantry divisions, the 4th Armoured Division also made another dash for the gap with their infantry following behind, ready to take over and hold positions taken by the tanks, but yet again the enemy repulsed them. In an effort to break the enemy resistance, RAF Typhoons made numerous attacks. 'The battalion could see the Typhoons attacking beyond the forest,' recorded the Argylls' War Diary. 'They would peel off and dive out of sight behind the trees, then suddenly reappear, zooming upwards and in a few seconds one heard the peculiar double crash of their missiles.' But the enemy was as obdurate as ever and kept attacking. By the following morning a pall of dirty smoke hung in the cold air over the Hochwald; both sides had worn themselves out and the fight had abated. Between the combatants lay burning and shattered trees, innumerable wrecked vehicles and hundreds of smoking craters, over which the snow settled. The Hochwald Layback, with its wide defences and open approaches giving excellent fields of fire to the gunners, had thus proved far more effective than the concrete defences in the Siegfried Line in the Reichswald. Schlemm had finally succeeded in stabilizing his front line and would hold it for several days against persistent Canadian attacks.

13 The Americans drive to the Rhine

Having dissipated their reserves in the Ardennes any German units moved now had to be taken from points considered less critical at the time; although Schlemm had sent units south to reinforce von Zangen, he was being reinforced from less active fronts in the Eifel, weakening in turn the forces opposing General Patton. The 338th Infantry Division, for instance, had been withdrawn from the Colmar Pocket and directed north to stem the British advance towards Geldern but von Zangen hastily injected it into Fifteenth Army's front to stop the Americans. Such a hastily conceived move could only proceed with difficulty as units were stopped, given new orders and moved in a different direction. They arrived at Erkelenz in dribs and drabs just before Gillem's XIII Corps arrived with elements of his 5th Armoured Division. The battle that followed was a foregone conclusion with the American infantry and armour rapidly encircling Erkelenz and driving out its defenders who lost heavily in men and equipment.

Tank for tank, the Panther and Tiger tanks were more than a match for the American Shermans, but they were inevitably outnumbered. The Germans screened their armour with anti-tank guns as they had been doing since the desert war three years before, forcing the Americans to run their gauntlet before getting within range of the big German tanks. In such a battle of movement the rapid American advances overran, or by-passed, German infantry units dug in with their *Panzerfausts* which then fired at close range. It was the GIs' job to winkle these out.

Irving Hopkins recalls that they 'quickly learned the danger of following our tanks too blindly. German infantry always popped out from cover, maybe a cellar or just a hole in the ground, with either a "bazooka" or a Spandau. I saw a group of our boys race across a field towards a block of ruined houses. Suddenly two Heinies popped up from nowhere with a Spandau which they placed on the lip of the shell crater, and opened fire on our soldiers, cutting them to ribbons before half a dozen grenades were chucked into the hole.'

The 11th Panzer Division withdrew leaving behind many casualties and prisoners from whom it was learned that their commander had been ordered by von Zangen to hold a line south of Munchen-Gladbach to Grevenbroich and was digging in with all available forces there. This news was welcomed by Simpson who had as yet committed only a fraction of his powerful armoured forces. So far his offensive had been a pursuit rather than a battle as the Germans had moved most of their best divisions against Canadian-British forces in the north. Simpson was eager to give battle and destroy the enemy west of the Rhine.

Simpson now conferred with XIX Corps' Commander, General McLain, to decide how to make the breakthrough towards Neuss which would be their first city on the Rhine itself, opposite Oberkassel and Dusseldorf. Their problem was which to commit first, 83rd Infantry or 2nd Armoured Divisions. There was a combat team of the 83rd under command of the 29th Division, already operating on the XIX Corps' left flank and also a combat command of 2nd Armoured up with the 30th Infantry on the right of the Corps' zone. But there was insufficient capacity on the Roer bridges to bring forward the rest of both divisions at the same time. The problem was a belt of German defences stretching south-east from Rheydt, on the southern outskirts of Munchen-Gladbach, to the river Erft at Grevenbroich. If the defences were strong enough to hold up the armour then the infantry would have to go first and clear the way for the tanks to break through. But if they weren't strong enough then the armour could go first and dash for the Rhine. But it would take two days to move the heavy armoured division through the bridgehead and only then could the infantry follow; but if the infantry went first the armour would only be delayed by one day. Simpson decided on the armour; it was a risk he thought worth taking. Without delay the 2nd Armoured was ordered to concentrate east of the Roer ready to drive on Neuss. Sidney Olsen, *Time* correspondent, described the move:

From the air in a Piper Cub the tank drive was a thing of the sheerest military beauty. First came a long row of throbbing tanks moving like heavy dark beetles over the green cabbage fields of Germany in a wide swath—many tanks in a single row abreast. Then a suitable distance behind, came another great echelon of tanks even broader, out of which groups would wheel from their brown mud tracks in green fields to encircle and smash fire at some stubborn strong point. Behind this came miles of trucks full of troops, manoeuvring perfectly to mop up by-passed tough spots. Then came the field artillery to pound hard knots into submission. . . . This was óne of the war's grandest single pictures of united and perfectly functioning military machines in a supreme moment of pure fighting motion.

While the 2nd Armoured Division ground inexorably onwards XIII Corps pressed forward without waiting for the XIX Corps to complete its left wheel to come alongside them. Simpson encouraged his forces to keep driving forward even if that meant ignoring the phase lines established in the pre-battle planning. Where the Germans were under constant pressure it worked, although had they been at pre-Ardennes strength they would undoubtedly have seized the opportunity to drive wedges into the gaps between the American corps. But they were no longer capable of this kind of reaction and tried to resist from defence lines. Several times in their headlong drive northwards US troops came upon startled Germans still facing west.

Exactly as Montgomery had intended, the Germans were being harried by two armies, and reinforcing the American front could only be accomplished by weakening their northern front and letting the Canadians and the British through to Wesel and the Rhine north of the Ruhr. Schlemm had by now sent the 15th Panzer Grenadiers to stave off the Americans. The Panzer Lehr Division, which the Canadians had defeated just west of Moyland Wood, had been sent to defend the approaches to Munchen-Gladbach but in the rapid mobile warfare their reduced numbers were insufficient to stop the Americans and once again they were defeated. Had the Germans sent Panzer Lehr to defend the Rheydt–Grevenbroich defence line, their heavy tanks and guns dug in amongst the trenches and wire entanglements would have been a far more stubborn obstacle to a rapid breakthrough than the open country around Rheindahlen, and might have delayed the expected attack towards Neuss.

On the last day of February 2nd Armoured Division accompanied by the 331st Regimental Combat Team of 83rd Division drove eight miles north-east and got within seven miles of the Rhine. 'The ground before Junchen was quite hilly and as we moved across a low ridge we came under fire from German positions in front of the town, which was smoking and there was a large fire,' wrote Eddy Dixon:

The armour fanned out and kept firing as it moved forward but the enemy had plenty of anti-tank guns and they were hitting us hard. I could see several tanks burning and one nearby stopped a shell which blew the turret open. Craters started to appear everywhere and there was so much smoke it was hard to see. We slewed to avoid a crater and a shell hit us in the engine compartment, the impact shaking us about. Next moment we were coughing in clouds of smoke flooding into the tank. In scrambling to open the hatch I slipped and cracked my head and only vaguely remember being shoved out of the turret and literally falling off the tank as a machine-gun splattered us.

The carnage went on for several hours as American tanks and tank destroyers crunched over the trenches, scattering enemy infantry and tearing up the wire. By the evening the Germans were beaten and 2nd Armoured was on its way to Neuss and the Rhine.

Equally important was the non-stop advance by 29th Division towards Munchen-Gladbach. Panzer Lehr again moved to block it but it now had so little fuel that most of its armoured troops fought on foot as infantry. To the west of the city Shermans and Tigers ploughed through the woods slamming away at one another. Thunderbolt fighter-bombers took advantage of an improvement in the weather and dived to attack the German tanks with rockets and bombs.

Von Rundstedt knew how desperate the situation had become and Model in particular saw the full implications of a pincer movement that would destroy the north wing of his Army Group 'B' as well as the south wing of Army Group 'H' to his north. Neither Fifteenth Army, nor Schlemm's First Parachute Army, had any reserves and would be wiped out unless evacuated. On the last day of February a conference was hastily convened at von Rundstedt's HQ near Koblenz. There were few options open to the commanders in the west, but as a staff officer later wrote, 'it was obvious that something had to be done. Von Zangen had shown himself inept and was more concerned about his front further south, where, he argued, a major threat was developing from the American First Army's gradual encroachment towards the Rhine south of Bonn. Model was adamant that no such threat existed and insisted the Americans were heading for the Ruhr.' The outcome of the conference was a pointless manoeuvre to

exchange zones between von Zangen's Fifteenth Army and Fifth
Panzer Army under the redoubtable General von Manteuffel, who
had masterminded Hitler's offensive in 1940. The Fifth Panzer Army
was better equipped to deal with the Americans' armoured drive, as
they had a headquarters schooled in such tactics. But time had run
out and along the front units were more concerned with extricating
themselves from the Siegfried Line defences south of Venlo. Around
Roermond where General Vadehn's vaunted 8th Parachute Division
had been pulled out to reinforce Schlemm's Hochwald defences the
replacement Volkssturm units began retreating as fast as they could.

By the sixth day of the attack Ninth Army was still accelerating
and while XIII Corps swung towards Krefeld and the Rhine, XIX
Corps sent 29th Division to take Munchen-Gladbach, a city of
170,000 people, located twelve miles from the Rhine and twenty
miles from the Maas—a daunting proposition that could hold up the
advance for days. Hitler had ordained that every German city had to
be defended to the last, and many remembered the bloody fighting
for Aachen. Senior Allied commanders had conjectured for hours on
the way von Zangen would incorporate the city into his defences and
decided it would have to be enveloped and if necessary besieged in
the manner of Brest, which had held out for months against persistent American attacks and had only fallen after British Crocodiles
had been used to burn out the defenders. The 175th Infantry Regiment led the attack to probe the city's defences, but to the astonish-
ment of regimental and army commanders it wasn't even defended.
By the end of the day a somewhat disbelieving regiment held the entire city.

Following its breakthrough at Junchen, 2nd Armoured Division
moved implacably through Glehn to attack Krefeld while the task of
capturing the important city of Neuss was relinquished to the 83rd
Division. Neuss was situated on the west bank of the Rhine opposite
Dusseldorf, to which it was connected by three bridges. Despite fierce
resistance, by 4.30 am on the following morning, March 2nd, the
Americans had captured the town and by 6.30 am they could see the
Rhine. The regiment had been ordered to capture the railroad bridge
at Neuss but while the Germans put up a desperate fight to hold the
bridge, using machine-guns backed by 20mm Flak guns, the Americans managed to secure the western end of the bridge. At this point
the Germans attempted to blow up the bridge. 'As we watched from
the east edge of Neuss', wrote the regimental commander of 329th
Infantry, 'there was a loud explosion and a big chunk was blown into

the air from the centre of the bridge. Major Sharpe's 2nd Battalion
was ready to cross and secure a bridgehead on the east side but the
blowing up of a chunk out of the bridge brought up problems. Would
it stand up under tanks? There was another span beyond the main
river span. Had it been blown? We had been two days and nights
without sleep. We took the easy and regrettable way out—we did not
cross. The following night the bridge was completely destroyed.'

Frustrated at Neuss the US 83rd Infantry Division commander
held a brief consultation with his regimental commanders and decided to try for a bridge at Oberkassel, a few miles downstream. As
far as possible the tanks were made to look German while the infantry kept close behind and to the sides. Any German-speaking soldiers
climbed aboard—to confuse enemy troops, if necessary, by talking in
German. The small column reached the bank opposite Oberkassel in
darkness and slowly made its way along a narrow riverside road. At
one point they moved quietly along on one side of the road while a
marching column of Germans passed by on the other. Americans on
the tanks conversed in German and several 'Heil Hitlers' were called!

In front they could see the bridge looming up in the darkness
against the silver-grey of the river. Guns thundered to their left but
here it was the eye of the hurricane, a strangely quiet place where
troops went about their business. They progressed cautiously until
the proximity of the bridge; ahead of them was a German sentry pac-
ing up and down in the cold pre-dawn. Hardly daring to breathe, the
men watched the sentry stamp his feet and rub his hands. Then he
stopped and stared, he raised his hand. 'Heil Hitler,' he called. 'Heil
Hitler,' German voices replied and then incredibly they were past.
More soldiers appeared, some carrying rocket launchers and, again,
greetings were called by the soldiers, who barely bothered to look at
yet more tanks.

Nearly at the bridge now the Americans prepared to fling themselves forward while the tanks raced across. Yet another column of
German troops tramped towards them, deep in thought, careless in
the cold of early morning, and paying little heed to the tanks and
men. But a lone soldier on a bicycle pedalled slowly along, then
turned in his saddle . . . a greeting was called to him in German, he
stared, then light dawned in his eyes; it was unbelievable but he saw
they were . . . 'Amis!'

'Halt!' an American shouted but instead the man yelled a warning.
The column faltered as men glanced towards the cyclist, then they
too started. Surprise gone, the tanks revved up while the infantry

blasted everyone with machine-gun fire. The cyclist swerved, screamed and was ripped from his bike in a blast of fire. German troops unslung rifles as they dived for cover but the American guns opened fire, wiping them out. Yells and screams were drowned by the whine of the town's air raid siren warning the garrison as the tanks raced for the bridge. Just as the first tank reached its western end, there was a great explosion that rocked nearby buildings and blew out windows, a rumble followed by a huge splash sending cascades of water everywhere and the bridge was gone.

'About 27th February,' wrote Schlemm, 'I learned that US armoured spearheads had reached Neuss.' This advance created a very dangerous situation since First Parachute Army was facing a British-Canadian thrust in the Marienbaum–Weeze area on 26th and 27th February. Following Fifteenth Army's collapse the Allies were between the Maas and Rhine along a thirty-five mile front, in the rear of his army's flank. 'I was sure that, after reaching the Rhine at Neuss and to the south, the US forces would turn to the north in great strength and attack my army in the rear. If they acted quickly and hurled their powerful armoured forces boldly and unhesitatingly along the Rhine to Wesel, the left bank of the river would be lost, and the army would be cut off from a retreat over the Rhine. There would have been no time to destroy completely the nine large bridges over the Rhine. It would then have been impossible to form a new defence front on the east bank of the river.'

Because he did not have enough forces to stop the American attacks he determined to slow the thrust northwards and form a bridgehead on the west bank to permit a withdrawal. Schlemm informed Blaskowitz that he intended to form a bridgehead on the line Marienbaum–Kevelaer–Kempen–Krefeld. But Blaskowitz took an incredibly optimistic view and forbade Schlemm to withdraw, explaining that he considered Fifteenth Army still capable of combat. Indeed, he ordered Schlemm to deplete further his forces on the British front and send troops south through Krefeld and Kempen to form a new front in co-ordination with Fifteenth Army opposite the Americans. 'Therefore, on about 27th February, I ordered General Abraham, Commander of LXV Infantry Corps, to build up and hold a new defensive front facing south between Maas and the Rhine.'

14 Defeat in the Rhineland

On February 24th Hitler called a Party meeting at the Chancellery in Berlin to which all the Gauleiters were invited. After lunch Hitler crouched at a small table, as though incapable of holding erect his worn body, but fixed them with eyes as clear and penetrating as ever. The Gauleiters waited to hear of the long-promised secret weapons, super rockets, gas, the atomic bomb, but they were never mentioned. Instead Hitler told them of their losses in heavy weapons and how in the west, his magnificent *Westwall* was holding back the Allies.

Hitler admitted he, too, was feeling the strain. At one point he took a glass of water, but his hand trembled too much and he replaced it on the table. Some thought he was acting as he gave a bleak smile and said: 'I used to have this tremor in my leg. Now it is in my arm. I can only hope it won't proceed to my head. But even if it does I can only say this: my heart will never quaver.'

Behind his optimistic façade, Hitler was shocked by reports of crumbling resistance. In the Rhineland people had suffered weeks of heavy bombing, and in their disillusionment with the war, they turned on their own soldiers: local farmers had attacked with pitchforks when German soldiers attempted to demolish small country bridges. When the deputy mayor of Ingelheim advised the people to permit the enemy to pass through, the SS publicly hanged him. White flags hung from houses in the path of the advancing Canadians, British and Americans. At Trier the hastily assembled Volkssturm battalions ran away at the latest American advance.

Hitler's response was predictable. Every town and village must be held, officers who failed to hold a position would be shot, their families would be shot . . . ! There would be no retreat. Not one soldier or tank could be withdrawn without his express instructions. . . . Hitler now took responsibility for command even down

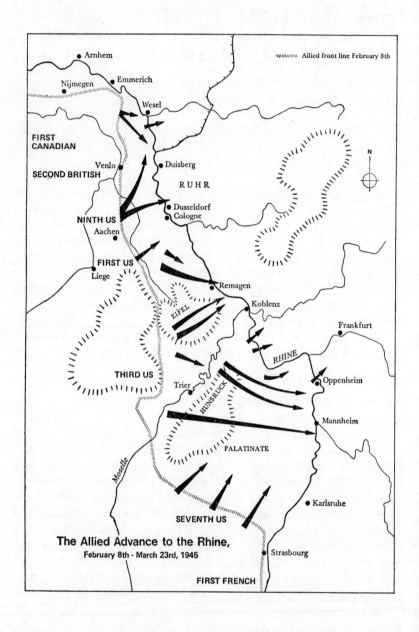

The Allied Advance to the Rhine,
February 8th - March 23rd, 1945

Allied front line February 8th

Arnhem

Nijmegen Emmerich

Wesel

FIRST
CANADIAN

SECOND BRITISH Venlo Duisberg

RUHR

Dusseldorf
Cologne

NINTH US
Aachen

FIRST US
Liege Remagen

Koblenz

EIFEL Frankfurt

RHINE

THIRD US Oppenheim

Trier HUNSRUCK

Mannheim

PALATINATE

Moselle

SEVENTH US Karlsruhe

Strasbourg

FIRST FRENCH

N

to battalion level. There would be no withdrawal, the garrison at Xanten would fight to the death!

At 1 pm on March 2nd the 53rd Welsh Division began its push towards the Americans and cut the German front in two. The 1st Oxford and Bucks Light Infantry with the Reconnaissance Regiment and tanks from 8th Armoured Brigade pursued the enemy south-east from Weeze towards Kevelaer. By 8 am on the 3rd, 158th Brigade was rolling fast towards the Americans. They encountered only slight opposition and 4th/7th Dragoons took the lead, pushing towards Geldern, eager to break through. Enemy tanks appeared over the crest of a rise and opened fire, their shells screaming across the snowy fields and plunging onto the ground ahead. The squadron stopped but didn't fire back; there was a familiarity about the 'enemy' tanks. A Dragoons' officer dismounted and took a recognition panel from the back of the tank. While the squadron waited, its guns trained on the approaching armour, ready to open fire, the officer walked cautiously forward, holding aloft the panel. Three hundred yards through the shells he walked, then stopped. The approaching tanks stopped, figures clambered out and waved. They were Americans!

The US 35th Division's 135th Tank Battalion rolled joyfully forward to meet the Dragoons. At long last 'Veritable' and 'Grenade' had met and severed the German lines. There were cheerful scenes in the snow as Allied soldiers mingled and exchanged cigarettes and the inevitable swops. When the American commander explained they were holding Geldern and about to begin clearing the town, 158th Brigade halted and awaited instructions from Divisional HQ. At 2.15 pm they were ordered to wheel north-eastwards towards Kevelaer and advance along the axis Geldern–Issum–Alpon. From now on the front was continuous and nothing could prevent them closing to the Rhine.

General Schlemm couldn't take much more. His confidence was ebbing in the face of appalling losses that would eventually reach 90,000 men. He could get no reinforcements. Ironically Blaskowitz was still ordering him to release groups to von Zangen's desperate Fifteenth Army. Schlemm said that: 'About the same day it became clear that divisions of Fifteenth Army were no longer available on the southern front of First Parachute Army. Panzer Lehr Division was the only division under LXV Infantry Corps . . . it had three battalions and 10 to 15 tanks.'

On the previous day he had again moved his HQ and was now established west of Wesel at the vital bridgehead. On March 3rd news arrived that the British and Americans had finally joined at Geldern, and were turning east in two armoured columns. General Blaskowitz, Commander Army Group 'H', ordered Schlemm to counter-attack at Xanten but with his weak forces he could do no more than consolidate his fairly solid front. He called von Rundstedt and told him: 'If you have a map before you, you will take in the situation at a glance. My divisions are surrounded, with the Rhine at their back. Under these conditions I cannot do anything against the enemy's superior forces. I am asking your authorization to withdraw to the east bank of the Rhine.'

But as Hitler had made clear at his recent Berlin conference, he now decided the disposition of his forces, and von Rundstedt, who complained that the only troops to whom he could give orders directly were those at the door of his HQ, could only answer Schlemm: 'I'll have to speak to Berlin.'

Hitler's military conferences at the beginning of March echoed to the Führer's condemnation of von Rundstedt's handling of the defence of the Rhine. Ever since the loss of Silesia Germany had become dependent on the Ruhr for its coal and hardware which could only be moved with the Rhine in German hands. Hitler raved about his troops' shortages and, of course, about how he had been let down by everyone—it was all the fault of others . . . 'Here on the upper Rhine front something has to be made out of rubbish piles—the troops just aren't there. Commands are given in vain. The Commander can give orders to his two corps every day, and both of the corps can give them to their divisions, and the divisions can send the orders on down; but there is nothing there . . .'

Jodl reminded Hitler that von Rundstedt still awaited authorization to consolidate his flanks. As Speer reports, Hitler snapped back that all von Rundstedt wanted was authority to retreat across the Rhine, and demanded that he continue his defence west of the river:

At any rate, I want him to hang on to the *Westwall* as long as it is humanly possible. Above all we have to cure him of the idea of retreating here (he referred to the Maas sector on Montgomery's front), because at the same moment the enemy will have the entire 6th English Army

(actually British Second Army) and all the American troops free, and
he'll throw them all in over here. These people don't have any vision.
That would just mean moving the catastrophe from one place to another.
The moment I move out of here, the enemy will have that whole army
free. He (von Rundstedt) can't promise me that the enemy will stay
here instead of going over here. There's no doubt that the building of
reserves at the most dangerous point here was not done with the energy
that might have been possible. That wasn't so much Model's fault—he is
concerned only with his own sector—that was the fault of the
Commander-in-Chief West . . .

All Hitler would agree to was the sending of observers to the front.
'We have to get a couple of officers down there, officers who are
good men, so that we get a clear picture.' The orders that were sent
to the C-in-C West were uncompromising; 'There can be no question
of General Schlemm withdrawing his troops west of the Rhine. On
the contrary he must hold on to the west bank at any cost with a
bridgehead stretching at the very least from Krefeld to Wesel.'

In the south Schlemm's line was based on Uerdingen and, in his
own words, 'OKW now ordered me to hold the west bank of the
Rhine at all costs and in such a manner as to secure the passage of
coal boats on the river from the mouth of the Ruhr Canal at Orsoy
and the mouth of the Lippe-Seiten Canal at Wesel. Otherwise the
supply of coal for the Navy in the North Sea ports by way of the
Dortmund-Ems Canal would break down.'

On the morning of March 3rd, Schlemm's 24th Parachute Regiment, backed by tanks and guns of 116th Panzers, again staggered
forward through mines and wire towards the Canadians. It was a
fruitless offensive. By the end of the day, under the Canadian artillery barrage, the Germans were pulling back, in reaction to XXX
Corps' outflanking march and to the threat of the Americans driving
from the south.

General Crerar reported to Montgomery, 'the enemy is executing a
withdrawal to a line before Xanten, Sonsbeck, Bonninghardt and
Rheinberg'. Obviously he would try to hold this narrow bridgehead
as it was his only hope of withdrawing the battered remnants of nine
divisions across the Rhine. On March 5th Schlemm ordered all the
Rhine bridges in his sector to be blown, except the one at Wesel
which he intended defending to the last. 'Everything depended',
Schlemm knew, 'on holding Wesel with its two bridges and numerous
ferries. I particularly reinforced the northern wing of Xanten with
local reserves, ammunition and the tanks that were still available. I

also had a third bridgehead position prepared on the line Birten–Ossenberg. This was accomplished with the aid of the security garrison at Wesel, two or three Landwehr battalions and construction units.' Resistance was diminishing as he pulled back what remained of 6th, 7th and 8th Parachute Divisions and his mixed panzer and infantry divisions, with scattered groups of anti-tank and flak units. Hardly had the new defence line been determined when a signal arrived at Xanten that the Canadians had taken Sonsbeck, and the line had to be redrawn.

On March 2nd General Simpson issued the last of his Letters of Instruction for Operation 'Grenade'. This confirmed the verbal orders he had given earlier, stressing the need to secure at least one bridge across the Rhine. His instructions included:

The enemy forces opposing Ninth US Army are weak. They display signs of disintegration. There are no major reinforcements in sight. There are virtually no field works south of the Ruhr, west of the Rhine, though it is possible that along the waterfronts of the larger towns, docks and houses have been prepared for defence.

The Directive concluded with the exhortation: 'be prepared to establish bridgeheads east of the Rhine if the situation permits, and exploit such bridgeheads to advance to the east.'

Simpson clearly wanted his troops to 'bounce' a bridge, and he had the backing of Eisenhower who, with Bradley, had paid a visit to Simpson's HQ at Maastricht on March 1st and 2nd. Both commanders showed great pleasure in his rapid advance and interest in his plans to seize a Rhine bridge. But Montgomery, Simpson's immediate superior, was at variance with the Americans. Eisenhower regarded the taking of a bridge as a priority, but he was careful to distinguish between Monty's front and those of the American commanders.

At a press conference on March 28th he explained his views, which were recorded by a Colonel Dupuy and later published by his Naval Aide, Captain Harry C. Butcher:

Since we did it (the campaign to close to the Rhine) on a one-two-three from north to south, immediately one was completed we started to prepare for the attack across the Rhine in the north. There we knew the resistance would be heaviest because it was closest to that extraordinary

region, the Ruhr. We knew it would be heaviest there. So, there,
deliberate plans were made. Army, Navy and Airborne troops
—everybody was brought to bear on that with all the strength it
was considered necessary to use. Troops to the south thereof as they were
finishing up their jobs had one order—over and above everything
else—that at any time they got a chance to jump a bridge over the Rhine,
or failing to get a bridge, jump a bridgehead with little boats or
swimming or any other way of getting across, to do it and do it quickly.

Montgomery always delegated authority for the day-to-day running
of the current battle, while he planned the next which now was going
to be for the road to Berlin. It was obvious to a man of his single-
mindedness that crossing the Rhine was only a means to an end; the
real purpose was to place his forces in a position from which they
could race for the German capital. To do that he needed not only a
firm base from which to start, but also the elimination of all immediate opposition, which justified the immense forces he would concentrate in exactly the right place. If Simpson was to grab a bridge, or
bridges, he would have to be supported and Montgomery must have
thought with consternation of the effect of such a drain on his resources. His eventual decision to limit the number of Ninth Army
crossings has also to be seen against this concept; he needed the
American divisions to follow through and maintain his long
cherished drive to Berlin to which Eisenhower seemed to have
agreed. Higher up the Rhine, where the Americans would cross, such
considerations were less important as the country east of the Rhine
was lightly defended and, being in the main mountainous, did not
lend itself to rapid advances into Germany.

The Germans, too, were concerned with the Rhine bridges. Hitler
had decreed that no ground was to be surrendered and no troops, not
even the wounded, were to be evacuated without special permission
from the Führer personally. The result of this diatribe was unparal-
leled congestion in the bridgehead as nine battered divisions, their
vehicles, their armour, much of it in need of repair, and truck loads
of wounded, all crowded into the small remaining bridgehead.
Schlemm received a spate of orders from Hitler, following one upon
the other. He was not to surrender the west bank at any cost; the safe
passage of Rhine traffic had to be ensured, from the Ruhr to the
Lippe and Dortmund-Ems Canals. Schlemm was to be personally responsible that none of the bridges fell into enemy hands.

Local commanders were fighting desperately to extricate all possi-

ble forces in preparation for the battle when the Allies began to
cross. Units of 15th Panzer Grenadiers, 190th Infantry Division, bits
of the 7th and 8th Parachute Divisions and an amalgam of units
known as 406th zBV (Special Operations) Division left rearguards
to delay the Americans while they withdrew over the river by ferry,
river craft and rafts, or by the few remaining bridges. The Allied air
forces struck at the bridges to prevent the enemy's escape, Lancasters
attacked bridges, while fighter-bombers and medium bombers harried
the enemy traffic. River barges were especially prone to air attack
and on March 3rd alone twenty-nine were claimed destroyed in addition to locomotives and railway trucks in daylight sweeps. But they
could not destroy them all and their inability to do so was one of the
failures of the Rhineland battles. Captain Butcher reported that Eisenhower said later:

Now I have read in the papers that there is some criticism that we did not
destroy the Rhine bridges. Naturally, we would have liked the Rhine
bridges destroyed. We weren't silly enough to think the Germans weren't
going to destroy them if they could . . . our bombers have been forced to
operate day after day through heavy cloud—to destroy a thing like a
bridge would require an air strength you couldn't afford to devote to
bridges alone . . .

On March 4th a new phase in the struggle for the bridges began.
With four bridges down, Ninth Army tried again, this time some
thirty miles downstream from Oberkassel at Uerdingen where the
1,640-foot Adolf Hitler bridge reached across just south of Duisberg.
Unknown to the Americans, General Lackner's 2nd Parachute Division, withdrawn from the Hochwald, had arrived to form the southern end of the last-ditch bridgehead to which von Rundstedt planned
to hang on as long as possible.

The bridge was in XIII Corps' zone and the likeliest candidate to
rush it was the 5th Armoured Division. But XIX Corps' 2nd Armoured Division was moving up from the south, although still beyond the Nord Canal. Deciding on a wait-and-see policy, Simpson
alerted XIII Corps to be prepared to shift northwards on short notice
to make room for 2nd Armoured.

On March 1st, 2nd Armoured's Combat Command 'A' found an
intact bridge over the Nord Canal and fought its way across, followed by the rest of the division. By nightfall they were at Krefeld,
only three miles from the Adolf Hitler bridge. About noon that day,

Colonel Armistead D. Mead, Ninth Army's G3, arrived at XIX Corps' HQ to check the progress of the attack and learned that 2nd Armoured was approaching fast. Simpson was away and, in his name, Mead issued the necessary orders changing the boundary between XIII and XIX Corps enabling 2nd Armoured to drive beyond Uerdingen for the bridge.

The 5th Armoured Division kept pressing for the bridge under orders from General Gillem, the Corps Commander, to stop only if 2nd Armoured got there first; meanwhile 84th Infantry Division had not been told of the changes and General Bolling had also ordered 334th Infantry Regiment with the 771st Tank Battalion to by-pass Krefeld and rush the Adolf Hitler bridge. The race was won by 2nd Armoured Division. They rushed Combat Command 'A' to seize the bridge but the enemy were well established in buildings covering the approaches and hit them with rocket launchers, *Panzerfausts,* machine-gun and small-arms fire. As the armour got nearer along the war-torn streets paratroopers added intense mortar fire to their onslaught. As night fell Uerdingen reverberated to the sounds of battle while smoke and flame swirled up into the night sky and were reflected in the dark waters of the Rhine.

Early in the night a six-man patrol slipped quietly through the ruins, crossing mountains of rubble until they reached the bridge. Incredibly they managed to get over to the far side then on their way back they cut all the demolition wires they could find, before making their way to Command HQ. Just after midnight German engineers were ordered to blow up the bridge. Their troops were withdrawn from the western end while artillery and mortars from the eastern end continued to hammer any American attempts to close up. When the charges were activated nothing happened! The German commander hastily got more demolition teams onto the bridge to renew the wiring which they thought had been cut by American gunfire. By dawn they were ready and as the Americans fought their way forward yard by yard the charges exploded one after the other and the bridge crashed into the river.

Based on his assumption of seizing a bridgehead between Dusseldorf and Mundelheim McLain now proposed an assault over the river by whatever means presented itself, followed by a drive east to envelop the Ruhr from the south. This would be followed by the capture of Hamm, an important rail centre north-east of the Ruhr. One corps would move along the route Dusseldorf–Wetter–Unna–Hamm; a second corps would clear and expand the bridgehead

north to the Ruhr river. Alternatively they would strike north from
the first bridgehead, go over the Ruhr river and then turn east to
seize Hamm. The operation would avoid Essen in the east and concentrate on clearing the banks of the Rhine to enable progressive
bridging by remaining forces with the aim of getting all three of
Simpson's corps across.

Simpson was elated at the prospect of getting over and driving into
the Ruhr, and if he had been under American command he probably
would have tried first and sought approval afterwards. Instead he
went to Montgomery and recommended that a surprise crossing
should be carried out either by capitalizing on a bridge capture or by
direct assault, arguing that Hitler's determination to fight west of the
Rhine had decimated his forces and little resistance would be encountered. Ninth Army were convinced they could penetrate the
Ruhr, but Montgomery said that such a scheme was not in line with
his plans: 'this was not the moment for giving subordinate Generals
the opportunity to advance their reputations by a display of technical
expertise.' Inevitably the Americans took umbrage and talked of
Montgomery's concern that an impromptu American crossing might
detract from the grand assault that he himself was planning. What really worried Montgomery was that an assault several weeks in advance of his planned crossing might be cut off if the bridge was
demolished, leading to a complicated and unnecessary rescue operation in the face of strong enemy forces. Also, he did not like the idea
of launching an assault into the heavily populated and very indus-
trialized Ruhr with some eighty miles of factories, warehouses and
housing where every tactical advantage would lie with the enemy.
'War correspondents might not mind, the widows would. Make it
sure and keep the losses small, was no great error at this stage of the
war.' But American pride, and especially Simpson's, was hurt and
Bradley seized the opportunity to express sympathy with Simpson's
plans.

Meanwhile at Rheinberg, three miles west of the Rhine, and until
recently the site of Schlemm's HQ, American infantry and a strong
force of tanks were opposed by about twenty German Panther tanks.
General Schlemm watched the battle from high ground at Moers,
anxious that his forces should hold the position which was a key approach to Wesel and his bridgehead. Although the superb Panthers
put up a stubborn and accurate fire the numbers of American tanks
began to tell and they had to withdraw back to Rheinberg. Schlemm
could only commiserate with himself on his lack of air support and

heavy artillery. But, contrary to his expectations, the Americans did not follow up their breakthrough, which, he believed, could have reached Wesel with little difficulty and cut off his retreat over the Rhine; another opportunity had been lost.

Xanten and the high ground south of the town were vital links in Schlemm's perimeter at his last bridgehead at Wesel. Within it were the remains of four corps that had been all but destroyed in Operation 'Veritable'. Von Luttwitz, Straube and Meindl had seen their forces reduced to these shattered remnants. Schlemm told von Rundstedt: 'In my opinion, the reasons for holding this bridgehead are outdated. American artillery on the west bank, to both sides, covers the river and shuts off all traffic.' He wanted permission to withdraw all his forces back over the Rhine, but was refused. It was made very clear to Schlemm that he was expected to hold the remaining bridge until the last possible moment to allow the retreating forces to get across, and only then was it to be blown. The message concluded with the superfluous but inevitable threat: 'Failure to carry out these orders to the letter means death.' Although he disliked the Führer's threats, when the German colonel holding the Homburg bridge hesitated to blow it up because he wanted to bring over more vehicles from the west bank, Schlemm commanded him to blow the bridge immediately, or he would personally shoot him.

On March 6th Schlemm began evacuating troops and equipment as fast as he could, his rear covered by 24th Parachute Regiment and two battalions of 116th Panzer Regiment ringing the shrinking bridgehead. There was an ironic comparison with Dunkirk; the Germans now queuing to escape, the Allies hammering Schlemm's ring of defenders into submission. Hugo Pritz's battalion, now little more than a couple of platoons, had been driven back from their positions at the Asperberg bridge and now held out in trenches on the outskirts of Wesel.

We were waiting our turn to retreat across the bridge at Wesel, but in the meantime had to bear almost continual shelling from Allied guns ringing us from north to south. Also, every evening their bombers came over and tried to destroy the bridge but our flak defences were too strong. The worst moments were always when fighter-bombers firing rockets attacked our columns, which was almost every few hours. They would roar in at low level from the direction of the Maas and tear along the roads firing machine-guns and rockets which would swoosh along to explode in terrifying sheets of flame. Whenever they attacked, the

columns would halt while men scattered and after a few minutes vehicles
would be blazing. Eventually our turn to be evacuated came and we had
to endure the approach march under shelling and bombing and then we
literally ran across the bridge, frightened of being caught upon it. We had
no sooner got across than aircraft attacked the columns still crossing and
slaughtered many men who had nowhere to run to.

Schlemm commented: 'While watching this artillery preparation in
the British-Canadian or in the American sector on the Wesel bridgehead I often believed that no German soldier could live through this
hell. Deep and narrow foxholes for one or two had to be dug. The
men had to have nerves of steel.'

The east bank had not been fortified for defence and was held only
by a few Volkssturm battalions. Schlemm asked Blaskowitz to let him
withdraw General Straube's LXXXVI Corps staff to prepare a defensive front on the east bank of the Rhine. 'There is only one available
bridge, the Wesel. If an enemy spearhead reaches it and I have to
blow it according to orders, we shall have no way of escaping. And
some of my men have had experience that would make them very
useful in preventing an enemy crossing of the river.'

Blaskowitz could hardly have had any illusions about the state of
Schlemm's front or the ability of the Allied armies to break through
the now flimsy screen protecting the remaining bridgehead, but his
discipline, or his fear of Hitler, forbade him to countermand OKW's
instructions. 'Berlin is dead set against any withdrawal,' was his stony
reply. Frustrated and anxious for his men, Schlemm insisted: 'Well,
please communicate what I have told you. If Berlin does not believe
me, or thinks I am painting too black a picture, let it send an ob-
server. But there's no time to be lost.'

Time was indeed running out for the Germans. Crerar was now determined to break the enemy positions at Xanten and eliminate his
remaining enemy west of the Rhine. Hitler ordered the rearguard to
fight to the death and no one doubted that the paratroopers would do
so. Xanten was protected on the west by a deep anti-tank ditch while
on the east the Rhine made a great loop right up to the town. The
whole area was protected by minefields and wire entanglements and
trenches. Crerar decided to make a frontal attack with 2nd Canadian
Division going for the western edge of the town while the Wessex
took the town itself, supported by special assault equipment.

On the right, General Mathew's 2nd Canadian Division's 4th In-

fantry Brigade ran into heavy machine-gun and artillery fire from
fortified houses. The Essex Scottish, who had suffered badly on February 19th, again took heavy losses, especially among its officers. But
their supporting armour took on the strong points: 'The Crocs put
the finishing touches to the Germans with shell and flame,' their War
Diary recorded.

Accompanying them, the Royal Hamilton Light Infantry broke for
the enemy defences and reached a ditch just as Spandaus got their
range. The Hamiltons dived for cover into icy water-filled ditches
where they were pinned down for several hours. They huddled up to
their necks in water, unable to rise as machine-guns swept the
ground. 'It was just like battle courses in England, but the bullets
aimed at them instead of over their heads,' one of the men remarked.
With companies cut off and vehicles bogged down, Brigadier Cabeldhu restored the situation by sending in the reserve Royal Regiment of Canada.

Late that night 5th Brigade took over with the South Saskatchewan Regiment under command, passed through 4th Brigade and captured the ridge commanding Xanten from the south. By this time resistance was crumbling as the Wessex drove in from north and west.

Major-General Ivor Thomas, commander of the 43rd Wessex,
which suffered more casualties than any other British division in
Europe, now elected to send 129th Brigade under Brigadier J. O. E.
Vandeleur to capture Xanten. Heavy bombers opened the attack
with a raid on Xanten which, in Vandeleur's words, 'blew it to bits.'
The Divisional artillery let loose a 'pepper pot' which stoked the already raging fires. Such was the conflagration that the enemy could
neither reinforce the town nor evacuate his wounded.

Vandeleur launched a two-battalion attack just before dawn in
order to cross the ditch before daylight. The 4th Somerset Light Infantry made for Xanten and 5th Wiltshires for the small village of
Luttingen which lay to the left and guarded the approaches across
the plain. Behind the Somersets, 6th Assault Regiment Royal Engineers were ready with a specially-constructed skid Bailey bridge
which would be pushed across the ditch by AVRE Churchills while
smoke poured across their front, hiding their operations from enemy
gunners.

Preceded by 22nd Dragoons' Flails at 5 am Major Hutchinson led
'B' Company of the Somersets forward behind a rolling barrage to
seize a crossing point over the ditch, under heavy fire from panzer
grenadiers and paratroopers. 'We had been ordered to prevent the

British taking Xanten no matter what happened to us,' recalls Wolfram Schaub, 'which did not please us because we knew we had little hope of getting out alive. Already the town was blazing and from our positions near the old stone gates we could feel the heat behind us. My Spandau was positioned in a concrete emplacement protected by wire. We seemed for once to have inexhaustible ammunition and I just kept firing, the spent belts piling up around us had to be cleared away every so often. My partner had a jerrycan of water and would splash water on the gun barrel to cool it whenever necessary.'

Crocodiles of the Fife and Forfar Yeomanry moved in to flame the defences but they couldn't reach across the ditch. Schaub's position was lucky to survive when a flame-throwing tank attacked it but 'the ditch was, fortunately, about forty metres wide, and the flames fell short. But it was very frightening.' Well-entrenched defenders withstood even the artillery concentration and kept firing. Major Hutchinson decided to get on without artillery support and sent his section forward independently. One by one they inched forward. 'I think Xanten was the worst,' one soldier recalled. 'There seemed to be no cover at all and I couldn't understand why I wasn't hit a hundred times. We reached the ditch eventually and fought our way to the other side where we pitched grenades at every Jerry we could see.'

About ten that night, when Vandeleur was preparing a new attack, word reached him that a German doctor had arrived at the Wiltshires's HQ carrying a white flag to ask for a pause in the battle while he evacuated his wounded. In Vandeleur's words: 'I went to see the doctor. He was a charming man and about six feet three inches tall. He was dressed in a white sheet marked with an enormous red cross, back and front. We smoked a cigarette or two together and I explained to him that war is not a tea party and that he would have an opportunity to recover his wounded when the battle was over. I personally conducted him from the front lines where we saluted one another with some ceremony.'

Schaub, meanwhile, continued to fire his Spandau into the smoke-filled night, illuminated by the roaring fires and gunfire. 'In the early hours of the morning the British put a long bridge across the ditch—we didn't believe it possible—and the shelling intensified while their engineers worked. We concentrated our fire in that direction but at two in the morning their tanks began to clatter across. Within minutes the area around the crossing was in flames as their flame-throwers set to burn everything in reach.' The Engineers' bridge was, indeed, barely finished when gun tanks, Crocodiles and Wasps thundered across.

The flame-throwers went into action straight away. Crocodiles destroyed enemy positions along the ditch while the Wasps burnt the enemy out of houses. The darkness was lit by roaring flames and the night echoed to explosions and hideous screams. The armour followed them into the town, against which the 116th Panzers threw their remaining Tiger tanks, scoring direct hits on several tanks and Crocodiles at ranges upwards of 200 yards. Fortunately there were only a few Tigers, and anti-tank guns, PIATs and gun tanks combined to drive them back. After examining a shattered Tiger the British discovered it was fitted with an infra-red gun sight—which explained their deadly accuracy. For Wolfram Schaub the end of the fighting came soon afterwards.

Our panzers made a brief attempt to halt the attack but they were heavily outnumbered. While they were fighting, British tanks made their way along the ditch towards our positions and shells began to blow the surrounding buildings down. We kept up a steady fire and in the flickering light from the many fires we saw the British troops working their way from door to door along a ruined and burning street. We prepared to hold out but a small flame-throwing tank (Wasp) burst into view from our right and set alight a house only twenty metres away; then the British troops charged down the road and we knew it was all over. We were very afraid the flames would get us but they stopped. I remember in the darkness that the British troops were very dirty but grinning with delight when we gave up.

By dawn the Somersets had secured Xanten and the Germans were finished.

The Allied net closed although the Germans fought to the last. When the 52nd Lowland Division attacked Alpon their 6th Cameronians were almost annihilated by German guns while the American armoured attack at Rheinberg cost them most of their Shermans. On the right of the Allied line the US XVI Corps, under General Anderson, was placed under Crerar's Canadian First Army and directed to liquidate the enemy bridgehead. The 52nd Division took Ginderich while the 4th Canadian Armoured Division finally destroyed enemy troops holding out in the monastery east of Veen. Small parties of paratroopers began dashing for the last ferries or the Wesel bridge.

Now, at the last moment, Berlin's promised officer arrived at Schlemm's HQ to report on the situation there. The now cynical commander of First Parachute Army invited the staff officer, whom he described as 'young and resplendent in a brilliant uniform', to view the situation. Schlemm's HQ rocked to continual explosions as aircraft and artillery kept up the pressure. With obvious reluctance the staff officer accepted the invitation and looked for a staff car. But Schlemm shook his head and said that there was no point since the front line was so near. With barely disguised satisfaction Schlemm 'hoped they wouldn't have to crawl'. By the time they returned to the command post Hitler's dashing officer was in a dishevelled state and sweating with terror. 'Well,' Schlemm asked, 'what do you think?'

The colonel cleaned his face with his handkerchief, visibly shaken. 'I agree the situation is desperate and the bridgehead must be withdrawn.' Soon he was gone. Schlemm wasted no time and gave orders for the immediate evacuation of the west bank.

March 10th dawned strangely quiet. The exhausted Canadian and British infantry waited for the command to rush the remaining German positions. Great clouds of smoke were pouring from enemy tanks and trucks blazing where the artillery had caught them. At 7 am a tremendous explosion shook everyone; then another and another, crashing and roaring across the shattered country. Great columns of smoke shot into the air. Men came to their feet and stared. The bridge at Wesel was gone. The battle for the Rhineland was finished.

It had taken Montgomery's armies a month, and cost the Canadians, British and Americans 22,000 casualties, to clear the country between the Maas and the Rhine. But they had destroyed the last German field army in the west—First Parachute Army had lost 90,000 men and most of their equipment—and elsewhere the German front was held by remnants backed by Volkssturm divisions of low quality. Of equal importance, they had brought about the destruction west of the Rhine of forces that should have been retained to oppose the crossing and to prolong the defence east of the river. 'The enemy,' Eisenhower stated, 'was now in no condition to hold fast in the defensive line to which he had been compelled to retreat . . . His defeat in the Rhineland led straight to his complete collapse less than two months later.'

Eisenhower wrote to Crerar expressing his admiration for the way the campaign had been handled and fought. He concluded: 'Probably no assault in this war has been conducted under more appalling conditions. . . . It speaks volumes for your skill and determination and the valour of your soldiers that you carried it through to a successful conclusion.'

On March 7th Eisenhower was at his Rheims HQ. At 7.30 he sat down to dinner with several of his airborne commanders. Captain Harry Butcher recorded the scene:

. . . Ike had said he didn't particularly care for the soup when Henry Clay answered the telephone in the next room. It was for the Supreme Commander who excused himself, and we soon heard his voice saying:
    'Brad, that's wonderful.'
    There was a pause and then he continued: 'Sure, get right on across with everything you've got. It's the best break we've had. . . . To hell with the planners. Sure, go on, Brad, and I'll give you everything we got to hold that bridgehead. We'll make good use of it even if the terrain isn't too good. . . . It's wonderful! Congratulations.'
    When Ike was talking, the airborne generals were all ears, as indeed was I. General Ridgway said: 'Butch, couldn't you get us in on this show? It sounds good.'
    When Ike sat down again at the head of the table, he said, 'Hodges got a bridge at Remagen and already has troops across.'

15 The bridge at Remagen

From its confluence with the Moselle at Koblenz, the Rhine flows northwards through mountainous country as far as Bonn, where it emerges into rolling country once more. Halfway through the mountainous stretch lies the town of Remagen, just north of the point at which the river Ahr flows from the rugged Eifel mountains to the west. It is country unsuited to armoured warfare because columns of tanks and trucks are tied to narrow, winding mountain roads. But this was the terrain that lay across the front of Bradley's 12th Army Group, comprising Hodges's First Army on the northern flank and Patton's Third Army to the south.

Opposing the Americans in this sector was the German Army Group 'B' under Field Marshal Walter Model, a tough and wholly uncompromising soldier who had won Hitler's acclaim commanding the 9th Army in Russia when in 1941 he had ordered the SS Regiment *Der Führer* to hold a position until he brought up reinforcements; although the Russians were heavily defeated, of the 2,000 men of *Der Führer* only thirty-five survived. If Model was resolute he was also known as a foul-mouthed bully and described by von Rundstedt as a 'good sergeant-major'. Although ambitious, he realized his own limitations as an administrator. When appointed C-in-C West, in succession to von Kluge, who had committed suicide, Model told Hitler he wasn't capable of commanding OKW West and Army Group 'B'; after only eighteen days he had been replaced by von Rundstedt. General Blumentritt, formerly Chief of Staff at OKW West, remembers Model spending most of his time in the field and avoiding paper work. Significantly, in view of his subsequent actions at Remagen, Lieutenant-General Zimmermann, Operations Chief at OKW West, thought Model always dissipated his forces and had poor staff work because of his frequent absences.

For several weeks Model had been predicting that the Americans would concentrate their forces on the Rhine near Bonn. This seemed logical in view of the difficult country further up the Rhine valley, and it was an obvious egress from which the mobile American forces could flood onto the country south of the Ruhr and meet with Montgomery's forces expected to cross the Rhine north of the Ruhr. During February Model continuously reinforced Bonn's defences from his Army Group 'B' forces further south. But his subordinate commander of Fifteenth Army, General von Zangen, who was then still fighting a desperate defensive action against US Ninth Army, held a different view to Model. He pointed out that the country which the US III Corps, under General Milliken, was penetrating, resembled a funnel along which their advance would close south-east to the river Ahr and the town of Remagen. The real danger, von Zangen correctly predicted, was not at Bonn, but at the outlet to the funnel at the town of Remagen. He wanted to block this outlet by withdrawing two corps from the *Westwall* defences and placing them at Remagen, otherwise, he argued, there was the danger of the Americans reaching the great Ludendorff railroad bridge at Remagen. Von Zangen needed the bridge as a supply route, or if necessary, as an escape route. To this end he was having the tracks planked over to improve its surface for trucks. Model dug his heels in and obstinately refused permission for any troops to be pulled out of the *Westwall* because, as he repeatedly pointed out, Hitler had decreed that not a single pillbox was to be abandoned without a fight. So, while Model, like Blaskowitz, his counterpart in Army Group 'H', stuck unfailingly to Hitler's orders, the army commanders, first Schlemm and now von Zangen, were unable to dispose of their forces as they thought the situation demanded.

After Collins's VII Corps had crossed the Roer on March 23rd to protect US Ninth Army's southern flank, Hodges sent the rest of First Army across on the right. All the troops crossed over one bridgehead, after which they fanned out to form other bridging sites. This was a part of Bradley's Operation 'Lumberjack' by which he intended his 12th Army Group to close to the Rhine. VII Corps escorted Ninth Army to the Rhine and then turned south along the river to take Cologne, Germany's fifth largest city.

March 1st found the German armies resigned to the impending American blow. One of Patton's probing attacks that day inflicted a serious reversal on the German Seventh Army and Model saw an immediate danger to his entire Army Group 'B' from the threat of Patton advancing over the river Kyll and completing his rout of the Seventh Army. It would cut off the remains of von Zangen's Fifteenth Army (which had by now changed places with the Fifth Panzer Army) in turn endangering the rear communications of Army Group 'G', which was defending the vital Saar industrial region south of the Moselle.

Bradley issued orders on March 3rd for Hodges and Patton to prepare their dash to the Rhine. Hodges was to close to the river north of Cologne after which he was to swing south-east for Koblenz meeting Patton there. These manoeuvres would, however, bring 12th Army Group to the Rhine in the most rugged section of the river, where the mountains on the east side fell sheer into the water; hardly a point at which a crossing could be exploited for a drive into Germany. Bradley's entire strategic concept was in fact still based on nationalistic considerations instead of on sound military logic: because America was providing the bulk of the equipment and manpower, then its direction and its triumph should also be American. Bradley could not accept that the mountainous country east of the Rhine in his sector was quite unsuitable for a rapid armoured thrust. At the beginning of the campaign in the Eifel he was approached by a SHAEF officer requiring troops from Bradley's forces for another operation. Bradley's retort was that if SHAEF wanted 'to destroy the whole operation, they could do so and be damned . . . much more than a tactical operation was involved in that the prestige of the American army was at stake.'

Patton launched his attack through the Eifel on March 3rd, heading for Koblenz. On March 5th, two days later, 4th Armoured Division was released, with Patton's usual exhortation to get to the Rhine. Under General Gaffey they drove headlong on a narrow front of a couple of parallel roads. A correspondent at Third Army HQ reported how Patton's tanks just took off, roaring along mountain roads and vanishing over the ridges. Leaving the infantry almost seventy miles behind, the columns raced across minor rivers and beyond the mountains regardless of the state of the roads. In fact Gaffey's forces overran many areas before the already-disorganized defenders knew what was happening. A German corps commander seeing a crowd of his soldiers gathered around a group of tanks went across to find out what was going on. An American lieutenant challenged him: 'Where do you think you're going?'

'It looks like I'm going to the American rear,' he replied as he realized that the tanks were American and the Germans prisoners.

By March 7th tank crews weren't stopping when encountering groups of German troops, but simply yelling to them to go to the prisoner-of-war cages! What remained of the German forces west of the Rhine and north of the Moselle straggled back in disorderly columns towards the Rhine in the hope of getting across on barges or on the remaining bridges.

On March 3rd General Collins had sent a combat command to capture the Rhine north of Cologne, and while the rest of his forces descended into the great city, General Milliken's III Corps continued its eastward drive along VII Corps' southern flank. Milliken had been given specific instructions by Hodges to head for the river Ahr to link up with Patton's Third Army, but he and his divisional commanders decided independently to disobey orders and close to the Rhine near Bonn. To keep Hodges happy, Milliken directed the 9th Armoured Division to the Ahr. But with Patton's spectacular advance towards the Rhine developing on his right, Hodges could not remain indifferent to Milliken's unauthorized drive to the Rhine at Bonn and he ordered him to make for the Ahr to link up with Patton. To satisfy his commander, Major-General John Leonard, commanding 9th Armoured, he reluctantly sent the bulk of his division down the funnel to the Ahr. But, still cherishing the thought of reaching the Rhine first, Leonard sent Combat Command 'A', under Brigadier-General William Hoge, towards the Rhine at Remagen, with a mixed force of tanks and infantry.

General Siegfried Westphal, von Rundstedt's Chief of Staff, was called to Berlin on March 6th, following the latest confrontation between his chief and Keitel, Chief of the High Command of the Armed Forces, who had kept his post by assiduously toadying to Hitler ever since February 1938. Keitel had telephoned von Rundstedt that as C-in-C West he would have to answer to Hitler for the continuing reverses on the western front.

Westphal was received by Hitler in the Reich Chancellery and for five interminable hours was subjected to his wrath. Westphal explained von Rundstedt's report: '. . . our fighting strength did not nearly suffice to man all these bunkers. For these reasons large increases in the length of the front merely for the sake of holding onto sections of the *Westwall* could not be justified. The whole front would only be rendered thereby the more liable to collapse.'

Hitler disagreed. He contended that infantry divisions, each averaging 5,000 strong, ought to be capable of holding a front of 15 kilometres. He raged at von Rundstedt's report, calling it a 'shameful fabrication.' Bravely Westphal stood up to Hitler and tried to reason with him. It was, he argued, imperative to hold the shortest possible front to make the most of their limited numbers of troops. 'Otherwise the danger of a breakthrough was acute. The Ob West must therefore again ask to be permitted to give up the fortified lines according to their merits.' Hitler promptly demanded to know the extent to which forces would be saved. Lamely, Westphal had to admit there would be no actual 'saving', but rather that the present overstretched front might be subjected to unforeseen pressure. Hitler retorted that if they shortened their front so too would the enemy, who would concentrate his forces even more decisively. At that Westphal returned to von Rundstedt's HQ.

The field commanders, and particularly von Zangen and probably Model, saw that it was patently absurd to hold onto the west bank of the Rhine. They were currently holding both sides of the Rhine but on the west bank they were at widely separated places covering the most likely crossing points at Bonn and Koblenz. Between them was a sixty-mile gap around Remagen, virtually undefended because Model thought the mountainous country beyond Remagen would dissuade the Americans from crossing there. Model's Intelligence staff kept telling him that his forces at Remagen were adequate because the Americans were definitely driving for Bonn.

Von Zangen, who was responsible for defending the Remagen area, worried greatly about the weak defences and, against orders to hold the dangerously long line west of the river, retreated his troops along an axis that would place them between the Americans and the Remagen bridge, and give him the time, he hoped, to strengthen his defences. Like Schlemm in the Reichswald, von Zangen was prepared to use his judgement and disobey his army commander, an extremely dangerous thing to do, for Hitler was quite capable of ordering his execution as a result.

Model had been so sure that Patton's forces further south constituted the major threat that he had removed the anti-aircraft guns on the 600-foot Erpeler Ley cliff that overlooked the Remagen bridge, and sent them to Koblenz. Replacement guns were only installed at Erpeler Ley in the first weeks of March. Model now complicated the already confused situation by establishing a separate command reporting directly to von Zangen's Fifteenth Army. He placed a junior officer in command of all army troops in the area, but then appointed Captain Karl Friesenhahn, an engineer, in charge of the Remagen bridge itself. Luftwaffe Captain Willi Bratge commanded a force of 200 anti-aircraft troops, 500 Volkssturm and 120 Russian 'volunteers'. In addition there were 180 Hitlerjugend he could call on, although they were officially answerable only to the local Nazi officials. Bratge persistently warned of an impending American attack—he could hear their tank guns firing—but was coldly told it was only a small force protecting the flank of the main drive heading for a crossing point north of the Drachenfels mountain.

All morning on March 7th the American 9th Armoured Division's column wound its arduous way over the road towards Remagen. About 1 pm, Second Lieutenant Emmet J. Burrows, leading an infantry platoon of the mixed infantry and tank force comprising 27th Armoured Infantry Battalion, emerged on a bluff overlooking the small town of Remagen. Below, they could see German forces streaming east across the bridge, moving in a disorganized mass of troops, trucks, field cars and even horse-drawn vehicles and a herd of cows. That the bridge was still standing did not sink in at first as they were more excited by the sight of the fabled Rhine, flowing at the foot of the cliffs. Paradoxically the troops had little intention of capturing a bridge, because Remagen was halfway between two previously-selected crossing points.

Once Burrows fully realized the importance of his find, he was all for directing their mortars onto the mass of enemy troops in the bridgehead. His company commander, First Lieutenant Timmerman, became as excited as Burrows and enthusiastically decided that they should employ artillery and tank guns as well as mortars. But his colonel refused permission, instead allowing tanks to fire only to prevent any attempted demolition of the bridge by the Germans. Eventually Brigadier-General Hoge himself arrived, saw the full potential of capturing the bridge intact, and without reference to his commanders, including General Hodges, urged his forces down through the town as fast as they could go. A platoon of the newly-arrived M26 Pershing tanks plunged downhill to aid the infantry.

By mid-afternoon Timmerman's platoon was running through the narrow streets of the old town, dodging the olive-green Pershing tanks as they ground past, crashing chunks off street corners. At the bridge entrance German troops fled for safety, knowing their engineers would blow the bridge as soon as the Americans got near enough to rush it. Already the roar of engines and clatter of gunfire were drawing very close and the German rearguard was retreating nearer to the bridge. Machine-guns mounted on half-tracks and tanks up on the bluff swept the bridge with a hail of fire to hinder German demolition attempts. Through the scything bullets, Captain Friesenhahn ran from the far end with a squad of his engineers, dodging behind the huge steel columns to avoid the bullets that whined off them. He had set out only to examine the bridge's structure and the charges, and intended to get back to the east bank, but the speed of the American advance changed all that.

The last German troops were crossing and with the Pershings only minutes away, Friesenhahn was ready to run back and set off the demolition charges, when he was infuriated to see a last German battery hastening from the town and racing for the bridge. Friesenhahn swore at them, exhorting the troops to get a move on as shells and mortar bombs crashed among the buildings only yards away. Then American tanks and infantry burst into sight, the GIs darting from doorways, firing carbines as they ran.

Timmerman yelled for his platoon to rush the bridge as the last German soldiers raced across. But from the far end and from positions on the Erpeler Ley, German gunfire now swept the western approaches, and Timmerman's platoon faltered. His men were reluctant to race onto the bridge; it looked suspiciously like a trap. At any moment the Germans might blow it up, either while they were on it, or to cut them off on the far end. Yelling to them to get a move on, Timmerman plunged forward as the Pershings' shells crashed into the enemy positions. They were only yards away when Friesenhahn detonated the charges. The end of the bridge erupted in a sheet of orange flame followed by the roar of explosives and tons of débris. Friesenhahn staggered from his firing position while rubble and dust still swirled around, ready to race back along the bridge but next moment another explosion flung him down. An American shell had crashed into the bridge just ahead of him.

Timmerman shook his head, looked up at the swirling cloud and staggered to his feet, expecting the Remagen bridge to have been blown into the Rhine. But incredibly when the dust and smoke cleared the bridge was still there. Friesenhahn had only exploded charges to blow a thirty-foot crater in the road in front of the bridge to slow up the Americans while the German battery got safely across. But instead of running for the bridge immediately, Timmerman hesitated, waiting for his platoon to recover.

Meanwhile as the American attack developed Bratge's security guards had been deserting, and reluctant Volkssturm and flak gunners had slipped away from the bridge area. By the time Friesen-hahn scrambled back only thirty-six men remained, all convalescents on 'light duties', quite inadequate to oppose the armoured force at the other end of the bridge. Bratge immediately intercepted Friesen-hahn and demanded he blow up the bridge. Friesenhahn said he didn't have the authority; only Major Scheller could give the order. But, Bratge reasoned, Scheller was at the far end of the railway tunnel. Friesenhahn told him to go and find the major as fast as possible. Bratge made a quarter-mile dash along railway tracks congested by civilian refugees sheltering in the tunnel. When he eventually located Scheller and hastily explained the situation the major, too, hesitated in view of Hitler's orders that the bridge should not be blown until the last minute. For several minutes Bratge fumed impatiently, then when Scheller consented, he dashed back again to tell Friesenhahn to blow the bridge. Friesenhahn promptly turned the key to explode the sixty charges separately placed on the bridge—but nothing happened. He tried three times but still got no response.

All this time American tanks had been sweeping the bridge with cannon and machine-gun fire and Friesenhahn concluded that this had cut one of the main cables, which prevented them from electrically detonating the charges. A 300-kilo emergency charge with a simple fuse could still be lit. One of Friesenhahn's sergeant engineers agreed to do the dangerous job and set off along the bridge, dodging behind the great steel columns to escape the hail of gunfire. For eighty yards he ran while bullets whanged and whined off the steel and stone structure, finally dropping to his stomach to fumble with the fuse. It spluttered a few times, then caught, and he started the desperate return race against the charge and the American bullets. As he reached the eastern end and dived headlong into cover, the charge went up with a terrific roar. Deck planking, railway sleepers, track, stone and débris whirled upwards in a cloud of thick smoke and flame.

Timmerman and his platoon emerged from cover to look at the wrecked bridge—if it had gone, well, that was a disappointment, but at least they wouldn't have to fight their way along it. As the clouds of dust-laden smoke drifted away, everyone gasped—the bridge was still there!

Recovering from his surprise Timmerman exhorted his troops to get the hell over it, but they were far from keen on what they thought was a suicide mission. Once on that bridge they had to keep going for if the Germans blew it again they couldn't survive the drop into the Rhine. However, ducking the German bullets, bobbing, swerving between the steel girders and columns, they gradually got across. German machine-guns mounted on towers at the far end opened fire, sweeping the bridge from end to end. Instantly the Pershing tanks fired their 90mm cannons, the heavy shells smashing into the stone tower and silencing the guns, while machine-guns mounted on American half-tracks tore into the enemy infantry milling around the tunnel mouth. German gunners opened fire from a barge moored in the river, but immediately American machine-guns directed such a hail of fire onto the barge that the gunners were torn from the decks. Behind the GIs the engineers scampered about cutting every wire and cable they could find on the bridge and within its structure, to which they had gained access by inspection hatches, expecting that at any moment they would be blown to. smithereens. Those cables they couldn't cut with hand tools they blasted apart with their carbines.

Alexander Drabik, a lanky, diffident sergeant, raced with his platoon along the last yards, dodging fire from positions in the right-hand tower which they rushed firing from the hip. This so frightened the Germans they threw down their weapons and surrendered. Drabik thus became the first man across the Rhine south of Holland. Timmerman and his men fanned out to race for the tunnel itself, dashing for cover on either side of the gaping hole. Timmerman's patrol entered with extreme caution, peering into the near total darkness, praying the enemy would not open fire with machine-guns.

The German civilians who had retreated well into the tunnel when American shells began bombarding the bridge and its approaches, attempted to get the troops to surrender, arguing with their officers to give up. Confusion reigned, Friesenhahn and Bratge tried to find Major Scheller to get fresh orders, but he had disappeared. Bratge decided to surrender.

Outside the tunnel, Timmerman's platoon, and those on the bridge, were coming under fire from the enemy flak positions atop the Erpeler Ley, so Timmerman sent troops scrambling up the sheer mountainside. Two additional companies of the 27th Battalion crossed to reinforce him, but as they had little more than infantry weapons the situation on the eastern bank remained extremely hazardous. While engineers searched the bridge for charges, a number of the infantry quietly slipped back again to where more engineers were busily filling in the huge crater which Friesenhahn had blown at the western end. Tanks stood waiting to cross at the first possible mo-

ment. Further along the bridge more engineers struggled to repair the
chaos of planking over the shattered rail track to facilitate the tanks'
crossing.

Corporal William C. Hendrix was with the 467th Anti-Aircraft Artillery (Automatic Weapons) Battalion whose half-tracks were operating in support of First Army. Their battalion had been directed to
Remagen where they assumed they were to support a crossing. At 5
pm on the 7th, as they waited in their staging area, cheering broke
out and everybody seemed to get excited. Moments later an officer,
Lieutenant Wallace Gibbs, drove up in a jeep, yelling for them to get
loaded. 'We have a bridge across the Rhine,' he shouted, 'and by
damn we're going to keep it there.'

General Leonard's main force of 9th Armoured Division was still
moving towards the Ahr and their projected junction with Patton's
forces when the signal arrived at his HQ that Hoge's combat command were across the Rhine and fighting to hang onto a bridge. In
great excitement Leonard ordered 9th Armoured to reinforce the
Remagen bridgehead, despite Hodges's orders. At the HQ of Milliken's III Corps, the telephone jangled in the late afternoon. A
switchboard operator answered the call. 'Hot damn!' he yelled,
throwing aside his headpiece. 'We got a bridge over the Rhine and
we're crossing over!'

Word was immediately sent to Hodges at First Army HQ who
promptly commanded additional engineers to be despatched to the
bridge and only then got onto Bradley at 12th Army Group HQ to
tell him the news. Bradley was then in an angry meeting with General Harold R. 'Pinky' Bull, Eisenhower's Operations Officer, their
discussion revolving about a SHAEF proposal to move four of Bradley's divisions to reinforce Dever's US 6th Army Group in the
south, to strengthen Patch's Seventh Army for its attack south of the
Moselle, on Patton's right flank. Their angry exchanges were interrupted by the phone call. Bradley's face changed as Hodges told him
that a First Army division had seized the railway bridge at Remagen.
'Hot dog, Courtney,' he exclaimed, 'this will bust him wide open!
Are you getting the stuff across?' When the conversation finished,
Bradley hung up and turned to Bull, slapping him on the back with
undisguised glee. 'There goes your ball game, Pink. Courtney's gotten across the Rhine on a bridge.'

Bull shrugged and retorted that it didn't make any difference because there was nowhere to go from Remagen. 'It just doesn't fit into

the plan. Ike's heart is in your sector, but right now his mind is up north,' he tried to explain to Bradley.

Bradley would not accept that Eisenhower could be so rigid as to ignore this bridgehead over the Rhine, no matter whether or not it fitted existing plans, and he saw Hodges's achievement as a way of restoring the main effort to his army group. He decided to call Eisenhower, who indeed promised to support him in his bridgehead while pointing out the limitations of the terrain.

After speaking to Eisenhower, Bradley authorized Hodges to send in the 99th Infantry Division in addition to the 9th and 78th Infantry Divisions that had already been told to exploit the 9th Armoured Division's thrust. But in spite of his indignation at Bull, Bradley was in a dilemma. He had already planned for Patton to seize a crossing further south, which SHAEF had not agreed to, and he was not really keen on diverting resources into Remagen, which even he realized only led to very difficult country. His impulsive reaction to Hodges's success would cause trouble with Patton.

While the top commanders patted one another on the back or argued the merits of the bridgehead, at the bridge itself engineers had succeeded in replacing the damaged planking. Hendrix's battalion arrived at the bridgehead about 6 pm. A big sign hung across the steelwork between the stone towers: 'CROSS THE RHINE WITH DRY FEET—COURTESY OF THE 9TH ARMOURED DIVISION'. But it was night by the time the Pershings began to cross. Five tanks inched along in absolute darkness, banging into one another, like so many over-sized Dodgem cars. They ground to the end of the bridge and then accelerated to make contact with the infantry ahead in the darkness.

After the five tanks, Hoge sent across a formation of tank destroyers belonging to 656th Tank Destroyer Battalion. Captain Forst Lowery, who earlier that afternoon had sunk a German patrol vessel on the Rhine by tank-gun fire, led his tank destroyers across at speed but the lead vehicle slipped on the hastily laid planking and one tank went through to remain lodged eighty feet over the river, completely blocking the bridge. The rest of the platoon juddered to a halt. Fortunately the enemy limited their counter-attacks to small-arms fire, but it was a desperately anxious night while engineers tried to move the tank destroyer. First they attempted to pull it out, then to drop it through into the river, but neither succeeded. It was not until dawn that their strenuous efforts were rewarded, the tank destroyer was removed and more armour and men streamed over.

The Remagen bridgehead concentrated the attention of Allied and German commanders alike. Strategically it was a blind alley and for both sides its danger lay in the forces which were already being sucked into this single bridgehead from more vital areas. If the process went on unchecked there was a real danger that Patton would find his supplies diverted to support Hodges's thrust instead of his own. Patton's drive was gaining momentum and would take his forces to a crossing point from which a breakout was possible. Montgomery's objections to a crossing by Ninth Army applied to Remagen as well, where there was a danger that the small bridgehead would have to be supported at the expense of more important sites. Its one benefit was that during the coming weeks the Germans would react by dissipating their weakened forces by trying to block off an Allied thrust that could not by itself affect the overall strategy. Hitler was not satisfied just to prevent a breakout but insisted the Americans should be thrown back, an infinitely greater task.

The day after the Remagen bridge was crossed, Hitler summoned Field Marshal Kesselring. Hitler was furious that the Wesel bridgehead was being evacuated and the British-Canadian army was about to reach the Rhine. He execrated the army commanders for cowardice but praised Kesselring, who, he pointed out, 'was a Luftwaffe officer'. Kesselring reached Berlin a little before noon on March 9th. Keitel and Jodl met him and wasted no time in telling him he was to replace von Rundstedt as C-in-C West. Kesselring took the news in his stride and replied that: 'I was needed in the Italian theatre and that not being fully recuperated had not the necessary mobility for this decisive mission. . . . They listened to my objections with understanding but thought it certain they would hold no water with Hitler.'

Hitler interviewed Kesselring that afternoon. The fall of Remagen, Hitler said, had made necessary a change of command in the west. 'Without reproaching von Rundstedt', said Kesselring, 'he gave as his reasons for taking this step that only a younger and more active commander who had experience of fighting the western powers and enjoyed the confidence of the man in the line could restore the situation.' Von Rundstedt was sacked for the last time, having been sacked and recalled several times previously.

Then Hitler gave a long résumé of the overall situation. The crux of this assessment was that a collapse on the Russian front would mean collapse everywhere. But since he was concentrating all his defensive strength on that front he was confident of eventually stopping the Russians. Hitler's confidence was hardly justified; German troops on the Eastern front at the beginning of February stood at an all-time high at just over 2,000,000, but Stalin had over 6,000,000 men with an overwhelming number of tanks and guns.

Once the Russian front had been stabilized, Hitler reasoned he would be in a position to feed replacements into the Western front. A steady flow of men and materials to the west would enable his forces to hold out behind the natural obstacles, essentially the Rhine. But, he admitted, 'the vulnerable spot was Remagen. It was urgent to restore the situation there; he (Hitler) was confident it could be done.'

Following his interview with Hitler, whose exposition was 'remarkably lucid and showed an outstanding grasp of detail', Kesselring had a further meeting with Keitel and Jodl when various points were discussed in more detail. 'My mission was clear: Hang on! It worried me the more because for the time being I was to command "anonymously", the idea being that my name should still be effective in Italy.'

During the night of 9th–10th March, Kesselring drove to the HQ of the C-in-C West, *Adlerhorst,* at Zeigenberg, near Frankfurt. He clearly had Hitler's promises of secret weapons much in mind for on arrival he announced to the gathered staff officers: 'Well, gentlemen, I am the new V3.'

Almost immediately Kesselring began talks with General Westphal, his Chief of Staff. Westphal reported: 'The main feature of the situation at the front is the enemy's extraordinary superiority in men and materials on the ground and his absolute ascendancy in the air.' They had fifty-five weak divisions to oppose eighty-five American, British, Canadian and French divisions. The strength of the German infantry divisions was on average down to 5,000 as against an establishment of 12,000, although the panzer divisions were better off at about 11,000. 'Altogether this meant at the very best 100 combatants to every kilometre of front. There could be no talk of back areas, of pulling out even small reserves from the line or of garrisoning the numerous pillboxes of the *Westwall*.' Westphal thought that on the whole morale was still generally high, but many men were war-weary and worried about their families at home. He concluded: 'They are alive to the importance of their task of keeping the rear of the Russian front free . . . every soldier in the West knows he has a part to play in saving the soil of our country and the Germans of the Eastern provinces from the Russians.'

That evening Kesselring telephoned Keitel and said that the situa-

tion was much worse than he had been led to believe. The next day
he began consulting his field commanders. To Schmidt, Air Officer
Commanding the Luftwaffe West, an independent command, he
made important recommendations: 'logical concentration for the moment necessarily in the Remagen area, and the intensification of all
efforts by the Luftwaffe and the navy to destroy the bridge at Remagen and any auxiliary pontoons.'

On the 11th March he went to Model's HQ Army Group 'B'
which totalled around 350,000 men, most of whom were concentrated in the northern part of his zone. The troops were dispirited
after successive defeats and many officers and men were in a dangerous state of exhaustion while the army in general was desperately
short of junior officers. Von Zangen and his subordinates thought two
American infantry divisions and one armoured division plus artillery
were across the Rhine and confessed that no 'equal strength could be
mustered to oppose them'. They had little prospects of liquidating
the bridgehead unless more supplies of ammunition and reinforcements could be quickly pushed in, especially on the vulnerable
flanks.

Later that day Kesselring conferred with Blaskowitz at Schlemm's
First Parachute Army. Army Group 'H' were confident, providing
they had a respite for about ten days to prepare their positions.
(Schlemm didn't know it, but this was the same amount of time
Montgomery would need to prepare his massive assault across the
Rhine.) Kesselring commented that this sector was in any case the
most heavily defended. In Holland Blumentritt's Twenty-Fifth Army
was 'weak and insufficient for the purpose.' His best troops protected
Schlemm's right flank and would have to bear the brunt of the expected crossing by Montgomery's forces. 'All I heard made, on
reflection, a good impression, so that, remembering the unique performance of the Parachute Army west of Rheims (and in the Reichswald), I felt I could look forward with confidence to the battle to be
expected on the right wing of the front.' He later added: 'With the
significant exception of the first-class paratroopers under Blaskowitz
up in Army Group "H" in the north, the morale of the German
troops in Italy was better than that of most of our troops along the
Rhine.'

By that night Kesselring had 'formed a superficial personal impression of the situation'. Because of the pressure of time and his own in-
juries he had been unable to visit front-line troops: 'This was a pity,
as I would have been able to form a more convincing picture of the

situation and the state of the troops and perhaps would have come to
another decision.' However, in his memoirs, Kesselring admitted it
was difficult to guess the Allied intentions but said he had seen three
possibilities:

1 To exploit their lucky success at Remagen either so as to split the
German western front in two and link up with the Russians by the
shortest route, or—which was less probable—to limit their forward drive
towards the east and to attack the Ruhr from the south and south-east.
2 An encircling offensive against the only remaining bastion west of the
Rhine, the Saar Palatinate, in order to wipe out Army Group 'G' and so
by crossing the Rhine to secure a jumping-off base for operations against
South Germany.
3 A British offensive to force a Rhine crossing on the Parachute Army's
front and so create a bridgehead which would give them strategic
possibilities in (several) directions.

It was the last of Kesselring's three possible options which the Allies
were to pursue in the final stages of the war. The Saar Palatinate
was, indeed, about to be wiped out, as he foresaw, but by Patton's
Third Army in conjunction with General Patch's Seventh Army to
his south; the Remagen bridgehead was not going to play a decisive
role in these events.

The American newspapers were ecstatic at US First Army's success,
but Eisenhower was irritated at them for habitually ignoring Hodges
by name, and for that matter, Bradley; for when Third Army took a
place the headline invariably read, 'Patton captures . . .'
    Publicity was an endless problem for American commanders.
Butcher reported on March 14th: 'General Marshall has been pressing to get more publicity for divisions and their commanders.' Eisenhower sent a memo to Bradley and Devers, commander of 6th Army
Group: 'Much of the publicity with respect to the achievement of US
ground units in this theater has been impersonal and generalized in
character. Many opportunities have been lost to publicize forcefully
the extraordinary achievements of particular commanders and units
in specified situations.' He pointed out that the action of 101st Airborne at Bastogne had been an exception. 'In the recent advance to
the Rhine, the names of Collins, Gillem and McLain have been mentioned in news stories only casually, whereas I believe that, with a little prompting, reporters would have made these men stand out
more clearly for the public.' He pointed out that the American prob-

lem was more difficult than was the British, because '. . . we do not
have the historical names of regiments and the concentrated interest
based on geographical recruiting at home.'

If the Press were in raptures at the Remagen bridgehead the
American command was not. Eisenhower was, as usual, all enthusiasm after talking to Bradley, but he later became distinctly cold
about the whole affair, forbidding any larger scale build-up across
the Rhine at Remagen. Brigadier-General Hoge became very apprehensive because he had deliberately disobeyed orders, although he
could point to the support and indeed encouragement of his Divisional Commander, General Leonard. He in turn could argue that it
had not taken much to persuade their Corps Commander, General
Milliken, to go for Remagen.

Eisenhower contacted Montgomery, anticipating the usual difficulties, and was surprised to find him extremely pleased. Montgomery
had been quick to realize that the capture of Remagen bridge would
force the enemy to send reserves into the bridgehead. It was the
opposite of Normandy and 'Veritable' when his forces had attracted
the enemy and allowed US forces to break out. Nevertheless Montgomery was worried in case this unexpected breakthrough provoked
Eisenhower into changing his mind again and encouraged him to
close along the Rhine prior to launching a crossing in the north
where the Siegfried defences had been cracked wide open. If Eisenhower did want that, it could only mean a bloody battle through the
Siegfried defences further south and would delay his crossing. Eisenhower was probably seeking assurances, for this was indeed his intention regardless of agreements already made. As the next ten days
would show, Eisenhower would close to the Rhine along its length,
provoking just the kind of hard-fought battle that Montgomery anticipated. But more than this, it was to bring about a radical change in
strategy that even Montgomery did not foresee, once the British had
crossed the Rhine.

In response to Kesselring's demands the Luftwaffe threw everything
they could find at the Remagen bridge. For nine days they kept up
the pressure, bombing the bridge, the tactical bridges put across the
river by American engineers, and the ferries in vain attempts to slow
down the American advance. The onslaught began to tell on the
American fighters who had no suitable bases close enough to the
bridgehead and were overwhelmed. The RAF was called in to help
and since only Tempests had the range to reach Remagen from Hol-

16 Shermans of the Fort Garry Horse waiting to attack in Operation Blockbuster

17 British and US troops meet at Issum

18 Montgomery, Brooke, Churchill and Simpson inspect the 'dragons' teeth' of the Siegfried Line at Aachen
19 Montgomery, Eisenhower, Bradley, Crerar, Simpson and Dempsey

20 Medium batteries massed along the Rhine

21 Smoke screen at Xanten

22 The greatest barrage of the war, 23rd–24th March 1945

23 Assault troops set out over the Rhine

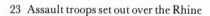

land they were sent in. For several days the RAF made several
sweeps down the narrow gorge, combating Luftwaffe bombing and
strafing raids.

When the Luftwaffe attempts failed the Germans fired V2 rockets
at the bridge, the only time they were used tactically during the entire
war. Their biggest artillery piece was moved into position, the giant
railway-mounted *Morser Karl,* weighing a stupendous 130 tons.
After hurling a few 4,400-lb shells it broke down and had to be withdrawn for repairs. From behind the mountains, enemy long-range
guns fired shells which plunged into the Rhine, again and again show-
ering the bridge with splinters and cascades of water. An officer of
the US 809th Field Artillery Battalion wrote: 'The dismal March
weather and the use of smoke generators obviously helped in preventing enemy air attacks from destroying it, although the near
misses and pounding that Remagen took must sure have helped
weaken it. During that period Remagen was a real hot spot, and with
the anti-aircraft guns surrounding the place there was the greatest
ring of conical firing one could ever hope to see.'

As Montgomery had feared, the Remagen bridge was now sucking
to its vortex the forces of both sides. The 99th Infantry Division, for
instance, was on its way to the Rhine north of Cologne when it was
diverted to Remagen. As they came into the town, said James Ri-
cardo, 'The streets were a shambles and there was a lot of dead lying
around. Most of the town was in ruins but troops were sheltering in
cellars. All the while we could hear shells screaming towards us and
pounding down all along the water front. Although we had been
marching for hours and were dead beat we were ordered across and
told to go to the stone towers at the end of the bridge. There were
stairs inside and they led us to the bridge. I vaguely remember shells
crashing into the stonework as we raced across and then I was huddled behind a building on the far side. We weren't given time to get
our breath before someone started yelling at us to get on . . .'

Kesselring, too, grew more anxious as these persistent American
attacks shoved back the German defenders in the north and north-
east. After securing the heights of the *Westerwald,* the range of
mountains behind Remagen, the Americans swung east, which Kesselring interpreted as an attempt to force a breakthrough. Fresh reports indicated that the attacks were broadening as the Americans
pushed out their perimeter to the south-east heading for the towns on
the adjacent hills.

Kesselring was becoming increasingly alarmed by Model's apparent reluctance to get to grips with the Americans in the bridgehead. For the few days immediately after the bridge was lost it was necessary only to mount a normal defence to hold up their advance while counter-attacks were prepared. This was possible until March 25th, while the American armour was still stuck in the bridgehead, but on that day the armour began to push rapidly ahead. 'Our counter-measures', wrote Kesselring, 'had to be adapted to the behaviour of the enemy', which meant that in the first phase one possibility only existed for success, to send in large closed formations.

Albert Speer now called at Model's HQ to discuss the problems of bridges that Hitler wanted destroyed, but which Speer deemed vital to maintain the cycle of production in the inter-related coal, steel and rolling mills. 'He (Model) was in a state of fury. He told me that commands had just come in from Hitler to attack the enemy on his flank at Remagen, using certain specified divisions, and recapture the bridge. "Those divisions have lost their weapons and have no fighting strength at all", he said. "They would be less effective than a company! It's the same thing all over again: At headquarters they have no idea what is going on. . . . Of course, I'll be blamed for the failure." '

To Kesselring it was obvious that the rapid expansion of the American bridgehead was more than Model's reinforcements could contain; he could seal off penetrations and even launch small counter-attacks, but he could not establish a front. Kesselring sought fresh reinforcements but OKW had no more divisions to send him. The Americans could not be stopped once they reached the autobahn east of Remagen and two days later they crossed on a wide front to tear Model's line wide open. Kesselring repeatedly warned Model to 'intercept the imminent breakthrough to the east' but it had no effect. Model's poor staff work and hesitant tactics had caused catastrophe, a great gap had been opened up from the river Sieg in the north to the Lahn in the south. In turn, this threatened the defence line between the Lahn and the Main, towards which Patton's forces were advancing from the south. The forces diverted to the north and the retreat of the corps defending that flank started the ultimate progress towards complete collapse.

The capture of the Remagen bridge led to discord among the Americans, too. Hodges, who had been eager to exploit the spectacular drive by his forces, had been frustrated by Eisenhower's subsequent decision to restrict his resources, and he suspected, erroneously, that Montgomery was behind the decision. Hodges was far from his normal placid self and getting more and more irritated by the failure of his forces to break out of the bridgehead in a sensational way that would make the American Press take notice. He blamed III Corps' Commander, John Milliken, for being slow and uninspired, and didn't hide his regret that the Remagen bridge had not been taken by VII Corps, under General 'Lightning Joe' Collins. All the while Hodges had wanted Milliken to drive north and clear a crossing for Collins, Milliken had concentrated instead on a southern attack to make a junction with Patton's Third Army. By the time Milliken got the message it was too late, for von Zangen had managed to establish a defence line across his path blocking any drive towards the Ruhr.

On the afternoon of March 17th, Hodges called Milliken by telephone. 'I have some bad knews for you,' he began, and told him he was relieved of his command. When Hodges finished talking Milliken replied: 'Sir, I have some bad news for you too. The Remagen bridge has just collapsed!'

For ten days the bridge had shuddered to a constant aerial bombardment, and reverberated to the march of infantry and the rumble of tanks and armour. The continual concussion of nearby guns and the enemy's battering was the final straw. Frederick Burger was with 9th Infantry, holding the Erpeler Ley: 'I had been resting for a while. Everything was quiet, no enemy planes and no shelling. I was looking down on a crowd of our engineers still working on the bridge, trying to improve its track. There was a terrific crack, I remember ducking because I thought it was a rocket, then there was another and the bridge began to shake, whipping from side to side. A strange sound came from it, a deep sonorous grinding and as we watched it fell into the river.' The Remagen bridge collapsed as engineers scrambled and slipped for safety but twenty-eight men died as the great structure fell into the Rhine.

After the collapse of the bridge Hitler set up a 'Flying Special Tribunal West' without waiting for the reports compiled by the command in the west. The Tribunal was headed by Lieutenant-General Hubner, a fanatical Nazi, who did not fail Hitler in using the extraordinarily wide powers he was given. Several officers, including Major Hans Scheller, were tried for cowardice and shot. Speer recalled that Model told him on March 18th 'that they were completely innocent'. What Speer called the 'shock of Remagen' put commanders in a state of terror until the war ended—it may have been the reason for Model's own suicide after he lost the Ruhr. Bratge and Friesenhahn were tried in their absence, the first was sentenced to be shot, the latter was acquitted. It hardly mattered as both were American prisoners by then.

16 Preparing for the crossing

The battle of the Rhine crossing, so far as the 44th Royal Tank Regiment was concerned, started on 7th March, when we were suddenly pulled out of the Hochwald battle. Puzzled and mystified, the tank drivers and commanders were whipped off their tanks and told to drive them to Nijmegen.

Dawn broke and the first crews climbed out of their trucks to have a look-see—'browned-off' but ready for the worst. Hm! Not a bad looking joint, no civvies about though? Surrounded by water: what's that smoke screen for? And look at that twelve-foot high screen on the other side —miles of it! What is this place anyway, a Zoo?

Just then a string of things looking like mobile hip-baths went clattering by, plunged in the water and proceeded to swim across. This was too much and there was a mad dash for breakfast, for no man can stand seeing things like that on an empty stomach!

Yes, it was all too true—we, the 44th Royal Tank Regiment, had joined the Wavy Navy and were to sail our way across the Rhine.

The strange contraptions that so startled Lieutenant-Colonel G. C. Hopkinson's men were Sherman tanks, developed by Hobart's 79th Armoured Division for the D-Day landings, and equipped with a propeller and a waterproof canvas screen which gave just enough buoyancy to keep afloat. As well as providing these tanks for the British, 79th Armoured Division also trained Canadian and American tank battalions for the Rhine crossings. 'Early on it was decided that we couldn't be expected to do a night crossing in view of the limited time available for training. So all final crossing practices and dress rehearsals were carried out at first light.'

The Rhine is a long river with great variation in its topography and its moods. On the upper Rhine where Patton would cross, and at the Remagen bridge, it was no more than eighty yards wide between

well-defined, at times rocky, banks. At Wesel the Rhine was nomi-
nally 400 yards wide between winding flood plains that were inun-
dated in winter when the river could spread for a mile or more in
places. Then when the floods subsided they left great lagoons and
creeks along the shores with sand-bars that changed shape almost
daily. Thus the land alongside lent itself to strong defences in depth.
The far bank was criss-crossed by a sophisticated trench system with
interconnecting saps enabling defenders to move between trenches,
fall back or to reinforce a position in secrecy. In front of the trenches
was a mass of concertina wire and acres of minefields, while further
back every house, farm and building concealed 88mm guns, anti-tank
guns, machine-guns and infantry. Still further back along the low,
wooded hills the Germans had heavy guns ready to bombard a
beachhead. Look-outs in the numerous church towers of the towns
and villages could see across the river and flood plain on the west
bank.

The American commanders went into the Rhineland battles with
every intention of seizing a bridge and getting across the Rhine without delay. Their good fortune and considerable bravery at Remagen
enabled them to do just that. But the British, too, wanted to 'bounce'
a bridge if they could. When the ground was still frozen hard Horrocks had had 'no doubt at all that we should break out very quickly
into the plain beyond and I had hoped secretly to bounce one of the
bridges over the Rhine.' Horrocks's enthusiasm was frustrated by the
appalling weather and floods which made rapid advances impossible.
The Guards Armoured Division, earmarked for the breakthrough,
had not been able to get to the battlefield from its assembly area. The
Roer floods had prevented 'Grenade' being launched and Canadian
First Army had fought a desperate battle to defeat the best remaining
units of the German Army in the west. They had suffered heavy casualties and when XXX Corps and 11 Canadian Corps reached the
Rhine at Wesel they were exhausted.

Above all the vicissitudes, however, Montgomery's character was
indelibly stamped on this, his last great assault. To achieve success he
had to be superior at the point where it was intended to strike. His
great battles—at Alamein, in Tunisia, Italy, Normandy and now in
the Rhineland—were all launched when he alone said so. Montgomery also emphasized the importance of sound pre-battle intelligence and intensive reconnaissance, from which the point of attack
would be chosen and forces concentrated to exploit it. His tactics
therefore included deception plans and feints to confuse the enemy

and cause him to dissipate his forces. As Sir Huw Wheldon says, 'you knew Monty would win and that gave you great confidence.'

On March 9th Montgomery issued orders for crossing the Rhine north of the Ruhr. 'My intention,' he wrote, 'was to secure a bridgehead prior to developing operations to isolate the Ruhr and to thrust into the northern plains of Germany.' Two factors were uppermost in Montgomery's mind in planning the assault over the Rhine. First he could not forget the extraordinary ability of the Germans to strike back after repeated defeats. In the months since the enemy had suffered their appalling débâcle at Falaise, they had several times reacted forcibly; Arnhem, Aachen, Hurtgen forest, the Ardennes and lately the Hochwald had been nasty shocks for the Allies. Now the Germans were preparing to fight on the far side of the Rhine, their backs very much to the wall, led by a fanatical Führer who had shown himself to be as ruthless to his own men who failed him as he was to his enemies. But Montgomery was also very concerned about the Russians. President Roosevelt was dying and the direction of the war in America had become noticeably lax; in the belief that the Russians did not constitute a threat to Western Europe the Americans did not have the same anxiety to penetrate as far into Germany as possible with all speed to deny territory to the Russians. By March 1945 the American people were anticipating that their troops would all return to America as soon as the war ended. The British, and Montgomery in particular, were very apprehensive of a powerful Russian presence in the North Sea ports, or Scandinavia, and Montgomery saw the urgent need to reach the Baltic coast before the Russians and deny them access to Denmark.

In outline (said Montgomery), my plan was to cross the Rhine on a front of two armies between Rheinberg and Rees, using Ninth American Army on the right and (British) Second Army on the left. The principal objective was the important communications centre of Wesel. I intended that the bridgehead should extend to the south sufficiently far to cover Wesel from enemy ground action, and to the north to include bridge sites at Emmerich; the depth of the bridgehead was to be sufficient to provide room to form up major forces for the drive to the east and north-east. I gave 24th March as target date for the operation. It will be recalled that the battle of the Rhineland was not completed until 10th March, so that the time available for preparing to assault across the greatest water obstacle in Western Europe was extremely short.

Speed then was of the essence, to keep up the pressure and not let
the enemy reorganize. He intended to attack with 'such drive and
strength' as to overwhelm the Germans; his forces would then drive
on 'quickly to final victory in the campaign.' Montgomery had three
armies poised for the assault. Simpson's US Ninth Army was arrayed
from Dormagen, south of Dusseldorf, to the river Lippe, upstream
from Wesel; they would assault across the Rhine at Walsum between
Wesel and Duisberg to secure the right flank. Simpson had three
corps comprising three armoured and nine infantry divisions, although his initial attack would be with General Anderson's XVI
Corps only.

From the Lippe to the Dutch frontier, eight miles west of Emmerich, was Dempsey's Second Army, with four armoured and eight
infantry divisions, plus five independent armoured brigades and an
independent infantry brigade; it also had attached a Commando brigade. It was to seize the town of Wesel, enabling the Ninth Army to
bridge the Rhine there, and to secure the bridgehead from Dorsten to
Pannerden. Then 11 Canadian Corps would send its forces through
the Rees bridgehead and exploit northwards towards Doetinchem
and Hoch Elten to secure Emmerich. Dempsey also had under his
command the US XVIII Airborne Corps, British 6th Airborne Division, with a Canadian airborne battalion attached, and the US 17th
Airborne Division.

The order of battle was: XXX Corps' 51st Highland Division at 9
pm on March 23rd; XII Corps' 1st Commando Brigade at 10 pm on
the 23rd; and 15th Scottish Division at 2 am on the 24th. The Americans would begin at 2 am on the 24th when XVI Corps' 30th Division would attack followed at 3 am by 79th Division. The Airborne
Divisions would begin dropping at 10 am on the 24th. Then 9th Canadian Infantry Brigade would cross with 51st Division.

Opposing the crossing on 21st Army Group's front was Blaskowitz's Army Group 'H'. Again the main opponents would be First
Parachute Army from south of Wesel to west of Emmerich, with
Twenty-Fifth Army from there to the North Sea. Intelligence estimated there were four infantry divisions opposite Ninth Army; between the Ruhr and Emmerich were the 8th Parachute Division
around Rees, with elements of the 6th and 7th Parachute Divisions
on the flanks, and 2nd Parachute Division was at Wesel. In mid-
March more parachute troops were sent from the 'island' between
Nijmegen and Arnhem to the Emmerich area. In reserve, some
fifteen miles north-east of Emmerich was von Luttwitz's XLVII

Corps, with 116th Panzer and 15th Panzer Grenadier Divisions. Just north of Wesel was Straube's LXXXVI Corps, including the 84th Infantry Division with three infantry regiments and supporting artillery, anti-tank and engineer battalions, but in all they only totalled some 1,500 men. But they were dug in across the route from the Xanten crossing sites to the wooded country upon which the airborne forces would land. Local training units and depots could produce a further three weak divisions while the Volkssturm and quasi-military organizations might form a further 30,000 men of admittedly doubtful value.

Kesselring knew he did not have much time until the Allies began to cross the Rhine. Already he was scraping together every reserve to stem Hodges's advance out of Remagen, while south of that bridgehead he watched with increasing consternation as another pincer movement was developed by Patton and Patch. On his northern flank he knew Montgomery was assembling a powerful force, while Blaskowitz was frantically re-equipping and regrouping such forces as he had. 'The enemy's air operations in a clearly limited area, bombing raids on headquarters and the smoke-screening and assembly of bridging materials, indicated their intention to attack between Emmerich and Dinslaken,' wrote Kesselring, 'with the point of main effort on either side of Rees.'

Kesselring spent hours contacting field commanders by telephone, something which von Rundstedt never did; like Montgomery, he used his Chief-of-Staff for all contacts with his subordinates which left him free to plan. 'The telephone conversation which I had with the Group commander (Blaskowitz) gave me fresh heart . . .' The Volks Artillery Corps and the Volks Smoke Corps had been kept in reserve instead of being used at Rees, and were now directed to strengthen von Luttwitz's forces. Kesselring was unhappy, though, that Blaskowitz had positioned both panzer divisions so far back, on the east side of the river Issel, and wanted this disposition corrected. Montgomery, he realized, would make full use of all the means at his disposal and that included his airborne forces. 'The cloudless spring weather gave Montgomery the opportunity for a large-scale airborne landing . . .' He thought back six months to the lessons of Arnhem, when the two panzer divisions, which by good luck had been refitting nearby, had broken up the British 1st Airborne Division. Blaskowitz argued that was just why he wanted to keep the reserves available for use anywhere to break up enemy landings before they could establish firm bridgeheads and bring in heavy weapons. By keeping the panzers in readiness he could move them to whichever landing threatened the major breakthrough. After discussion Kesselring agreed.

Montgomery was likewise assessing his opponents' likely moves and when reconnaissance aircraft reported that they had deployed formidable anti-aircraft defences he feared the worst. 'From their location', he wrote, 'it seemed clear that the enemy anticipated the use of airborne forces in our crossing operation.' Faced with these preparations, Montgomery was clearly sensible to use such forces as he did. 'On his side', said Kesselring, 'Montgomery had the most difficult assignments; his armies, which had suffered great losses in the preceding battle west of the Rhine, were confronted by a most formidable obstacle, defended by divisions with a recognized combat tradition, which, moreover, had had a respite of ten days, and were backed by adequate reserves. The technical preparations for this manoeuvre were exemplary, however, and the massing of forces was commensurate with the undertaking and the Allies' resources.'

Overall planning for Operation 'Varsity'—the airborne assault across the Rhine—was delegated to First Allied Airborne Army which was responsible for pre-assault training and planning, as they had been for 'Market Garden'. Once landed, Lieutenant-General Matthew B. Ridgway's US XVIII Corps would take command, with British General Richard Gale as deputy. The entire formation was placed under Dempsey's Second Army.

The British 6th Airborne, which under Richard Gale had made the D-Day assault in Normandy, was now commanded by Major-General E. L. Bols, whom Sir Huw Wheldon describes as having an air of easy elegance always about him. The US 17th Airborne was under Major-General William Miley and had been reorganized and equipped after fighting as infantry in the Ardennes.

Ridgway's XVIII Corps was to drop its airborne divisions directly onto the high ground about the Diersfordterwald, between the rivers Rhine and Issel, with 6th Airborne on the northern flank and 17th Airborne to the south. The main objectives were behind the Diersfordterwald where troops were to seize and hold the important crossroads at Hamminkeln, and the bridges over the river Issel and the Schneppenburg feature where the Germans were concentrating their artillery. They were to defend these until British XII Corps' ground forces broke through to them, which should be within twenty-four hours. The strongly reinforced 116th Panzer Division was concentrated on the north-east, and possession of the bridges over the Issel river and canal would stop these tanks being rushed to the bridge-head and so enable the ground forces to land with the minimum of interruption and breakout rapidly. As each crossing was started, from XXX Corps at Rees, to the two American crossings, an hour apart, near Rheinberg, the enemy would hesitate before committing his armour until it became clear which site was the biggest threat. By that time the airborne forces would be down and controlling the approaches. In effect they would create a *cordon sanitaire* extending from Wesel, east to the Issel and back to the Rhine at Xanten, into which XII Corps' armour would erupt.

After the bitter experience of Arnhem the attack was to be concentrated in the shortest time as well as into the smallest area; at Arnhem troops had been faced with long marches from their dropping zones giving the enemy ample time to recover from the surprise. This would not happen at the Rhine crossings as the entire assault would go in one enormous airlift as quickly as technical considerations allowed. It was a bold plan but the risk of dropping onto the German's main positions would be reduced both by the preceding attack by 15th Scottish Division and 1st Commando Brigade and by the enemy's assumption that an airborne attack would not be launched *after* the ground attack.

The huge armada would leave from eleven airfields in England and fifteen in France and would converge over Belgium before crossing the Rhine. They would be escorted by 5,000 fighters while 3,000 bombers attacked German battlefield positions and airfields. Within two hours of the landing 120 American Liberator bombers would drop supplies. Since most troop carriers held less than twenty men it would take too long for the stream to pass over. IX Troop Carrier Command, under Major-General Paul L. Williams, had found a way to reduce this time by flying their planes in tight formations of 'Vs' with nine planes flying abreast. This enabled a parachute brigade to drop in only two minutes instead of the usual ten. But it was less easy to reduce the time factor for the gliders. Because of their tow ropes the gliders and tugs required a long space which stretched the columns too far, and they could not fly in tight formations as they were unable to maintain a true course and were subjected to buffeting from the wind. It would therefore take three or even four times as long to cast off a glider unit as to drop the same number of parachute troops.

The gliders would be preceded by the paratroopers who would all land within twenty minutes in parallel streams of the two divisions.

Then the gliders would go in carrying all the support and HQ echelons, taking forty-five minutes to land 6th Airborne and 108 minutes to land the 17th Airborne. Thus no matter how efficient the RAF and Glider Pilot Regiment and the American Air Corps Troop Carrier Groups, the landings would go on over a long period and the later American gliders, especially, would have little chance of surprise.

Also, enemy flak would be a serious menace to the gliders on their long, slow glide-in to the landing zones. At one time a night attack had been considered, but the dangerous German night fighers, still very active, offset the reduced flak. There were also objections on navigational and tactical grounds to a landing in darkness. Although a daylight landing could incur a considerable loss of life, this was more than offset by the ability of the troops to see where they were, locate units and see the enemy.

On March 10th, Brigadier James Hill, commanding 3rd Parachute Brigade, visited the 9th Parachute Battalion in its camp at Netheravon in England. He held a briefing for all the COs, seconds-in-command and battalion adjutants using huge three-dimensional models, prepared from aerial photos and maps, to show exactly what they were to do. Major Napier Crookenden was at the briefing and recalls how, 'as he went on to describe the task and the plan of the Brigade, the dozen people present pressed a little closer to the model, breathed a little more quietly and gave that concentrated silent attention to the one man speaking, characteristic of all briefings for a battle.' Exercises early in the winter had given the battalion experience of dropping right on to enemy positions, 'but the presentation of such a plan in practice produced a queer but well-known feeling in the stomach.'

James Hill explained everything in his usual decisive and enthusiastic manner. 'Three thousand yards east of the Rhine and north of Wesel', recalls Major Crookenden, 'the ground rose into a low ridge, dominated by the Schneppenburg feature. Covered with thick woods of the Diersfordterwald, interspersed with a few clearings, this ridge could overlook the flat fields sloping down to the Rhine. German positions had been located by the Air Forces along the western and northern edges of these woods, and gun positions and tank harbours were thought to lie hidden in them. The German 8th Parachute and 84th Infantry Divisions were known to be holding this area, and although badly mauled in the heavy fighting west of the Rhine, it was established that the parachute troops at least would fight hard for this last German defence line. Beyond these woods to the east was the river Issel and beyond that again the beginnings of the great North German plain, into which it was Field Marshal Montgomery's plan to launch his armoured divisions as soon as possible.'

A final briefing was held on March 13th by General Eric Bols, at Divisional HQ at Aldershot. 'After General Bols's summary of the division's job', says Major Crookenden, 'each Brigadier explained his own plan in detail, and the programmes of supporting air effort and artillery were explained by the commanders and staff concerned. Eric Bols, quietly explaining the job to be done as if describing arrangements for a party, carried conviction and increased people's confidence. Nigel Poett's detailed and rather worried explanation of 5th Brigade's plans was as clear as a bell but boring to hear. James Hill's short, ardent description of 3rd Brigade's action made his three battalion commanders grin derisively at the rest of the division.'

'Gentlemen,' James Hill said, 'the artillery and air support is fantastic. And if you are worried about the kind of reception you'll get just put yourself in the place of the enemy. Beaten and demoralized, pounded by our artillery and bombers, what would you think, gentlemen, if you saw a horde of ferocious, bloodthirsty paratroopers bristling with weapons, cascading down upon you from the skies?' He finished off with an exhortation: 'But if, by any chance, you should happen to meet one of these Huns in person, you will treat him, gentlemen, with extreme disfavour.'

On March 17th the British commanders flew to meet their American counterparts. Accompanying Bols were Hill and Brigadier Bellamy, Commander 6th Air-Landing Brigade, Lieutenant-Colonel Darell-Brown, commanding the 52nd Division's light infantry and Lieutenant-Colonel Gerald Rickard, CO 1st Royal Ulster Rifles of 6th Air-Landing Brigade, who would be on the right of 6th Airborne and make contact with the Americans. They flew from Netheravon in an American C-47 (Dakota), with, as Major Crookenden records, 'an obliging pilot who gave lessons in flying to all applicants.' They touched down some twenty miles from Chalons and were rushed in a jeep caravan along dusty roads to 17th Divisional HQ. 'Here a profusion of glistening sentries and saluting orderlies escorted the British party into the General's room where General Miley and his regimental commanders were already assembled.' There was coffee and small-talk and then the party went to the briefing room.

Miley described in general terms the background picture of the battle and the particular tasks of his division. He was full of humour and confidence, but questioned his chief staff officer whenever he was stumped by some fact or place name. To the British his plan seemed incredibly vague. After Miley the fire support programme was detailed by the artillery commander and then the commander of each regimental combat team explained his proposed actions. The first to speak was Edson P. Raff, commander of 507th Parachute Infantry Regiment. He was well known to British commanders as 'a tough, opinionated and cheerful leader', as Crookenden recalls. 'In answer to Miley's request for a plan, he looked around slowly and began: "Well, General, it's like this. In these woods there's a bunch of Heinies. We drop here, 'bout half a mile away, and we just go and sort 'em out. We fly in West to East and I jump No 1 from the lead ship." Raff sat down amid muffled laughter.'

The other commanders were more detailed in their briefing but it was still a very loosely organized affair, in contrast to the detailed 6th Division briefing, but the Americans seemed satisfied. 'To the British this American vagueness seemed excessive and only the obvious high fighting spirit and remarkable discipline of this American division prevented a feeling of uneasiness.'

On Monday, March 19th, a convoy of lorries took the 6th Airborne to their transit camps in East Anglia. The 3rd Brigade went to a disused mushroom farm in Essex. Les Jones says 'they spent most of the time in physical training and checking equipment. All of us wrote letters and in the evenings there were concerts. The RAF at Earls Colne allowed us the use of their cinema and a lot of us went there one night, otherwise it was confined to camp. Made you realize the show had started.'

In France much the same thing was happening to 17th Airborne troops. The division, rested and re-equipped, left in secret for a dozen marshalling fields. Frank Langstone and Justin P. Buckridge, write of the official history of 17th Airborne Division:

The airfields were not too bad, the GIs opined as they inspected their temporary homes. For one thing, it was no longer so cold that tents were uncomfortable. They had a little time to rest or bat the breeze or do whatever they pleased without having a three-striper looking for them for some detail. Phonographs kept grinding out good old American music, over the loudspeaker system. The Red Cross was on hand, providing a real link with home as smokes, gum, doughnuts and coffee were dispensed. The troopers of the 17th were getting a lot of attention. And they were to get a lot of attention of another kind in just a few days.

Meanwhile, US Ninth Army was preparing for the assault over the Rhine. The 30th and 79th Divisions were to spearhead XVI Corps' attack. A site was carefully selected on the river Maas that closely resembled the actual crossing point of the Rhine. The regimental reconnaissance team had already advised that the crossing should be made in a column of battalions and as 2nd Battalion, 119th Infantry, was selected to lead, they were given priority in training with assault boats. Accompanied by their supporting 187th Engineer Combat Battalion they settled down to train and establish close liaison with each other.

It was essential not to give the enemy any warning of the attack and so the boats would not be taken over the dyke until the troops were on their way. As the lead force the 2nd Battalion had the most difficult task as they would have to carry their boats over the twenty-five foot high dyke to launch them into the water. This condition existed on both Maas and Rhine, so they had plenty of practice. According to Private Ralph Albert, he and his group just couldn't get the knack of carrying the boat: 'although we practised over and over again, every damn time one or other of us would trip, slip or drop the boat as we raced up the slippery bank in the dark. After several days it was no longer a joke and we dreaded the real thing.'

Enough assault boats would be available to carry 2nd Battalion infantry in two waves with groups organized on a permanent basis, each teamed with their respective engineer boat crews with whom they stayed in close contact until landed on the far shore. Like the infantry and tanks, this marrying up of different supporting units was essential to mutual confidence.

Gradually by improvisation and trial and error the many snags were ironed out. Outboard motors needed a special oil that eventually turned up after long delays. Life jackets were in short supply and the promised Storm boats never arrived. The Buffaloes developed a maintenance problem which prevented them being used in water! That, too, was eventually overcome. Practices went on until teams neared perfection by going over and over the same routine. 'This was done,' reported Colonel Van Bibber, 'to set a definite pace for the training and to impress the seriousness of the project and the necessity for precision on the troops. When the leading battalion could complete its crossings in twenty-five minutes we knew we were ready.'

At the point selected for 79th Division's crossing, the bank sloped quite steeply towards the water, while on the far side the bank was more gentle and ideal for a landing beach; beyond that lay green fields. Patrols on the west bank believed there were only listening posts on the far side. But aerial observers were sure the far bank was occupied, probably by a single company. Although 'confirmed' by prisoners, it was later found to be untrue. The dyke was held in strength, while the river bank had only listening posts at night. Nearly a mile back from the dyke was a railroad embankment where the enemy's main reserves were located. American patrols discovered the front was held by elements of the 2nd Parachute Division and the 180th Infantry Division.

On the British front reconnaissance was difficult. The extensive smoke screen which was intended to hide British operations from German eyes obscured the far bank and so on two occasions the smoke was stopped for the commanders to have a good look. Security measures prevented battalion commanders taking their officers nearer than 1,000 yards from the bank, the only exception being the extreme left where there was good cover almost to the dyke.

Horrocks did not want reconnaissance parties on the flat polder land and ordered his Chief Staff Officer, Brigadier C. B. 'Splosh' Jones, to establish an office at XXX Corps HQ. This was known as 'The Pig Hotel', after the Corps' sign, a wild boar. Nobody was allowed forward without visiting the 'hotel' where on a map they were shown the 'rooms' allocated them. There were large numbers of aerial photos and each brigade was provided with an accurate ground model which enabled each man to know his role, and equally important, to know what the flanks were doing. This was very much a Montgomery touch, again resulting from his experience in World War One, when few officers, let alone men, even knew where they were fighting. After a visit by Montgomery, a veteran RSM in the desert had said how he 'talked to the officers, then to the NCOs. He told us everything; what his plan was for the battle, what he wanted the regiment to do, what he wanted *me* to do . . .' That was his way. According to Brigadier Villiers, commanding 46th Brigade of 15th Scottish Division, 'It was this detailed briefing which contributed considerably to the high morale, which was evident in all units, in spite of the obvious magnitude of the tasks ahead. The preparations were very thorough: every single driver "walked the course" from the marshalling area to as near the river as it was safe to go; and every officer of those units which were to approach the river on foot also walked the course.'

The movement of the vast assembly of vehicles had to be arranged under the control of the Bank Group, which in addition to the Royal Berkshires also included Royal Signals and REME detachments. Every vehicle due to cross within forty-eight hours was given a serial number listed in divisional priority tables. It was the responsibility of each unit to ensure their vehicles left the marshalling area in the right order. But if a tactical development required particular vehicles to go forward, word would be passed back to alter priorities. 'One of the biggest problems for the "G" staff at Divisional HQ was deciding on priorities. A very large number of non-divisional vehicles had to be included on the priority list—these included Corps and Army Troops, recce parties of all arms, and the land-tail of the 17th US and 6th British Airborne Divisions.'

The crossing places were determined by bridging sites, which in turn depended on the ability of the Buffaloes to enter and leave the river. 8th Battalion Royal Scots, for instance, practised at Houthuizen on the Maas. Night crossings of rivers were nothing new to them but they had never used Buffaloes before. Lieutenant-Colonel Barclay Pearson, their CO, went to the Xanten area to reconnoitre and scanned across the swiftly flowing grey waters. The heavy smoke-screen was all but impenetrable, except for a few thin patches when the far bank could be glimpsed. The flat, almost bare flood plain, which could be swept by machine-gun fire from the dyke, presented a discouraging view. The ground seemed excessively muddy and there were doubts about the ability of the Buffaloes to get across. By good fortune, though, a German soldier gave himself up and, seeking to ingratiate himself, revealed a much better track for the Buffaloes. Engineers could blow gaps in the dykes at that point to let the Buffaloes through.

After the carnage of the Rhineland battle, 51st Highland Division had been pulled out of the line and sent back to Holland and Belgium for special training. Their attack, spearheading XXX Corps, would be a secondary assault to the main bridgehead of XII Corps from which the armoured 'expanding torrent' would begin. The division would cross at Rees, between Wesel and Emmerich, enabling the Engineers to construct bridges to carry the heavy equipment into Germany. 153rd Brigade, with 2nd Seaforths under its command, were to take Esserden and Rees, while on their left 154th Brigade would capture Speldrop and Beinen and then move on to Esserden to link up with 153rd Brigade and consolidate the bridgehead. The 2nd Seaforths were to lead in Storm boats about 500 yards left of the main 153rd Brigade crossing, at H-Hour plus three hours, to pass through 5th Black Watch at Esserden and head for the main road running north out of Rees which they would block to prevent the Germans moving reinforcements in to the bridgehead from Emmerich.

After spending nearly two months training and re-organizing in Sussex, 1st Commando Brigade had moved to Asten on the Maas in January where they had taken part in fierce ·fighting around Roermond, while attached to US Ninth Army. The Brigade comprised No 3 and No 6 Commandos from the Army and No 45 and No 46 from the Royal Marines. On March 6th they concentrated at Venray and immediately began two weeks intensive training for the Rhine crossing, using a creek at Wansum on the Maas, at the end of which time they were confident they could tackle any river crossing.

When Lieutenant-General Dempsey, Commander of Second Army, visited them to watch them practise with Storm boats, Brigadier Mills-Roberts, their commander, took the opportunity to point out their inherent problems; they were 'unreliable, high-revving monstrosities and remained so despite all the efforts by REME', who did their best to improve the boats. He asked Dempsey for permission to bring from the Channel a number of Dories, small whalers with reliable engines that the Commandos had used many times, as rescue boats to pull any casualties from the water. Dempsey was undecided and asked that he should first take a trip on the Maas in a Storm boat, which broke down in midstream, necessitating his rescue: Mills-Roberts got his Dories.

Once the ground between the Maas and Rhine was cleared Mills-Roberts organized a reconnaissance. With his Brigade Major, Donald Hopson, and his four Troop Commanders, he took a look at their objective: 'Looking across the river I saw the town of Wesel rising up from the high ground, with the tall spires of several churches reaching up to the sky. It was going to be difficult to marshal over 1,600 men for the crossings without being observed.' Dempsey had already explained that the town was their initial objective as it was the key communications centre and was believed to be strongly held by the enemy. Prior to the attack Bomber Command would 'strike a sharp blow' on Wesel to destroy as much of the enemy as possible.

In operation 'Plunder', the overall code-name for the Rhine crossings, 21st Army Group had assigned a specially important task to 1st Commando Brigade to capture and hold Wesel in a separate operation called 'Widgeon'. It was unlikely they could seize the entire

town before the Germans counter-attacked but they were to grab a
compact area including a large factory in the northern suburbs. After
landing at Grav Insel, a most unpromising site of mud flats which the
enemy would least suspect, the Commandos would abandon the
bridgehead completely and disappear into the ruins of Wesel. They
would have to hold the town until morning and then clear a route to
the river bank for a Buffalo ferry service to carry across the Cheshire
Regiment to reinforce them. By holding Wesel they could deny to the
enemy the routes through the town by which they could counter-attack the bridgehead. Then 17th Airborne Divisions, dropping at 10
am, would move to link up with the Commandos and between them
would hold Wesel for another four hours while the Airborne operation was completed.

On the evening of March 19th, the Brigade's transport loaded at
Venray with troops and equipment. The trucks drove away into the
night and for four hours the convoy moved steadily towards the
Rhine. They passed through Venlo, crossed the German border and
rumbled on to their destination west of the main Xanten road and
about five miles west of the river near Wesel. It was bitterly cold and
persistent drizzle fell as troops disembarked in strict silence and were
directed to billets, many in disused factories.

On the following morning the Commandos stared at scenes of incredible activity. In every direction were masses of guns, tanks and
every kind of supplies for what Churchill described as the 'last great
heave'. Thousands of troops were encamped on the approaches to
the Rhine. A never-ending stream of trucks travelled every route
bringing in ever more men and equipment, all largely hidden from
German view by the smoke-screen.

Soon everything was ready, the vast stores had been stock-piled
and the men were trained. From its positions some thirty miles back
the huge army prepared to move forward without lights, on the night
of March 20th. Through Nijmegen there passed immense columns of
trucks, tanks, transporters, armoured bulldozers, sledges, winches
and fifty-foot long pontoon trailers carrying landing craft from Belgium. By dawn on the 21st the army was ready on the banks of the
Rhine hidden by specialist American camouflage experts. The next
night the huge mass of artillery moved in, under cover of a continuous RAF attack. To their south the American 30th Division
moved up its forces, its troops, armour, bridging materials and the
big guns. Everything was in place for the great crossing.

17 'Take the Rhine on the run!'

Eisenhower's firm decision not to push any big force through the Remagen bridgehead was received by Bradley with bitter resentment. His normally laconic composure gave way to righteous anger made all the more acrid as he saw everywhere the hand of Montgomery. Outwardly Bradley was mild-mannered, his slow Missouri drawl suggesting an easy-going person, but he was in fact quite temperamental and easily took offence. Writing much later, however, Bradley thought the British plans for the drive on Berlin and the Baltic had been 'shrewd', and he admitted that he and other American generals were at that time politically naïve; they had thought only in terms of the current military situation and did not comprehend that every military decision would subsequently shape the political and economic order of Europe in the years to follow. Some felt that Bradley carried more blame for this than Eisenhower.

The crossing of the Rhine was the biggest military challenge since Normandy, offering the prospect of a rapid breakout into Germany. This was the redeeming goal that would restore Bradley's image. It was also important to Bradley that the world's press should proclaim that it was American troops that were first over. Bradley fumed that when American troops did get to the Rhine opposite the Ruhr, Montgomery had refused permission for Simpson's forces to make a surprise crossing and he had no doubts that the devious, self-righteous British Field Marshal had persuaded Eisenhower to stop Hodges's Remagen bridgehead from receiving the support it needed to break out. Bradley was peeved about the orders relegating his forces to a secondary role and saw in Hodges's bridgehead and Patton's powerful drive an opportunity to get his two armies so deeply involved in the Rhine crossings that Eisenhower would not be able to order them to withdraw.

The US Third and Seventh Armies were now arranged about the triangular enclave of the Saar-Palatinate. 'Sandy' Patch's Seventh Army had been reinforced with divisions from General de Lattre de Tassigny's French First Army, his task to occupy the attention of German First Army while Patton burst over the Moselle. To the east lay the Rhine, on the north-west was the Moselle, while the south-west was bordered by the Lauter-Sarre river line. The threat was obvious to all but the most obtuse German commanders. General Paul Hausser cried out for reinforcements from anywhere to stiffen the remnants of his new command, Army Group 'G'; he could see only annihilation facing both Seventh and First Armies if they were forced to hold onto the *Westwall*. But Hitler would not budge; at all costs, he thundered repetitively, the troops must hold the *Westwall!*

At 1 am on March 15th the sky over the Blies river on Patch's Seventh Army's front shook to the roar of the bomber streams converging on the east bank. The 'heavies' of Bomber Command and US 8th Air Force opened their bomb doors and down went hundreds of tons of death and destruction. Even before the ground had settled and the bombers were out of the area, XXI Corps with the 3rd and 45th Divisions of XV Corps broke from their start-lines and headed for the enemy positions. They were followed at 6.45 am by the main force of VI Corps and the 3rd Algerian Division which attacked at 7.15 am.

With the banks of the Blies cleared of mines in the selected footbridge and ferry sites, 45th Division went over in assault craft and soon four companies of 180th Infantry Regiment were across. The 120th Engineer Battalion had two footbridges operational and the rest of the regiment were crossing fifteen minutes later. By dawn 180th Infantry were pushing northwards along the west bank of the Blies while 157th Infantry Regiment drove ahead on their right. Behind them the 179th Regiment mopped up the enemy by-passed in the leading assault. Taken by surprise, the demoralized German troops fell back to their main defences, the formidable steel and concrete fortifications of the *Westwall*. At 5 am 100th Division began its attack on Bitche, the last French town before the border. The 397th Infantry streamed forward to capture the high ground to the north of the forts and after a hard fight entered Schorbach by midday. Troops from the 398th Infantry going for Forts Freudenberg and Scheisseck, and from the 399th Infantry attacking the Reyersvillers Ridge, encountered moderate resistance. At the same time, the 2nd and 3rd Battalions with the 399th Infantry fought their way into Bitche itself, taking seventy-five prisoners including the garrison commander. For this action, 100th Division's commander, General Burress, was made the first 'citizen of honour' in the town's history. Then 71st Division, under General Grow, took over Bitche while the 100th moved on towards the *Westwall*. To the east of Bitche, VI Corps began clearing Alsace.

In five days US Seventh Army rolled forward until all its divisions reached the German border. By this date General Felber, commanding the German Seventh Army, could no longer ignore the imminent threat of being cut off. He personally, with his Chief of Staff, had been forced to hide in the forest when American Thunderbolts and Mustangs had raced overhead and an American armoured column had roared by in their full view. In their steel and concrete defences, the German First Army could not resist indefinitely against increasing American pressure. The long awaited spring weather had at last given the fighter-bombers absolute mastery over any armour or trucks that were foolish enough to move by day.

XXI Corps started close to the Siegfried Line defences to take Saarbrucken and the nearby towns on their way to the Rhine. Inevitably it was a hard-fought slogging match through built-up areas, and their artillery and tank destroyers fired over 5,000 shells at all identified gun emplacements and bunkers. But the enemy kept replying. Finally on March 18th, XXI Corps' HQ was relieved to hear that Patton's Third Army advancing from the Moselle had reached St Wendel, some thirty miles north of Saarbrucken. This thrust threatened to cut the Germans off from the Rhine and they were bound to withdraw. On March 17th Kesselring, ever mindful of Hitler's dictates, ambiguously gave instructions to hold the positions but not to get trapped. That was enough for Hausser to justify retreating from the most dangerous positions, if not authority for wholesale withdrawal. Gradually divisions began to slip away from the *Westwall*.

General Eddy's XII Corps in the centre then easily forced a river crossing over the Moselle. Ahead lay the Hunsruck mountains which Bradley doubted Patton's armour could get through without delays and casualties. His fears were groundless; Hugh Gaffey's 4th Armoured, Patton's favourite division, swept forward and in two days reached Bad Kreuznach, only about fifteen miles from the Rhine and almost cutting the Saar-Palatinate in two. There, Patton halted his tanks; intuition told him the enemy would soon counter-attack. His judgement was to prove correct.

Kesselring again went to Hitler on March 15th. The Saar-Palatinate, he insisted, had no decisive importance for the campaign, although Kesselring acknowledged that, as a soldier, he had to respect the high-level views of OKW. The portly Bavarian knew he commanded some respect from Hitler as a result of his skilful defence of Italy so he went on to explain carefully that while the Palatinate probably could not be held, the American advance could be delayed by fighting a rearguard operation in the mountainous country that was extraordinarily difficult for the attackers, who were too dependent on armour. After some discussion, Hitler reluctantly agreed and gave general approval that Kesselring could evacuate the *Westwall* on First Army's right, providing they only withdrew to the next defences. With that Kesselring had to be satisfied, but knowing the Führer's capacity for changing his mind, he wasted no time and telephoned Westphal, his Chief of Staff, even before he left the Führer's HQ.

Immediately on arrival back at Ziegenburg, he set Felber's Seventh Army the task of covering the northern flank of First Army by 'local defence'. Hausser at Army Group 'G' would have to co-ordinate the manoeuvres of the inner flanks of his two armies with those of the right flank of the Seventh Army. 'This required energetic tactical control from close to the front', wrote Kesselring. He thought that at this stage it would serve little purpose to consider the strategic implications simply because the evacuation of the Palatinate had been delayed too long. He learned then of Patton's breakthrough at Bad Kreuznach and hoped it could be blunted by a 'counter-attack with sufficiently powerful panzer support'. This must have been wishful thinking as by that time such forces did not exist in the Palatinate and were scarcely possible anywhere south of the Ruhr. When they did attack, Patton's armour was ready and, with the aid of US XII Corps' fire power, cut Kesselring's forces to ribbons. By March 19th the situation was desperate; the right wing of Seventh Army 'had been unhinged'. There was an immediate danger of Patton's army thrusting for Oppenheim as his armour drove beyond Kreuznach towards Worms-Ludwigshafen which would cut off the whole of Army Group 'G' and destroy it. There was little doubt in Kesselring's mind that he could no longer defend the Palatinate.

More news soon arrived that American tanks had reached Kaiserslautern. The counter-measures Kesselring had directed Seventh Army to carry out had at least slowed down the American advance and now Felber was desperately trying to extricate his forces through the bridges at Speyer and Germersheim, which Kesselring personally as-

24 Buffaloes move forward

25 The 15th Scottish Division troops landing on the east bank of the Rhine

26 Commandos in Wesel

27 Cheshire Regiment arriving in Buffaloes at Wesel to reinforce Commandos

28 'Here come the Airborne'

29 Airborne troops deploying from gliders

30 Airborne troops digging-in along the Issel canal

31 Second Army tanks link up with the Airborne

sured him were safe for the time being. The bridges here, as at Wesel, were heavily reinforced with flak and each night after the 16th, Kesselring watched his forces streaming back across the Rhine.

General Kurt Student, Schlemm's predecessor as commander of First Parachute Army, had been severely wounded when the RAF had raided his HQ at Dinxperlo, and now Schlemm was destined for the same fate. On March 21st the RAF staged one of its many raids on the Wesel area and caught Schlemm's HQ. He was severely wounded and had to be evacuated. General Blumentritt, Commander of Twenty-Fifth Army, relates that 'the Commander of "Heeresgruppe H", General Blaskowitz, informed us that General Schlemm . . . had suffered a brain concussion from an air attack and was hardly able to fulfil his duties in that capacity any more. On 27th March, I received an order over the telephone from the "Heeresgruppe" which stated that I was to take over the command of *1st Fallschirme Army*. I was to leave without my staff and take over this command temporarily as General Schlemm's condition had become worse.'

Forbidden to pull their meagre forces back over the Rhine the German commanders desperately struggled to form new defence lines; trenches were dug and log road blocks constructed in a vain attempt to hold up the onward thrust of tanks and half-tracks. But it was hopeless as American columns burst through the wooded country along every track and road, often appearing behind half-finished defences which then had to be abandoned. Karl Sommers, a German engineer, remembers how 'For hours we struggled to build a road block across a winding road in the wooded hills south of Kaiserslautern. A gang of Polish workers had been sent to help us by cutting logs and carrying them to the road. The sound of gunfire had been getting nearer by the hour and we could hear the rumble of tanks, but our commander, a SS Lieutenant, insisted they were ours. About mid-afternoon, the sounds of battle grew much louder and then the Poles came running from the woods. The Lieutenant yelled for them to stop but next moment there was a great crashing and American tanks burst from the forest. . . .'

That day Hitler finally and with bitter reluctance consented to Felber's Seventh Army withdrawing to the east bank of the Rhine and what was left streamed back in disorder. The remnants of First Army desperately held on to three shrinking bridgeheads, their commanders faced with near-impossible conflicts; if they blew the bridges too soon even more of their troops would be lost, too late and it could be another Remagen.

On March 22nd Patton's Third and Patch's Seventh Armies linked up. Patton had successfully penetrated through the Saar-Palatinate and deprived the Germans of its industrial resources, making them wholly dependent on the Ruhr. By crossing the Moselle he had by-passed the Siegfried Line defences while Patch's Seventh Army had painfully butted its way through, taking the enemy's main attention. Time and again Patton had ruthlessly crossed the boundary between his and Seventh Army without consulting Patch. Now his Third Army was overrunning the remaining enclaves in order to close to the Rhine from Koblenz in the north, through Mainz to Mannheim. He had done his bit to fulfil Eisenhower's wish that his armies 'close the length of his entire line to the Rhine', even if the drive, which was later designated the 'Palatinate Campaign', was never fully authorized by SHAEF. Patton's motivation was clear enough—he was determined to get back into the limelight. He was shrewd enough to realize that he had not simply struck a weak section of the enemy front, but that it was collapsing before his forces. Nevertheless it was an opportunity to get over the Rhine and win more popular accolades and get one up on Montgomery.

Patton, Bradley and Hodges were worried lest Montgomery should succeed in persuading Eisenhower to let him have more American divisions to support his scheme to drive into Germany. But in fairness to Montgomery, he was, as we have seen, no longer thinking just of beating the German Army, but of frustrating the undisguised Russian advance into Scandinavia. Unlike Montgomery, whose austerity sometimes bordered on the recluse, Bradley at least had Eisenhower's ear. For some while the Supreme Commander's Chief of Staff, Bedell Smith, had been urging him to take a short rest before the final thrust in spite of Eisenhower's protests that he didn't need one. Eventually, when an American citizen offered him the use of his villa in Cannes, Eisenhower agreed, provided Bradley went with him. So, while Montgomery and Devers struggled with the immense complexities of their army groups, Bradley went on holiday to the Riviera.

There, in the seclusion of the villa, Eisenhower and Bradley could converse long and quietly on the moves after the Rhine. 'Since January, and especially after Remagen, his inclination had been to keep increasing the strength of the attack on Bradley's front.' Originally he had viewed this as a diversionary attack, and then as a secondary attack to Montgomery's main thrust. Then in his mind it took the form of an alternative major drive 'should Montgomery's become halted'. Now, as they sat in the sun, he saw it 'equal in scope and importance to Montgomery's'. On March 21st, two days before Montgomery's crossings, he contacted General Bull and discussed his ideas with him. The SHAEF staff were instructed to arrange a directive to Bradley to 'establish a firm bridgehead over the Rhine in the Frankfurt area, then make an "advance in strength" towards Kassel', there to make a junction between Hodges's forces driving east from Remagen and Patton's going north from Frankfurt. South of the Ruhr there would conveniently be a force equal in strength to 21st Army Group's north of the Ruhr. Cock-a-hoop at the decision, which removed any chance of his losing divisions to Montgomery, Bradley told Patton: 'Take the Rhine on the run!'

Patton needed no urging and drove for the Rhine, not bothering to clear up pockets of resistance, which Montgomery would have insisted upon, and which, it must be remembered, was one of Eisenhower's previous reasons for closing to the Rhine along its length—that no German forces should remain on the west. The columns threading along every road created the utmost congestion as they met Patch's Seventh Army moving up from the south. 'It was one hell of a traffic jam,' recalled one truck driver. 'When we ran into other columns it was like New York in the rush hour.'

Determined that he was going to cross not later than the night of the 22nd/23rd March, the night before Montgomery's assault, Patton wasted no time in bringing forward his engineers and their convoys of bridging materials. To cross a major river successfully assault troops need a great deal of support. A mass of construction and support troops provided the rubber boats taking the first troops over, rafts to ferry across armour and built the permanent bridges to stand up to flood and adverse weather. Patton had already collected together a huge train of engineering supplies for his bridges. Crossing in the Mainz area, where the river was no more than 300 feet wide, according to Bennet H. Fishler, commander of the 8th Tank Battalion of 4th Armoured Division, certainly did not present the same magnitude of problems facing Montgomery's forces. But the American Engineers who laboured long and hard to build the bridges did not get much publicity for their effort. The world gained the impression that Patton had raced up to the river, leapt into boats and paddled across. With his bridging convoys rumbling forward, Patton exhorted his commanders to get across a day or so earlier than they were prepared for. To the background of roaring artillery pounding enemy positions along the east bank before Darmstadt, Patton confronted General Manton S. Eddy, the bespectacled, portly commander of US XII Corps. Mincing no words he demanded: 'We've got to get a bridgehead at once! Every day we save means the saving of hundreds of American lives!'

Eddy had planned to cross on the 23rd when he would have been organized: 'General,' he protested, 'I'm not ready yet', at which Patton acrimoniously demanded to know why, proclaiming that 'they could take the Rhine on the run'. Patton went to a large map of the sector on which red and blue arrows marked enemy and Allied troops. He and Eddy studied it for a while and concluded that the enemy expected them to cross at Mainz; they would therefore use that site only as a diversion. Patton scrutinized the map a while longer, then jabbed his finger onto the village of Oppenheim, fifteen miles south of Mainz. 'We'll cross here tomorrow night', he commanded. Eddy had actually earmarked this site as an alternative to Mainz if that should prove too heavily defended. It was a good choice because there was a small barge harbour which could be reached from the village but could not be seen from across the Rhine, making it ideal for launching the Storm boats. Meanwhile to keep the enemy guessing about Mainz, they laid on a heavy smoke screen around that site.

But, in fact, around Mainz, Felber's Seventh Army was quite incapable of putting up serious resistance. He had only one corps, a collection of mostly old men, depot and supply troops grouped into four loosely organized divisions which had no regular fighting soldiers amongst them, and only five effective Jagdpanther guns. 'To those of us who were in ignorance of what the Germans had,' wrote one soldier of 26th Division, 'it was certain that all hell would break loose once we started across.' While commanders 'couldn't wait to be committed', junior officers and men had neither illusions of valour nor enthusiasm. The tension, the fear and bravado were all a part of Patton's stage management for the waiting press. But the infantry didn't know that and their courage was real enough as they set out to cross the Rhine.

Patton called in his Chief Engineer, Major-General Conklin, and told him to get his assault craft forward immediately. Patton had built up a stock of assault boats well behind his lines and held onto them since the autumn. He had also 'acquired' twelve landing craft under naval personnel who had been rehearsing a crossing at Toul, so in spite of his derision at Montgomery's preparations, he, too, had collected everything necessary.

Robert Welch of the 23rd Regiment remembers that they 'spent the last hours in houses and buildings along a narrow street in the village. About 10 pm we began to file out and moved quietly down to the small harbour. Although there was plenty of gunfire to the north and south of us, where we were was too quiet. At the harbour the engineers had the boats ready launched and waiting. As luck would have it the moon came out as we were pushing off and it seemed too damn bright as we dipped our paddles and pushed across . . .' Softly-paddling echelons of 23rd Infantry boats cut their way through the current across the 300 feet or so of the river. 'The river seemed so wide', said Robert Welch, 'from that little boat and it seemed ages before the far shore came into view, shelving and muddy. My boat nosed into the bank and we stepped out into the water, which was very cold.'

The leading boat touched the bank and its men went silently ashore literally bumping into some German soldiers who threw their guns down and their hands up in sheer terror. But their exclamations alerted a party manning Spandaus only yards away. 'We scrambled onto the bank and I flung myself flat as the machine-guns ripped away. Some of the boys flung grenades and the gun fire stopped after a few searing flashes and bangs, leaving us to race further ashore. But then others opened up and we were pinned down for a while.'

Twenty men were killed or wounded along the banks as the 23rd Regiment fought its way ashore. Behind them more assault boats streamed across while ponderous rafts manned by engineer assault troops ferried over more infantry and anti-tank guns. The infantry streamed off into the darkness to deploy and hold the bridgehead. Groups of enemy troops appeared with machine-guns, or more often old rifles with which they put up a stubborn but short-lived resistance. When dawn broke on the 23rd, 5th Division had six battalions across the Rhine.

The telephone call caught Bradley having breakfast in the sun-filled room at his HQ, Château de Namur. It was Patton, his high-pitched voice even higher with excitement:

'Brad, don't tell anyone, but I'm across . . .'

Bradley almost choked on his coffee: 'Well, I'll be damned,' he exclaimed and spluttered. 'You mean across the Rhine?'

'Sure I am. I sneaked a division over last night. There are so few Krauts around they don't know it yet: we'll keep it secret until we know how it goes . . .' So, while Patton was jubilant at beating Montgomery across the Rhine, his excitement was contained, just in case he didn't manage to hold on.

But the effervescent Patton could not contain himself for long. A few hours later, his Liaison Officer at 12th Army Group, Lieutenant-Colonel Richard Stillman, released details of Patton's latest stroke, with a few taunting references to Montgomery's detailed preparations: 'Without benefit of aerial bombardment, ground smoke, artillery preparations or airborne assistance, the Third Army at 22.00 hours, Thursday evening 22nd March, crossed the Rhine.' His words were not quite true, since there had been preparations and smoke at Mainz in a successful deception plan. But Patton couldn't restrain himself and that evening he telephoned again: 'Brad,' he piped, 'for God's sake, tell the world we're across. We knocked down 33 Krauts today when they came after our pontoon bridges. I want the world to know the Third Army made it before Montgomery starts across.'

18 The storming of the Rhine

It dawned fine on March 23rd 1945 with a slight haze that had swirls of smoke mingling in it. By mid-morning the sun blazed from a cloudless sky upon the placid waters of the Rhine. Trooper Bob Nunn of 46 Royal Marine Commando sat on an abandoned oil drum in the factory where his troop had been billeted, cleaning his Sten yet again. 'It was not', he reflected, 'a morning upon which I was likely to be called to fight.' But an hour later he was with the rest of his Commando gathered around Lieutenant-General Ritchie, Commander of XII Corps, who told them they were going to cross the Rhine that night. With a sinking feeling in his stomach Trooper Nunn realized he might not see another dawn. Ritchie went on: 'I think, although my knowledge of military history is a little rusty, that you will be the first British troops ever to cross this river. Not even Marlborough attempted it . . .' (He had apparently forgotten Guards Armoured who crossed at Nijmegen the previous September.)

The Rhine crossing was an event second only to Normandy and the top brass assembled to witness their forces. Lieutenant-General Horrocks left his XXX Corps' HQ to go to an observation point on high ground which overlooked the Rhine. Eisenhower travelled up from Cannes to spend the night of March 23rd with Simpson at General Anderson's XVI Corps' HQ. He and the other senior American commanders were to stay up all night to watch from a church tower at Rheinberg. Churchill did not want to miss the great event either and, accompanied by Field Marshal Sir Alan Brooke, flew from England to Montgomery's HQ. And at 3 pm, while the Prime Minister was flying over Belgium, Montgomery gave the order: 'Over the Rhine, then let us go. And good hunting to you on the other side.'

Montgomery had decided that 'Plunder', the overall operation covering the crossing of the Rhine, would go ahead together with its subordinate operations, 'Widgeon', the Commandos' attack that night, while 'Varsity' the airborne assault, would be launched the following morning. It was about the time that Patton's Liaison Officer was releasing the details of Third Army's crossing, but if Montgomery had heard the news by then, it was never mentioned.

During the afternoon, too, Brigadier Mills-Roberts, Commander of 1st Commando Brigade, addressed his troops. He spoke loudly and clearly, his words full of fire and fervour for the coming operation. The listening troops were whipped into a frenzy of enthusiasm for the assault. The Brigadier went over the plan in detail.

No 46 Royal Marine Commando and Brigade Tactical HQ would cross first in Buffaloes of 77th Assault Squadron, Royal Engineers. Their task was to seize a bridgehead at Grav Insel. No 6 Commando would leave soon after in Storm boats from a creek a mile downstream and divert German attention from the main crossing. Engineers would send them up empty, 'flat out', to take on the Commandos opposite their beachhead. Next, No 45 Royal Marine, with No 3 Commando bringing up the rear in Buffaloes. No 46 Royal Marine Commando was to break into Wesel while No 6 Commando marked the route with white tape for the brigade to follow in Indian file. The sappers were responsible for launching the Storm boats, clearing the minefields on both sides of the river and establishing routes on the other side. The Brigadier then listed the mortars and guns, detailed the rest of the weapons and told them what help they would get from the RAF, and how the Airborne Divisions would arrive on the following morning. The men were cheering by the time he concluded with the rousing entreaty: 'Never in the history of human warfare have so many guns supported so few men. When you go in tonight, cut *hell* out of them!'

It was over. The men knew what they had to do and when they would do it. They were dismissed and told to rest for the remainder of the day. But as Bob Nunn recalls: 'We were too enthused, too excited and could talk of nothing but the operation. We just lay about on our bunks or gathered in small groups to talk while checking weapons and ammunition yet again. I remember I couldn't even eat, and one of my mates, who did get his dinner, went sick with nerves not long after.' They went over the plan endlessly.

Eventually Friday evening came. A correspondent from *The Times* watched the events building up. There was no abnormal traffic on the road that evening, he noted, nothing different from the previous days. At HQ men were queuing with mess tins in hand waiting

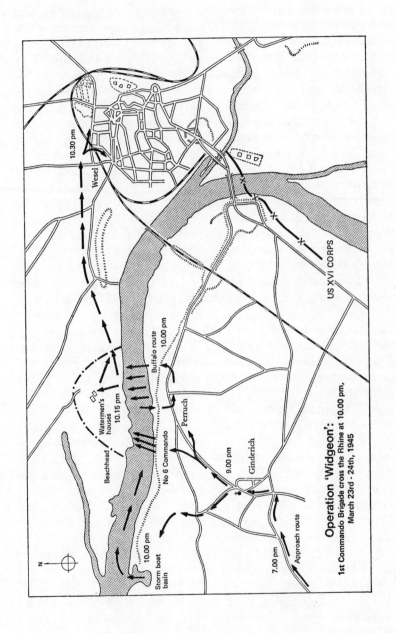

Operation 'Widgeon':
1st Commando Brigade cross the Rhine at 10.00 pm,
March 23rd - 24th, 1945

US XVI CORPS

Wesel

10.30 pm

10.15 pm
Watermen's
houses

Beachhead

No 6 Commando

Buffalo route
10.00 pm

Perruch

10.00 pm

Storm boat
basin

9.00 pm

Ginderich

7.00 pm

Approach route

N

for their evening meal. Groups of officers were talking at tent flaps
and around half-screened lamps, everywhere things were purposely
casual, but there was an underlying atmosphere of suppressed excitement, a heartening feeling that everything was ready now. Bob Nunn
was walking back with his dinner when he and a couple of friends
stopped to watch a preliminary air raid. 'It was about half-past five
when a flight of RAF medium bombers (Bostons) roared over very
low and headed out across the river. Because of the distance to the
river and the dykes we couldn't see Wesel, but after a few minutes we
heard the flak opening up and then the crash of bombs. Only a few
minutes later the bombers came back and we could see thick smoke
rising from the direction of Wesel.'

At 7 pm the whole of 1st Commando Brigade moved up to the
Rhine and formed up just short of the west bank. A chill crept into
the air as evening drew on and the smoke drifted sluggishly along the
river. The men lay in scattered groups, quietly talking and smoking.
Dave Morris recalls: 'We had all blackened our faces and were
loaded down with equipment. The quartermaster issued each of us
with rum and biscuits and just after that there was a final mail deliv-
ery. It was difficult to read the letters because it was pretty dark by
then but we had a few hurricane lamps and even a few candles.' As
the Buffaloes manoeuvred noisily into their formations on the far
side of the Rhine RAF fighter-bombers continued to roar back and
forth, their engines intentionally drowning out the noise of the
Buffaloes.

At 7.25 pm the Sappers and a Gunner working party went silently
to the Storm boat basin. 'They worked like beavers', wrote Major
Groves of the Royal Engineers, 'smoothing off the launching ramps
and filling slit trenches which traversed the edge. There was a thick
thorn hedge through which the engineers had previously cut gaps, but
so as not to alert the enemy, they had tied the cut sections together
with pickets and wire; these were now quickly pulled aside. They
quickly taped the traffic circuit and at 7.55 pm the first lorries appeared, and the Sappers and Gunners really got down to it. There
were a few old-fashioned remarks flying about but by 8.40 pm the
last of the Storm boats was afloat and the job done.'

Meanwhile, further north opposite Rees, the 51st Highland Division had been preparing for its crossing, the first of the many to be
made by 21st Army Group that night. Buffaloes of the 4th Royal
Tanks and the Northamptonshire Yeomanry rumbled forward to
their assembly points. Ahead of them white tapes stretched towards

the water leading them on their way. They took on four companies;
7th Black Watch, 7th Argylls and 1st Black Watch of 154th Brigade
plus the 5th/7th Gordons of 153rd Brigade. Then at 9 pm, just
twenty-three hours after Patton's crossing, the first wave set off. The
154th Brigade led with 1st and 7th Black Watch. The water was
choppy and the Buffaloes spewed up a high back wash. The far shore
could just be glimpsed when the enemy opened fire with Spandaus
and mortars, sending tall plumes of water cascading over the craft.
The Buffaloes' 20mm cannon opened fire, too, their gunners hanging
on grimly as the craft pitched and tossed. The amphibians nosed to
the bank, tipped up and crawled out, the men leaping ashore. Colonel Alan Jolly, CO of 4th Royal Tanks, planted his old regimental
flag; they were across the Rhine.

It was 9.04 pm when the signal reached Horrocks: 'The Black
Watch has landed safely on the far bank.' But after landing safely
with very few casualties they met regular formations of the German
Field Army, mostly paratroopers of high quality and battle began.
Reinforcements arrived as the Buffaloes surged back and forth carrying 7th Argylls and 5th/7th Gordons. While 154th Brigade captured
the villages north of the main town of Rees, 153rd Brigade were attacking some three miles to their right on either side of Rees. The
2nd Seaforths surged across in their noisy Storm boats on the left of
the Brigade on their way to pass through 5th Black Watch to cut the
main road leading north from Rees and prevent the enemy counter-
attacking the main bridgeheads. Having paddled across under inter-
mittent shelling, they scrambled ashore, up the muddy banks while
Spandau fire whizzed overhead and mortar bombs exploded in rapid
succession. They assembled on the bank, then started off along 5th
Black Watch's axis towards Esserden, following a reconnaissance
party which had gone with the Black Watch to find a forming-up
place.

As the Germans made their first moves to oppose the landings at
Rees, it was the turn of the Commandos to launch their assault.
Mills-Roberts and his team started out for the forming-up positions
at a little before 9 pm. Donald Hopson, the Brigade Major, produced
some champagne to send them on their way. They all clambered into
a jeep and within a few minutes had reached the long lines of
Buffaloes drawn up in formation. Mills-Roberts and his team could
see that Lieutenant-Colonel T. M. Gray's No 46 RM Commando,
the spearhead unit, were already on board and with a sense of occa-

sion they, too, climbed onto their waiting Buffalo. 'Don't worry,' quipped Mills-Roberts, doing his best to keep up morale, 'Hannibal was the first man to cross the Alps on an elephant, you'll be the first to cross the Rhine in a Buffalo.' Everyone laughed dutifully at his threadbare but reassuring crack.

Just before 10 pm the gunners opened their softening up programme on Grav Insel. Within seconds the air was filled with the rumble of heavy guns, the thunder of the 5.5s of the Medium Regiments, the crack of 25-pounders, the pop-popping of literally hundreds of mortars and the persistent chatter of Vickers machine-guns. At precisely 10 pm the first Storm boat turned out of the basin and led the flotilla upstream to where No 6 Commando were waiting behind the flood bank.

A couple of hundred yards ahead of the marshalling area the ribbon of the Rhine was almost hidden with the ochreous bursts of thousands of shells, each one increasing the intensity of the thick clouds of smoke. On the right flank, around the town of Wesel, it looked to observers as though thousands of candles had been lit over the town as orange-coloured tracer shells from the Bofors guns made graceful curves towards their targets. The dull night sky glowed with the reflections of many fires. Then the last-minute preparations went on.

A BBC commentator wandered around the Buffaloes stopping here and there to talk to the soldiers. He cheerfully asked a young North Country Marine Commando:

'Do you think you'll be the first across?'

The answer came promptly back: 'Not if I can bloody-well help it mate!'

Beneath the thin veneer of calm, Mills-Roberts knew only too well the danger he and his men faced in the coming hours. He glanced towards the dyke behind which was the Rhine and, 500 yards further on, the first German defences, and fervently hoped the Commandos' marshalling areas would not be beaten up too badly when the German guns opened fire. The vast array of XII Corps' artillery was giving the enemy on the flood plain and in the defences beyond a terrific pasting. He glanced at his watch; there were ten minutes to go. All around the Buffaloes' engines were throbbing as they warmed up. As Mills-Roberts leaned forward to speak to Terry Donelly they came under starter's orders. With a steadily increasing roar, followed by a sudden jerk, the first wave of four Buffaloes raced for the water's edge. Mills-Roberts's big vehicle lurched forward, thrusting the men backwards. They were off. The assault had begun.

With a great roar the Buffaloes raced for the dyke which loomed in front, sixteen feet high. With tracks flying the Buffaloes topped the rise, slithered down onto a short beach of mud and raced for the swirling river.

'Our Buffalo skidded on the top of the dyke and seemed to slide down sideways,' recalled Bob Nunn. 'We entered the water with a huge splash that drenched most of the men inside. But the Buffalo ran quite smoothly although very low down, which seemed safer as the enemy shells which were pitching into the river appeared less dangerous. This was a fallacy we realized soon after when shrapnel and bullets began to hit us.' It took three and a half incredibly long minutes to cross the river to the landing bays which were being shelled heavily. *The Times* correspondent could not help wishing that these 'wonderful armoured amphibious vehicles' had been available at Arnhem six months before. The Buffaloes churned out of sight in the smoky darkness. 'We waited', he reported, 'while nothing happened save for our tracer. We began to wonder if something had gone wrong then the signal came in, slightly incredible at first, but confirmed by others: "First wave across. No opposition."'

Without warning the bank of Grav Insel was suddenly in front of the Buffaloes. Almost simultaneously the four Buffaloes in the first wave of 46 RM Commando touched together. The men leaped over the side into the water and were splashing ashore before the vehicles had stopped. First ashore was Captain J. D. Gibbon, commanding 'B' Troop. From the trenches a few yards ahead those Germans who had survived the artillery barrage began firing but the Commandos were already racing towards them, Tommy guns blazing, bullets slashing into the soft ground around the trenches. Captain B. W. Pierce's 'Y' Troop rushed the Germans and within a few minutes had taken sixty-five prisoners. As one German put it: 'We couldn't see anything properly. The noise was terrible and we were blinded by the flashes. We thought they had landed tanks and couldn't understand where all the men had come from.'

Dave Morris was in a later wave of 45 RM Commando:

We had sat tight and pretty apprehensive while the first waves launched their attacks. Once the signal came back that they were landed our follow-up waves set off. The Germans had woken up by now and were shelling the river, sending huge spouts of water shooting upwards and pouring back over the craft. A Buffalo following us got a direct hit that lit the river like a beacon but we made it with no worse than a wetting, splashing ashore onto a muddy bank and immediately joined in the scrap raging over the first line of trenches. A burst of enemy gun fire tore my beret off and cut my head, but I didn't even know where it came from as I fired blindly into a trench. Next moment a bunch of Germans were yelling and throwing down their weapons.

No 6 Commando was having a rough time in their noisy Storm boats. The German gunners had quickly aligned their weapons on the creek and their shelling and mortaring were deadly accurate. Casualties began to mount as the Commandos struggled the 400 yards to their narrow bridgehead. Several outboard motors packed up. Other boats disintegrated in the devastating hail of steel and explosives, flinging men into the chilly water. The Dories, so insistently called for by Mills-Roberts, did valiant work, rushing to fish men from the water or snatch them from sinking Storm boats. Gradually they got across and as they drew near to the bank, No 6 Commando fired into the German troops on the bank, and when they landed tore straight into the German defenders and smashed their way clean through the line of trenches in the darkness. Many fell wounded and dead but the defence was driven in and the increasing noise as the main force was ferried across in the Buffaloes had the effect of further confusing the enemy. Within twenty minutes, No 6 Commando troops were sending back their prisoners and setting off in single file along the bank to join the rest of the Brigade.

Mills-Roberts was especially concerned about two Watermen's houses lying further inland, known to shelter batteries of guns which could threaten the bridgehead. Two troops of Commandos from the first wave were ordered to attack them. They set off at the double, unhesitatingly blasting away at any Germans who got in their way. Captain Gibbon's 'B' Troop successfully took the left hand Waterman's house, about 500 yards inland across the flooded plain, while a few hundred yards to their right two other troops, 'A' and 'Z' under Majors Campbell and Buscall, went all out for the second Waterman's house. In both places the Germans fought as well as they could but had no real chance and were swiftly and ruthlessly overrun.

The Buffalo ferry service was going flat out in the meantime and had brought across both 45 Royal Marine and No 3 Commando. With No 6 Commando advancing along the river bank the whole Brigade was across the Rhine. A tape-laying party of No 6 Commando now marked the route with thick tape and led the way to guide the following troops, as had been done at Normandy.

German prisoners had been pressed into service to carry part of the Commandos' equipment and the newcomers were surprised at the strange sight of enemy soldiers dotted about the column and loaded with equipment. While the column quickly wound its way across the shell-torn flood plain, snatches of conversation were to be heard. One Commando was heard to say to a pal about the German prisoners:

'I've got a fine big bugger 'ere, 'e's doing a grand job.'

There was a short pause after which his pal reluctantly agreed, but then added defensively: 'My little bugger isn't too bad neither. . . .'

The men from No 6 Commando spread out on reaching the outskirts of Wesel, just before 10.30 pm. They lay in the dark, their blackened faces close to the ground, waiting and listening as the bomber force came over. The murmur grew to a tremendous roar that bounced back from buildings and shook the ground. Men held their breath as huge bombs whistled down to pulverize what was left of the once-thriving town. The shock waves were so fantastic that Commandos were lifted bodily from the ground and thudded back, winded by the violence. Major P. I. Bartholomew wrote in his diary that it seemed 'as if more than mortal powers had been unleashed'. Corporal Ramsey, with a Royal Engineers bridging party waiting on the Allied side said, 'It was like fireworks. First a rain of golden sparks as the leading aircraft dropped the markers right over an enormous fire that already lit the town like a beacon. Then we heard the main force. It was a terrific sight. All colours of sparks flying everywhere, red, green, yellow and the fantastic concussion as the bombs went down. On our side of the river the ground shook and we could see waves of light shooting up into the smoke. It was like stoking a fire, the dull glow burst into flames and it was like daylight.'

Within fifteen minutes the last of the 'heavies' wheeled away from the swirling smoke and sparks that roared up from Wesel, now finally reduced to rubble and blazing embers. The men of 6 Commando arose, shaken and dazed, some even deafened, and led the way into the swirling smoke, sparks and dust. But even as they entered the wrecked town, the remaining Germans were recovering. The parachute troops of 180th Division set up their Spandaus and resisted. 'We were absolutely amazed', Dave Morris remembered. 'After the devastating RAF raid, it didn't seem possible for anyone to survive. But there were plenty of German paratroopers left and ready to fight it out, too.'

While the RAF was reducing Wesel to rubble, 51st Highland Division's assault was developing in the Rees area. The capture of Rees itself was assigned to 1st Gordons, landing left of the town and swinging right in their advance to assault the enemy defences. As Lindsey described the scene there was 'a tremendous rumble of guns behind us, their shells whistling overhead, and the nice, sharp, banging, bouncing sound of our 25-pounder shells landing on the far bank. But a mortar was still smacking down right in the loading area, and one dreaded the thought of a mortar bomb landing inside a Buffalo with twenty-eight not-so-gay Gordons inside.' At 11.15 pm it was their turn to cross and they made their way to the Buffaloes. The Buffaloes carrying 'B' and 'C' Companies of the Gordons crawled away across the fields, past the dyke and dropped into the water. 'The Buffaloes became waterborne, and then we had the feeling of floating down out of control, yet each Buffalo churned without difficulty out of Germany's greatest barrier.' On the far bank they disembarked and deployed towards the town.

While the 51st Highland Division was crossing and getting a foothold, to their south 15th Scottish Division was preparing for its later assault in the XII Corps' zone. '44th Lowland Brigade was to assault with two battalions', wrote Brigadier Cummings-Bruce, 'crossing in Buffaloes, and one battalion in Storm boats.' Cummings-Bruce thought it likely the enemy was dug in along trenches behind the dyke, ready to open fire on the troops as they scrambled from the river. Cleverly he sited his massed 'Pepper-pot' guns on the bank around the bend in the river from where they could actually 'see' behind the enemy dyke. During the barrage the Germans were swept by a storm of Bofors and machine-gun fire directed right into their weapon pits. The resulting carnage threw their defence plans into chaos and thoroughly demoralized them before the assault began. 'The principal memory of the Rhine crossings', says Major B. A. Fargus, 8th Royal Scots' adjutant, 'is the complete confidence we all had in the success of the operation. This was the result of the detailed and competent planning and the two rehearsals we had all taken part in on the Maas.'

At the dispersal point a thousand yards from the river, the carriers fanned out into three columns line abreast, 'C' Company on the right, 'B' in the middle and 'A' on the left; 'D' Company followed in reserve. Then, forming into nine columns abreast, the force went

through the dyke breached by the Engineers, across the mud flats and
into the water punctually at 2 am. 'About this time', said Fargus, 'the
enemy had come to life, and some shelling and mortaring were met
on the near bank. Several Spandau machine-guns opened up from the
dyke on the far side. But the fire was inaccurate and there were no
casualties.'

In three waves, at four-minute intervals, the 8th Royal Scots Battalion crossed. At the far bank all the troops scrambled out and the
carriers and anti-tank guns were driven from the Buffaloes as fast as
their drop-tails could be opened. Major D. McQueen led 'A' Company 'hell-for-leather' to seize enemy-occupied houses on the far
bank at Ronduit. 'B' Company under Major D. R. O. Drummond
passed through to capture a crossroads near a large farm at Gossenhof, but they ran into Spandaus and were held up for a time until
'D' Company, which had by then landed, sent a platoon into their
area which enabled them to extend their attack to Gossenhof.

Meanwhile, Major A. MacIntyre's 'C' Company on the southern
flank of the battalion ran into a particularly stubborn German machine-gun post. MacIntyre went forward to try and locate this gun:

I made my way up the bund (dyke) and, on looking over the top, saw
some Germans dashing about among some farm buildings, which as far
as I can remember, were on fire as a result of our preliminary barrage. I
took one or two pot shots at those Germans who didn't appear in the
confusion to be front-line troops, and then was myself hit, presumably by
this Spandau or Schmeisser, and toppled down the bund where I was 'out'
for some minutes and then came round minus my steel helmet and with a
lot of blood around. I staggered about for a few minutes and then spotted
my helmet which I was amazed to notice had no less than six bullet holes
through it! Whereas I had suffered a fairly superficial head wound.
However, the MO who happened to come along at this point decided to
evacuate me in case any more serious damage had been done which he
couldn't determine in the darkness and confusion.

Captain J. G. Kiddie took command and eliminated the German
post. All the companies had their objectives, sending patrols to wipe
out any remaining Germans still hanging on in houses and trenches.
Thanks to the counter-battery bombardment which had successfully
prevented much retaliation the battalion was fairly free of mortaring
and shelling, but a stray shell unfortunately landed on the mortar
platoon while it was in action.

The 15th Scottish Division's other leading Brigade, 227th, had also crossed by Buffaloes of the East Riding Yeomanry, to capture and hold the areas of Haffen and Mehr. At the briefing on March 20th, Barber, the Divisional Commander, had told them: 'I must impress on you the need to push on quickly. It looks from the map and air photos as though you may find yourself on an island in your brigade area, and we must therefore try and bounce the bridge north-east of Mehr intact and as early as possible; otherwise we may never get 46th Brigade through you, and the whole party will be in danger of congealing. I think we shall find the enemy pretty thin on the ground, although I have no doubt their 7th Para Division will give a good account of itself as usual. I am inclined to believe it will go for a series of strong points holding such places as the farm houses at Lohr and Sandenhof.'

The 10th Highland Light Infantry was to cross on the right in the Wolffskath area, a large farm which dominated the bridge site and was known to be strongly held by the enemy, and then push on to Mehr. On the left the 2nd Argylls would cross to the creek at Hubsch and attack Weyerhof; both battalions were to clear the dyke in their sectors while the Argylls also took the sluice gates at the junction of their sectors. According to Brigadier R. M. Villiers, 'there were not enough Buffaloes to lift more than two battalions in the assault wave, and the 2nd Gordons had to follow by Storm boat. We were impressed by the need for speed, so as to overwhelm the enemy before he could recover from the hammering he was to get in the initial bombardment. Above all, it was important to be at least well on our way to our objectives before the artillery had to stop altogether on account of the airborne landings. It was therefore decided that the assaulting battalions should push right on to the brigade objective and the follow-up battalion would come in behind them, taking over the ground they had won.'

At 11 pm the 10th Highland Light Infantry loaded into their Buffaloes, and set off on the drive to the river. Three hundred yards from the bank the Buffaloes fanned out and splashed into the Rhine, while to their south, heavy shelling and a bright glow attested the Commandos' fierce fight in Wesel. Between them the Royal Scots were charging into the water at the same time as the great assault began to accelerate.

Villiers was exhilarated: 'Everybody was keyed up for this great enterprise. There was the sound of firing on the far bank, but the river mist precluded us from seeing exactly what was happening. Everyone had been told to get their heads down below the waterline, except commanders, who could look out when they wanted. The mist was extremely thick; it was a combination of the river mist, the smoke screen which had gone on to the last moment, and the bursting of artillery shells. During the last five minutes before H-Hour our artillery had plastered the edge of the far bank.'

The 2nd Argylls crossed with three battalions in Buffaloes of the East Riding Yeomanry. But the 2nd Argylls and the 10th Highland Light Infantry encountered fierce resistance in getting their objectives —as fierce as anything they had met so far. The mist and speed of the river led to confusion in the crossings and in the attacks on Wolffskath the HLI lost a lot of men. In fact it was not until around 6.30 am that 'A' and 'C' Companies finally swept the enemy from their strong-points at Overkamp, permitting 46th Brigade through to take the vital bridge just beyond Mehr and enable the Brigade to get off the 'island'. The two companies charged with fixed bayonets, yelling and shouting, at the four houses and drove the enemy out. There they dug in to hold the position until 46th Brigade's 7th Seaforths and DD Shermans passed through.

At Wesel the Germans were beginning to realize the importance of the Commando raid and, as 46 Royal Marine Commando, the last away from the bridgehead, was hastening after the rest of the Brigade across the floodplain, the enemy artillery opened a heavy concentration; they had finally decided the Commando attack was not a feint. 'It was about midnight', Mills-Roberts wrote, 'that the Hun got properly under way with his counter battery fire and plastered our bank with mortars and everything else he had got, but he had missed the boat in more senses than one.' Although there followed an hour or so of bitter fighting amongst the ruins of Wesel by midnight the Commandos had fought their way deep into the suburbs of the town. Bob Nunn paused in the shelter of a collapsed shop front:

There were two of us crouched in what had been the shop window. My mate took out some cigarettes and we were just lighting them when a Spandau opened fire from a ruin across the way, wounding my friend. I pulled him further back into the shop over a mass of broken glass on which I cut my hand badly. We kept down and then risked a look to find the German gunner. His fire was coming from the darkness in the ruin and we couldn't see him, so I hurled a grenade over which hit a wall and bounced back into the road before exploding. Then my mate fired a long burst from his Sten which drew an even longer burst of machine-gun fire. By that time the exchange had attracted attention and another German gun joined in, but our own lads also came up and a couple more grenades silenced both Germans.

It was 1 am when the entire brigade eventually reached the centre of Wesel and set about trying to dig in. Their maps were by this time useless since most of the town no longer existed. The Commandos moved in two single-file columns along either side of the main street and at last reached a corner which led northwards to a wire factory which was 45 RM Commando's final objective for the night. As Brigadier Mills-Roberts stopped to talk to Lieutenant-Colonel Nicol Gray, their CO, without warning a 'dead' German SS soldier suddenly leapt to his feet clutching a *Panzerfaust* which he fired at point-blank range. The blast knocked nearly everyone off their feet as it exploded with a vivid flash. Nicol Gray fell wounded. Two of the HQ staff were killed by the explosion. Instantly the night was rent with the tearing chatter of several Stens as magazines were emptied into the SS soldier. Furiously the Commandos blasted every corpse in sight, just in case; the SS man had taught them a bitter lesson.

At about 2 am 45 RM Commando reached the wire factory. A platoon cautiously entered, the others waited expectantly and were puzzled to hear the sound of laughter from within. The advance platoon had found that the factory made not wire, but lavatory seats! They thought it very appropriate. But there was no time to rest. Immediately they set about strengthening their position, by barricading all exits and windows, utilizing whatever came to hand—machinery, doors, benches, tables, timber and coils of wire. It was their job now to sit tight, deny Wesel to the Germans and prevent them moving armour through the town to attack the bridgeheads until the Airborne arrived in several hours' time.

On the night of the 23rd Bradley announced Patton's 5th Division's crossing of the Rhine to the Press, and he could not resist giving a final twist to the knife: 'American forces', he announced, 'could cross the Rhine at practically any point, without aerial bombardment and without airborne support. The Third Army had crossed during the night of March 23rd without even so much as an artillery preparation.' While this ignored Patton's quite extensive engineering preparations and the topography of the river, it also was an unfair comparison with the British sector in terms of enemy strength; Patton had been opposed by a motley collection of Volkssturm Divisions with virtually no armour, while opposing the British 21st Army Group were the parachute divisions and the remaining German armour. Indeed, the pattern was evolving and as von Luttwitz prepared to move in one direction, the Americans of Ninth Army began their assault at the other end of the front.

At 1 am on the 24th 40,000 artillerymen of US Ninth Army loosed off another massive bombardment of the Rhine's far bank at Walsum opposite XVI Corps. Vehicles and supplies had been secretly moved into assembly areas as close as security permitted. 'Their movements to the crossing sites', wrote Colonel Van Bibber, 'had to be timed so that they would meet the specialized craft designed to move them. They then had to move into predetermined areas on the far shore.' To back up the infantry the plan called for supporting vehicles to cross as soon as possible, although '. . . serially numbered, the vehicles could be called for in any order, depending on the changing tactical situation or the availability of craft.' Top priority was given to Weasels with ammunition supplies, then anti-tank guns and tank destroyers, followed by tanks, communications vehicles, jeeps with more ammunition and the rest of the support train.

At 2 am US 30th Division took off, three battalions of 119th Regiment abreast, the leading waves of troops gasping and swearing as they manhandled the heavy assault boats over the dyke, slipping and sliding down the far side to the water. Ralph Albert's group that had had so much trouble in practise now set off for the real thing, but as he remembers: 'We got the boat over the dyke and seemed to have mastered the technique, but then someone tripped and we dropped the damn thing down the other side. It was a bit flustered for a few minutes but eventually we got the boat onto the water and piled in.' Infantry and engineers moved their craft to the water, and through the smoke they glimpsed the enemy on the far bank, illuminated against the fiery background. To either side machine-guns sent red tracer streaking across the water to mark their route. Then they were splashing into the Rhine; frantic pulls of starter cords, roars of engines like mad hornets and they were away, shoals of small boats scudding across the water. 'We all got as low as we could', said Ralph Albert, 'because there was a lot of enemy fire coming across, as well as water spraying over us which made it difficult to see. A boat alongside us was hit by a burst of gunfire, which killed the engineer steering it, and slammed into us, almost capsizing our own boat before it rocked away and turned over. I think it was hit by a cannon shell.' Minutes later the boats rubbed the far bank and troops splashed out and ran ashore, three regiments abreast heading for the enemy positions. On the west bank the assault came to life as American bulldozers tore away the dyke ready for the bridging teams to begin their work.

An hour after 30th Division's attack, battalions of the 313th and 315th Regiments set off as 79th Division began its assault. Their artillery had been pounding away so fiercely that, as Colonel Van Bibber put it, 'We couldn't believe that anything could stay alive on the other side of the river.' The units moved over the huge dyke in perfect alignment and slid into the water at exactly 3 am, while the division's machine-guns fired non-stop to drown the sound of the assault boats.

Like the other assault troops that night they found the enemy shocked by the suddenness of the attack. 'The first few hundred prisoners reached the army cage within six hours after capture,' an army report recorded, 'many still being in a stunned or dazed condition. "Hellish, terrifying" was all some of them could say at first. One officer apologized for his seemingly incoherent answers, saying his head still felt thick and numb from his recent ordeal.' Others expressed wonder at the barrage, calling it 'colossal'.

American troops were pouring over the river by the early hours of the morning, in assault boats and Buffaloes; ponderous fifty-foot landing craft carried sixty men and their equipment, ploughing majestically through the water. Clanking and rumbling, a troop of DD tanks entered the water, sinking almost to the tops of their screens and then, with screws thrashing, chugged the 400 yards to the far bank. Tracks slipped on the muddy shore opposite but eventually they succeeded in gaining the wide flood plain before the far dyke, and, with screens lowered, moved forward providing welcome fire power. Heavy rafts bearing tank destroyers and Shermans also began their slow journeys across. By morning on March 24th eight infantry battalions of US 30th Division and five of US 79th Division were over the Rhine.

19 Battle for the bridgeheads

By the early hours of March 24th all the British thrusts were across the Rhine and preparing to break out. The 51st Division in the north, the 15th Division from Xanten and the 1st Commando Brigade in Wesel were well entrenched. The Germans had taken a severe hammering from the thousands of guns and the RAF had dealt a *coup de grâce* at Wesel. On the German side urgent signals were flashing back and forth between Army Group and its corps and divisions. But as Wolfgang Holtz, at Blaskowitz's HQ, points out, decisions were being delayed for fear of an airborne assault; 'some staff officers were advocating the dispatch of the panzer corps to Rees where a powerful assault was in progress and which some saw as the main attack because, like Wesel, there were good communications very close to the Rhine. It would also lead to a quick advance to Emmerich where there was a bridging site, which the Allied resources would soon have working again. But Blaskowitz counselled caution because by this time, early morning, an American attack had just begun to the south of Wesel, which he saw as being connected to the British attack and heavy bombing of the town, and probably the main area for the breakout.' Otto Diels, with the 146th Panzer Artillery, north of Emmerich recalls: 'We knew there was a big offensive taking place. For hours the Allied bombing and shelling had become very intense and I knew it would not be long before we were sent to make a counter-attack. My battalion was at readiness from about midnight, but to our surprise no more orders came and we waited until the morning.'

All available panzers were ordered to attack Wesel, while to the north, the re-grouped First Parachute Army prepared to counter-attack. The telephone lines between Blaskowitz's HQ and that of Kesselring began to buzz about midnight. Kesselring had rightly predicted the enemy's intention to attack Dinslaken and Emmerich and

since 9 pm that evening British forces had been landing either side of
Rees. But there was another strong British attack at Wesel, heavily
supported by air attacks and artillery concentrations while more British troops were crossing near Xanten. The wary Kesselring took note
of the fine weather and of the lack of information about the whereabouts of the British 6th Airborne Division and guessed that Montgomery intended to use airborne forces. But vital decisions were
delayed as a result of deliberating until the British intentions could
be clarified, and movement of the panzer divisions was held in
abeyance for the time being, although von Luttwitz was warned to be
ready to move in the morning.

Back in Wesel, Mills-Roberts was anxious to get his brigade well settled before the Germans got back on balance and attacked with their
full force. Accordingly, while Commandos dug in, offensive patrols
went out into the town and scoured the surrounding area, encountering numerous parties of German troops. In one skirmish a patrol
seized a cellar and when Regimental Sergeant Major Woodcock descended the stairs he found, to his surprise, the German Garrison
Commander, Major-General Deutch. The General refused to surrender and in the ensuing scuffle with his staff, he was killed by a burst
of Tommy gunfire. When the Commandos examined the HQ they
were delighted to find a map giving full details of all the enemy's flak
positions which would be invaluable for the Airborne's landings. It
would now be possible for XII Corps' artillery to concentrate on the
flak positions and smash them before the aircraft came over. Immediately the map was taken to Brigade HQ where Ted Ruston the
Gunner representative for 1st Mountain Regiment radioed it back on
his signal network.

   At this time everyone was optimistic although the battle was far
from over. In particular 45 RM Commando was having a rough
time. A German self-propelled gun was sniping at them from behind
a cemetery when word came in of the noise of tracked vehicles and
heavy engines. Each of the four Commandos reported the noise and
were asked for map references. When all these were checked and
verified by compass bearings they crossed in the vicinity of a small
copse where several roads linked, near the cemetery. Ted Ruston
pointed out that they still had the Corps' artillery on call for a bit
longer; it couldn't shoot once the time approached for the Airborne
landings. 'Shall we give them a pasting?' he asked.

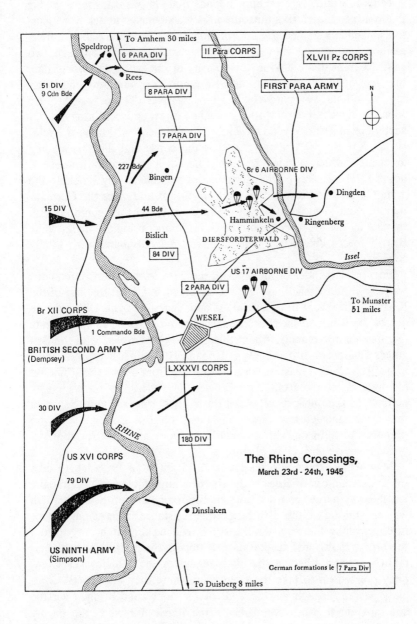

The Rhine Crossings,
March 23rd - 24th, 1945

Mills-Roberts agreed and added that it would make a big difference to the battle's outcome to deter a counter-attack now. Ruston's signallers passed the information back. Trooper Bob Nunn remembers squeezing into a ridiculously small corner between two ruins. 'I think the clanking and roaring of the tanks was worse than the sight of them. But then, out of the non-stop slamming and banging behind us we heard shells whistling over. There wasn't much room in my small corner but I crouched down and next moment our shells began crumping down and we could hear all kinds of explosions.' XII Corps' artillery plastered the copse and the surrounding area, after which nothing more was heard of the enemy for several hours. The location of the Commandos was effectively blocking the main German routes towards the bridgeheads and since the Germans had no clear idea of the size of the force in Wesel they could not risk by-passing the town. For those essential hours during the night, while British forces crossed at several points, the Germans were totally confused.

For the remainder of the night of the 23rd March the Commandos waited, while the shelling went on unabated. At 3 am the first of the RAF's sorties went in as Typhoons and Tempests from Holland tore across the Rhine to shoot up trains and convoys trying to concentrate German reinforcements. About this time Major Groves, with the Brigade's Engineers, drove back to Brigade HQ and just reached them in his jeep when a blast of machine-gun fire from across the Rhine on his right burst the front tyre. It was the Americans on their way across. On the outskirts of Wesel the available panzer units began to move in, ready for a dawn onslaught on the Commandos who prepared to hold on with automatic weapons and wait for the Airborne to arrive and relieve them.

Meanwhile, 2nd Seaforths left at 2.45 am from Esserden to take the main road out of Rees at the site of a large factory. 'A' Company led the way across country towards the road junction beyond which was an anti-tank ditch. Brushing aside resistance from enemy troops in cover along the way, the Seaforths reached the ditch only to find the bridge blown and several deep craters in the road. While the battalion's sappers filled in the ditch ready for the vehicles, 'D' Company pressed on to take the main road where they dug in. 'B' Company passed through and headed for the main road bridge over the anti-tank ditch. Both companies came under fire when the enemy launched a counter-attack along the roadsides. But the Seaforths simply shoved a Bren into position and hosed it up and down the road, its short bursts forcing the German infantry to give way. But they soon reformed and the Scots were under heavy attack again. The position was too big to be held with just two companies and 'A' Company was sent up as reinforcement, less a platoon that remained to guard the battalion's flank.

At dawn local patrols went out to probe the factory at Rees and gradually drove off the enemy. It was a tough job fighting through the maze of buildings and the CO called for a troop of tanks. He was told there were none to spare for the time being. 'So', recorded the regimental Historian, 'we just had to sit in our hedgehog, having no transport of any description with us, keep the enemy quiet, and take what local offensive action we could.' For the next few hours they held out and watched large numbers of enemy troops moving out of Rees along a road running due east. The Seaforths were well off for radios, including some heavy sets on old prams they had salvaged. They reported to Brigade headquarters the enemy movements and then sat back to watch the artillery shooting up the retreating enemy.

It was 4 am when 44th Royal Tanks moved from their concentration area at Xanten, after the crews had all had a steaming mug of tea well laced with rum. They slowly moved downhill, through Xanten. Their reconnaissance parties had crossed earlier and a report came back that the right hand one had been badly hit by Spandaus, mortars and shelling, and had casualties, but that it expected the tanks on time. The tricky business of erecting the flotation screens went on while sporadic shells whistled across but fortunately none slammed down near them.

'Both exits had by then been completed', wrote Hopkinson, 'and soon the river was full of tanks, looking rather like floating baths drifting downstream. Over half of "A" Squadron was waterborne when the enemy started shelling the tanks. One tank was hit as it left the shore and sank like a stone, all the crew abandoning ship and making the shore safely. (This crew later carried a swastika flag, emblazoned "First to the bottom of the Rhine, 2 Baker".) The last tank of "A" Squadron was hit as it was going down the runway to the water, but it managed to reverse out and retired for patching. Regimental HQ nipped in while the enemy was adjusting for range and, except for a few splashes in midstream, had no trouble.'

On the other side 1st Gordons were having a rough time. Alec Lumsden's 'D' Company had crossed the dyke but came under heavy shelling. 'B' and 'C' Companies had fought their way across the dyke and into a housing estate on the outskirts of Rees, occupied by 19th

Parachute Regiment who fought desperately, making the Scots contest every yard. As it grew light more paratroopers in the houses further along joined in the fight. Wireless messages passed back and
forth between company commanders; Lindsey picked them up on the
west bank: 'The next thing I heard was an acrimonious conversation
between Alec ('D' Company) and George Morrison ('B' Company). Alec was telling George that he hadn't put a platoon where he
said he was going to, and that the enemy had in consequence been
able to get round his flank. He was pinned down in the open with
Huns on three sides of him and had to withdraw to "B" Company as
he was getting casualties, could not get forward and his position was
untenable. But, having got permission from the Colonel to withdraw,
he decided to hold on, and began to feel his way forward once more.'

By this time the Black Watch had finished loading and Lindsey
could start loading the Gordons' vehicles. A jeep drove up and a tall,
lean figure climbed out to talk with them. It was Major-General
Thomas Rennie, Commander of the Highland Division. He exchanged a few pleasantries, and told the Gordons that all was going
very well and that the bridgehead was now about eight miles wide
and some two miles deep.

All night row after row of American Dakotas stood silent in East
Anglia, until at 2.45 am a bugle blared reveille. Men scrambled from
bunks, washed and shaved rapidly in time for bacon and eggs at 3.15
am in the blacked-out mess halls. As they fell in on parade they
shuffled and bumped into one another, a cheerful banter belying the
anxious excitement each man felt. 'It was cold when we paraded cluttered up with as much as we could carry', Major Crookenden recalls.
'But it was a fine morning and by the time trucks arrived to take us
to the transports, the sky was blue and there was bright sunshine.
The usual complaints were heard about it being too late to cancel,
but even the Jonahs were soon on board.'

At the stroke of 7 am a green light winked in the control tower,
American pilots opened the throttles, engines thundered, brakes were
released and they were off. Rapidly increasing their speed, the leading echelon tore down the runway, followed 200 yards behind by the
next echelon, and so on. 'The noise and acceleration and pace of any
take-off,' said Crookenden, 'is always exciting but that American
mass take-off with something like eighteen to twenty-seven Dakotas
moving down the runway together in successive waves was a revela-
tion of skill and nerve.'

At Rivenhall, Great Dunmow and Matching the glider series were formed up behind their tugs, Dakotas, Albemarles and Stirling bombers with specially equipped Halifax bombers to pull the giant Hamilcar gliders. Flight-Sergeant R. S. Trout was the pilot of a four-engined Stirling bomber destined to tow a Horsa carrying men of the 12th Devons, under Lieutenant-Colonel P. Gleadell, the battalion providing the 6th Air-Landing Brigade HQ. He recalled how he wandered across to talk to his intended passengers. One Major among them had become very upset because his tug was piloted by an NCO when others were flown by officers. Trout sent his navigator, a Flying Officer, to encourage him. As Trout put it: 'If the troops were edgy, they had my entire sympathy—I hoped to be back in England by teatime.'

Major Huw Wheldon was in a Horsa glider carrying a jeep loaded with stores. They took off with the rest of their battalion of the Royal Ulster Rifles, of 6th Air-Landing Brigade, from Rivenhall. 'Our pilot was a young chap, very competent, very efficient. The take-off was exciting, we sat back and we could hear the tug's engines roaring away and then, there was a jerk and the tow rope tightened and we were off. The tug pulled us up, bobbing along behind.'

Lieutenant D. S. M. Turner of the Glider Pilot Regiment flew one of the gliders carrying Lieutenant-Colonel Rickards's 1st Royal Ulster Rifles, which with the 2nd Oxfordshire and Buckinghamshire Light Infantry was a *coup de main* party briefed to take the Issel bridges. Turner and his squadron had been training to land individually on spot targets. 'On the morning of 24th March the visibility was good and all combinations were airborne except for one which was unable to take off owing to the tug's undercarriage collapsing. The stream formed up over Hawkinge and flew from there to Wavre.'

At Earl's Colne airfield were Horsa gliders and Halifax tugs of 195th Air-Landing Field Artillery. At 7 am the troops clambered aboard, their guns, ammunition and jeeps were stowed, and the tugs set off. The gliders became airborne at around 70 mph and rose above the tugs still staggering along only just above stalling speed, pilots praying the engines wouldn't cut out. But they all struggled into the blue sky. By 8 am the huge armada was heading eastward. In the Medway towns and along the Essex coast people stared upwards.

The departure of the 17th Airborne went as planned from fifteen airfields near Amiens, Paris and Rheims in France. The 507th Regimental Combat Team took off first and soon rows of C-47s (Dakotas) were roaring down runways. They were followed by 72 C-46 Commando aircraft; these were new, larger troop carriers that tragically were to be found to have a fatal flaw. Soon the entire column was airborne, over two hours long.

Howard Cowan of the Associated Press, travelling with the 194th Glider Infantry Combat Team, was thinking how easy it all seemed, when a sergeant sitting next to him leaned across and said: 'Now is when you pray.' Cowan began praying when the silken rope stretched taut from the tail of the C-47 ahead. He watched the flimsy craft start down the runway, its sides vibrating in the prop blast. He heard the tyres singing over the concrete, a reminder that it had no engine, 'that it was just a crate, a big crate with wings. You felt something akin to horror as you read the label on a case lashed by heavy rope to the floor . . . "five anti-tank mines . . . Five". And you wondered why they had to go in this glider with a bunch of medics, a radio operator, a lineman, a photographer and war correspondent. You wondered just how much of bump it would take to set them off as the glider rocked and jerked and swayed in the slip stream of the powerful tug ship ahead. You thought of the landing and suddenly remembered the pictures of gliders in Normandy and Holland, all smashed and splintered . . . and you prayed some more.'

The great column of 6th Airborne turned over the south of England and headed for the Channel at Dover. The waters of the Channel glinted blue and green far below them, patterned by the flitting shadows of hundreds of aircraft. Many of the gliders were twinned to the same tug and looking to left or right troops could see the wing-tip of their sister glider undulating very near. 'What would it be like', thought Howard Cowan, 'if the two wings locked and the pair plummeted to the green fields of France below? Why don't they give you parachutes to wear in these gliders? Or wouldn't it do any good? A bit of thinking and it is soon decided . . . it wouldn't.'

Across the Channel, across the Seine, flew the airborne divisions until they met at Wavre. The formations wheeled over Belgium, 'a great fleet of troop carriers appeared out of the south-west stretching back as far as the eye could see', recalled Major Crookenden. 'They took up a course parallel to our own aircraft about a mile away to the south. This was the 17th Airborne Division coming up from the Châlon–Paris area and they made a magnificent and heartening picture.'

'Ricky' Richards, with the 507th Parachute Infantry, recalls being 'in a troop carrier on the northern flank of the column and dozing a

bit, when the next guy nudged me. The fellers were excited and looking out of the window. I struggled to turn around and saw another
enormous column coming alongside us. It was fantastic, we hadn't
seen ourselves and didn't know until then what the armada must
have looked like. But here were the British airborne roaring alongside us; it was a marvellous feeling.' Now side by side, 'Pegasus' and
'Talon', 6th and 17th Airborne Divisions, headed for Germany in the
biggest airborne assault in history.

All the DD Shermans of 44th Royal Tanks were across the Rhine by
8.15 am and ready to go. Contact was made with 9th Cameronians
and 'A' Squadron of the Royal Tanks was sent to help them enlarge
their bridgehead. The Shermans 'waded in' with their 75mm guns
crashing shell after shell into enemy positions. On their right 15th
Scottish's 44th Brigade was firmly holding Bislich but couldn't go
further, while some three miles to the left 227th Brigade was separated by German positions along the river bank.

The 8th Royal Scots called upon the tanks for help in capturing
their objective, ready to push forward to meet the airborne troops. A
squadron of DD Shermans trundled along to the Scots' positions at
Gossenhof farm where they 'married up' with Major Drummond's 'B'
Company directed on Vissel and Major Cadzow's 'D' Company attacking Jockern. The attacks went in with great élan and the enemy
troops were 'steamrollered' by the combined assault.

No 45 RM Commando waited in their concentration area across
the Rhine as dawn slowly lightened the sky. It was about 5.30 am
when they were aroused by the sounds of a column of German soldiers cycling along the road towards them. The Commandos waited
silently until the column was passing then, in a hail of fire, swept the
Germans from their bikes. But the numerous assaults during the
night had by now dispelled any German doubts that the Commandos'
crossing was only a feint; clearly the Commando assault had
achieved its objective of capturing Wesel before the Germans could
realize the threat and reinforce the area. Wolfgang Holtz recalls that
it was only around 5 am that orders were given that Wesel was to be
denied to the British at all costs.

At 9 am the Germans counter-attacked in bright sunshine. Waves
of grenadiers backed by Mk IV tanks and *Sturmgeschutz* assault
guns closed in. Commandos with Brens and Stens cut down the infantry as they crossed the open ground, leaving the tanks behind; the

earlier artillery concentration had made the Germans wary of losing precious tanks, unsure how much fire-power the Commandos had available. Had they made a determined attack then the Commandos had virtually nothing with which to stop them, except captured *Panzerfausts* and some PIATs, both weapons having a short range. A Mk IV swung into view and started to grind and rattle ominously along the road, its long 75mm gun waving. 'Easy' Troop watched it advance, pushing the PIATs through gaps in the rubble ready to shoot when it got near enough. Then 150 yards away it stopped, seemingly unable to decide which way to go. Major Beadle got every available *Panzerfaust* and PIAT into position and they waited with bated breath, fingers on triggers. The tank roared, sending a cloud of black exhaust shooting out, and began to come forward again, slewed to one side and stopped, its gun slowly traversing; the Commandos tightened their trigger fingers. The tank slewed right around and retreated; with audible sighs of relief 'Easy' Troop magnanimously let it go.

At the lavatory-seat factory another battle raged. Scattered bands of Germans were in a small hamlet about 300 yards away. They were trying to close in but could not get across the open ground because the Commandos sniped with great accuracy whenever they showed themselves. Time and again parties broke cover and ran forward only to be mown down by Brens. Several times a *Sturmgeschutz* moved forward, fired a few rounds and withdrew after which the infantry attacked, to be driven off by Brens. There is no doubt these constant small failures prevented the enemy mounting a full-scale attack. It was the same on No 3 Commandos' front. They, too, spent the morning ambushing German patrols. 'One patrol', reported a sergeant, 'came down the railway lines and we waited until we could literally see the whites of their eyes before killing them with Bren and Tommy guns. Later, a section of Germans came across the fields . . . we just picked them off like sitting birds. They had no idea where the fire was coming from and simply lay on the ground ready to be shot.'

Around Wesel the First Parachute Army was bolstered by a number of Volkssturm battalions that did their best. Von Luttwitz was committing to the hilt his tanks and self-propelled guns, and the fighting was intensifying by the minute. This was no unopposed crossing and while the initial bombardment had allowed the assault battalions to cross the wide river with relatively few casualties, its effect had worn off and the battle that had developed was as fierce as any in the Rhineland. Trooper Bob Nunn remarks that

It was getting distinctly unpleasant. We had been told the ground troops were across and the 'Jocks' were fighting their way inland to link up with us, but we wondered if we'd be shelled to bits first. Enemy tanks were knocking holes in the buildings and their troops kept coming at us. Suddenly it fell quieter and the continual rumble of guns stopped. Then we heard it, and the Germans, too; we could see them staring up at the sky. The air filled with the drone of thousands of aircraft. We couldn't see them at first but then they were there, huge lines of Dakotas. It was a marvellous sight and everyone stopped to cheer them. Somebody started yelling; 'Here come the Airborne!'

20 'Here come the Airborne!'

To the Germans entrenched on the far bank of the Rhine, the aircraft seemed to swarm across the water barrier like locusts, filling the sky. They flew in three columns, each some 150 miles long, taking more than two hours to pass. As the troop carriers, tugs and gliders approached, Typhoons and Thunderbolts struck at every flak position and gun site they could find. In size, Operation 'Varsity' dwarfed both D-Day and Arnhem.

In the words of *The Times*

The battle had already receded from the Rhine leaving nothing to disturb the illusion of a peace-time beauty and tranquillity. The wide ribbon of water shimmered in the summer-like sunshine. Here and there the sparkle was broken by the waves of assault craft ferrying over reinforcements and supplies—from the height at which we were flying they might have been pleasure steamers. But just beyond the east bank the illusion was quickly shattered. For mile after mile the brown-coloured countryside presented a picture of utter desolation. From the air it looked as though there was a bomb crater every few yards. Tank tracks criss-crossed the broken surface and showed what had called down this avalanche of explosives.

Among the distinguished observers was Churchill who wrote: 'In the morning Montgomery had arranged for me to witness from a hilltop amid rolling down-land the great fly-in. It was full daylight before the subdued but intense roar and rumbling of swarms of aircraft stole upon us. After that in the course of half an hour over 2,000 aircraft streamed overhead in their formations. My viewpoint had been well chosen. The light was clear enough to enable one to see where the descent on the enemy took place. The aircraft faded from sight.' The

Prime Minister turned to Eisenhower and said, 'My dear General, the German is whipped. We've got him. He is all through.'

Each parachute battalion had been assigned thirty-five Dakota troop carriers, two Horsa and one giant Hamilcar gliders, making a total lift for 3rd Brigade of 122 Dakotas, twenty-seven Horsas and three Hamilcars. The leading aircraft of 3rd Brigade were on course for the run-in to the dropping zones, where their glider element would arrive at P (the time of the parachute drop) plus 60 minutes. Below, the dense woods of the Reichswald and the ruins of Cleve and Goch slipped behind as they neared the Rhine and multiple-barrelled 20mm flak guns swung to meet them.

'At 9.46 am', Lieutenant-Colonel Hewetson, of 8th Parachute Battalion reported, 'we were given the order "Five minutes to go", and at 9.51 we crossed the Rhine with the usual sinking feeling of impending "Baling out". I remember looking forward from the door and seeing the fog of battle on the ground, the aftermath of the terrific pounding from our massed artillery.' Les Jones was first man in his stick of paratroopers:

I held onto the door frame, the wind whipping past was very cold. Down below I could see a great curve in the river and the Buffaloes churning across. Then we were over green and brown fields and I could see burning buildings and smoke everywhere. There was the smoke screen rolling in clouds, too, but we were past that. The bottom light flashed green. The stick commander yelled 'Go!' and slapped my shoulder and out I went.

In a different Dakota Ken Williams jumped number 3: 'The first men jumped and I took my place ready to go when the plane next to us was hit. It shuddered in the air and I saw a propeller fly apart and smoke poured from the nacelle, then the man behind shoved me out. But I remember looking up instinctively and seeing flames burst from the aircraft.'

Troops cascaded down from the planes. 'Red light—green light—out— parachute open—ground fairly hard—sigh of relief!' was how Hewetson recalled it. From each plane the sticks tumbled followed by the stick commander and soon the sky was filled with billowing parachutes, flak bursts exploding amongst the troop carriers, and machine-gun bullets. 'It was murderous,' recalls Ken Williams; 'I couldn't believe so much stuff could be flying about. Shells and shrapnel were tearing pieces off the Dakotas. One piece of metal tore a hole through my parachute making me so worried that I didn't notice the ground coming up fast and hit it a hell of a wallop which completely winded me.' Hewetson's 8th Battalion landed on dropping zone 'A' and immediately set about grabbing weapon-containers. Companies then scattered to each corner of the field to hold the enemy back. A tongue of woodland jutted into the open field to their south from which heavy fire was coming—later found to be held by two platoons of German parachute troops. The enemy also held woods to the north-east as well as orchards and farm buildings to the north-west. 'By the time I got my breath back,' said Ken Williams, 'the field was covered by parachutes, all blowing about in the wind, and among them were scores of our lads lying, kneeling or gathering weapons from cases. Jerries were firing at us but nobody seemed to pay them much attention, they were all too busy getting ready to attack them. After a few minutes, we were ready and attacked German positions about our landing zone.' While 8th Battalion deployed, the armada continued to fly in more paratroops, a continual thunder of aircraft.

3rd Parachute Brigade HQ was down by now and 1st Canadian Parachute Battalion was being followed by 9th Battalion. 'Initially there was very little flak,' said Hewetson, 'although one or two planes were shot down. I remember as I was getting out of my parachute watching a Dakota returning with flames streaming out of the engine; probably No 1 plane flown by the colonel (the American commander of the Troop carriers), which crashed west of the Rhine.' A Canadian paratrooper saw a Dakota roaring in much too low with flames licking along the fuselage. There were men in the doorway, some of whom jumped out, but it was too late and their parachutes didn't open. The plane screamed overhead and plunged into the woods a mile away.

Corporal Roberts remembers that the dropping zone was covered in smoke and laced with flashes as guns fired on both sides. He ran to recover a container that had fallen about thirty yards away but was fired at by a Spandau. Roberts tried to crawl towards the container but bullets tore up the turf ahead and another paratrooper was shot down as he ran for the container. The smoke was swirling so much that Roberts couldn't see where the gun was located, but some troops still descending spotted it and put it out of action.

The 1st Canadian Parachute Battalion, under Lieutenant-Colonel J. S. Nicklin, was included in 3rd Brigade. Its task was to clear the remaining south-west corner of the dropping zone and then seize the western edge of the woods atop the Schneppenburg feature. It called for quick and determined action. The men tumbled from the planes in swarms but many landed along the fringe of the woods and got caught up in the trees. The Germans began shooting at the helpless troopers as they dangled and twisted to free themselves. Some released their harnesses only to make bone-breaking falls to the ground. The Field Ambulance dropping with the Canadians also lost a number of men who fell into the trees and were killed by the enemy with small arms fire. Sergeant-Instructor Slater of the Army Physical Training Corps dropped into a tree and was caught by his left webs twenty feet above the ground. Enemy soldiers were shooting men all around him so Slater unhesitatingly drew his knife, slashed the webs through and dropped to the ground unharmed. Nicklin himself, however, was not so lucky and was shot dead as he tried to get out of his webbing.

Enough Canadians, however, had landed safely to open a fierce fire on the Germans. A trooper with a Bren hammered away while another let off yellow smoke bombs to direct incoming troops to the rendezvous. One German sniper flushed from the woods ran towards the Canadians, his hands tight on his helmet. The Canadian trooper whom he met unhesitatingly swung the butt of his Sten into the man's face lifting him from the ground with the force, as the troops met. They could see 8th Battalion similarly engaged in their section of 'suicide woods', while 250 yards away the Canadians' 'C' Company grabbed a small hamlet and fought off an attack by several tanks.

The 8th Battalion's task was to seize the dropping zone and hang on to it while the rest of the division came in. 'C' Company's objective was the triangular strip of woodland jutting into the drop zone, which they rushed and took with little opposition. 'A' Company also got its objective, a wood 500 yards or so to the north. But 'B' Company landed rather widely dispersed and had to run for their objective in small groups of two or three. The Germans were entrenched in strong positions from which they kept up rapid fire. Hewetson, in the triangular wood, could see 'B' Company's men through the drifting smoke, many coming from north of the wood straight into the small-arms fire criss-crossing their drop zone. Hewetson sent his second-in-command to find out what was happening. The wood had just been attacked by another platoon, that had assembled north-east of it, which now pelted the enemy with grenades, throwing them into confusion while paratroopers leapt into their trenches and fought with knives and Stens. A large number of Germans were shot and knifed before the remaining officers and men surrendered.

The first Americans to jump were 507th Regimental Combat Team. 'The order had come, "stand up and hook up!"' the official Historian recorded. 'The number 1 men were standing in the doors as their planes rocked and bucked and flak tore through wings and sides as some of the troopers were hit.' Below they could see the rolling smoke but it was the smoke up top that really frightened. In spite of the Allied counter-battery fire and the pounding by Allied fighter-bombers the flak was now appalling, far worse than they had expected. At about 600 feet the Americans were flying lower than the British, which gave their paratroopers a better chance of surviving the descent through the flak and small arms fire; conversely their troop carriers were almost sitting ducks and they lost many more than the British. The incoming American serials were badly hit although with great gallantry the pilots flew unerringly on towards the dropping zones.

The leading serial of 507th began jumping at 9.50 am just to the north-east of Wesel, their camouflaged parachutes dotting the sky as they drifted down towards Diersfordt Castle. The planes swept on to turn for home, their place taken by another serial coming in with the 464th Parachute Field Artillery Battalion. But after landing, 1st Battalion and HQ commanders could not fix their positions. Troopers deployed around the dropping zone firing from kneeling and prone positions, many in a small orchard, while platoon commanders consulted maps. Colonel Raff and his men eventually decided they were about a mile and a half north-west of their intended dropping zone on mainly open fields. To their north was a wood from which the enemy was firing at them.

Men were still landing, releasing parachutes and grabbing weapons; others raced for containers, tore them open and took out heavier weapons. Colonel Raff assembled those nearest to him and led them quickly towards the woods. Several machine-guns were emplaced at the edge while nearly a mile further on a battery of heavy guns was shelling the landing zone. In open order troopers raced across shell-torn ground, some falling to the Spandaus, others fanning out and returning the fire.

As the first American paratroopers sorted themselves out and made for their objectives, to their north the British 7th Parachute Battalion of 5th Brigade, under Lieutenant-Colonel Pine-Coffin, literally dropped straight into trouble. Enemy flak guns until then had been shooting at the Dakotas without too much success but they now switched their attention to the paratroopers, firing air-bursts among the bunched parachutes as they drifted down. This was horrifyingly effective as concussion and shell splinters tore them from the sky, and the battalion suffered heavy casualties before they even landed. Pine-Coffin had experimented several times to find a way of avoiding the hopeless confusion after a mass drop. As a result his serial was organized with the flanking aircraft assigned to separate companies and the middle to Battalion HQ. The commander of HQ Company, Major J. D. West, intended landing as near as possible to the rendez-vous and did so, right on top of it, in a tree. He was fortunate there were no Germans there because the next arrivals found he had for-gotten to put a magazine on his Sten. Pine-Coffin said: 'My battalion was ordered to establish itself at the end of the DZ and to take on all opposition which might interfere with the other two battalions which were to capture the brigade objective. In short 7th Battalion came down looking for a fight, which is not a bad role for any battalion.' They hoped the mass drop would frighten the enemy and prevent de-termined resistance. On the ground troops rallied to the hunting horns and cries of 'Tally Ho!'

'A' Company jumped directly into a small wood where there was a troop of 88mm guns. The mass drop, however, had by now so terrified the German gunners that they had panicked and begun run-ning away through the woods. Their commander ran after them and by threats and commands turned back the crew of one gun and got them to open fire on 'A' Company and on the mortar and medium machine-gunners who had landed with them. As far as Corporal Evans was concerned, 'The rest of the battalion were away behind us and we were cursing and blinding our luck when a Jerry gun began firing at us. We thought it was a couple of guns because the shells were falling so quickly. Every fifteen or twenty seconds one whistled in and we all dropped to the ground as it smashed down. Somebody copped it every time.' Pine-Coffin himself was injured. Finally, Lieu-tenant P. Burkinshaw, leading a platoon, broke his way in through the trees and seized the group of gunners.

The battalion also had to seize and hold an important road and rail junction in an opening in the woods between 5th and 3rd Bri-gades. Pine-Coffin wanted to send an officer and a party with a radio to spy out the area after which a platoon would be sent to clear it. But he found that the designated officer had already been killed on the dropping zone. Having no alternative he sent an 'A' Company platoon off without prior reconnaissance, led by Lieutenant Patterson, a Canadian who had joined the battalion in Normandy.

Time and again the platoon was ambushed but it managed to keep going. They reached the junction and hung on there using 'Patterson's Method'; when an enemy counter-attacked Patterson and his men held them off as long as they could, then, when the enemy made his most determined attack, they would move suddenly to the flank. The enemy would storm in with guns firing and find to their consternation that the positions had been abandoned. While they were wondering what to do next Patterson's platoon struck. In this way they killed a great many Germans and hung on for an amazing twenty-two hours.

The C-46 Commando aircraft carrying the American 513th Combat Team was new. This was its first operational mission. Because of the C-46s' higher speed they had left later than the C-47s which they were to overtake on the way but in the event the timing went wrong and they arrived after them. They dropped 2,049 paratroopers, nearly as many as the whole 53rd Wing, and half the quantity of equipment delivered by each of the 52nd and 53rd Wings. However the C-46s had one terrible weakness that only became apparent after they droned over the Rhine at around 500 feet and met intensive flak. If flak or shrapnel punctured a wing tank, the leaking fuel ran down along the fuselage; it then took only a single incendiary shell to turn the plane into a flying torch. General Ridgway, in his report on the mission, wrote that 'With 20mm incendiaries especially lethal, approximately 72 per cent of the losses were estimated to have been inflicted during the first thirty minutes of battle.'

The first serial arrived to the right of a serial of C-47s over the dropping zone at 10.20 am, with several aircraft on fire. They had been badly hit by flak and altogether twenty-four were shot down. 'I was standing at the starboard side door, number three in the stick,' Sergeant Taylor recalled, 'and couldn't get out fast enough. Flak was peppering us and I saw pieces of the plane's skin tearing off when shells whizzed through. There was another C-46 alongside us with the jumpers already in the door. Suddenly it was hit and flames shot from its wing roots. We saw the guys inside flapping a bit but our jump lights flashed and out we went. I think the other aircraft crashed.' Glen Davis with 513th also saw a C-46 aircraft on fire: 'I was standing in the big doorway watching the other planes as we made our run in. It was very frightening because all along I had been telling myself it always happened to someone else when suddenly the guys were yelling and shoving, and when I turned I felt my scalp prickle, there was fuel running around our feet! Thank God the jump light went seconds after and we all leapt out damned fast.'

Regimental-Commander Coutts's aircraft was already burning when it crossed the Rhine, hit by long-range enemy flak. When the green light flashed Coutts went out quickly with his men, thankful to leave the burning plane but anxious for its crew; it crashed on the way back. Hordes of American paratroopers hit the ground and found themselves immediately under intense small-arms fire. Coutts slipped from his harness and hurried through carbine fire to begin attacking the enemy, even before he had formed a battalion, never mind found his regiment. (An American 'regiment' was equivalent to a British Brigade)—'I started looking for terrain features that I had memorized, but I couldn't find them.' All he could see were increasing numbers of British paratroopers, wearing their red berets instead of helmets. British Horsa gliders swept in, skidding along the ground and being unloaded. He assumed the British had come down in the wrong place.

Coutts was able to establish that he was about 2,500 yards to the north-west of Hamminkeln and had landed in the British zone. But a large part of the battalion had landed much further away and considerable confusion reigned. Similarly, 2nd and 3rd Battalions also landed under heavy fire in the wrong area, further south. Lieutenant-Colonel Ward Ryan from Fort Atkinson, Wisconsin, landed right in the middle of a German artillery command post and many of his men were killed as the enemy infantry fired up at them. Sergeant Curtis Gadd, from Cleveland, was swinging down when he saw a German soldier on horseback beating a hurried retreat. Gadd unslung his carbine in mid-air and raked the soldier with fire, killing him instantly. Private Lynn Vaughan of Georgetown landed in a tree, unhitched his 'chute and slid down just as three Germans ran past; he shot the first and the others surrendered.

Meanwhile Colonel Raff had sent a patrol of his 507th Parachute Infantry Regiment along the woods to capture the battery while his men dealt with the machine-guns. Close to the battery, the American paratroopers hurled grenades before rushing the enemy gunners, whose infantry opened fire with rifles before falling back in the face of the determined assaults. A runner soon got back to Raff with the news that the battery had also fallen; they had taken a full German colonel, about 300 prisoners and had killed fifty men.

With the majority of his 1st Battalion assembled, Raff ordered an

attack on Diersfordt Castle. 'A' Company were sent ahead towards
the castle while the rest of the battalion formed up, but they had not
left when the third wave of transports began dropping 507th's 3rd
Battalion, to whom the capture of the castle had originally been assigned. Raff now reverted to the original plan and let 3rd Battalion
take the castle. 'A' Company could not be recalled so he left them
but sent the rest of the 1st Battalion into regimental reserve. Smith's
3rd Battalion pressed on to the castle where they aided 'A' Company
in a room-by-room battle. 'Ricky' Richards recalls racing towards
the old castle: 'The enemy were firing from positions inside and on
the walls. We were directed towards a sort of back door, a big affair
flanked by stone pillars. It had already been blown open and we
dived through to fan out in the courtyard. It was only minutes before
the battalion had gotten into the building itself and we were soon
shooting it out through corridors and huge rooms. The German position was pretty hopeless and it wasn't long before they were surren-
dering. But not all gave up easily. I remember a couple of Germans
who drove our guys off a stone stairway with Schmeisser fire, dodging from behind columns to let rip as we tried to get up to them.
Someone threw a grenade but it bounced off the stone balustrade and
came hopping down stair by damn stair—I dived into a small ante
room but a couple of fellers were hurt. The next grenade didn't miss
and one German suddenly catapulted over the banisters; the other
one gave up.' Within an hour they had captured all the castle except
a group of enemy officers holding out in an isolated stone turret, supported by quite sizeable forces. They were in contact with 15th
Panzer Grenadiers who sent several Tiger tanks to relieve them.

As luck would have it, the 507th Parachute Infantry Regiment had
been recently equipped with the new 57mm recoilless anti-tank gun
which they quickly brought forward and sited in time to take on
these tanks. They also sent back a runner to Battalion HQ who made
contact with the 464th Parachute Field Artillery, who now directed
their howitzers on to the targets. The paratroopers took cover while
the guns also took on the tanks, destroying two. In the face of such
unexpected resistance from the paratroopers the remaining tanks
withdrew. A strong attack was then launched against the turret which
finally surrendered, yielding around 500 prisoners.

When the 466th Parachute Field Artillery was landing the enemy
were sweeping the area with machine-gun fire and many casualties
were incurred as the troopers dangled earthwards. Unlike his British
counterpart who carried his extra weapons and supplies in a kitbag

which he released just before landing, the American had his things stowed in a weapons bundle with which he landed still attached, often violently. But the moment he hit the ground the trooper rolled over, tearing off his harness and releasing his weapons. So the 466th began replying to German fire within moments of landing, covering the actions of those concerned with other loads. Initially the battalion fought as infantry on one of the most hotly-contested landing zones, while their 75mm howitzers were dropped, recovered and assembled.

Before leaving base, Lieutenant-Colonel Kenneth L. Booth, from Fort Smith, Arkansas, had examined a map of the area and pinpointed where his command post should be. As his parachute descended into an orchard he was keenly searching for his chosen spot and, to his amazement, saw that 'there was something awfully familiar about the buildings beyond the trees.' It was the command post he had picked, then occupied by enemy infantry who fought stubbornly for a while until the arrival of more American paratroopers pushed them out and Booth moved in.

Within thirty minutes of landing some of the howitzers were ready to lay their guns onto enemy positions in their immediate vicinity. Round after round was shoved into breeches as fast as they could go, while groups were still recovering air-dropped loads of ammunition. German guns replied with such fervour, however, that all the officers of one battery were killed or wounded. The Germans only began to pull back when other units dropped onto their flanks and the 466th turned their guns onto other targets around the drop zone.

Meanwhile, Coutts's group of 513th Parachute Infantry Regiment had reached their objectives to find that the 507th had already cleared it for them. His 3rd Battalion had had difficulty in organizing due to heavy fire but they had set off to the north-east which they believed was where their objective lay. After about ten minutes, though, it was realized that by orientating themselves on Hamminkeln, they were going the wrong way. So they changed direction and marched back to the south-east to reach their assembly area about 1.30 pm. The second group of the battalion had done the same except that their officer had set up a hedgehog to protect their positions while he and his senior NCO worked out where they were by sending out a recce party. This came back with the information they were going the wrong way and he, too, reformed and led his men back again. On their way they had to clear the enemy from several positions including an 88mm gun site. But then they came under fire from a 20mm flak gun which turned its attention from incoming gliders to the paratroopers. 'For a long while things were difficult', said Glen Davis, 'this gun was spewing a real hail of shells across the fields. We fired back without much luck. Later a fighter-bomber flashed in and hit it with a rocket.' One section found itself under fire from a farmhouse which they attacked and captured. Lieutenant Peter Scotese of Philadelphia, with Privates Dobridge and Braun, took over the farmhouse and were staggered to find the enemy's payroll, equivalent to $40,000!

The 194th Combat Team comprising the 194th Glider Infantry Regiment, and the 681st Glider Field Artillery Battalion in support, was the first double tow of gliders into combat. It was also, along with British 6th Air-Landing Brigade, the first time that gliders had landed on fields not previously secured by paratroopers. Planned in meticulous detail, every man had been carefully briefed and knew what he should do. Colonel James R. Pierce, commanding the 194th, and Lieutenant-Colonel Joseph W. Keating, commanding the 681st, had between them supervised the operation.

Yet plane after plane was hit as they flew in to release their gliders. Frank L. Lloyd with the 194th Infantry was horrified at the sight of C-47s blazing as they flew straight on into the searing lines of tracer and flak. After landing he and others watched the dreadful sight of aircrews standing in the doors of burning planes, unable to jump because of the low altitude and having to go back inside to take their slender chances when the plane crashed. 'One guy gave us a "V" sign as he went back and the plane arrowed straight into the ground a mile away and blew up.' Other aircrew jumped when their pilots managed to coax their stricken aircraft just high enough, but in their anxiety and fear many forgot to remove their anti-flak jackets which prevented their parachutes opening and they plunged to their deaths.

Howard Cowan sat tight in his glider for the three agonizing hours of the flight, swinging and twisting over the Seine, the Maas and then the great winding snake of the Rhine:

Then things began to happen fast . . . too fast. Above the sustained roar of the wind whipping past cloth covered ribs of the glider, you began to hear crack! pop! . . . snap!
Bursts of fire were accompanied by the popping of machine guns and the guttural whoomph of 88mm flak shells. Unconsciously you lift your bottom off the seat and brace as if to meet hot metal singing through the smoke. You find yourself dodging and weaving from something you can't even see.

Then the pilot's hand goes up and forward. 'Going down!' he shouts, and the nose pitches forward steeply. The speed slackens and the roar of the wind dies down to an audible whisper and the battle noises suddenly are magnified into a terrifying din.

The right wing tilts sharply as the shadow of another glider flits past. It almost hits us. Smoke is thick and acrid, almost as though you were in a burning house. You can see half a dozen buildings aflame on the ground. Dozens of gliders are parked at crazy angles on every field. Everyone with a weapon has it cocked and across his lap. And almost before you know it, the ground is racing underneath. You are in a pasture, crashing through a fence, bounding across a gully, clipping a tree with a wingtip. You've made it . . . landed and nobody hurt.

Company 'G' landed first at 10.30 am, three minutes ahead of schedule, and rushed across fields lashed by automatic and machine-gun fire. The enemy were slap in the middle of their landing and dozens of pitched battles went on as more gliders emptied. At least the unexpected descent onto a single field by dozens of gliders coming in from all directions confused the enemy, as the airborne had planned, and gave some protection to the paratroopers.

The 681st Artillery also came down in the middle of a strongly defended enemy flak gun position. For a while after landing the battalion could not get its guns into play until the enemy had been cleared from their immediate surroundings. The Battalion Commander, Keating, had plans to bring his guns to bear on the enemy but they could not position them while the German 88mms continued to plaster them. However, they got their radio working and were soon in contact with the British 81st Light Regiment, waiting on the far side of the Rhine and assigned the task of reinforcing the 681st. The gunners of the 53rd Welsh Division responded immediately, and the vicious cracks of the 25-pounders reverberated across the Rhine. To the delight of the American paratroopers the concentration wiped out several batteries. Throughout the rest of the day a 194th Combat Team Cub aircraft circled the area, spotting for the guns and calling up the 81st Regiment who fired several supporting missions, as did the other field regiments of 53rd Welsh.

'Able' Company of 194th Glider Infantry Regiment came down fairly close together and, scrambling clear under sporadic machine-gun fire, set off for the bridges across the Issel. Their front extended along 1,000 yards of river towards the British 6th Air-Landing Brigade's positions. Germans manning a strong-point in a house were not so easily overcome and constantly machine-gunned the Americans, forcing 'Able' Company to take cover. 'Charlie' Company tried to relieve them but they were pinned down, too, until 'Baker' Company forced the enemy out of the strong-point with grenades. While the other companies got going again, 'Baker' Company attacked a gun position where German crews were trying to bring two 88mm guns to bear on new targets. Cutting them down with machine-guns, troopers overran the position. Taking advantage of the stocks of shells alongside the guns, the company's anti-tank platoon took over the guns to good effect.

The airborne landings, although anticipated by Kesselring, nevertheless took the Germans by surprise. All previous Allied airborne attacks—in North Africa, Normandy and Arnhem—had been made *before* the main assault. Wolfgang Holtz, at Army Group HQ, believes that by early on the 24th the Army Group Commander had largely discounted an airborne attack which is why he had moved some of his armour towards Rees and Wesel. 'The sudden appearance of a vast airborne army at 10 am on a sunny morning stunned everyone. Signals were immediately sent asking for confirmation of the size of the attack. Von Luttwitz was officially alerted, although the size of the attack was such that he was already aware of it. Once it was established that airborne forces were landing on the Diersfordterwald, it did not take long to guess that the Allies were going to seize the bridges over the river Issel and the Issel Canal, and the adjacent autobahn. Orders were therefore sent to XLVII Corps to get across these bridges without delay. There were a number of tank harbours in the woods on the Diersfordterwald where limited numbers of tanks were positioned to defend the artillery emplacements, which were shelling the river crossing sites, and these were instructed to break-up the airborne landings.'

Von Waldenburg, Commander of 116th Panzer Division, had by this time sent several Mk IV tanks into battle, which encountered the anti-tank platoons of the American 194th Glider Infantry Regiment, losing several after which the others withdrew. They now attacked in a different direction and this time ran into 194th's 2nd Battalion which were moving off their landing zone. The American troops faced the tanks with bazookas, taking what cover they could as the monsters clanked forward through the drifting smoke. Private Robert Geist lay low and waited until a tank got within only fifteen yards before he fired his bazooka and saw the tank blow up. Private William Palowida fired at 100 yards range and knocked out another. Private

Robert Weber fired what seemed an impossible shot at another tank at 600 yards range and watched fascinated as the projectile looped high in the air and smacked straight into the open turret! Instantly the tank burst into flames and they could see the crew scrambling frantically to get out.

The gliders of the British 6th Air-Landing Brigade were now arriving—12th Devons to take Hamminkeln, 2nd Oxfordshire and Buckinghamshire Light Infantry to seize and hold the railway bridges between Hamminkeln and Ringenberg and the 1st Royal Ulster Rifles to try and capture intact the bridge over the river Issel. Major Huw Wheldon recalls that more than half of this battalion were volunteers from the Republic of Ireland. *The Times* correspondent reported that:

As we approached the DZ the danger of collision became very real. The Halifax rocked dangerously in the slipstream of machines in front, and perspiration trickled down the pilot's face as he tried to keep the tug in level flight, while the glider was preparing to cast off. In the haze and smoke ahead one could see a straight stretch of railway and a lake, landmarks which served as unmistakable guides to our DZ. 'Two miles to go,' the pilot shouted into the microphone to the pilot of the glider swaying along behind. 'O.K. Tug,' came the reply. 'Can you take us a little lower?' The nose of the Halifax dropped down slightly. Then we heard the voice of the glider pilot again. 'Hello, Tug, I am casting off now. Cheerio, Old Man. Good luck, see you again soon.' The Halifax gave a bound forward as it was relieved of the load of the glider. The Horsa started to dive steeply away to the right and we turned upwards and to port to get out of the tangled stream of gliders and tugs. Within a mile or so of sky were dozens of similar gliders, skilfully manoeuvring for position before landing.

Major Crookenden already on the ground with the 9th Battalion recalls the arrival of the gliders with their support weapons.

One of them flew straight in towards the battalion, touched down about 100 yards from the edge of the wood, and ran into the trees with a rending crash. Both wings broke off, but the men inside were unhurt. . . . A minute later a second glider approached the same corner of the woods. As he neared the trees the pilot must have realized that he had too much height and speed, for the glider swung sharply a few yards before it hit the wood, men of the 9th Battalion scrambling to get out of its way. It then crashed heavily on top of 8th Battalion headquarters, at close on 100 mph and was completely shattered. All the men inside were

killed and the jeep and trailer badly damaged; the Intelligence officer of
the 8th Battalion was also killed and the C.O. slightly injured. . . . There
was no sign of the Hamilcar.

Major Wheldon's flight was uneventful if nerve-racking but eventually crossed the Belgian coast and converged on to the Rhine. It was
then that things began to go wrong. There was far too much smoke
from the screen laid by the ground troops and this, mingled with the
battle smoke from guns and fires raging all over the place, made it almost impossible to see any detail of the ground. Dodging, swerving
and dipping, the pilot sought his landing zone, but could not recognize any landmarks. Wheldon stood behind him peering at the
ground and trying to identify features which showed briefly through
the rolling smoke. He saw that the pilot's knuckles were white as he
clenched the wheel and sweat was streaming down his neck; it was
hot behind the perspex but this was the sweat of extreme fear. Wheldon momentarily wondered if he, too, was sweating as profusely but
then they saw a church spire: 'Do you think that's Hamminkeln?' he
shouted in the pilot's ear, 'that church spire?' The pilot shouted
something that Wheldon couldn't catch and then he was diving for
the ground. They had a glimpse of gliders on the ground and in the
air, one shot overhead, there was a building in the smoke, a shell
burst, then they were tearing along the ground in a rending, screaming skid that sent earth and turf flying over them. With a terrific
crash the Horsa slammed its nose into a farmyard, rose in the air and
crashed down again.

The brief silence was broken by yells to get out. The Horsa was a
shambles, the jeep seemed to have come adrift and several men were
obviously already dead. The young pilot had died instantly. The
colour-sergeant remembers Wheldon shouting: 'Get out, get out
quick!' With German guns quickly ranging on every glider that
landed there was no time to lose. The colour-sergeant whipped out a
machete and began furiously hacking at the door which had buckled
and jammed on impact. After several mighty swipes it burst open
and he tumbled out followed by the survivors.

They had landed in a slight hollow, not directly under fire; the
enemy's tracer shells were skimming overhead. The sergeant got out
in such a hurry he forgot his Sten gun and had to run back for it.
Then as a couple of netting-covered helmets poked above the bushes
everyone instantly dropped into cover, swinging their Stens to cover
the intruders. A voice called out: 'Christ, are we glad to see you!'

About eight Americans from 513th Regiment scrambled over the top to join them.

They were in a farmyard about a mile or two east of their zone, but beyond that they were lost. A rattle of machine guns could be heard quite close and mortars were thumping down not far away.

The parachute landings and the fighting had produced so many casualties that by 10.30 am the Field Ambulance Medical Team had all but run out of supplies. In particular they were desperately short of stretchers so that when the gliders arrived their supplies were badly needed.

Private Lenton knew each glider carried further medical supplies and suggested going out to retrieve stretchers. He was told by his section NCO: 'You'll never get there and back alive', for the open ground was being swept by machine guns. Lenton, joined by Private Downey, was sure he could and they set off for the wrecks. The two men managed not only to bring in supplies of invaluable stretchers but also struggled back with some of the wounded that lay on the dropping zone.

Cries for help were heard from a wounded trooper lying in the open. Two orderlies from 224th Parachute Field Ambulance promptly ran out to help him, heedless of the enemy fire from every side, but were killed by a machine-gun burst. Corporal F. G. Topham, a Canadian medical orderly, witnessed the killings and, in the words of his subsequent vc citation, 'Without hesitation and on his own initiative . . . went forward through intense fire to replace the orderlies who had been killed before his eyes. As he worked on the wounded man he was himself shot through the nose. In spite of severe bleeding and intense pain he never faltered in his task. Having completed immediate first aid, he carried the wounded man steadily and slowly back through continuous fire to the shelter of a wood.'

For the next two hours Topham refused medical attention but went on retrieving wounded. A couple of hours later a carrier loaded with mortar ammunition received a direct hit which set it ablaze. An order was given that no one was to go near it as it might explode at any moment, but Topham ignored this and on his own managed to drag three men from it and take them back one at a time while the enemy fired at him.

When the Devons landed the Germans were concentrated in Hamminkeln behind a screen of light flak guns, manned by an assortment of troops from the Luftwaffe Regiment, Volkssturm and Parachute

Divisions. The landing ground was held by Battle Group 'Karst', a special airlanding unit composed mainly of paratroopers, mostly SS or Waffen SS, who were helping to stiffen the 84th Infantry Division grenadiers. A number of armoured cars and half-tracks were cruising about the landing zone shooting up gliders and paratroopers with 50 mm cannon and machine guns. Further back three self-propelled guns and a couple of Mk IV tanks were firing heavier shells.

Lieutenant-Colonel P. Gleadell, CO 12th Devons, and his party joined up with a platoon of 'D' Company, whose commanding officer's glider had force-landed on the way, and concentrated about a road that was to be captured by the company with the anti-tank platoon. At the same time 'A' Company with another anti-tank platoon were to land south-west and west of Hamminkeln to isolate the village from enemy attacks. 'B' Company with two 17-pounder anti-tank guns had the task of holding the west of Hamminkeln while the reconnaissance platoon which landed with them went to make contact with the 1st Royal Ulster Rifles. The objective of these moves was to prevent enemy reserves breaking through to troops holding the Issel bridges and exploiting west to the Rhine.

Gleadell's group fought their way to the northern end of Hamminkeln by 11.30 am on March 24th where they made radio contact with the Battalion HQ. He gave orders for the next phase of the operation, which required 'D' Company to clear the enemy out of Hamminkeln and defend the village from the east and south-east while 'A' Company held the opposite end of the village. 'C' Company was held in reserve in case of counter-attack. They would also establish road blocks, but these were to be capable of quick removal when the ground forces came through.

The Devons set about their tasks vigorously. About forty Germans were holding out in a windmill and were attacked by a section under an NCO. Bren fire and grenades broke the enemy's spirit and after several Sten bursts killed any soldier who ventured to show himself, the rest gave up. A counter-attack launched by German infantry, with a couple of tanks and half-tracks, towards 'A' Company's positions, was quickly beaten off, then the battalion further consolidated its positions.

Lieutenant-Colonel P. E. M. Bradley, the 6th Airborne Divisional Signals Commander, was in a glider that should have landed near Kopenhof farm but skidded down near a large wood. All the men leapt out and lay flat while the GSO 1 and senior pilot tried to work out where they were. Bradley confessed to having no idea where they had landed but to everyone's relief the pilot pin-pointed their position. The GSO 1 ordered them to unload as more Horsas came overhead. A huge Hamilcar thudded heavily down only yards away and had barely stopped sliding when the nose opened and its crew hauled out a big 17-pounder anti-tank gun.

Bradley thought they were a long time unloading, but in fact it was no more than five minutes before they were moving in open order across the landing zone with a jeep and trailer behind. Other groups were hurriedly driving away to their objectives, often cutting across one another's paths, all keeping their heads down. It was a bit unreal, Bradley thought; only hours before they had been in the quiet East Anglian countryside and now they were under fire in Germany.

Skirting the big wood Bradley's group headed for Kopenhof which they reached just after 11 am. To their surprise General Eric Bols, Commander of 6th Airborne Division, had already arrived, dapper as ever with his inevitable silk scarf, and had established his own HQ. The 'A' Command radio opened at 11 am and immediate contact was established with 3rd and 5th Brigades who both reported themselves well placed. This pleased General Bols immensely as one of the great difficulties at Arnhem had been the near-complete breakdown of communications. Brigadier Hugh Bellamy, Commander of 6th Air-Landing Brigade, had also landed nearby, and contacted Bols earlier. With the Commander, Royal Artillery and his forward observers established and through to XII Corps' guns, things were looking good, although they still had not managed to reach General Ridgway's XVIII Corps HQ.

Major Wheldon's men in the meantime were still trying to get their bearings, having realized they were at least two miles from their objective at the river Issel. It was strangely quiet, small groups of men organizing about their gliders, then forming up and marching off to their objectives with apparent calm and lack of concern as though 'going off to their committee meetings'. By now more Americans had attached themselves to Wheldon's group and they all set off for the Issel. They reached the woods and began trekking around the edge towards the bridge. Wheldon remembers feeling distinctly agitated that he should have had affairs more under control, although in the circumstances there was not much else that could have been done. He was leading the way when he walked straight into a group of three German soldiers. 'I reacted instantly and swung my Sten gun up to cover them, only to realize it didn't have a magazine on it. But the Germans were pretty well all in and surrendered. I decided to be very stern with them and told them in no uncertain terms that they were prisoners.' But they were hardly in a position to encumber themselves with numbers of prisoners, so they sent them to where they thought the Brigade HQ was. 'It was remarkable really; just like directing tourists in London. I gave them very precise directions: "Take the left fork, left, do you understand? Then follow the woods for about 100 yards . . . you've got that!" and so on . . . and off they went.'

Moving through woods they heard tanks approaching. Wheldon remembers a 'terrifying, grinding sound, much worse than the sight of them.' Two huge Panther tanks rumbled into view, 'going athwart of us, and we wondered why they were moving in the open. We had no anti-tank weapons and with the guns we had we might as well have thrown handfuls of peas at them. The tanks had seen us, no doubt about that, but they didn't bother us, just kept going. We were pretty relieved.'

When Wheldon's company reached the Issel bridge it was to find that the 513th, who had dropped there in error, had already fought a terrific battle. The fields nearby were a charnel house with dead and wounded Americans who had been caught in the air and mortared and machine-gunned on the ground. Many experts attributed their terrible casualties to their practice of bunching together in attacks; the British, by contrast, nearly always spread themselves out along both sides of a road. At the time lack of experience might have been an excuse, but the practice was still in evidence in Vietnam twenty-five years later.

But the Royal Ulster Rifles were grateful to the Americans for clearing their objective and did what they could for yet more of their wounded. Wheldon's most vivid impression of the day was its complete difference to Normandy; there they had dropped by night and met so little opposition that after twenty minutes, he had been drinking tea in a woodland shed. Here they had paid the price of dropping onto the enemy and lost nearly a third of their battalion. But the drop threw the enemy's plans to counter-attack the bridgehead right out of gear. Instead of von Luttwitz being able to move XLVII Corps' armour over the Issel bridges from his reserve area, as intended, once the main thrust had been identified, they were the wrong side of the line of the Issel and the canal. Although the airborne had taken heavy casualties when the enemy artillery was turned onto them, it diverted the fire from the bridgehead and in consequence the ground troops' casualties were relatively light. They could break out from the Rhine in hours rather than days.

As the sunny day wore into afternoon, the Germans began a series of localized attacks with tanks along the line held by 6th Air-Landing Brigade. It was doubtful if the paratroopers could hang on much longer in the face of armoured attacks. A couple of German planes appeared around noon to disrupt the landings but were pounced upon by patrolling Tempests from Volkel in Holland. One German fighter was shot down, its pilot landing on the dropping zone in front of the Canadian's 'C' Company. Private J. A. Collins saw him land between the two armies, then both sides began yelling and the pilot seemed unsure which way to run. Three Canadians sprinted out, grabbed him and bundled him back to their lines. The German was very cocksure and offensive at which a Canadian sergeant got tired and challenged him to a fist fight there and then while the 88mms were still shelling. Arrogantly the 'Luftwaffe pilot took the challenge and did quite well before the sergeant laid him out with a piledriver'.

During the afternoon the first supply mission was flown when 120 shiny new Liberator bombers roared across the trees dropping their tons of supplies. They flew rather too low and many parachutes failed to open in time, their loads thumping into the ground endangering troops in the area. Worse still, their low level presented easy targets for the still very active German gunners. Americans and British alike watched anxiously as one Liberator after another was caught by the flak, set alight or torn into shreds, many staggering on, some crashing in flames. Immediately the drop was over troops rushed to gather in the supplies, using every jeep they had, farm carts and even wheelbarrows.

The 681st's 'G' Company was to secure the Issel Canal running from the river to the Rhine, as far west as Wesel where they were to make contact with the Commandos, who had the town sealed off. Lieutenant Fred B. Wittig's platoon tried to infiltrate through the German lines which were particularly strong on the exposed flank of the 194th Combat Team. The platoon was soon pinned down by enemy fire. A runner returned to report the situation and a platoon from the reserve company was sent to aid them. As darkness fell, Wittig's platoon advanced into the town, made contact with 1st Commando Brigade and spent the night in Wesel.

Isolated pockets of German troops and armour were now fighting desperately in various places across the battlefield between Wesel

and the river Issel. A band of about 150 Grenadiers from the unlucky 84th Infantry Division tried to fight their way out from the
woods, with a single Mk IV tank, an armoured car and a self-
propelled gun. With the American 435th Group across their path
they had no alternative but to attack them. The 435th Group was
supported by 'B' and 'E' Batteries of the 155th Airborne Anti-
Aircraft Battalion which had landed in the same two serials as 194th
Regimental HQ, under Lieutenant-Colonel Paddock, and Keating's
681st Artillery. The glider pilots held their fire until the enemy were
only yards away and then opened up with everything they could
muster—machine guns, infantry weapons, anti-aircraft guns and bazookas—killing about fifty men and knocking out the armoured car.
By the time the Germans reached 681st's 'G' Company near Wesel
only thirty troops remained with no vehicles.

It had been thought that Ringenberg, just over the Issel and the
autobahn, would be used as a forming-up place for the enemy's
counter-attack. So, every time forward observers spotted enemy
tanks and infantry assembling, the call went back and the guns fired.
The RAF also struck at Ringenberg. Pierre Clostermann's 274
Squadron machine-gunned an armoured train near Ringenberg and a
convoy of panzers in the streets of Bocholt itself. 'It was a hair raising business. We came down at roof level, all four cannon spitting
fire. Tiles flew all over the place, flak shells exploded along the walls,
lorries burned, the panic-stricken inhabitants ran in every direction
and sheltered in doorways.'

Enemy attacks were still pressed home at several points. The 2nd
Oxford and Bucks Light Infantry on the left of 6th Air-Landing Brigade were holding the road and rail bridges between Hamminkeln
and Ringenberg with about 200 men. They had, as instructed, prepared the bridges for demolition, but they could only be blown on
the orders of Brigadier Bellamy, or any officer to whom he delegated
the responsibility on the site. The enemy kept trying to get their armour to the Rhine before the bridgeheads expanded. Wolfgang Holtz
believes that by nightfall on the 24th March, Blaskowitz was realiz-
ing how little time was left before the British broke out from the
bridgeheads and began to overrun the flat country north of the Ruhr.
Von Luttwitz was urged to get across the Issel at all costs; many at
Army Group 'H' could not understand why they could not get
through an airborne force, and it was only later that reports of the
heavy weapons they had landed reached HQ. Von Luttwitz, XLVII
Corps Commander, in turn pushed General von Waldenburg to get

his 116th Panzers across the Issel. The British armour, already moving out of its bridgehead, was expected to reach the paratroopers the following morning; there was no doubt among the German commanders that once that happened the British forces would rapidly fill the area within the perimeter held by the airborne divisions and their own limited forces would not be able to stop them driving for the Ruhr or the important town of Munster, or heading northwards into Holland which would trap the German Twenty-Fifth Army.

Now 116th Panzer Division sent a number of tanks driving along the road with the intention of crossing the bridges and breaking loose among the paratroopers. But the gliders had delivered a troop of 17-pounders, of which half had survived the landing, which took on the tanks as they approached and pushed them back. Fresh German attacks were mounted after dark when the much depleted Oxford and Bucks LI was forced to call Brigade HQ for help. 'A' Company of 12th Devons were sent to reinforce them, north-east of Hamminkeln. More enemy tanks could be heard rumbling towards the bridge. A desperate fight developed with the paratroopers raking the bridge with Brens while the anti-tank guns 'cracked' repeatedly. The German armour made every effort to break through in the last hours remaining to them and attacked ferociously. Faced with this big push, the Oxford and Bucks' Commander dared not hold out any longer and in the night the bridge was blown up. At that the Germans fell back to re-group for another attack across the rail bridge at first light.

The airborne assault, with its sudden impact and sheer spectacle and size, had temporarily stopped the ground battle, but now the latter was renewed as determined German infantry fought to hold off the advancing British troops, hoping that their panzer divisions would somehow reach them before it was too late. Kesselring reflected that, 'The cloudless spring weather gave Montgomery the opportunity for a large-scale airborne landing, making full use of his airmen for ground support, thus facing Army Group "H" with the greatest difficulty of movement.' With the Allied forces about to break out, the enemy command was close to panic as the British and American bridgehead expanded north to the Ruhr. 'I agreed with the group commander's idea of smashing both by every means at his disposal. But the result was that the Army Group had used up its main reserves before the situation at the front nearly clarified. That was an error which was paid for later.' Wise after the event Kesselring said that:

'As it was, the location of these reserves, which I had omitted to correct, and the ill-judged use of them not only lost the battle for the Rhine, but also shaped operations to come.'

Both the 1st, and the 5th/7th Gordons, with the 5th Black Watch at Rees, fought savagely against Meindl's II Parachute Corps, clearing them from strong-points amid a torrent of grenades and machine gunning. The 454th Mountain Battery fought their first battle, manoeuvring their 3.7 howitzers in Rees into mounds of rubble to fire a few rounds, then dragging them to a new position. Captain McNair was loudly applauded by the Gordons' CO: 'For each situation in his street to street battle, McNair had some suggestions for using his gun. He hauled it over rubble, rushed it around corners, laid it on a house that was giving trouble, dodged back again, prepared his charges, and then back to fire again. He even took it to bits and mounted it in an upstairs room. "Exactly which window is the sniper in?" he said and then, the sniper fired at him, "Oh! that one!" and laid his gun on it. It set houses on fire as well as any Crocodile and the effect on the enemy was devastating . . .'

Major Lindsey, of 1st Gordons, eventually crossed the Rhine at 3 pm in his jeep and was amazed at the number of sappers working on the bridges in full view of the enemy a half-mile up river. Now and then a shell plunged into the bank or the water, but clearly the airborne attack had completely disrupted the enemy artillery sited on the high ground to the east. When Lindsey arrived at the east bank near Rees a conference was in progress about the night's operations to clear Rees. Lieutenant-Colonel Grant Peterkin, the 1st Gordons' CO, broke to Lindsey the sad news that Major-General Thomas Rennie, to whom Lindsey had been talking only hours before, was dead. He had been driving to 152nd Brigade HQ when a mortar bomb had smashed into his jeep. Lindsey comments that 'he always set great, perhaps exaggerated store by personal bravery and example of officers and so scorned to drive about in an armoured car like brigadiers so sensibly did. His death was not so surprising in view of the risks he took.'

In the 15th Scottish Division zone at the Xanten crossing site, the 8th Royal Scots, of 44th Brigade, had succeeded in capturing and consolidating at Gossenhof farm. From there they had watched the airborne assault passing over and had then taken up the task of fighting their way forward to link up with the paratroopers, just over three miles away. Patrols were dispatched to the nearby villages of Vissel and Jockern and reported that the enemy were still holding them. Major Fargus recalls: 'The operation to clear these two villages began at 9.45 am. Two companies were used, the left hand company attacking Vissel was supported by a squadron of 44th Royal Tanks DD tanks and resulted in the capture of twenty-eight German prisoners.' Once the two villages had been taken and the threat of an enemy counter-attack on Gossenhof farm removed, the Battalion HQ was moved to the farm, while troops pressed forward towards the Diersfordterwald.

The battalion had been allocated an American crystal-controlled wireless set for communication with the airborne troops after landing. Major Fargus, the battalion adjutant, was manning the rear link radio in a white scout car while a portable link went across the river. When the forward set failed, Fargus's priority was advanced and he was called forward about 4 am. 'Such was the organization that my vehicle was waved past all the waiting queues, on a special lane, and without any delays or problems I had an uninterrupted journey out to the Battalion HQ at Gossenhof farm on the east bank of the river.' He set up the radio in an upstairs room at the farm and began sending signals to the airborne but without success until around 2 pm a voice was picked up.

'Fargus: "Hello, can you hear me? Over?"
Voice: "Hear you O.K. Over."
Fargus: "Are you the Airborne? Over?"
Voice: "Yes we are. Are you the ground troops? Over?"
Fargus: "Yes. Who are you and what is your location? Over?" '

They were in contact with 3rd Parachute Brigade and learned that 'the final task of 8th Royal Scots was rendered unnecessary as the bridge and high ground were firmly in the hands of 6th Airborne Division.' The airborne troops, under Brigadier James Hill, were at a road junction about two and a half miles north-east of Vissel. Fargus passed on the information to Lieutenant-Colonel Barclay Pearson who ordered a section of the Battalion's carrier platoon to patrol north-east to contact the airborne; nine carriers set off led by Captain E. A. Wall. They drove through open country straight along the road running northward from Vissel towards Bergen, alert for German troops still lurking in the nearby woods. Just past the bridge over the Bislicher Lay, a troop of Germans broke from bushes at their approach and fled towards the forest, and as they did so, paratroopers came from the trees and opened fire, cutting the Germans down. The carrier platoon waved excitedly when they saw the familiar red berets —air and ground forces had linked up.

These airborne troops were mostly from the Canadian parachute battalion and Trooper Acton recalls how they had been sent from their dropping zones on the north-western edge of the Diersfordter-wald, to clear the enemy from a small extension to the woods. 'It was early afternoon and very hot for March in Europe. We had been pushing on without pause and the sweat streamed off me. We heard the rattle of an armoured vehicle and were prepared for a German tank, but as we cautiously crept forward through scrubby under-growth a platoon of Germans suddenly ran towards us. I was to-wards the rear of the group but the lead troops opened fire. Only minutes after that they began cheering, and pushing between them I saw Bren carriers trundling along a track towards us. The sense of relief was overwhelming and certainly I, at least, felt intense relief that we weren't going to be isolated as had been the troops at Arnhem.'

Immediately word was received at Battalion HQ Barclay Pearson went forward with Brigadier Cummings-Bruce. He said, 'I was im-mensely relieved we had made contact with the airborne. It was a momentous occasion and we wasted no time in going forward.' He and Cummings-Bruce were driven by jeep to 3rd Parachute Brigade HQ and were soon being greeted by Brigadier James Hill. All the 44th Brigade battalions had now reached the airborne as Cummings-Bruce wrote: 'Contact was made with the airborne troops first by 6th KOSB at 14.00 hours, then by 6th Royal Scots Fusiliers at 15.10 hours and 8th RS at 15.15 hours.'

The KOSBs' vehicles were already passing through, pressing on after an enemy in general retreat. Over the Diersfordterwald parties of the enemy were trying to break through the encircling British and American forces, while von Luttwitz's panzers were trying to break in from the other side, but the lessons of 'Market-Garden' had been well learned and the gliders had brought in ample heavy weapons to support the paratroopers. Things were moving faster on the front of 44th Lowland Brigade and that evening 8th Royal Scots were or-dered to pass through the Airborne Division at 7 am the following morning. Fargus was surprised 'at the immaculate turn-out of the dead parachutists. Their brand-new battledresses, blancoed equip-ment and clean boots were in sharp contrast to the infantry who had been engaged in operations throughout the winter.'

Moving forward the next morning they ran into stubborn German troops who fired a heavy mortar barrage but the 8th Royal Scots pushed them back and moved up to positions astride the autobahn to the Ruhr. On the right the 6th Royal Scots Fusiliers crossed the Issel in the face of enemy reserves rushed from Bocholt. The 8th Royal Scots then advanced to protect their flank and after a terrific battle in which Spandaus fired continuously the entire 44th Brigade pushed forward to spread out into open country across the enemy communications and headed into the German interior.

On the west bank the 43rd Wessex Division and 53rd Welsh Division, which had played such prominent roles in the battle of the Rhineland, were to cross in the coming hours and drive inland. The 2nd and 3rd Canadian Infantry Divisions were preparing to follow their 9th Brigade, which was still attached to 51st Highland Division, through to begin their drives along the east bank of the Rhine, westwards into northern Holland. Most important of all, Montgomery's armoured divisions, 7th, 11th and the Guards Armoured, were ready to begin the massive punch that would sweep them deep into Germany.

21 The breakout

While the airborne troops battled on the Diersfordterwald, at Oppenheim General Patton made a personal crossing of the Rhine. He passed through the town to the barge harbour and thence across by a footbridge. Halfway over he stopped. 'Time for a short halt', he remarked and stood on the edge of the bridge to urinate into the Rhine. He buttoned his breeches, saying: 'I have been looking forward to that for a long time.' Patton then walked to the far bank where he deliberately tripped, fell to his knees and grasped German soil.

Patton's forces were at that moment preparing to make another crossing of the Rhine at Boppard. Before daylight on March 25th US Third Army launched its attack. The crossing site at Boppard had been Patton's first choice and was in a narrow gorge where the steep sides rose from the river to leave only the narrowest space for a road and railway. The site was attractive only because it lay to the north of the confluence of the Rhine and Main; although to the south of that confluence the country was open it would have meant another river crossing over the Main to reach Frankfurt.

But Kesselring had transferred to von Zangen a corps that had formerly been a part of Felber's Seventh Army and as the 87th Infantry Division crossed in assault boats the enemy opened a devastating fire. Shells tore apart boats and ripped men to pieces as they battled across the swirling, bouncing current. Conditions were so bad at the first site that one regiment had to abandon it and try further south at a different site.

Patch's Seventh Army reached the west bank a week after launching their offensive through the Saar-Palatinate. On March 23rd XV Corps took over the river bank from Third Army troops in its zone and prepared to mount its own crossings. Reserve regiments of 3rd and 45th Divisions moved in for the assault. On the 24th, while Montgomery's British and American forces were fighting their way out of the northernmost bridgeheads, XV Corps assembled its boats and drew up vehicle priority lists with all the detailed planning that Americans had so ridiculed in Montgomery's preparations. Two huge engineer columns, each thirty-five miles long, meandered to the crossing sites with all the vast array of equipment needed for bridges.

Their crossing sites were threatened in the same way as had been Ninth Army's on the Roer by nine dams which controlled the flow of the Rhine. The previous October the RAF's 'Dambuster' Squadron, 617, had attacked the big Kembs dam with 12,000 lb 'Tallboys' and succeeded in breaching it. The dams were operated under a joint German-Swiss agreement and diplomatic pressure was put upon the Swiss to ensure they prevented the weir gates being opened. At that point the Rhine was nearly a thousand feet wide and some seventeen feet deep. On both sides the country was sparsely wooded, fairly flat and open to enemy observation, so Patch's forces resorted to move-ment by night. About eight miles east of the Rhine ran a ridge of mountains, the Odenwald, extending some forty miles north and south and thirty miles in depth. These would not interfere with the crossing but if the enemy artillery dug in there it could seriously hold up any breakout to the east.

The plan was for 45th Division to make an assault over the river just north of Worms, while 3rd Division crossed just to the south, their objective being to cut the Gernheim to Mannheim railway, after which the divisions would turn east towards the Odenwald. Behind the assault divisions 63rd and 44th Divisions assembled ready to follow.

The opposition was believed to be about twenty divisions strong, although, according to Kesselring, most of the forces had been shifted north in an attempt to contain the Remagen bridgehead. To ascertain the extent of the opposition on the night of March 24th/25th, the commander of the 1st Battalion of the 180th Infan-try Regiment paddled across the river in a rubber boat accompanied by three men, landed near the Alter Rhein Canal and spent about thirty minutes moving quietly up and down the banks. They found no defences worthy of the name, no mines, wire or emplacements.

At 1.52 am on March 26th US Seventh Army guns opened fire. Twelve thousand rounds saturated the far shore, hitting identified enemy positions, while 45th Division remained silent, in the hope of maintaining some secrecy; at 2.25 am the guns ceased firing. Five minutes later the assault boats set out and by 2.31 am four regiments were seizing a bridgehead. The 179th Regiment of 45th Division

were furthest north near Hamm with the 180th in the Rheim Durk-
heim area. Shells and mortar bombs plunged into the river during the
crossings and casualties mounted. The next wave of assault troops
really caught a packet; almost half its boats were lost and a great
many troops drowned in the dark, swirling current.

To the right, 3rd Division encountered light opposition and
pushed inland rapidly, but the enemy began to fight back on the left
flank as 30th Infantry Regiment crossed near Worms. The Germans
were holding an island in midstream from where they shelled the
crossing. The 15th Infantry Regiment sent their 3rd Battalion to
clear them out and after a difficult landing managed to capture the island by noon. Two other battalions went directly over the river and
struck out through the Loracherwald for the autobahn.

Behind the assault troops Patch's armour was massing and on
their cue DD swimming tanks were launched into the river, and, although several were lost, the majority clambered out safely. As the
tanks advanced, 540th Engineer Combat Group set about building
bridges. By the end of the day they had a treadway bridge and a
heavy pontoon bridge across while in 45th Division's zone the 40th
Engineer Combat Group had similar facilities installed. Within
twenty-four hours over 1,000 vehicles were across the Rhine, including battalions of tank destroyers and tanks.

By March 27th the enemy were breaking off and making a run for
the Odenwald. The commanders of both 3rd and 45th Divisions sent
their infantry in hot pursuit; it became a race for the hills with the
American regiments rolling forward line abreast. The remnants of
Felber's armies, mostly old men of the Volkssturm stiffened by a few
regular battalions, had broken. They had virtually no artillery support apart from scattered anti-aircraft units. An irate Hitler immediately sacked General Felber for his failure and replaced him with
General der Infanterie Hans von Obstfelder. Model, meanwhile, was
massing all his available forces in the Ruhr. To his north Blaskowitz's still strong forces in Army Group 'H' were falling back as British forces crossed the Issel and the Lippe on the northern side of the
Ruhr. Felber had been isolated, there were no reinforcements to be
spared and, according to Kesselring, the Germans did not regard the
Frankfurt-Mannheim area of great importance. With Patton and
Hodges linking up from their Remagen and Oppenheim bridges the
drive for the Elbe was forming up.

Only the French had not yet crossed and De Gaulle, already
smarting because France had not been allocated a zone of occupa-

tion, was determined that his forces should carve one out for themselves. Thus, on March 29th he sent a telegram to General de Lattre
de Tassigny, Commander of French First Army: 'My dear General,
you must cross the Rhine, even if the Americans do not agree and
even if you have to cross it on rowboats. It is a matter of the greatest
national interest.' De Tassigny had, however, already arranged with
General Devers, Commander of 6th Army Group, to cross and then
head south and south-east. A mere twenty assault boats set out. The
Germans flayed them with cross-fire, sinking all but three. For hours
thirty men held on to a tiny bridgehead while French artillery protected them. Then more boats arrived and this time they crossed in
force, to begin their drive to Stuttgart.

In the meantime on British Second Army's front, 43rd Wessex Division had crossed, by-passed Rees and pushed east to the Issel. On
the extreme left flank 9th Canadian Infantry Brigade were fighting
their way along the road to Emmerich. The North Shore Regiment
cleared the German village of Millingen and the 3rd Canadian Division took over the left flank of the front from XXX Corps. From
across the Rhine every tank in 4th Canadian Armoured Division
was used as artillery to reduce Emmerich to rubble. When 8th Brigade occupied the wooded hills of Hoch Elten to the east of Emmerich, the Canadians were ready to drive for Arnhem to liberate the
rest of Holland.

On XXX Corps' northern bridgehead the battle raged for two days
as 154th Brigade of 51st Division tried to by-pass the stubborn German resistance in Rees. But when the 1st Black Watch tried to clear
the village of Speldrop they were met by the German 7th Parachute
Division under General Erdmann. Every house had to be cleared at
the point of the bayonet. Wasp flame-throwers drove in and flamed
the cellars while artillery reduced the houses to rubble. To counter
this, General Rott's 15th Panzer Grenadiers, back in the north again
holding the Alter Rhein and the road junction at Bienen, surrounded
the Black Watch who fought them off time and again with grenades,
bullets, bayonets, even spades and pickaxes when ammunition ran
out. In the same area the Canadian North Nova Scotias were so
heavily engaged at close quarters that their artillery could not fire in
support. Eventually the Highland Light Infantry of Canada were ordered forward and advanced to relieve Bienen. The HLI advanced
with fixed bayonets to find the remnants of the Black Watch holding
out in cellars. In the savage fighting that followed the Canadian Scots

finally got the upper hand, and the Panzer Grenadiers staggered back leaving over 400 dead.

On March 25th the 15th Scottish Division troops passed through along the line and made rapid advances towards Bocholt and Borken. The 53rd Welsh and 52nd Lowland Divisions crossed and headed eastward, pushing the enemy back. The bridgehead swelled until Montgomery had six British armoured brigades ready with a thousand tanks. On March 28th he unleashed his armoured divisions. 7th Armoured went through the bridgehead, clean through the enemy lines and defences and disappeared into Germany; by evening no one knew exactly where they were but it was believed they were heading for Berlin. Next day Guards Armoured rolled through, paused only to pick up the US 17th Airborne troops, and then this lethal combination also set off into Germany. By the time the tail of the division was across the Rhine the Reconnaissance Regiment was approaching Munster, over thirty miles away.

With his Canadian, British and American armies driving into Germany, Montgomery issued a new order directing 21st Army Group to seize Berlin. Then Eisenhower dropped his bombshell. Going back on his earlier assurances he informed Montgomery that once the Ruhr was sealed off, US Ninth Army would revert to the command of Bradley's 12th Army Group. With General Grow's US Fifteenth Army now coming into the battle as well, it meant that Bradley had four American armies under his command.

Coming when it did, the British smarted under a downgrading of their role and when Eisenhower then communicated his intentions direct to Stalin, without going through the Combined Chiefs, hurt turned to resentment. There is little doubt that in the back of Eisenhower's mind there remained the niggling irritation of Montgomery's post-Ardennes press conference which had so upset the Press in America. No doubt he was also nursing some animosity, from Montgomery's outspoken criticism of his abilities as a field commander. Whatever irritations he felt were also likely to have been fanned by Bradley during his several days of sanctuary in the south of France just prior to the Rhine crossings. In the event, Devers's southern group of armies, one French and one American, and Montgomery's northern group, now only British and Canadian, were relegated in the final weeks to protect the flanks of Bradley's enormous American central group. Once again the British and Canadians had been used as an anvil to prepare the way for an American breakthrough and triumph.

*   *   *

The Rhine had dominated British, American and German planners alike ever since the Allied breakout from Normandy in July and August 1944. Eisenhower had all along favoured his armies closing to the Rhine more or less in unison, partly because of the supply problems which loomed large in his strategy, partly to satisfy his ever-demanding army commanders.

Montgomery, for whom Eisenhower's supremacy had meant his own *de facto* demotion from overall commander, was single-minded in what he saw as the twin objectives of defeating Germany as soon as possible, to relieve the strain on a British economy crippled by six years of war and his dwindling manpower, and of halting the Soviet advance into western Europe as far east as possible, which did not figure large in American planning. To Montgomery, problems of supply and maintenance were of secondary importance—they should be overcome by a bold policy of allocating as much as necessary to one decisive thrust while the rest of the front held firm. He pursued deliberate strategies designed, not just to capture ground, but to inflict major defeats on the enemy by means of set-piece battles. Montgomery had the patience to set up and fight a battle on his own terms and ground, while Bradley, on the other hand, believed in movement and individual flair. This essential incompatibility between their two preferred styles of warfare dogged the Allied campaign until the end.

Was Montgomery correct in his belief that given sufficient support by Eisenhower he could have succeeded, with a combined British and American force, in crossing the Rhine, driving around the Ruhr and racing on to Berlin? With the advantage of hindsight it is evident that if this force had been dispatched immediately after the German débâcle in France, it would have encountered little initial resistance from the disintegrating German army. But as the Germans fell back towards the Rhine they were shortening their supply lines from the armouries of the Ruhr, becoming less dependent on rail and road supplies and withdrawing into the prepared defences of the Siegfried Line. Conversely the Allied lines of communication were extending and, in the absence of a major port, the facilities in Normandy, upon which they were relying, were inadequate for a thrust beyond the Rhine.

Seen in this context, Montgomery's failure to clear the Scheldt estuary and the approaches to the port of Antwerp, when the city was captured in September 1944, was a major tactical error. He missed the chance to do so because of his preoccupation with crossing the

Rhine at Arnhem and outflanking the Germans before they could re-group after their flight from France. Had the attack at Arnhem succeeded it would have provided a bridgehead over the Rhine, outflanked the Siegfried Line and allowed a swift drive along the east bank of the river which in turn should have forced a German with-drawal from the Rhineland. Hitler would have been hard put to hold on west of the Rhine once the German supplies were cut and the Ruhr threatened.

But Arnhem failed (although the operation as a whole provided the vital Nijmegen bridgehead across another branch of the Rhine), Montgomery's reputation was badly dented and the Antwerp docks were not opened for several weeks. However, even if the port had been seized and opened promptly, there is no reason to suppose that Eisenhower would then have permitted the kind of thrust Mont-gomery advocated. Indeed, given the animosity between Montgomery and the American commanders, the influence Bradley exerted over Eisenhower, together with the pressure of American public opinion for American successes, it is hardly conceivable that Eisenhower could have allowed Montgomery's thrust. Therefore to suggest, as some authorities have, that Antwerp was the decisive factor delaying the advance to the Rhine is conveniently to ignore Eisenhower's pre-occupation with closing to the Rhine on a broad front and his need to act towards his commanders in a manner that would not arouse public hostility in America.

Eisenhower was taken by surprise by the German eruption through the weak American lines in the Ardennes in December 1944, and from then on he became convinced that the Rhine was the only really secure line he could economically hold to ensure there was no German counter-attack while his forces were crossing the river. But the Ardennes offensive had already sapped the last German reserves and while they were able to put up a determined resistance to the British and Canadians in the Rhineland, it was only at the expense of stripping their other fronts. Eisenhower was therefore too cautious in insisting that all his armies close to the Rhine preparatory to any crossings being attempted.

Montgomery's eventual attack into the Rhineland was opposed by the strongest German field army in the west, well entrenched in their Siegfried Line defences. His plan to force mobile warfare upon them in the knowledge of their dire fuel shortages, and catch them in a pincer movement, was almost foiled by Bradley's failure to capture the Roer dams in time. Nevertheless it did virtually destroy the best remaining German army and made the subsequent crossing of the Rhine and the rapid breakout into Germany a certainty.

Much has been made of what Charles B. MacDonald called 'Montgomery's prideful refusal to allow Simpson's Ninth Army to jump the Rhine', and of the American claim that he wanted all the prestige. There is no evidence that having driven from the Roer virtually unopposed, the Ninth Army could have bounced a bridge. Certainly they made several attempts but each failed when the Germans blew up the bridge. It is significant, however, that at the 'Adolf Hitler' bridge at Uerdingen, American engineers surreptitiously crossed the bridge by night, reconnoitred the far side and then found time to cut the German demolition cables on their way back. But no attempt was made to get combat troops over and the enemy even had time to lay new charges with which they blew up the bridge the following morning. If Simpson was serious in his desire to jump the Rhine he had the opportunity at Uerdingen. The Germans believed an American assault in the Neuss-Dusseldorf area was planned, as is evident from retention of significant forces in that area awaiting the American attack even after the crossings of March 23rd/24th. This suggests that Simpson's attempts were planned feints for the benefit of German Intelligence—in which case they succeeded—although the records are hazy on this matter. Certainly any crossing of the Rhine directly into the Ruhr would have resulted in the fiercest of street fighting in the miles of industrial conurbation and as American troops were not well trained in street fighting their losses would have been catastrophic.

Hitler's intransigent domination of German strategy held together his shattered armies after the loss of France and Belgium. But he, too, was obsessed with the importance of the Rhine both to German industrial output and as a final barrier of the Reich. First his attitude produced the disastrous offensive in the Ardennes, then his determination to hang on to the Rhineland at all costs meant that the remaining German forces retained the outdated Siegfried Line until they were almost annihilated in February and March 1945. Had they been withdrawn east of the Rhine, as General Schlemm wanted, they would have forced the Allies to make a very costly invasion against much stronger German forces. Of course, Hitler knew, as did others, that if they did withdraw and hold the river, they would inevitably lose the all important traffic it carried; it was very much a case of 'Hobson's choice'.

Much criticism was levelled at Montgomery's huge and elaborate invasion force that crossed the Rhine, but he was faced with quite different conditions, both geographically and militarily, than either Hodges or Patton further south. To him, though, crossing the Rhine was only a means to an end. He wanted a firm base from which to launch his armoured thrust into Germany, which Eisenhower had agreed would be the main Allied effort. The ground forces, the artillery, the landing craft (which Patton also had) and the airborne forces were all to ensure the rapid capture and consolidation of his bridgeheads ready for the breakout. There really was no alternative to this maximum force given the presence of a strong German armoured force which could have seriously disrupted the landings and forced a protracted and costly battle on the Allies. Thus the several crossing points and the different times of the crossings all confused the Germans long enough for bridgeheads to be won. Then, when the Germans finally used their armour the airborne troops had seized the vital Issel bridges and blocked their way, and the build-up could begin. To quote General Essame: 'Never before had such a mass of armour been placed so securely and with such speed. The complete destruction of the German armies was in sight.'

The Rhine crossings placed massed Allied armies on the east bank from Switzerland to Holland and they began their powerful and rapid thrusts into the German heartland. That most of Germany was taken by the Western Allies rather than by the Russians was largely due to the defeat of the Germans west of the Rhine and the success of the crossings. Montgomery was diverted to the Baltic and reached Lübeck only hours before the Russians, but in time to stop them getting to Denmark and thence to Scandinavia. The Americans rapidly drove into Germany, Simpson to meet the Russians on the Elbe while Patton sent part of his army into Czechoslovakia (only to be recalled by Eisenhower in spite of the appeals of the Czechs) and the rest into Bavaria, and through the Alps to meet Alexander's forces coming up from Italy. Patch's US Seventh Army and Lattre de Tassigny's French Army turned south and cleared the remainder of Germany. Six weeks after the Rhine crossings the war in Europe was over.

Bibliography

My research for this book has followed two broad lines, personal interviews and correspondence with people who were involved in the campaign, and a widespread examination of the literature. The latter has included a wide range of books, including many private publications by military units, magazines and newspaper articles and reports compiled in the immediate post-war years by Allied organizations, including accounts by German commanders.

Many of the publications deal with wider aspects of the war and touch on the Rhine campaign only in passing and the compilation of this book has of necessity required the collection of a great deal of information, often in small items from a wide range of books. Other books have provided specific information especially those personal accounts by Allied and German personalities. Much of the German viewpoint is derived from the reports compiled by them at Allied instigation in the post-war years and throws much light on their confusion and the paucity of their resources.

1 Principal sources

I have tried to isolate the more important sources for this book in the following separate list, although I stress it is only in conjunction with other sources that their real value becomes apparent.

Battlefield Tour: Operation Veritable: 30 Corps Operations between the rivers Maas and Rhine, 8–10 February 1945. (G(Training) HQ B.A.O.R. 1947)

Battlefield Tour: Operation Plunder: Operations of British 12 Corps crossing the Rhine, on 23, 24 and 25 March 1945. (G(Training) HQ B.A.O.R. 1947)

Battlefield Tour: Operation Varsity: Operations of XVIII US Corps (Airborne) in support of the crossing of river Rhine, 24–25 March 1945. (G(Training) HQ B.A.O.R. 1947)

The three above publications provide very detailed accounts presented as lectures and usually given by officers who directed, or at least participated in, the actions. They contain many eye-witness accounts and frequently explanations of actions and what might have occurred had they not been attempted.

Fiebig, Major-General Heinz. 84th Infantry Division (19th January–25th May 1945) (Office of the Chief of Military History. B-843 1948)

General Fiebig's 84th Division held the front against which the main attack in Operation Veritable was launched. They bore the brunt of the fighting in that campaign and later in the Rhine crossing. Fiebig's account of his operation gives interesting insights to the extreme problems his division encountered.

Geyer, Oberst i. G. Rhineland Campaign (Answers to questions) 25th November 1944–March 1945)

Kesselring, Field Marshal A. Memoirs of Field Marshal Kesselring (London: William Kimber Ltd. 1953)

Kesselring, Field Marshal A. Remagen and the Ruhr. Interviews (Office of the Chief of Military History. Date unknown)

Kesselring, Field Marshal A. Remagen and the Ruhr. (Answers to questions) (Office of the Chief of Military History. Date unknown)

The publications by Kesselring shed much light on the dilemma of the Commander-in-Chief West, who replaced von Rundstedt. They also give a great deal of information on his relationships with and opinions of his subordinate Army Commanders, their strengths and dispositions. He makes interesting comments on the Allied Commanders who opposed him and their actions.

Mission Accomplished: A Summary of Military Operations of the XVIII Corps in the European Theater of Operations, 1944–1945. (Schwerin, Germany: HQ XVIII Corps. Date unknown)

Mission Accomplished: The Story of the Campaign of VII Corps, United States Army, in the War Against Germany. (Leipzig: HQ VII Corps 1945)

Both the above are concise, detailed reports on the operations of two corps that played major roles in the Rhineland campaigns.

Meindl, General der Fallschirmtruppen Eugen. II Parachute Corps. (Office of the Chief of Military History. MS B-674. 1947)

This corps played an important role in the battle of the Rhineland and Meindl's report deals with its injection into the battle and its actions as they formed part of the defences in the area around Wesel.

Miley, William, Papers. Report of the 52nd Troop Carrier Wing for Operation Varsity. (HQ 17th Airborne Div. 1945)

This gives a very detailed and comprehensive account of the troop carrier operations with maps and charts illustrating material deliveries and casualties.

Miley, William, Papers. Intelligence Annexe, Operation Varsity. (HQ 17th Airborne Division. 1945)

Miley, William, Papers. Varsity: Enemy Order of Battle (HQ 17th Airborne Division. 1945)

Miley, William, Papers. Varsity: Counter Intelligence Annexe. (HQ 17th Airborne Division. 1945)

Miley, William, Papers. Varsity: G-2 Estimate of the situation. (HQ 17th Airborne Division. 1945)

Miley, William, Papers. 17th Airborne Division Report. Historical Report of Operation Varsity. (HQ 17th Airborne Division. 1945)

All the above William Miley papers throw much light on the division's operations and the enemy dispositions. The counter-intelligence annexe in particular is most interesting as it lists all the German military and civil offices considered by the Americans to be important sources of intelligence.

Ridgway, Matthew, Papers. IX Troop Carrier Command Report. (XVIII Corps HQ. Office of the Corps Commander. 1945)

Ridgway, Matthew, Papers. XVIII Corps Report. Study of Ground Forces, Participation in Operation Varsity. (XVIII Corps HQ. Office of the Corps Commander. 1945)

These two reports by the Corps Commander give interesting accounts of this lesser known but biggest airborne operation.

Schlemm, General der Fallschirmtruppen, Alfred. First Parachute Army. 20th November 1944–21st March 1945. (Office of the Chief of Military History. MS 1947)

The Commander of the Army opposing the main British and Canadian forces in Veritable has left a valuable account of his actions and directives. He also makes interesting comments on the role of von Zangen's Fifteenth Army in its fight against the US Ninth Army.

Speer, Albert. *Inside the Third Reich.* (London. Weidenfeld and Nicolson Ltd. 1970)

Albert Speer's role as Hitler's Minister of Armaments gave him a unique opportunity to liaise between the higher echelons of the political power and the military command. His book is a valuable source of information on the way the German commanders struggled to continue the fight under Hitler's ever more stringent demands and threats and with diminishing resources.

Zangen, General d. Inf. Gustav von. Battles of the Fifteenth Army between the Meuse-Scheldte Canal and the lower Meuse 15th Sept.–10th Nov. 1944. (Office of the Chief of Military History. MS B-475 1947)

Although this particular account deals with the period before the Rhineland campaign really began, it is an important source of information about the period during and after Arnhem and leading up to the American attacks against the Hurtgen forest and the Roer dams.

2 Secondary sources

Ambrose, Stephen E. *The Supreme Commander: The War Years of General Dwight D. Eisenhower* (New York: Doubleday. 1970)

Argyll and Sutherland Highlanders of Canada (Princess Louise's), The. *War Diary 1st Feb. 1945 to 31st May 1945.*

Barclay, C. N. *History of the 53rd Welsh Division in War* (London: Clowes. 1956)

Bird, W. R. *No Retreating Footsteps: The Story of the North Nova Scotia Highlanders* (Nova Scotia: Kentville Publishing Co. 1947)

Blake, George. *Mountain and Flood: History of the 52nd (Lowland) Division* (Glasgow: Jackson. 1950)

Blumenson, Martin. *Breakout and Pursuit: US Army in World War II.* (Washington D.C., Office of the Chief of Military History, Dept. of the Army. 1961)

Blumentritt, General d. Inf. G. *Positional Warfare of 25th Army in the Netherlands 3.2.45–28.3.45.*

Bradley, General Omar N. *A Soldier's Story* (London: Eyre and Spottiswoode. 1951)

Brereton, Lieutenant-General Lewis H. *The Brereton Diaries* (New York: Wm. Morrow. 1956)

Brickhill, Paul. *The Dam Busters* (London: Evans Brothers. 1951)

Bryant, Sir Arthur. *Triumph in the West: The War Diaries of Field Marshal Viscount Alan Brooke* (London: Collins. 1959)

Bullock, Allan. *Hitler: A Study in Tyranny.* (London: Odhams Press. 1952)

Butcher, Captain H. C. *My Three Years with Eisenhower* (New York: Simon and Schuster. 1946)

Chalfont, Alun. *Montgomery of Alamein* (London: Weidenfeld & Nicolson. 1976)

Chamberlain, Peter, and Ellis, Chris. *The Sherman* (New York: Arco. 1969)

Chatterton, George. *The Wings of Pegasus* (London: Macdonald. 1962)

Churchill, Winston S. *The Second World War Vols. 1–6* (London: Cassell. 1955)

Clarke, W. S. *The Story of the 34th Armoured Brigade* (HQ 34th Armoured Brigade. 1946)

Bibliography 301

Clostermann, Pierre. *The Big Show* (London: Chatto & Windus. 1952)

Cole, Lieutenant-Colonel Howard N. *On Wings of Healing—The Story of the Airborne Medical Service, 1940–1960* (London: Blackwood. 1963)

Compte Rendu des entrevenues avec le Général von Manteuffel, le 7 Decembre 1957, et le 8 Juin 1958.

Crabhill, Buckshot. *The Ragtag Circus from Omaha Beach to the Elbe* (New York: Vantage. 1969)

Cross of Lorraine, The. *A Combat History of the 79th Infantry Division, June 1942–December 1945* (New York: Army & Navy Publishing Co. 1946)

Davies, Bramwell, Collection. *21st Army Group, Operation Blackcock: Clearing the area between the river Maas and the river Roer, 15th–20th January 1945.*

Davies, Bramwell, Collection. *21st Army Group; Operation Veritable. Clearing the area between the Maas and the Rhine, 8 Feb–10 March 1945.*

Davies, Bramwell, Collection. *Bde Command. Problems and Solutions, 146 Bde. Rhine.*

Davies, Bramwell, Collection. *Lecture: Assault Crossing of the river Rhine, 23rd & 24th March 1945.*

Davies, Bramwell, Collection. *Notes of the Operation of 21st Army Group. 6 June 1944–5th May 1945.* (In the Imperial War Museum.)

Draper, Theodore. *The 84th Infantry Division in the Battle of Germany, November 1944–May 1945* (New York: Viking. 1946)

Duncan, Major-General N. W. *79th Armoured Division: 'Hobo's Funnies'* (London: Profile Publications Ltd. 1972)

Eisenhower, General Dwight D. *Crusade in Europe* (London: Heinemann. 1948)

Ellis, Major L. F. *History of the Second World War: Victory in the West. Vol II: The Defeat of Germany* (London: HMSO. 1968)

Elstob, Peter. *The Battle of the Reichswald* (London. Macdonald. 1971)

Erman, John. *History of the Second World War: Grand Strategy. Vols V and VI* (London: HMSO. 1956)

Essame, Major-General Hubert. *The 43rd Wessex Division at War* (London: Clowes. 1952)

Essame, Major-General Hubert. *The Battle for Germany* (London: Batsford. 1969)

Essame, Major-General Hubert. *Patton the Commander* (London: Purnell. 1974)

Fargus, Major B. A. *Action of the 8th Battalion Royal Scots during the attack on Goch 18–19th February 1945* (The Thistle, April 1948)

Fargus, Major B. A. *The Action of the 8th Battalion Royal Scots in Operation Torchlight* (The Thistle, July 1948)

Fitzgerald, Major D. J. L. *History of the Irish Guards in the Second World War* (London: Gale & Polden. 1949)

Forbes, Patrick. *6th Guards Tank Brigade* (Sampson Low, Marston and Co. Date unknown)

Futter, Geoffrey N. *The Funnies—a history, with scale plans, of the 79th Armoured Division* (London: Model & Allied Publications. 1974)

Gardner, Brian. *The Wasted Hour: The Tragedy of 1945* (London: Cassell. 1963)

Gavin, Lieutenant-General James M. *Airborne Warfare* (Washington D.C. Infantry Journal Press. 1947)

Gersdorff, Frhr v. General-Major and Chief of Staff, 7th Army. *The German Westwall Defences.* (Answers to questions, date unknown)

Gilbert, Felix. *Hitler Directs his War* (New York: Oxford University Press. 1950)

Goodspeed, Lieutenant-Colonel D. J. (ed.) *The Armed Forces of Canada 1867–1967: A Century of Achievement* (Ottawa: Canadian Forces HQ. 1967)

Grant, Roderick. *51st Highland Division at War* (London: Ian Allan. 1977)

Groves, J. J. D. *The Assault upon Wesel on the Rhine* (The Royal Engineers Journal. Date unknown)

Guingand, Major-General Sir Francis de. *Operation Victory* (London: Hodder & Stoughton. 1947)

Hastings, Macdonald. *The Rhine Crossings* (*Picture Post.* Vol 27, No 2 April 1945)

Hayhow, Ernie. *The Thunderbolt Across Europe: A History of the 83rd Infantry Division, 1942–1945* (Munich: F. Bruckermann. 1945)

History of the XVI Corps: From its Activation to the End of the War in Europe (Washington D.C. Infantry Journal Press. Date unknown)

Hoegh, Leo A. and Doyle, Howard J. *Timberwolf Tracks: The History of the 104th Infantry Division 1942–1945* (Washington D.C. Infantry Journal Press. 1946)

Hopkinson, Lieutenant-Colonel G. C. *44th Royal Tanks Across the Rhine* (Royal Armoured Corps Journal. Date unknown)

Horrocks, Lieutenant-General Sir Brian. *A Full Life* (London: Collins Ltd. 1960)

Humble, Richard. *Hitler's Generals* (London: Arthur Barker. 1973)

Huntly Express, The. *Gordons to the Rescue* (March 1945)

Huston, James A. *Out of the Blue. US Army Airborne Operations in World War II* (West Lafayette, Indiana, Purdue University Studies. 1972)

Hutnik, Joseph J. and Kobrick, Leonard (eds.) *We Ripened Fast: the Unofficial History of the 76th Infantry Division* (Privately Published. Date unknown)

Irving, David. *Hitler's War* (London: Hodder & Stoughton. 1977)

Ismay, General Lord. *The Memoirs of General Lord Ismay* (London: Heinemann. 1960)

Jackson, Lieutenant-Colonel H. M., MBE (ed.) *The Argyll & Sutherland Highlanders of Canada* (Princess Louise's) 1928–1953 (Hamilton: Canada. 1953)

Keitel, Field Marshal Wilhelm. *The Memoirs of Field Marshal Keitel.* (London: William Kimber Ltd. 1965)

Kennett, Brigadier B. B. CBE, *Signal Planning for Operation Plunder.* (Date and publisher unknown.)

Kennett, Brigadier B. B. and Tateman, Colonel J. A. *Craftsmen of the Army: the story of REME* (London: Leo Cooper. 1970)

Lewin, Ronald. *Montgomery as Military Commander* (London: Batsford. 1971)

Lewin, Ronald (ed.) *The War on Land 1939–1945* (London: Hutchinson. 1969)

Liddell Hart, B. H. *History of the Second World War* (London: Cassell. 1970)

Liddell Hart, B. H. *The Other Side of the Hill* (London: Cassell. 1948)

Liddell Hart, B. H. *The Tanks: the History of the Royal Tank Regiment,* Volume II (London: Cassell. 1959)

Lightning: The History of the 78th Infantry Division. (Washington D.C. Infantry Journal Press. 1947)

Lindsey, Lieutenant-Colonel Sir Martin of Dowhill, KBE, CBE, DSO. *So Few Got Through* (London: Simon Books. 1956)

Macdonald, Charles B. *By Air to Battle* (London: Macdonald. 1969)

Macdonald, Charles B. *The Last Offensive* (Washington D.C. Office of the Chief of Military History. 1973)

Macdonald, Charles B. *The Mighty Endeavour* (New York: Oxford University Press. 1969)

Macdonald, Charles B. *The Siegfried Line Campaign* (Washington D.C. Office of the Chief of Military History. 1963)

McKee, Alexander. *The Race for the Rhine Bridges* (London: Souvenir. 1971)

Macksey, Kenneth. *Armoured Crusader—Major-General Sir Percy Hobart* (London: Hutchinson. 1967)

Macksey, Kenneth (ed.) *The Guinness Book of Tanks, Facts and Feats* (Enfield: Guinness. 1972)

Martin, Lieutenant-General H. G. *The History of the 15th Scottish Division, 1939–1945* (London: Blackwood. 1948)

Mattenklott, General d. Inf. *Werkreiss VI 15.9.44–31.3.45* (Office Chief of Military History. MS B-044)

Mellor, Major J. F. C. *The Rhine and Beyond* (Publisher and date unknown.)

Mick, Allan H. *With the 102nd Infantry Division through Germany* (Washington D.C. Infantry Journal Press. 1947)

Mills-Roberts, Brigadier Derek. *Clash by Night—A Commando Chronicle* (London: Kimber. 1956)

Montgomery, Field Marshal, The Viscount. *Normandy to the Baltic: A personal account of the conquest of Germany* (London: Hutchinson. 1947)

Moore, Captain John, and Phillips, Colonel W. L. C. *The Story of the Monmouthshire Volunteer Artillery* (Pontypool: The Griffin Press. 1958)

Moorhead, Alan. *Montgomery* (London: Hamish Hamilton. 1946)

Muir, Alastair. *The First of Foot.* (Publisher and date unknown.)

Nobecourt, Jacques. *Hitler's Last Gamble: The Battle of the Bulge* (New York: Schoecken. 1967)

North, John. *North-West Europe, 1944–5: The Achievement of the 21st Army Group* (London: HMSO. 1953)

Parker, Colonel T. W. *Conquer—The Story of Ninth Army* (Washington D.C. Infantry Journal Press. 1947)

Parkinson, Roger. *A Day's March Nearer Home* (London: Hart Davis, MacGibbon. 1974)

Patton, General George S. Jnr. *War As I Knew It* (London: W. H. Allen. 1948)

Pay, D. R. *Thunder From Heaven: Story of the 17th Airborne Division, 1943–1945* (Birmingham: Mich Books. 1947)

Perrett, Bryan. *Through Mud and Blood: Infantry Tank Operations in World War II* (London: Robert Hale. 1975)

Preparation for the Rhine Crossing. The Oak Tree. (Date unknown)

Pritchard, Paul W. & Dozier, William T. *Engineers and Chemics at the Roer Crossings* (The Military Engineer. May–June 1950)

Randel, Major P. B. *A Short History of 30 Corps in the European Campaign* (BAOR. 1945)

Remagen Bridge, The. 7–17th March 1945. Research and Evaluation Division US Armoured School. (US Armoured School. Date unknown)

Rhine Crossings, 24th March 1945, The. The Oak Tree. (Date unknown)

Ridgway, Lieutenant-General Matthew B. *Soldier: The Memoirs of Matthew B. Ridgway* (New York: Harper & Bros. 1956)

Royal Welch Fusiliers. *A Short History of the 6th (Caernavon & Anglesey) Battalion of the Royal Welch Fusiliers. North-West Europe, June 1944 to May 1945* (Dusseldorf: 1946)

Ryan, Cornelius. *A Bridge Too Far* (London: Hamish Hamilton. 1974)

Samian, Brian. *Commando Men* (London: Stevens. 1948)

Saunders, Hilary St George. *The Green Beret* (London: Michael Joseph. 1949)

Saunders, Hilary St George. *The Red Beret* (London: Michael Joseph. 1950)

Seaforths, 2nd Battalion: *An Account of the Battle of the Rhine* (Caber Feidh. Date unknown)

Shirer, William L. *The Rise and Fall of the Third Reich: A History of Nazi Germany* (London: Secker & Warburg. 1960)

Shulman, Milton. *Defeat in the West* (London: Secker & Warburg. 1947)

Shuster, George M. *Our Part in the War: Third Battalion 330th Infantry* (Publisher unknown. 1945)

Smith, General Walter Bedell. *Eisenhower's Six Great Decisions* (New York: Longman. 1956)

Stacey, Colonel C. P. *The Canadian Army, 1939–1945* (Ottawa: Ministry of National Defence. 1948)

Stanley, George F. G. *Canada's Soldiers: The Military History of an Unmilitary People* (Toronto: Macmillan Co. of Canada Ltd. 1960)

Straus, Jack M. *We Saw it Through; History of the Three Thirty First Combat Team* (Munich: F. Bruckermann. 1945)

Strawson, John. *The Battle for the Ardennes* (London: Batsford. 1972)

Sym, John. *Seaforth Highlanders* (Aldershot: Gale & Polden. 1962)

Talon Crosses the Rhine, The. 17th Airborne Division. US Army (Date unknown)

de Tassigny, Marshal de Lattre. *The History of the First French Army* (London: Allen & Unwin. 1952)

Taurus Pursuant: A History of the 11th Armoured Division. (BAOR. 1945)

Taylor, A. J. P. *English History 1914–1945* (London: Oxford University Press. 1965)

Tedder, Lord. *With Prejudice: The Memoirs of Marshal of the RAF Lord Tedder* (London: Cassell. 1966)

Toland, John. *The Last 100 Days* (London: Arthur Barker. 1966)

Tugwell, Maurice. *Airborne to Battle* (London: William Kimber. 1971)

Turner, John Frayne and Jackson, Robert. *Destination Berchtesgaden* (London: Ian Allan. 1975)

U.S. Forces, European Theater, General Board. Armoured Special Equipment. Study No 52. (USFET. 1945)

Van Bibber, Colonel Edwin M. *Objective Perfection* (Washington D.C. Infantry Journal Press. 1946)

Vandeleur, Brigadier J. O. E. *A Soldier's Story* (Aldershot: Gale & Polden. 1967)

Verney, Major-General G. L. *The Guards Armoured Division: A Short History* (London: Hutchinson. 1955)

War Monthly No 42. Rhine Crossings: The Final Assault (Marshall Cavendish. 1977)

Warlimont, Walther. *Inside Hitler's Headquarters 1939–1945* (London: Weidenfeld & Nicolson. 1964)

Watkins, G. J. B. *From Normandy to the Weser: The War History of the 4th Battalion, The Dorset Regiment* (Dorchester: The Dorset Press. 1952)

Westphal, General Siegfried. *The German Army in the West* (London: Cassell. 1951)

White, B. T. *British Tanks and Fighting Vehicles, 1914–1945.* (London: Ian Allan. 1971)

Whiting, Charles. *Hunters From the Sky* (London: Corgi. 1975)

Whiting, Charles. *Patton* (London: Pan/Ballantyne. 1973)

Wilmot, Chester. *The Struggle for Europe* (London: Collins. 1952)

Woolcombe, Robert. *Lion Rampant: The 15th Scottish Division—Normandy to the Elbe* (London: Leo Cooper. 1955)

Zangen, General d. Inf. Gustav. *Battles of the Fifteenth Army Between the Meuse–Scheldt Canal and the lower Meuse, 15th September to 10th November 1944* (Office of the Chief of Military History, MS B-475)

Index

Index

Index

AMERICAN FORCES cont.

83rd Infantry Division, 136, 162, 163, 165-6

84th Infantry Division, 12, 136, 138, 141, 177

87th Infantry Division, 287

94th Infantry Division, 115

99th Infantry Division, 197, 203

100th Infantry Division, 224, 225

102nd Infantry Division, 136

104th Infantry Division, 142

106th Infantry Division, 10

15th Regiment, 289

23rd Regiment, 231

30th Regiment, 289

47th Regiment, 37

119th Regiment, 217

175th Regiment, 165

179th Regiment, 224, 288

180th Regiment, 224, 288

194th Glider Infantry Regiment, 256, 271, 272, 273, 281

311th Regiment, 70

313th Regiment, 248

315th Regiment, 248

329th Regiment, 165

331st Regiment, 163

334th Regiment, 177

338th Regiment, 161

397th Regiment, 224

398th Regiment, 224

399th Regiment, 224

513th Regiment, 267, 270, 276, 279

507th Regiment, 216, 255, 256, 265, 269

8th Tank Battalion, 229

27th Armoured Battalion, 192

120th Engineer Battalion, 224

155th Airborne AA Battalion, 281

187th Engineer Battalion, 217

295th Engineer Battalion, 139

464th Parachute Field Artillery Battalion, 265, 269

466th Parachute Field Artillery Battalion, 269-70

540th Engineer Combat Group, 289

656th Tank Destroyer Battalion, 197

681st Glider Field Artillery Battalion, 271, 272, 281

743rd Tank Battalion, 139

771st Tank Battalion, 177

823rd Tank Destroyer Battalion, 139

IX Tactical Air Command, 13

IX Troop Carrier Command, 213

XXIX Tactical Air Command, 83

52nd Wing, 267

53rd Wing, 267

Anderson, Major-General John B., 136, 143, 183, 233

Antwerp, 2, 9, 10, 293

Ardennes, 10, 13, 16, 18, 21, 22, 24, 209, 293, 294

Armstrong, John, 153

Arnhem, 3, 8, 18, 74, 209, 211, 213, 261, 293

Asperberg bridge, 98, 99, 106, 109, 173

Barber, General, 26, 45, 78, 130, 244

Bartholomew, Major P. I., 241

Beadle, Major, 258

Beckhurst, Major, 108

Bellamy, Brigadier H., 215, 278, 281

Bibber, Colonel van, 248

Blaskowitz, General Johannes, 21, 30, 33-4, 35, 42, 56, 60, 74, 75, 91, 167, 172, 180, 188, 200, 211, 212, 227, 249, 281

'Blockbuster' Operation, 147-59

Blumentritt, General Guenther von, 21, 32, 35, 187, 227

Body, Major, 148

Bolling, General, 177

Bols, Major-General Eric, 212, 215, 278

Booth, Lieutenant-Colonel Kenneth L., 270

Boppard, 287

Bradford, Lieutenant-Colonel Bill, 120

Bradley, General Omar N., 2, 3, 4, 5, 7, 8, 9, 10, 11, 14, 15, 16, 18, 38, 84, 85, 113, 115-16,